O the depth of the riches and wisdom and knowledge of God! How unsearchable are his judgements and how inscrutable his ways! "For who has known the mind of the Lord? Or who has been his counselor? Or who has given a gift to him, to receive a gift in return?" For from him and through him and to him are all things. To him be the glory forever. Amen.

ROMANS 11:33-36

For this reason I bow my knees before the Father, from whom every family in heaven and on earth takes its name. I pray that, according to the riches of his glory, he may grant that you may be strengthened in your inner being with power through his Spirit, and that Christ may dwell in your hearts through faith, as you are being rooted and grounded in love. I pray that you may have the power to comprehend, with all the saints, what is the breadth and length and height and depth, and to know the love of Christ that surpasses knowledge, so that you may be filled with all the fullness of God.

EPHESIANS 3:14-19

John Hynes
Sabbatical— 2006

SACRA DOCTRINA

Christian Theology for a Postmodern Age

THE DEPTH OF THE RICHES

A Trinitarian Theology of Religious Ends

S. MARK HEIM

WILLIAM B. EERDMANS PUBLISHING COMPANY
GRAND RAPIDS, MICHIGAN / CAMBRIDGE, U.K.

Wm. B. Eerdmans Publishing Co.
255 Jefferson Ave. S.E., Grand Rapids, Michigan 49503 /
P.O. Box 163, Cambridge CB3 9PU U.K.

Printed in the United States of America

06 05 04 03 02 01   7 6 5 4 3 2 1

Library of Congress Cataloging-in-Publication Data

Heim, S. Mark.
The depth of the riches: a Trinitarian theology of religious ends / S. Mark Heim.
p.   cm.   — (Sacra doctrina)
Includes bibliographical references and index.
ISBN 0-8028-4758-7 (alk. paper)
1. Theology of religions (Christian theology)
2. Trinity. I. Title. II. Series.

BT83.85.H45   2001
261.2 — dc21

00-063666

www.eerdmans.com

For
Sara Fae Metzger Heim
Whose open-hearted love and wisdom have blessed
widening circles of family, friends, church, and community

She opens her mouth with wisdom,
And the teaching of kindness is on her tongue.

PROVERBS 31:26

Contents

CONTENTS

PART FOUR
ESCHATOLOGY AND PLENITUDE

Preface

This project has been supported by many people, with criticism, suggestions, and encouragement. If it does not always show the benefit of that support, the fault is mine. The following acknowledgments are at least a representative offering of thanks for the vast preponderance of this work that comes *from* me only because of the appropriation *in* me of the research and thought of others.

I am grateful to have received an Evangelical Scholars' Research Fellowship from the Pew Charitable Trust for the academic year 1997-98 which allowed me to complete the first full manuscript of this book. I particularly want to thank Nathan O. Hatch, the director of the Evangelical Scholars' Program, and Michael S. Hamilton, its coordinator, for their help and support. At the summer conference of research fellows in 1998 I was able to present my work in progress and to receive valuable criticism and suggestions. Andover Newton Theological School granted me leave during 1997-98, and I thank those colleagues who were willing to take over responsibilities left aside for that reason. The Christian Theological Research Fellowship's editorial board did me the signal honor of including this work in the fellowship's series, *Sacra Doctrina*. I thank general editor Alan Padgett and other members of the board for their comments. The series is quickly establishing a high standard for constructive Christian theology, a standard to which this book hopes to rise. It is a pleasure to associate myself with the aims of the Christian Theological Research Fellowship and with the authors who appear in *Sacra Doctrina*.

A host of individuals have offered assistance and insight in the course of this work. I especially want to thank John Carman, Christopher Chase, Frank Clooney, Sarah Coakley, Paul Griffiths, Roger Haight, John Hick, Roger Johnson, Patrick Keifert, Michael LaFargue, Anselm Min, Fred Norris, Clark Pinnock, Thomas Thangaraj, and Andrew Walls. All my colleagues at Andover Newton Theological School made knowing and unknowing contributions to this project, particularly my colleagues in theology, Sam Solivan and Gabriel Fackre. Mark Burrows and Robin Jensen offered good counsel in regard to Dante and medieval theology. Sze-kar Wan has opened to me many issues regarding Chinese traditions, and I am particularly grateful for a trip to China that he organized for us in 1998. I would like to thank Dr. Chun-chieh Huang, President of the Chinese Association for General Education, for his invitation to take part in an international conference on "Chinese Classics as Core Curriculum" at the National Taiwan University in Taipei, and Dr. Yez-zen Tsai for his gracious hospitality during that visit. Within the structure of the Boston Theological Institute, the Boston Theological Society and the Society for Comparative Theology have provided challenging conversation, stimulating colleagues, and many fruitful leads.

The Pluralism and Mission study group of the Faith and Order Commission of the National Council of Churches of Christ in the U.S.A. and the council's Interfaith Working Group have both been venues in which the themes of this book have been explored in ecumenical dialogue. I thank the members of those groups and their staff leaders, William Rusch and Jay Rock. The meeting of the World Council of Churches Faith and Order Commission in Moshi, Tanzania, in 1996 was an opportunity to learn more about the relations of Christianity with Islam and indigenous religions in that country and in Africa more widely. I was privileged in recent years to take part in a consultation on teaching world religions in a theological context, sponsored by the Wabash Center for Teaching and Learning in Theology and Religion. Thanks are due to all who took part in that consultation, particularly to its leaders, Frank Clooney and Judith Berling, and to Raymond Williams from the Wabash Center. I am grateful also for the opportunity to take part in the Conference on World Mission held at Luther Seminary in 1998, under the direction of Roland Miller. The other members of its theology colloquium provided a great deal of food for thought.

Melissa Lewis Heim offered a great deal to this project on the plane of these prior acknowledgments: ideas, editorial wisdom, a patient ear for new versions of the same thing. Given the demanding schedule of her own work, that was a labor of love. She contributed much to this book; I want to thank her for everything else. Sarah and Jacob have been more industrious than I. Between the first time they had to sit through talk of this book and the time of its publication, one finished college and the other high school. They have applied that increased wisdom to their father only gently. I am grateful for their conversation and their support.

May whatever proves of value in this work endure, and may whatever proves mistaken be quickly forgotten, whatever the proportion of the two may be, to the glory of one whose will truly is our peace.

Newton Centre, Massachusetts
August, 1999

In Christ,
S. MARK HEIM

Introduction

Today Christians and others who affirm the distinctive truth of their religious convictions are faced with two telling challenges. The first challenge is to be faithful to the "one and only" dimension of their faith. This is not just a claim handed down from the past, but a fundamental feature of the believer's experience and confession. For Christians this involves witness to the decisive, distinctive power of relationship to God in Christ. The witness can be explicit testimony that in and through Christ humans encounter possibilities open in no other way. It can also be participation in forms of life — service, prayer, ritual — which are grounded in that uniqueness. We can confess that Christ is the pivot point of relation between God and creation. We can act out lives that rest on that point. Christians aspire to do both.

The second challenge is to honor truth, virtue, and integrity in believers of other religious traditions, and in the substance of those traditions themselves. Some Christians cling to simple categories of evil, ignorance, and "pre-Christianity" to define other religions, despite the uncomfortable suspicion that these categories would soon break down in light of too much exposure to the reality of other faiths. Other Christians rush to affirm all religions as versions of the same generic truth, transcendence, and human goodness, despite the uncomfortable suspicion that such abstraction betrays a benign contempt for the concrete aims and practice of the religions as they actually exist. These two different perspectives agree in preferring to avert their eyes from the thick texture of religious diversity.

Many traditionalist Christians find that taking the religions seriously on their own terms shakes exclusivist assumptions about Christian superi-

1

ority. There is too much wisdom, truth, and human transformation integral to the differing religious paths to ignore. Many revisionist Christians find that taking the religions seriously on their own terms shakes pluralistic assumptions about their interchangeability. There is too much particularity in the wisdom, truth, and human transformation in the differing religious paths, seamlessly woven into the concrete, unique textures of these traditions, to ignore. It is hard for more evangelically inclined Christians to believe that the Dalai Lama's virtue and wisdom are unrelated to the specific Buddhist convictions he holds. It is hard for more secularly inclined Christians to believe this too. The connection can be a problem in both cases. For the conservative, the problem is that it is not just some moral conscience or general revelation that accounts for this goodness, but something substantive in the religious tradition itself. The religion has validity not despite its difference from Christianity but *because* of its difference. For the liberal, the problem is similar. It is not some abstract common truth "behind" the religion, some vague universal revelation, that explains the tradition's power. It is the specific convictions the believer takes to define the nature of things, and the specific practices undertaken on those assumptions that are crucial. One doesn't accidentally and automatically get the benefits of Tibetan Buddhism in all other traditions. The explicit "exclusivity" of the tradition is somehow necessary to its validity.

The traditionalist Christian who finds too much in order in the varying faiths raises doubts about the need for a universal Christian witness, about the uniqueness of Christ. The pluralistic Christian who finds the goods of the various religions too stubbornly particular raises doubts about the dogma that they all have the same aim, that there is nothing important missing in one that could be found in another. The two perspectives take their stand on slightly different principles: "What is contrary cannot be true" and "What is different cannot be important." More conservative Christians interpret the second in terms of the first: difference primarily means error. More liberal Christians interpret the first in terms of the second: religious truth claims can conflict only on matters of secondary significance. What one religion could be wrong about and another right, must not be important for "salvation."

If two religions conflict, then at most one can be correct. Wishing to affirm Christianity, Christian exclusivists seek out conflicts and in each case affirm the error of the differing tradition. If your religion differs from mine, you must be wrong. Wishing not to attribute error to one religion against another, pluralists recognize difference but sever it from religious validity. They are convinced that where religions differ, the differences are only apparent (because of the metaphorical and symbolic character of religious language) or are real but irrelevant in attaining the one true end of religion. If you think your religion is a real alternative to mine, you must be wrong.

To move past these two inflexible perspectives, we must reconsider some presuppositions. Anyone who pays passing attention to discussion of religious pluralism is familiar with the conventional question that dominates that conversation: Can religions recognize other ways to religious fulfillment than their own, and if so, how? The common typology of views — exclusivist, inclusivist, pluralist — presumes there is and could be only one religious fulfillment or "salvation."[1] The typology then divides people according to their convictions about the *means* that are effective to attain this single end. Exclusivists contend that their tradition alone provides those means; inclusivists argue that other faiths than their own may prove functionally effective as implicit channels for the truth and reality most adequately manifest in the inclusivist's tradition; pluralists maintain that each religious tradition provides its own separate and independent means to attain the one religious end.

The presumption of a single religious fulfillment is usually not a tentative claim but an axiom: there *could be* no more than one. The axiom challenges religious believers to recognize that those of other faiths actually are (in all truly important respects) seeking, being shaped by, and eventually realizing the same religious end. All paths lead to the same goal. One can freely acknowledge that the paths are truly different in many ways: they cover different ground, have different scenery, and perhaps require somewhat different skills. But in relation to what the paths are for and where they are going, no difference is conceivable.

I suggest a different assumption. Christian theologians have spent a great deal of time considering whether there are varying ways to salvation. They have spent little time considering whether there are different, real religious ends that are not Christian salvation at all. This book asks what sense Christians could make, theologically, of that possibility. Rather than a general Christian theology of religions, it is a Christian theology of religious ends.

---

1. This widely accepted typology of approaches to religious pluralism provides for three categories: exclusivism, inclusivism, and pluralism. The typology is set out by Alan Race (1993). The typology has been developed within Christian theology, but applied analogously to other faiths. Christian exclusivists believe the Christian tradition is in sole possession of effective religious truth and offers the only path to salvation. Christian inclusivists affirm that salvation is available through other traditions because the God most decisively acting and most fully revealed in Christ is also redemptively available within or through those traditions. Christian pluralists maintain that various religious traditions are independently valid paths to salvation and Christ is irrelevant to those in other traditions, though serving Christians as *their* means to the same end.

INTRODUCTION

"What is contrary cannot be true." This principle is certainly correct when applied to two logically opposed propositions, or to two mutually exclusive states of affairs in the world. And yet we must be careful to see its limits. One set of paths may be valid for a given goal, and thus final for that end, while different ways are valid for other ends. "The ascetic life leads to peace" and "The sensual life leads to joy" might both be true confessions. There are personal states that cannot both hold at the same time for the same person. Yet there is nothing contradictory in affirming that they are realized by different people at the same time, or even by the same person at different times.

If the statements above were rephrased to read "The ascetic life is the only path to salvation" and "The sensual life is the only path to salvation," we would have two conflicting claims. What is contrary cannot be true. So at least one of them would have to go. Yet this absolute exclusion might be an illusion, fostered by the fog of ambiguity around the word "salvation." If the word has the same concrete meaning in each of those sentences, then there is a conflict. But if in fact it stands for a different concrete end in each case, then the conflict is not real. To say the two paths both lead to "salvation" then is only to say they lead to *some* type of desired end, not necessarily the identical one.

J. A. DiNoia has made this point tellingly.[2] His argument has been summarized this way:

> . . . a Christian need not feel anxious if informed by his Buddhist friend that he cannot attain Nirvana except by following the Excellent Eightfold Path. If this is true, and if he does not pursue the Path, it follows he may never reach Nirvana.

But, DiNoia continues, "since I have as yet no desire to attain and enjoy Nirvana, I am not offended by this reasoning. I have not been persuaded that Nirvana is what I should be seeking." In the same vein, DiNoia quotes the revealing remark a rabbi once made to him: "Jesus Christ is the answer to a question I have never asked."[3]

The question is not "Which single religious tradition alone delivers what it promises?" Several traditions may be valid in that sense. If that is so, the truly crucial questions become "Which religious end constitutes the fullest human destiny?" and "What end shall *I* seek to realize?" Both questions have a clear objective dimension. I cannot effectively seek an end that is not actually achievable. Real human fulfillment has to be rooted in the way the world actually is. And it may objectively be the case that some ends encom-

2. (DiNoia, 1989; DiNoia, 1992).
3. (Walls, 1998, p. 34).

pass more possibilities than others. Both questions also include an irreducible evaluative dimension: What is to *count* as human realization?

This contradicts the second principle we noted above, the one that asserted what is different cannot be important. Different religious aims are profoundly important, if we once suppose that they relate to distinctively different religious ends. The "one and only" testimony of the religions is truthful and trustworthy in presenting us with true alternatives.

Christians believe God is the creator and fulfiller of the universe. They believe this is truly the way the world is. Buddhists, for instance, likewise believe there is a way the world is (even if they maintain that the particular way it is makes metaphysical terms themselves problematic) and it is undeniably different from the Christian conviction in crucial respects. There is a foundational level at which it is correct that what is contrary cannot be true. If there are such things as distinct Buddhist and Christian religious fulfillments, then one of three situations must follow. Ultimately, such Buddhist and Christian religious fulfillments as exist are embedded in a universe that more nearly accords with Christian convictions than Buddhist ones. Or such Christian and Buddhist religious fulfillments as exist are embedded in a universe that more nearly accords with Buddhist convictions than Christian ones. Or both are embedded within a universe which best corresponds to some other account.

But there is another sense in which what is contrary can also be true. Based on their views of the way the world is, Buddhism and Christianity both seek particular religious ends. The contrast in these ends may not be only apparent but quite real. And each end may be attainable. Whichever of the three scenarios above holds true, the religious ends themselves may still be real alternatives. In that case, adherents of religions with contrasting religious ends are quite right to see them as important alternatives, and to commend their own faith as the unique path to a distinctive religious fulfillment.

These changes in perspective do not eliminate the tension between the two challenges with which we began, but they recast it. In recognizing that what is "contrary" in two religious traditions may in fact represent a forced choice between two real alternatives (and not the logical contradiction of two states, one actual and one impossible), we do not eliminate the "one and only" dimension of Christian faith. We transpose it to a different key, one that contrasts the specific Christian hope of salvation with other distinctive religious ends. In recognizing that what is different is often decisively important, we do not diminish the significance of other religious traditions. We actually enhance the imperative to learn about them in their unique concreteness, to credit the "one and only" dimension they claim for themselves.

The various traditions cannot be put on a single scale and the discussion limited to the question of how much of some single human possibility each one can achieve. The faiths are cross-woven in a variety of dimensions, and even to place one entirely on the evaluative matrix of another yields no simple verdict. There are likely to be, for instance, a number of views among Buddhists on what to make of Christianity, on purely Buddhist grounds.[4] There is no "metatheory," no neutral place that allows us to judge from above the religions rather than among them. I believe that it is inevitable and appropriate that religions interpret each other and the world within the categories of their own tradition. My interest is that they include in *what* they interpret the true difference, the true otherness of alternative religious life. The aim of a theology of religions is to find, however imperfectly, an understanding of the other in its own integrity within the faith that is part of one's own integrity.

I am convinced that the fruitful and viable path for interfaith relations lies in each tradition developing, from its own particularistic grounds, frameworks for the fullest legitimate recognition of the *distinctive* qualities (those that finally resist assimilation) of the *positive* religious aims of other faiths. This path differs from the abstract view of many pluralistic theologies, which wishes to maintain that what is truly religiously important is either an indeterminate point of convergence beyond the particularities of all faiths or some analytic, generic essence of their current functions in human life. It also rejects the convictions (shared by the most pluralistic theologians and the most exclusivistic ones) that there is one and only one actual religious fulfillment on offer to humanity, that any claims to the contrary are pernicious and ought to be eliminated, and that the only live religious question concerns the number of religious paths that can deliver this payoff.

This last set of convictions is generally defended either by an argument that all humans in the end do and must desire one identical state as their highest good or by an argument that, whatever humans may seek as religious goals, a transcendent being or order forcibly limits them to one option. I believe religious traditions are committed to (indeed constituted by) the claim that there is one particular, best human destiny that corresponds to the true nature of the world. But I want to argue in this book that (for Christianity at least) this conviction does not foreclose enduring plural possibilities, in both human aims and human ends.

Rather than "one way — all others error and torment" or "all ways — equivalent religious outcomes," the grammar of religious diversity is more complicated. Faith traditions inevitably apprehend some specific religious

---

4. See, for instance, the variety of views expressed in Part III, "Buddhist Perceptions of Christianity in the Twentieth Century" (Griffiths, 1990).

end as the highest and fullest available to humanity. They may well see extraordinary ways to attain this end through religious traditions and practices other than their own. The grammar of religious diversity should also allow for the attainment of religious fulfillments other than the one a given tradition holds to be supreme. And it should allow for the possibility of religious failure, utter lostness. This grammar is neither a two-option view (a right way and a mass of indistinguishable wrong ways) nor a no-option view (all ways inescapably right, and right about the same thing). Instead it has four options: a specific and ultimate religious fulfillment, an "inclusivist" way by which others may converge toward that fulfillment (even while initially unaware that they do so), achievement of religious fulfillments that are concretely quite different from the ultimate one, and a state without religious fulfillment at all. This four-term grammar is an appropriate one for religions to use in their interpretations of each other. I contend that the relations between the religions would be most fruitful and peaceful if each encountered the other with the full range of such a grammar in place. It is particularly appropriate for Christians to use this grammar in facing the complex world of religious diversity, as it can be grounded in a trinitarian understanding of God.

It is the third term in this grammar, an actual variety of religious fulfillments, that is the most unusual note. It is not a common idea in traditional Christian theological reflection on these matters. It is entirely absent in the (ironically titled) pluralistic thinkers who attack that tradition. The latter group's hostility to the idea appears to be not just a fact but a principle. As I will argue in this book, I believe orthodox Christian theology can be more open to the possibility, a possibility that could in principle be accommodated within a traditional distinction between salvation and estrangement from God. Nor would it necessarily foreclose the existing debate within Christian tradition regarding universalism.

The Christian imperative to preach the gospel "to the ends of the earth" is an authentic counsel of Christian revelation. This book affirms the legitimacy of Christian confession of Christ as the one decisive savior of the world. But it does so by means that will no doubt seem unusual and perhaps paradoxical to many Christians: affirming that other religious traditions truthfully hold out religious ends which their adherents might realize as alternatives to communion with God in Christ. These are not salvation, the end Christians long for. But they are real.

There is good reason for Christians to commend and proclaim what they believe is the true end of human life, the reality that undergirds it, and the means of realizing it: the life, the truth, and the way. This is the Christian response to the challenge to maintain the "one and only" dimension of the faith.

7

At the same time, there is good reason for Christians to approach the various religions and particularly their very concrete and particular claims with an open mind and a readiness to recognize their truthfulness. One need not believe that alternative religious aims are illusory or without value in order to decline them or commend another. I believe such a perspective offers a refreshing vision for Christian witness, one in which the focus shifts away from acrimonious debates over whether such witness ought even to take place and instead focuses on the substance of religious aims, those of Christians and their neighbors. What might it mean for Christians to recognize concrete, distinctive truth in the particularistic witness of Buddhism or Hinduism, for instance, while still maintaining Christian witness and universal claims?

This book makes one attempt to answer that question. Although I treat many of the topics most Christian theologies of religion address, the frame is different. The innovation as well as the limitation of my approach is expressed in the subtitle: a trinitarian theology of religious ends. My aim is to explore whether a theology of religions can be transformed and enriched by the recognition of diverse religious ends. I want to explore the way such a thesis fits with basic Christian convictions.

I do not devote much space to discussions that often dominate Christian theologies of religion, particularly the questions over whether or in what ways people might have access to Christian salvation though they belong to other religions and/or have never heard of Christ. These are important matters, but they are not my primary concern here. I am a convinced inclusivist. The typology that defines "inclusivist," however, deals with only one aspect of religious pluralism. This book attempts to work with rather different categories.

I will use "salvation" to refer to the human fulfillment that Christians believe is offered to us by God through Christ. This is the characteristic use of the word in Christian theology. It is rarely used in other religious traditions to describe their ends. When speaking of those ends, or sometimes when speaking collectively or comparatively of the Christian end and others, I will use terms like "religious aim" or "religious fulfillment" or "religious end." In this way I hope to be consistent and to draw our attention to the importance of these distinctions. This convention does not mean that I rule out the possibility that two religious ends, described in differing terms, might turn out in fact to represent the same condition, imperfectly expressed in both descriptions or more adequately perceived in one than the other. This is a question that will have to be considered on the merits in particular cases. I have argued elsewhere that it cannot be presumed wholesale.[5]

5. See Part One (Heim, 1995).

It will be readily apparent that the Trinity plays a key role in this book. I am hardly alone in regarding the Trinity as the key that opens Christianity's theological interpretation of other religious traditions and its capacity to respect and learn from them.[6] But the topic remains in an early stage of development, and I hope that this work will be a small contribution to that process. The Trinity in this area as in Christian theological history generally is *both* an affirmation about God and a regulative scheme for keeping "in play" all the fundamental elements crucial to Christian faith and life. It is both a first order and a second order or regulative theological affirmation. Our focus is not on the Trinity as a particularly esoteric and mysterious doctrine, but on the basic features of Christian faith and practice which it integrates.

I contend that distinctive religious ends sought and realized in other religious traditions are grounded in apprehension of and connection with specific dimensions of the divine life of the triune God. They become separate ends by virtue of isolation and limitation, but this does not compromise their reality. Because the nature of God is a communion of the three divine persons, that nature itself has a variety of dimensions. Salvation, the religious end Christians know and seek, is a relational state and not a simple one. It is this composite character that opens the possibility of different but real religious ends, ones whose limitation leads to distinct definition, whose isolation leads to a special purity.

Trinitarian theology is a vast area in its own right. To attempt to connect the complexity of Christian trinitarian thought with the complexity of even one great religious tradition is a daunting project. I do not claim to be adequate to that task in any comprehensive way. I have drawn gratefully on recent works renewing trinitarian theology. It is not discouraging but reassuring to know that in light of the richness of the resources on both sides, the project I join here will in time be done better and more thoroughly by others.

This discussion touches on so many areas that some questions must simply be left aside. For instance, there is no effort here to specify exhaustively what qualifies as a religious tradition and how many religious ends there might be. I use several examples, but that broader question must wait for another time. Likewise, my discussion of salvation and religious ends is limited almost entirely to human persons. There are wider issues relating to the Christian belief in the redemption of all creation that could be considered,

---

6. Chapter Five goes into this in greater detail and touches on the work of a number of theologians (Panikkar, 1973; D'Costa, 1990; Smart and Konstantine, 1991; Williams, 1997).

but for the sake of focus they are left aside here. Similar disclaimers might be offered about other topics as well.

There is one very important point which will be made at several places in the book but which should be stated at the outset. I spend significant time discussing theological views of the life to come. Special attention is given to Dante's vision of the next world in the *Divine Comedy,* for instance. At first glance, then, the subject may appear to be exclusively life after death. I hope it will soon be plain to any reader that this is not the case. One of the reasons that I focus as I do on the *Comedy* is because the structure of the poem perfectly reflects what in my view should also be a characteristic of the theology of religions.

The *Comedy* can be read simultaneously on several levels. It visits the afterworld not primarily for a cautionary glimpse of the future, but to map the human situation in all its dimensions, present as well as future. This allegorical character does not mean that Dante does not believe in the future states he imaginatively portrays. He does. And so do I believe in those that I discuss. But one of the primary themes of my work is to stress the continuity between such eschatological suppositions and current analysis. This can be stated quite simply. All things being equal, I hold that theological interpretation to be more convincing which can show the way in which its eschatological visions reflect realities we can already see in some measure now, and which can show how such eschatological visions actually clarify these realities themselves.

Finally, a related point should be made. Paul Griffiths helpfully distinguishes between transitional eschatology and final eschatology.[7] Transitional eschatology describes events and conditions leading up to the final completion of creation, while final eschatology has to do with that ultimate state itself. Christian theology necessarily has something to say about each of these subjects, something substantive as well as regulative. But in both cases, and especially in the second, we must acknowledge that any description which is even moderately concrete (and for theological discernment we often need such concreteness) must trade heavily in speculation. Even within strictly Christian terms, it must include much detail that only *might* be the case, in proportion to a smaller number of points that are essential. For instance, it is a substantive Christian confession that in both transitional and final eschatology the saved remain distinct individuals, in personal relation with God and with other creatures. But any specific attempt to picture what features of our unique historical individuality and relations endure in that final transi-

---

7. (Griffiths, 2000, pp. 19-20).

tion, which are transformed nearly beyond recognition, and which are burned away, can only be an exercise in speculation. Not only will the conditions of knowledge be changed, but we the knowers will be changed as well. We are mistaken if we claim the same importance for that speculation as for the basis on which it rests.

On the other hand, there is real value in such speculation, not only for prayer, worship, and meditation but also for instruction. Not all speculation is the same. Some is more consonant with the overall grammar of Christian faith. For example, as I argue in this book, some types of speculation fit more coherently with Christianity's specified trinitarian doctrine than others do. Dante's *Comedy* is an example of such speculation, where the substantive and formal basic Christian qualities of salvation are expressed in a form that admittedly and gloriously includes imaginative, dramatic elements that cannot be put on the same level as that basic core. And yet they make the substantive convictions more vivid than they could ever be otherwise. There is much in the *Comedy* that is permissible and edifying, though not regulative for Christian theology.

A similar thing can be said of my much humbler sketches of both transitional and final eschatology. I try to make clear when I am speaking of substantive and formal Christian convictions and when I am speaking more imaginatively, but this will not always be plain. So it is important to remember that this book in no way aims to provide a definitive statement about topics where Christian theology must be agnostic. I enter such a speculative area not to claim certainty for the details but to illustrate the systematic cogency of elements of Christian confession that are often criticized as incoherent. So, for instance, some insist that Christian belief in the unique decisiveness of Christ must negate the content and aspirations of all other religions, discourage respect for adherents of other religions as neighbors in the human community, and finally consign them to eternal torment after death. This book aims to illustrate that none of these things need be true, by offering one consistent construal of the tradition in which orthodox views of Christ and salvation are maintained but these supposed results do not follow. Quite the contrary: the distinctively Christian perspective offers more support for the distinctive value of these other faiths than does a more secular or pluralistic perspective.

*   *   *

This work is the last act in an unanticipated trilogy dealing with religious pluralism. In 1985 I wrote a largely apologetic book which attempted to deal

11

with several aspects of the conventional wisdom that seemed to control discussions of religious diversity.[8] In a 1995 work, *Salvations: Truth and Difference in Religion*, I suggested a general interpretive perspective on religious diversity rather different from those common in recent academic discussion.[9] The key element in that perspective was a willingness to entertain the possibility of various actual religious ends. Chapter One summarizes this thesis.

The discussion in *Salvations* left many questions still unaddressed. The thesis argued there grew out of a critique of "pluralistic theologies" and a general defense of the particularist claims of religious traditions. I sought to explore how far one might consistently affirm the concrete truth of truly diverse, particularistic religious claims. It was a Christian proposal, in the sense that it was grounded in my own Christian faith. But it was posed in terms that I hoped could be tested and hopefully appropriated by those from other religions, who were likewise committed to specific features of their tradition as constitutive of religious fulfillments, not simply emblematic of such fulfillment.

In that work I was able only briefly to indicate what I found to be the distinctive Christian grounds for my approach.[10] Therefore a question remained, and was raised by many readers. Was the proposal I made an acceptably Christian one? Was it truly rooted in and consistent with Christian scripture and theological principles? This book attempts to answer that question directly, to map a Christian theology that has place for distinct religious ends. Another common response to that earlier work asked for full examples of the comparative theology that would flow from consideration of particular religious traditions in light of my thesis. This book does not claim to meet that request. It offers some brief examples and points to the work of others that I feel fits consistently and fruitfully with my perspective.

The book proceeds in the following way. Part One (Chapter One) offers a definition of religious ends and summarizes a perspective on religious pluralism that would recognize a variety of such ends. I end the chapter with two questions such a vision poses for Christian theology. These become the focus of Part Two.

Part Two (Chapters Two and Three) focuses on Christian tradition itself. The first question asks what Christians mean by salvation. Chapter Two reviews this topic, with special effort to draw on the ecumenical diversity of

---

8. (Heim, 1985).

9. (Heim, 1995). For two different brief summaries of my proposal see (Heim, 1994 and 1996).

10. See chapter six (Heim, 1995).

Christian tradition. The second question asks how Christian tradition has conceived religious ends, particularly heaven and hell. Chapter Three takes up this issue and explores whether we find any precedents or resources in the tradition for understanding multiple religious ends.

Part Three (Chapters Four, Five, and Six) turns to the doctrine of God and draws out a trinitarian framework for understanding religious ends. Since Christians believe God is the creator and sustainer of the world, the existence of diverse religious ends would have to be consistent with God's ordering of the universe and would have to be consistent with God's own character. At this point, the primary focus of our study becomes the Christian understanding of God as Trinity. Chapter Four outlines the significance of the Trinity as the framework for any Christian approach to the issues of religious diversity. It goes on to examine two important recent trinitarian theologies of religion. Chapter Five draws together trinitarian theology and our discussion of religious ends to specify a trinitarian theology of religious ends. It attempts to explain how various religious ends can be grounded in the distinct dimensions of the divine life that exist because God is Trinity. Chapter Six tries to illustrate the way this perspective can be applied in understanding specific religious traditions, particularly Islam and Advaita Vedanta.

Part Four (Chapters Seven and Eight) turns to a global but unavoidable question: Is the prospect of varied religious ends consistent with the Christian eschatological hope? Does such a vision fit with the affirmation that God will bring creation to a consummation marked by a plenitude of goodness, justice, and love? This is the subject of Chapter Seven. Finally, Chapter Eight offers a summary of our project and its implications for interfaith relations.

Part One

The Aims and Ends of Religions

Chapter One

Saving the Particulars:
The Diversity of Religious Ends

The most rigid liberal and conservative theological approaches share a largely undefended assumption that there is and can be only one religious end, one actual religious fulfillment.[1] They then differ fiercely over the means to that end: one way or many ways. From the "one way" side, there is a tendency to homogenize all religions except the home tradition. Despite the explicit testimony and evidence for each faith's unique profile, these particulars are dismissed. All that really needs to be known about other religions is that they are inadequate to achieve religious fulfillment, the one end concretely described by the "home" tradition. From the "many ways" side, there is a tendency to homogenize all religions without exception. Despite the explicit testimony and evidence that seem to set the traditions on diverse paths, any real divergence is dismissed. All that really needs to be known about other religions is that they achieve the same religious goal. Both standpoints are committed to downplay the particular claims and aims of the religions. The first view downplays them in all religions but one; the second view downplays them in all religions without exception, in favor of one particular type of philosophy about religion.[2]

1. This is perhaps most striking in recent "pluralistic theologies" which attack the exclusivism of traditional religious perspectives. Despite their title, this is one point at which these theologies are not pluralistic at all. True difference in religious aims and ends is what they directly deny. For a fuller discussion see (Heim, 1995, chapters one through five).

2. The first view has a specific picture of the religious end, and tends to lump all the

17

These approaches generally see no connection between the concrete particularities of a religion and the end its adherents may attain. On the face of it, this is an odd conviction, since one thing religious traditions seem to agree about is that the ends they seek are rather closely linked with the distinctive ways of life they prescribe. This conviction also seems to offer no rationale for a serious study of traditions in their thick concreteness, since such specific differences do not correspond to any variation in religious outcomes.[3] It is hard to see how we can take the religions seriously and at the same time regard all the distinctive qualities that are precious to each one as essentially unimportant in terms of religious fulfillment.

There is a way we can save the validity of a great deal of the particular testimony of the religions, the qualities that make each substantively unique. We can do this if we entertain the possibility that religious paths in fact lead persons to the distinctively varied states they advertise and on which they set such transcendent value. We can avoid the stale deadlock of the instrumental question over what will get you there ("one way or many ways?") by asking with real openness "way to *what?*"

Gandhi wrote that "[r]eligions are different roads converging to the same point," and asked, "What does it matter if we take different roads so long as we reach the same goal? Wherein is the cause for quarreling?"[4] (Actually, it turns out that it is all too easy to quarrel on exactly this assumption.) But I ask, "What if religions are paths to different ends that they each value supremely? Why should we object?"[5] A famous verse of the *Bhagavad-gita* is often quoted on the presumption that it indicates the identical goal of all religions: "In whatsoever way men approach me, in that same way I receive them."[6] But Krishna's declaration in the voice of supreme *Brahman* appears an equally good charter for a diversity of religious ends, affirming that people will realize the different receptions corresponding to their different ap-

---

other religious traditions together in one general category. The second view tends to accept the various traditions as having their own different historical characteristics, but to homogenize them in terms of an identical religious end, which is therefore typically quite vague.

3. There may be good reasons to study religious differences in regard to cultural or social or historical issues: I mean that the views I have just outlined provide no rationale for being *religiously* interested in the specific character of religious diversity.

4. (Gandhi, 1939, p. 36). Quoted in (Burch, 1972, p. 111).

5. (Burch, 1972, p. 111).

6. *Bhagavad-gita* IV.11 This is the first half of verse 11. An alternative translation, including all of verse 11, is given by Anantanand Rambachan as "Howsoever people approach Me, even so do I welcome them, for the paths people take from every side are Mine." See (Rambachan, 1999, p. 39).

proaches to ultimate reality. If human beings form their ultimate desires freely from among many options, and then through devotion and practice are able to see those desires actually realized, there is no reason to complain about the process but ample room to differ over which end we should seek. There is good cause to give profound attention to the concrete variety of religious traditions, to give the most serious consideration to their particularistic witness, and to expect that nothing will shape our destiny more distinctly than our religious commitment.

As we will discuss in the next chapter, salvation is communion with God and God's creatures through Christ Jesus. It is the Christian religious end, if you like. This does not mean that there are not other religious ends, quite real ones. It only means that Christians hope to be saved from them, and believe that God has offered greater, more inclusive gifts. Christians believe that salvation, the God who offers it, the relations it presupposes, and its priority in divine purpose are objectively real. But salvation has to be accepted. It has to be evaluatively true, or it is not realized. As far as I can tell, other religious traditions can and legitimately do take the same reciprocal view of their own religious aim: it is real and supreme but it can be realized only by those who accept it as so.

In this chapter, I will clarify what I mean by a "religious end" and develop the hypothesis of multiple religious ends. These are key background elements for the theological discussion in the balance of the book. The first section in this chapter will outline the hypothesis. The second section will provide a more detailed discussion of religious ends in relation to religious experience. The final brief section will outline the theological work to follow.

I

Pretend for a moment that we had an angelic visitor who could tell us the future, and that we asked whether some person known to us would be "saved." Consider two possible answers. Suppose on the one hand that our visitor said, "No, she will not be saved, instead she is going to get what she truly wants." Suppose on the other hand, that our visitor said, "Yes, she will be saved, though she will never come to know Christ or have communion with the triune God." Both of these predictions may seem a bit odd to us as Christians. They point up an ambiguity in our use of "salvation." People tend to use the word as if it could refer to only one thing, which in some way embodies all possible good, and as if there could be only one alternative to it, which was completely evil. Thus in common conversation the notion of salvation as a

Christian term, referring to a concretely Christian hope, is often rather thoroughly blurred with the notion of some general positive possibility.

Grace Jantzen has pointed out the false unity implied by transporting the term "salvation" into interreligious discussion. She cautions against the assumption that "all religions have a concept of salvation at all, let alone that they all mean the same thing by it or offer the same way to obtain it."[7] In an important article, Joseph DiNoia faults many Christian theologies of religion on the same ground.[8] Some focus on the manner in which those within other religious traditions may achieve a specifically Christian religious fulfillment. Others stress a common generic goal in the various faiths, perceived behind their specific accounts of their own ends. DiNoia maintains that in both cases the distinctive features of the traditions' varied religious aims fall into the background. They do not "survive their transposition to pluralistic and inclusivist theological contexts."[9] It would be much preferable to find a way to recognize the integrity of the religious traditions in their own terms rather than to denature them in either of these ways.

Those who affirm the validity of one religion and the utter emptiness of all others are ready to deny other traditions any but the most limited, "natural" truths that might be discovered by human reason. Those who affirm the validity of many religions insist that important truth contained in any one religion should be of the general and abstract sort that they can then argue is equivalently available in the others as well. In contrast with both of these approaches, is there a perspective that allows us to affirm, as religiously significant, a much larger proportion of the *distinctive* testimony of the various faith traditions? Are there conditions under which various believers' accounts of their faith might be extensively and simultaneously valid? If there is a positive answer to these questions, it would affirm the various religious traditions as truthful in a much more concrete sense than either the most liberal or most conservative options in the current discussion allow.

The key to such an answer is the availability of more than one realizable religious aim. If different religious practices and beliefs in fact aim at and constitute distinct conditions of human fulfillment, then a very high proportion of what each tradition affirms may be true and valid, in very much the terms that the tradition claims. This is so even if deep conflict remains between the religions regarding priorities, background beliefs, and ultimate metaphysical reality. Two religious ends may represent two human states that

7. (Jantzen, 1984, pp. 579-80).
8. (DiNoia, 1989).
9. (DiNoia, 1989, p. 252).

it is utterly impossible for one person to inhabit at the same time. But there is no contradiction in two different persons each simultaneously attaining one of the two ends. Adherents of different religious traditions may be able to recognize the reality of both ends, though they are not able to agree on the explanation of how and why the two ends exist or on the priority they should be given. On these terms, salvation (the Christian end) may not only differ from conditions humans generally regard as evil or destructive but from those that specific religious traditions regard as most desirable and ultimate.

A religious end or aim is defined by a set of practices, images, stories, and concepts which has three characteristics. First, the set provides material for a thorough pattern of life. The ultimacy often spoken of in definitions of religion is here given a quite concrete meaning. The religious end and the path that leads to it do not address only a limited dimension of life or one particular human need among others. They are ultimate in providing a framework that encompasses all the features of life, practical and sublime, current and future.

Second, at least some of the elements in the set are understood to be *constitutive* of a final human fulfillment and/or to be the sole means of achieving that fulfillment. For instance, for Christians, there is a texture of such elements making reference to Jesus Christ. Relation with Christ is believed to be integral to the deepest human fulfillment itself. Some Buddhists may maintain that all the teachings and instruments used to follow the dharma way are ultimately dispensable, even the eight-fold path itself. But they can only be discarded *after* use, and nothing else is fit to serve the same purpose: one may pass beyond them but everyone must pass through them.

Third, for any individual or community the religious pattern is in practice exclusive of at least some alternative options. Living in accord with the set of stories and practices necessarily involves choices. "The ascetic life leads to peace" and "The sensual life leads to joy" may both be true reports. But we can practice the observance of one more comprehensively only at the expense of the other. For our purposes it makes no difference that there may be a tantric claim that some particular combined practice of asceticism/sensuality will lead to peace *and* joy. This is itself a practice which, if followed, rules out either of the other two paths in their particularity. There is a distinct purity to an exclusive ascetic path or an exclusive sensual path. A path that is some determinate mix of the two excludes either of those other distinctive ends.

The relations among religious ends are, then, as diverse as the ends themselves. Some fulfillments may be similar enough that the paths associated with them reinforce each other to some degree, as typing and piano playing may both train the fingers. Other ends may simply pose no direct obsta-

21

cle, one to the other, save the intrinsic division of finite time and effort needed to pursue both, like marathon running and single parenthood. Yet other ends are so sharply divergent that a decisive step in the direction of one is a move away from the other: strict nonviolence and participation in armed revolution. It is obvious that there may be many goods or secondary goals that "overlap" on the paths to different religious realizations. Discipline is a quality essential to learning the piano or a new language. It is connected with both these different ends, but it is not identical with either of them. If discipline itself were the primary aim, then music or a language would themselves become instrumental means and not ends at all. What for some is an instrument is for others an end.

There is an interesting dynamic balance in the relation of religious ends. The more similar the aims, the more sharply contention arises over whether one path should supersede another. If the aims are nearly identical, this tendency is very powerful. To take a trivial example, if the end in view is word processing, few would not take sides between computers or typewriters as the more adequate tools. It is also true that in the case of such convergent goals, the common features of the religious aims provide a compensatory shared ground on which to struggle and work toward agreement, a set of shared criteria. On the other hand, the more incommensurable religious ends appear, the less they contend for the same "space." Losing weight and learning Spanish are separate aims with their distinct requirements. Though they have less concretely in common, there is a proportionally smaller impetus to substitute one for the other. These dynamics are key elements in understanding religious conflict and the possibilities for mutual understanding.

The religious goal sought by any religious community is integrally related to a comprehensive pattern of life. A particular religious tradition would regard someone as fulfilled or liberated whose life had been most fully shaped by the distinctive pattern it fosters. Religious ends are not extrinsic awards granted for unrelated performances, like trips to Hawaii won in lotteries. To take a Buddhist example, no one is unhappy "in" nirvana or arrives at it unready. This is because the state of cessation is an achievement that life on the right path makes possible. The end is not "enjoyed" until a person becomes what the path to the end makes her or him.[10] The way and the end are one.

Most religious traditions offer strong caution about descriptions of their ends, even descriptions provided by the tradition itself. The caution is

10. This paragraph paraphrases several points made by DiNoia in a very helpful discussion of religious aims (DiNoia, 1992, pp. 6-7, 56-58).

that these can only be provisional accounts: true understanding of the end can come only from direct participation in its actual realization. Such realization lies at the far end of a long process of transformation and/or heightened insight. It is our own lives, our capacities of discernment, our understanding, our emotions, even perhaps the constitution of our nature, that will be different in this new condition. Not only will our circumstances be different, but the means by which we apprehend them will be different. Any presumption that we can describe or grasp such a condition within the terms of our current life is problematic. Devotees of a religious tradition will often readily acknowledge that they are unclear about the full dimensions of the goal they seek. There is mystery that only "being there" can dispel. Some mystery may be part of the arrival itself.

In a religiously plural situation, this presents an obvious problem. If traditions maintain that the only way to know the end they offer is to spend your lifetime actually attaining it, how might one decide which end to pursue? Despite the reservations just noted, religions have to invest real value in descriptions of their aims. These descriptions claim to provide outsiders and beginners, initiates within a tradition, with a true witness about the path and the goal before them. This may not be an exhaustive account, but it is adequate to begin the journey and to differentiate the end in view from others. Apart from explicit descriptions of religious fulfillment, special weight falls on the close association religious traditions make between their end and the path that leads to it. While the goal itself may not be fully understood, we can understand that it stands as the culmination of this distinct set of practices, beliefs, and relations. People may reasonably decide that they will seek an admittedly mysterious end because of the nature of the way that leads to it: an end that is the culmination of *that* practice is given highest value, even if it cannot be fully described. Likewise, people may reasonably decide to follow a particular way (while knowing little or nothing about the specific practices it requires) by reference to the embodiment of its end they have observed in someone else's life.

To frame discussion of religions in terms of "ends" may appear already slanted toward certain faiths. The implication that religion requires a transformation or journey perhaps fits better with so-called "historical" traditions than those that might view the religious good as an already existing reality or situation into which insight is needed. But the definition of religious ends we have offered attempts to honor this distinction. More important, to focus on ends is to focus particularly on the perspective of persons living in pluralistic environments. Study of religions may be undertaken for the sake of purely historical or cultural understanding. But surely it exists primarily in the context of the human religious search, and this search is basically oriented to the ultimate conditions people hope to realize as individuals and communities. To consider religions in the framework of ends is, in part, to stress the connection of the study of religion to the concerns of people who are religious.

We should pause to note that it is certainly possible to fail to actualize any religious end. Instead of achieving one among alternative fulfillments, a person may attain none at all. There are human conditions, whether contemporary or eschatological or both, that no valid religious view seeks as its final end or regards as consistent with its end. Such would be states of perennial suffering, of thorough ignorance, of malicious destructiveness towards self or others. On this point there is ample room for common cause among the faiths, for spiritual and practical cooperation to overcome these conditions, even from differing perspectives. There is an enormous difference between a lack of religious fulfillment of any description and the achievement of *some* religious fulfillment.

In its simplest form, the hypothesis of multiple religious ends is not committed to any particular metaphysical view. Obviously, the universe does have some ultimate character or order. One or more of the religions may in fact offer descriptions of that order that are substantially better than others. But the hypothesis requires only that the nature of reality be such as to allow humans to phenomenally realize varied religious ends. There are many different constructions of reality that might allow this, including ones that correspond closely to particular religious visions.

Coordinate with accounts of their religious ends, faith traditions make at least implicit philosophical and empirical claims. Investigation and argument about these is possible, and sometimes necessary. Religious apologetics remain a viable and honorable discipline, in which faiths defend and advocate both the worldview within which their religious end is situated and the evaluative ultimacy of that end.[11] Though we recognize there are other religious perspectives from which varying conclusions can be reached, it is appropriate for each to make the case for the universal validity of their perspective. It is this impetus toward the universal that forces us to take the reality and the truths of varying traditions seriously.

Though we cannot now resolve the differences among religions at this level, these are matters of supreme importance for the objective relation that

---

11. By "apologetics" I mean both "negative" arguments that there is no internal incompatibility in the primary convictions of a religious tradition and "positive" cumulative arguments that one religious tradition's conceptual scheme is superior to another. This formulation is borrowed from Paul Griffiths (1991).

exists among religious ends. Each faith's conception and pursuit of its end is inextricably bound up with these ultimate empirical questions. Yet even without being able to resolve these differences, it may be possible for religions to reciprocally recognize the actuality of multiple religious ends. For instance, even if the Buddhist account of dependent co-arising is not an accurate metaphysical description of the inner nature of the world (which turns out to be better described in Christian tradition), yet an experiential religious fulfillment described by the category of nirvana may be an actual human state. Even if there is neither a triune, eternal God nor a created universe (and the universe turns out to be better described by Buddhist metaphysics), Christians might actually experience communion with a personal divine being. Christians would have their own explanations of the first case and Buddhists their own explanations of the second.

The hypothesis affirms the reality of different experiential states of religious fulfillment. It does not require that all of the elements a tradition associates with attainment of that state are also empirically true. One religious fulfillment may be associated in its tradition with an affirmation of the eternity of the universe, another with affirmation of the creation of the universe. One may be associated with a theory of the self and another with a theory of the no-self. To regard the religious fulfillments as real does not entail accepting in their entirety both sides of these oppositions.

Realization of one of these religious ends, or the realization of several of them by different persons, leaves the metaphysical questions still undecided. The answers to those questions will determine the ultimate status and relation of those existing fulfillments, and determine which religion or religions, if any, provides the ultimate and more inclusive framework for the truths in others. It is possible, of course, that all religious persons experience only illusion in this life and extinction in the next and are part of no coherent order or purpose. The religions are collectively committed to the proposition that the universe is such as to allow some fuller end than this.[12] The various religious traditions can agree that their ends are not only a transient phase in a person's earthly life, but have a more permanent or transcendent character. All would seem to agree that though their religious end is not merely such a phase, it can in fact constitute a distinctive form and condition of life here and now for adherents. Our religious choices, practices, and formation do determine distinct religious fulfillments in this life and in the next as well.

Recognition of diverse religious ends is the condition for recognition of

---

12. It is the validation of this fundamental positive claim that is the primary concern of John Hick (1989).

the decisive significance of our religious choices and development, a signifi-cance that the particularistic witness of the individual religions collectively affirms. We can expect a fulfillment in line with the "one and only" path that leads us to it. There is no cogent reason to assume that all of us — the vast majority against their prior conditioning and desires — will experience only one among these religious ends or some undefined condition beyond any of them. We may readily pose this question in terms of postmortem destinies. But the point holds also if we consider religious diversity entirely in an earthly frame. Indeed, one of the recommendations of my approach is the way in which it envisions some consistency in the way religious ends are achieved in the historical realm and in any transhistorical realm. Whether in an eschatological future or here and now, our conditions of religious fulfill-ment are significantly constituted by the expectations, relations, images, and practices that we bring to them.[13]

This is plainly the case with proximate historical forms of religious ful-fillment: living a Christian life or following the dharma, for instance. The meaning, overcoming of selfishness, moral discipline, and hope which per-sons experience in such fulfillments are permeated with the concrete ele-ments of a tradition. The lives that lead to the rewards of a Buddhist monas-tic, a Muslim imam, a Hindu brahmin priest or a Baptist deacon have unique textures. It is not hard to note generic similarities in these cases: textual devo-tion, communal structures, ritual practices. But for any person who wishes to attain a religious fulfillment, generic elements alone are entirely insufficient. The person will need particular texts, a specific community, discrete rituals.

We become different persons through our concrete choices and religious practices. Through these means we may increasingly realize a distinctive aim. In the characteristic religious dialectic, as we progress toward the realization of the

---

13. I have pointed out elsewhere (Heim, 1992, pp. 39-40) that despite John Hick's contention that there is and can be only a single ultimate religious end, his own vision of eschatology appears to expect that the experiences of a world to come could only be taken by the human subjects involved as concrete confirmation of *particular* religious expecta-tions. He emphasizes that postmortem experiences of human consciousness would bear the shape of the categories an individual's history had provided for them. This would not require of course any thoroughly literal conformity to the detail of such expectations. To take one of his examples, experience of communion with a personal God and a risen Jesus would confirm a Christian's expectations beyond a reasonable doubt, with or without robes and wings. If in fact such events are significantly conditioned by our prior practice and commitment, then it would seem there is good reason to credit the "one and only" tes-timony of various religious traditions. It is unlikely that one can attain to an end in any other manner than by following the way that aims at or near it in preference to other pos-sibilities.

aim, we at the same time develop an ever deeper and clearer desire for that end itself above all others. Finally, religious consummation is the entrance into a state of fulfillment by one whose aspiration has been so tuned and shaped by particular anticipations of that state, and by anticipatory participation in aspects of that state, that this end represents the perfect marriage of desire and actuality. It is the reception of a perfect gift by one whose expectation has been tuned to the specific desire for that particular gift and no other.

We can certainly point to great figures in varied religious traditions who exhibit some common moral and spiritual qualities. But we can hardly deny the different textures of these achievements. The examples are clearly not identical, however similar selected items may be. If there is some sense in which our selected devotees all strike us as having a claim to be "good" people, it still appears that one would have to choose between one way of being good and another. It is also clear that people in various traditions pursue and claim to participate in religious attainments other than or in addition to moral transformation. The thesis of an identical religious end for all can be proposed with rather more impunity for the world to come than the current one, but in neither case is it persuasive if we are serious about the cultural-linguistic component of all experience.

If we take religions in their thickest historical, empirical description, then "one and only" judgments appear inevitable, almost tautological. In this life, there is no way to participate in the distinctive dimensions of Buddhist religious fulfillment but the Buddhist path. The only way to Jewish fulfillment is the Jewish way. The same is true of each tradition. Here again, the hypothesis of multiple religious ends coheres with the data we have before us, with the importance of a religion's concrete texture. The impetus for study of religious diversity is the realization that we cannot assume we already know what it is like to be a Sikh or a Sufi. The only way to find out is to approach that tradition and its adherents directly. If we do so, we discover a unique complex of elements, interlocking patterns of life, which cannot be descriptively equated to anything else.

We may speculate about convergence on a metaphysical plane between, say, Buddhist "saints" and Jewish "saints." We may be able to specify some similarities in the effects of their practices. However, the premise of the whole discussion is that we have no difficulty generally distinguishing between them to begin with, for they are embedded in communities, practices, images, and doctrines that are distinct. If for the moment we leave aside religious ends as postmortem or transhistorical states, it would seem that religious traditions are simply, descriptively exclusive. To know one is not to know the others. Each is a "one and only," and their religious ends are many.

The difficulty of our human condition comes from a mixture of suffering, evil, and ignorance. The religions diagnose these in different patterns and address them in diverse ways. There is no need to deny validity to any pattern save that of our own tradition. But there is every reason to expect that the specific nature of our destiny hangs upon adherence to one rather than others. Living in accordance with religious commitments, our life is formed by them. They make us who we are. We can judge how well we have abided by our commitments, but we cannot judge with certainty the grounds for the commitments themselves. We could no more judge what our life might have been like as a Methodist instead of a Sikh than we can compare the children we might have had with those we did.[14]

There are of course interesting cases of the combination of religious traditions: cases where people may follow both Buddhist and Confucian paths, for instance. This only reinforces the point we have been making. Were they not exclusive paths to unique ends, there would be no need to follow two ways, since the same range of ends could be achieved in either one alone. Both are practiced because each constitutes a unique pattern, yielding distinct benefits, benefits in this case regarded as compatible and complementary.

Religious ends are constituted by a unity of various discrete elements. In this sense, there is inevitable and extensive overlap among religious aims. As an aggregated sum of practices, doctrines, and injunctions, no faith is without duplication elsewhere. If it is a Christian virtue to honor one's parents or to keep a Sabbath, then these virtues are realized in and through other religions as well. Truth or benefits that attach discretely to these elements in one faith must also attach to them in another. These truths are available in more than one tradition. However, both the mix of elements and the integrative principles that unify them vary significantly among the religions.

If we abstract from the specific aims of actual religious traditions, we can formulate other, more general functional ends that religions serve. They may organize and sustain major civilizations, as the world religions all have. They may foster certain generic moral attitudes. They may structure human institutions like the family. By substituting aims like these in place of the primary, explicit, and final aims of the religions themselves, one can judge the religions, correctly, as roughly parallel means of fulfilling these social functions.

These last two dimensions we have discussed — the similarity of specific items across traditions and the generic associated functions that reli-

14. The previous two sentences paraphrase (Burch, 1972, p. 20).

gions may serve — coexist in every religious tradition with the unique particularities and the integrating ultimate vision that constitute the whole. The religious end of a particular faith is a compound of these three dimensions. If we give "religious end" an abstract meaning — the achievement of *some* religious fulfillment among several possible alternatives and/or the successful function of religion to serve some generic social role — then we can say that many if not all paths truly achieve religious ends. There is an "any way" sign at most forks on the religious journey. A number of turns will get you to a real destination, but not the same destination. If on the other hand "religious end" is a concrete religious fulfillment of some determinate nature, as described by one of the traditions, then it is clear that it is constituted by certain features to the exclusion of others. There is an "only way" sign at many turnings on the religious journey. In either case we must acknowledge that all these paths link with each other, that "cross-over" travel is a real possibility. At most points a "two way traffic" sign is appropriate. Roads can bear travelers over the same ground toward different destinations, whether those travelers pass in opposite directions or go side by side for this overlapping leg of their trip.

The hypothesis of multiple religious ends offers the best account of this geography. It provides the only coherent foundation that can uphold each of three elements that I believe are essential for an effective and responsible understanding of religious pluralism. These three are ordinarily not thought compatible with each other, and many would not desire to see them as compatible. The first of these is the religious significance of careful study of faith traditions in their particularity. The second is the recognition of distinctive and effective religious truth in other religions, truth that contrasts with that of my own faith. The third is the validity of witness on the part of any one faith tradition to its "one and only" quality, indeed to its superiority in relation to others. I argue for an authentic religious pluralism, in which the distinctness of various religious ends is acknowledged. This implies that the validity of religious witness must also be acknowledged. Where witness can have no meaning, it is dubious if dialogue may either.

This hypothesis presumes an open set of varied religious ends available for realization both within the historical horizon of human life and beyond it. The historical and eschatological sets may differ. For instance, some religious fulfillments that appear irreducibly distinct within the historical frame may ultimately collapse together in some future state. But this hypothesis does not presume that all faith-fulfillments do in fact reduce to one, either in the historical frame or eschatologically. Individuals and communities live their way through a cloud of live, alternative possibilities. In their passing, they make some of these possibilities rather than others concrete, as the act of detecting an electron "collapses" a quantum probability distribution into an actual location or velocity.

In summary, let us consider several features of this hypothesis of multiple religious ends. First, this hypothesis directs us unavoidably toward the religious traditions themselves and their accounts of their own religious aims. It is the religions as they actually exist — as patterns and complexes of life directed toward particular textures of human fulfillment — that are addressed, not a generic construct imposed on them. I grant a high priority to perspectives on religious diversity that allow for religious significance and validity in the particularistic features a religious tradition itself values. Such perspectives indicate the intrinsic value of study and dialogue that deal with the "thick," distinctive natures of the religion. The hypothesis of multiple religious ends clearly provides a basis for such study and impels us to take the testimony of the traditions and their believers with great seriousness.

Though this approach affirms the value of confessional witness, it also relativizes any one tradition's claim to have an absolute monopoly on truth. It indicates that more than one faith tradition may be correct in claiming to offer a distinctive human religious fulfillment. That is, it relativizes any single tradition not by the dubious claim to impose a philosophical interpretation from an absolute vantage point above that possible for any actual religion, but precisely by the actual validity of other religious traditions themselves. It is not one imperialistic and absolute theory about religions that finally can or should curb any tradition's grandiose claims, but direct encounter with the concrete living reality and truth of other religious paths.

The second notable feature of this hypothesis is the manner in which it deals directly with the cultural and historical conditioning of all religious life. Some interpreters put extreme stress on this conditioning, to disparage the capacity of any religious tradition to offer a distinctive, universal truth for all people. If we are to maintain any consistency in the way we treat religious subjects and the way we deal with other realities, it seems we ought to recognize that human knowledge and experience are partially constituted by the contexts and categories we bring to them.[15] This includes the experience of religious fulfillment, both now and in the ultimate future.

15. See (Davis, 1989, chapter six) for a very helpful discussion of the necessary and legitimate role of mental models or "cognitive sets" in perception. "Preconceptions" are not only inextricable from most experience but play a crucial role in putting us in touch with specific aspects of reality in specific ways.

Religious ends are not conditions that obtain on some absolute "other side" of these parameters of humanity itself. We cannot posit some event that would be experienced as having the identical content and the identical meaning by persons who come to it with entirely different expectations, formation, and categories. It is interesting that this kind of "blinding revelation," wiping out all the mediating structures that have been built up in a person's distinct culture, tradition, and personality, is often an axiomatic end point in both very conservative and very liberal theologies of religion. But any revelation consistent with humanity as we know it will condescend to the conditions of our knowing (even if stretching those conditions), not violate them. Revelation in history has to do precisely with God's acts to provide "preconceptions" we could not otherwise bring as constitutive elements of experience.

The third feature I would note is that with the hypothesis of multiple religious ends our perspective on religious differences shifts somewhat in focus. Contrasts in ultimate metaphysical visions remain. And these remain deeply significant, as we indicated earlier. But we shift from dealing solely with flat issues of truth and falsehood to facing alternatives. We ask not "Which religion alone is true?" but "What end is most ultimate, even if many are real?" and "Which life will I hope to realize?" Let us presume for the moment that the following ends are actual possibilities: the cessation of self, the realization of an absolute single self which is "non-dual," communion with the triune God, living on only in my effects on historical posterity. These are real human states, whose attainment depends significantly on the practice and aspiration of the person who attains them. And these practices and aspirations can only be acquired through the medium of religious tradition.[16] The ends are not identical, and in reaching one we will not automatically attain others. That is, in approaching religious differences emphasis falls on the contrast of their *positive* ends.

As a Christian, it appears to me to make perfectly good sense to say two kinds of things. First, we may say that another religion is a true and valid path to the religious fulfillment it seeks. We may agree with the Dalai Lama for instance, when he says, "Liberation in which 'a mind that understands the sphere of reality annihilates all defilements in the sphere of reality' is a state that only Buddhists can accomplish. This kind of *moksha* or *nirvana* is only explained in the Buddhist scriptures, and is achieved only through Buddhist practice."[17] There is no way to the Buddhist end but the Buddhist way.

16. Or, in the case of the last option, through the medium of a purposely non-religious tradition, which has some of the same formal features.
17. (Lama, 1990, p. 169).

Second, we may say what the book of Acts says of Jesus Christ, that "there is salvation in no one else, for there is no other name under heaven given among mortals by which we must be saved" (Acts 4:12). There is a relation with God and other creatures made possible in Christ that can only be realized in communion with Christ.

On these terms, each tradition can acknowledge the *reality* of the religious end sought by the other, in terms largely consistent with those used by that tradition itself. After describing the Buddhist end, the Dalai Lama says, "According to certain religions, however, salvation is a place, a beautiful paradise, like a peaceful valley. To attain such a state as this, to achieve such a state of *moksha,* does not require the practice of emptiness, the understanding of reality. In Buddhism itself, we believe that through the accumulation of merit one can obtain rebirth in heavenly paradises like the Tushita."[18] The Christian end, then, is something like one of the pleasant interludes that Buddhists may enjoy between births as a reward for merit on their path toward true release. As a kind of mirror image, consider the statement of a Christian theologian: "Buddhists do not attain Christian salvation, since their Way does not lead to that personal relationship with God which is salvation. They attain a high degree of compassion and inner peace; and their unselfish devotion to the truth as they see it will surely fit them to receive salvation from a personal God when his saving activity becomes clear to them."[19] The Buddhist end is a kind of compassionate selflessness that would be an appropriate preparation for relation with God.

These are classically inclusivist views, which interpret other faiths ultimately in the categories of the home religion. But each recognizes the distinctive reality of the other's religious end, and so recognizes a diversity of religious ends. Each regards the other's ultimate as penultimate, leaving open the further possibility of transformation. There is no necessary contradiction in these two accounts of possible human ends, though there is a decisive divergence in their evaluative frameworks for these ends and there are contradictions in the metaphysical assumptions associated with each framework. Both accounts could be flatly wrong. But there is no logical reason that both cannot be descriptively correct. In fact, if one of the writer's characterizations is correct, it implies a very substantial measure of truth in the other.

Both writers might agree in broad terms to the existence of one "salvific process." But they would mean by this that a person can move in succession from the pursuit of the aim of one tradition toward that of another. This is

18. (Lama, 1990, p. 169).
19. (Ward, 1990, p. 16).

emphatically not the same thing as insisting there is one and only one religious fulfillment. Accepting different religious ends allows for mutual recognition of extensive *concrete* substantive truth in another tradition. Ironically, this degree of mutual agreement is ruled out by those who insist on one truth in all religions and so insist that the Buddhist end and the Christian one must be the same.

In a moment, we will pursue our hypothesis a bit further. But first we should acknowledge that many people find it self-evident that there can be only one real human religious end. Those who hold the popular view that various religions are different paths to the same goal and those who insist that all are lost unless they adopt one particular faith agree on this dogma. It is not very common to suggest that both are mistaken. Yet we would be wiser to presume that a variety of actual religious ends are open to humanity, a fact to which the existence of diverse religions testifies. Pluralism looks real. The best explanation for this appearance turns out to be that it is real.

Why do so many dismiss this possibility out of hand? The first reason is that the simplest formulation of such pluralism is a "polytheistic" one that has become highly problematic. The easiest way to imagine a different set of religious ends is to picture them in connection with a set of different objects. Let us suppose one group of people worshiped trees, another worshiped Apollo, yet another worshiped their ancestors, and yet another worshiped an angelic power from the planet Neptune. Let us further suppose that the beliefs of each of these groups were essentially correct. What the worshipers expect from these relationships is truly realized. We can well understand how these communities would lead different kinds of lives and reach different ends. Because there are various actual "gods" or religious powers, it makes sense that they might have quite diverse (even opposing) characters and constitute quite different conditions for people who relate to them. Devotees of one religious power need not deny or ignore the reality of another, nor the reality of the religious fulfillment it offers. In fact, it might even be possible to benefit from more than one of these powers, so long as direct conflict was avoided. The steps required to gain Apollo's assistance in love might pose no serious inconvenience for the steps required by piety toward one's ancestors. However, the two would clash if both required comprehensive or ultimate commitments.

This situation (which was apparently characteristic of the first-century Graeco-Roman world) made a pluralism of religious ends appear quite natural. Our cultural assumptions have changed. Whether we are theists or not, we all tend to participate in a monotheistic consciousness: there is, at most, one religious ultimate. This reflects our general expectation (supported by the rise of modern science) that there must be one, consistent "set of rules" for the universe rather than arbitrarily different laws in different cases or places. There then could be no more than one ontologically ultimate, perfect, maximally powerful divinity. The question focuses on what the character of that one is, if it in fact exists. To many, a short additional equation plainly follows: one religious ultimate equals one religious end. Even the fiercest arguments about religious pluralism today tend to take place between those who are agreed on this point but disagree over who may attain the one end, and by what means.[20]

In truth, these assumptions do not rule out a pluralism of ends. Even if there is one truly ultimate religious reality, there is no reason that human beings might not attach themselves to some lesser power or entity, give that power final priority in their lives, and so realize some end commensurate with that relation. From one point of view this could be called "idolatry," but it does not follow that idolatry is without its own rewards. Suppose, for instance, that the one religious ultimate were as it is described in Buddhist tradition. Even within that tradition, it has been common to acknowledge that there may well be divine powers ("gods") with whom humans might have interactions, leading to certain results. Buddhist iconography is rich in heavens and hells, with attendant divine and demonic figures. These are all given penultimate status in the larger Buddhist religious scheme, but they are recognized as real conditions. There is no logical reason why a universe with a single religious ultimate might not also encompass a variety of religious ends. The variety could follow because some people establish a primary religious relationship to something other than the religious ultimate or because there are distinctly different ways to relate to that ultimate or for both reasons.

As I noted, in its simple form the hypothesis of multiple religious ends is not committed to any particular view of the religious ultimate or even to the principle that there must be one fully perfect and all-powerful ultimate. All that is required is that the universe have the objective features necessary for at least some of the religious fulfillments proposed in the varied religious traditions to be real human possibilities. I subscribe to the monotheistic assumption, and I believe that the structure within which religious ends unfold is given by the triune God of Christian confession. There are Christian reasons that I have developed the hypothesis of multiple religious ends, though I have argued at length that it can make its way quite adequately without any

---

20. This is the general framework for a collection of pluralist essays (Knitter and Hick, 1987) and an opposing collection by inclusivist authors (D'Costa, 1990), though a contributor like Panikkar resists the typology.

particular confessional support.[21] However, in this book I want to outline a concretely Christian theology of religious ends. Before we turn to the beginnings of that task in Chapter Two, I would like to offer some further specification of the hypothesis, by considering the issue of religious experience.

II

If there are numerous religious ultimates as the objects of various faiths, and a number of religious ends in connection with those different objects, then variety of religious experience would be exactly what one would expect. The fact that such variety is plainly to be observed has always been an item in favor of a more polytheistic outlook. From that outlook, religious experiences vary because there are differences on the "object end" of the experience. Since such a perspective has increasingly been rejected in favor of a monotheistic assumption, the diversity of religious experience has become more problematic. One religious ultimate and one religious end seem to suggest there should be uniform experience. Variety requires some explanation.

If the polytheistic outlook explains the diversity of religious experience largely by variety on the object end, it is common for contemporary versions of the monotheistic outlook to stress diversity on the subject end. If the same religious ultimate figures in all true religious experience, it is the different cultural locations and psychological states of the experiencers that account for the distinct character of those experiences. If we add to this an axiom that there is no reason to privilege any particular set of experiences or associated religious beliefs, we get the very influential contemporary perspective on religious pluralism perhaps best expressed in John Hick's "pluralistic hypothesis."[22] On this view, the religious ultimate is in itself unknowable, but varied religious experiences arise in response to encounter with that ultimate. We can only say that in this or that particular cultural context humans expressed their encounter with the ineffable mystery in these terms. As Stanley Samartha puts it, "Although each response to Mystery has a normative claim on the followers of that particular tradition, the criteria derived from one response cannot be made the norm for judging the responses of other traditions."[23]

The polytheistic outlook tells us there are many religious objects and

---

21. (Heim, 1994).
22. (Hick, 1989, p. 240). A similar perspective is worked out in (Samartha, 1991).
23. (Samartha, 1991, p. 83).

ends, and religious experiences give us concrete, valid information about them. From the "monomystery" outlook, there is a single religious ultimate and a single religious end, but religious experiences give us no concrete information at all about them. All the particularity in the experiences comes from the subject side. It tells us where people were coming from when they met mystery. John Hick, who has developed this view most rigorously, goes to this extreme for a reason that appears to him cogent both philosophically and religiously. He wishes to defend a religious interpretation of reality as reasonable, in the face of rational critiques of all religion as illusion. A key element in that defense is the evidence of religious experience. Hick argues that in the absence of definitive rational proof for or against religious interpretation of the world, it makes sense for people to take religious experience as a deciding factor in favor of religious faith.

However, which way the weight of the evidence of religious experience will fall seems to depend on what it is taken as evidence for. If it is supposed to be evidence for some particular, confessional religious reality — for a specific kind of religious ultimate or a concrete religious end among others — then only some of it counts for that thesis and much of it goes in another direction. Religious experiences vary and may even conflict at many points, seeming to cancel each other out. They don't uniformly testify to a single, detailed description of the religious ultimate. This could be taken as providing good reason *not* to believe in any specific religious ultimate or end. Some philosophers of religion suggest that if we were to take the traditions' specific claims seriously in any concrete sense we would undercut the value of *all* religious experience as evidence, since it would then support a mass of conflicting propositions. On the other hand, if religious experience is weighed as evidence for *some* kind of religious ultimate, a mystery unknown in itself, then it might all be taken to point in the same direction. If religious experience is to count cumulatively as evidence for the same proposition, that proposition will have to be one of extraordinary generality.[24] If we are looking only for evidence that humans are in contact with "something more," with an "x," then we can count all religious experience as evidence in favor of our thesis. The

---

24. This is precisely John Hick's argument, which runs as follows. If one maintains that there is real, cognitive truth in religion, a primary pillar of this contention must be the validity of religious experience. But if religious experience is to testify consistently to any truth, it must be one that is beyond the obvious contradiction of various concrete religious experiences. Therefore one who wishes to defend a religious interpretation of reality is in fact compelled toward some version of the "pluralistic hypothesis," which construes the experiences as conditioned versions of the same encounter with the "Real" (Hick, 1989, pp. 233-36).

testimony no longer conflicts. It all agrees: there is something out there, even if all we can say about it is that humans adopt this series of dispositions toward it. Religious experience will rule against each religion taken one at a time, but it will support religion collectively, all at once.

There seems to be some sleight of hand in co-opting the specific accounts of varied religious ends as evidence for belief in one mysterious and virtually unspecified goal as the reality referred to in each case. The argument in defense of that move goes as follows. Since religious experiences are varied and even conflicting, there are only three options: to reject them all as illusory, to take a few as reliable and reject all others as false, or to take them all as symbolic or mythical representations of a real but mysterious reality. If one is committed to a religious outlook, the first option is ruled out. If one adopts the second option, then you have to explain away the religious experiences that do not have the "right" confessional features without undercutting the validity of the experiences that do — a difficult task. Some version of the third option then must be defended as the best way to validate religion, because one can argue that all the evidence supports the religious hypothesis (though admittedly in a very loose sense).

This analysis of religious experience is flawed. In any other area when we are faced with diverse perceptions (including conflicting ones), it is extraordinarily unusual to conclude that none of these perceptions are in touch with the world itself but all are responses to an "unexperienced noumenon."[25] The more common strategy is to seek some reconciliation of the inconsistencies. If this can be done by "saving" the validity of the perceptions themselves, this is rationally preferable to advancing a theory which drastically undercuts confidence in any connection between the perceptions and reality.

In other words, when confronted with quite diverse experiential accounts of an object or a person or an event, we do not usually limit our alternatives to the three given above. Those three options would be to take all the accounts as illusory, to hold that the different accounts cancel each other out and therefore make any particular description of the object improbable, or to conclude that all the experiences do reflect encounter with a single reality, but don't tell us anything about that reality in itself, only about the kind of dispositions people develop after meeting it. This last approach especially seems very strained. When applied to the evidence of religious experience, it imposes a high level of consistency, even uniformity, on that experience, but at the cost of reducing its referential value to near zero. The three options leave out a better alternative.

25. (Gellman, 1997, p. 115).

In a recent book, Jerome Gellman has made a careful and convincing case for a quite different approach to religious experience and religious pluralism.[26] Gellman's larger argument is that philosophical consideration of religious experience provides strong rational support for the existence of God. He considers the diversity of religious experience as a possible challenge to this argument. He notes that most of what is regarded as incompatibility in religious experiences can be dealt with in the same way that we deal with discrepancies in other varied experiences of the same reality. Different aspects of one reality may come uppermost in experience at different times and for different people. Here the cultural conditioning and personal idiosyncrasies which Hick wishes to make the sources of the entire content of religious experience (with a bare stimulus alone coming from the religious ultimate itself) are given full scope as significant factors.

Gellman's thesis stresses that it is fully possible to have a determinate view of the religious ultimate and still to retain the evidentiary value of religious experience. In order to conclude that two experiences of God are incompatible,

> what we need is at least some alleged experiences showing that God's character is *exclusively* of one sort, with other alleged experiences showing that God's character is exclusively of another, *logically incompatible* sort. Or we need alleged experiences showing that God's character is exclusively of one sort, and that God never can seem to act out of character, with alleged experiences showing God acting out of *that* character.[27]

Though such pairs of experiences exist, Gellman maintains they are fewer than often supposed. And major religious traditions have developed ways of harmonizing the dissonant experiences, ways not philosophically inferior to Hick's "pluralistic hypothesis." Gellman says, "The attempt at harmonization should be guided by the desire to accommodate as much of the appearances as is possible as indicative of reality. Any adjudication which in this regard saves more phenomenal content than another is to be preferred, everything else being equal."[28] Though conflicting religious explanations for the data of religious experience cannot all be correct, this does not remove the presumptive value of the data.

This is particularly so if the divine object is understood to have a complex nature. Gellman says that if some people experience God as loving and

26. (Gellman, 1997) chapter four is devoted particularly to this issue.
27. (Gellman, 1997, p. 102).
28. (Gellman, 1997, p. 112).

others experience God as just, "they may both be experiencing the true nature of God, a nature both loving and just."[29] Within most religious traditions, a certain spectrum of varying religious experiences is presumed. And within most religious traditions the religious ultimate is characterized in some way by having multiple attributes, even "polar attributes."[30]

More to the point, Gellman notes that alleged experiences of God "often include the perception of God's inexhaustible fullness."[31] He suggests that in religious experience something about God is openly revealed or directly encountered, but that typically the same experience also includes a perception of God's "inexhaustible plenitude, a plenitude only intimated but not open to view."[32] Gellman believes this is what religious people often mean in referring to their experiences as "ineffable." Clearly such experiences are not literally and absolutely indescribable, since the same people who call them ineffable take great care in describing and distinguishing them from other experiences. Gellman suggests that it is the dimension of plenitude, of unknown further depths in the one being experienced, that is indicated with this language. In a simple analogy, we might compare this to our experience of a person we know in a certain context as a neighbor or a coworker. At some time we might hear from others who claim to know a quite different dimension of this person: perhaps they served with him in a war or know him as an outstanding musician or as a former professional athlete. We would respond one way to these alleged experiences if we felt confident we had a near-exhaustive familiarity with the person. We would respond quite differently if our own experience already included intimations of unknown spaces, years unaccounted for, signs of a prior life, even an indefinable sense of depth in the person. Strictly speaking, we had no experience of these other facets. But we might receive these new "contradictory" accounts as reasonable *confirmation* of our prior intimation of something undisclosed. "I might have known that something like this was the case."

Gellman, who holds God to be a personal being, says God is not *only* a personal being. God is

> an inexhaustible being, possessed of an inexhaustible, hidden plenitude, save for that part of the plenitude with whose open, revealed presence the subject is graced. Given all of this, *judging from what is revealed of God in experience,* we can readily see how it could be possible for God to be experi-

29. (Gellman, 1997, p. 101).
30. See (Carman, 1994) for an excellent discussion of this point.
31. (Gellman, 1997, p. 116).
32. (Gellman, 1997, p. 117).

enced in ways other than and contradictory to His being a personal being. For instead, other features of God could emerge into the open out of the plenitude, just as God's personhood does. God could be experienced wholly as an impersonal being. And we can readily understand how it could be possible that the experience of God as a wholly impersonal being would be pure "bliss and joy," as are experiences of impersonal Brahman.[33]

Experiences of God as personal and experiences of the divine as impersonal are thus reconciled, with each retaining cognitive validity. It would not be possible to effect this reconciliation if the experiences in question were of the divine as nothing but personal and experiences of the divine as nothing but impersonal. It is the dimension of plenitude in the experiences that makes this possible.

Gellman's concern is to rescue the maximum volume of religious experience as rational warrant for the existence of God. He offers this harmonization of diverse experiences simply as an example, showing that it is possible and therefore that diversity of religious experience cannot be used to rule out its validity as evidence for the existence of God. He also shows that to achieve this end it is not necessary to go to the extreme of denying that God is experienced as God actually is in *any* of these experiences. Instead, Gellman's example indicates that contrasting experiences may both reflect encounter with real aspects of one God.[34]

---

33. (Gellman, 1997, p. 118).

34. This also points up a problem or at least a deep ambiguity with Hick's contention that we can with equal validity regard the one religious reality, "the Real," as either impersonal or personal (Hick, 1989, chapters fourteen, fifteen, and sixteen). If this means that people are right to regard the Real as either solely and exclusively impersonal or solely and exclusively personal, then the statement tells us nothing except that it is acceptable to believe logically contradictory things about the Real, and any other contraries could be substituted for these. If Hick's contention means that there is an obligation of some sort on those who represent the Real in one of these ways to recognize validity in the alternative representation, then the apparent even-handedness cannot hide inescapable asymmetries. A definite advantage attaches to personal representation of the Real, since it includes intrinsic impersonal dimensions while the reverse is not true. That is, the personalistic view can affirm the validity of "impersonal" religious experience in a way (as true experience of real aspects of the divine nature) that no impersonalistic view can reciprocally affirm the validity of experience of a personal God. Most recently, Hick has argued that both terms can be used because the Real is "beyond characterization by the range of concepts available to human thought" (Hick, 2000, p. 35). Their parity lies in their similar inadequacy, since no positive concept can refer to the Real. This would seem to imply that one can call God "personal" or "impersonal" because one can call God literally anything, to equal lack of effect. But Hick himself does refer positively to the Real, a practice he justifies by classi-

This also indicates that not all proposed reconciliations of this diverse data are equal. Gellman's reconciliation of the data in terms of a personal God differs strikingly from another version offered by the venerable tradition of Advaita Vedanta. From this perspective, experience of a divinity with personal characteristics is experience of *saguna Brahman* (the ultimate with attributed qualities) as opposed to *nirguna Brahman* (the ultimate without such qualities). There is a clear hierarchy between these two. *Saguna Brahman* is a lower level of truth, suitable for people at an earlier level of spiritual development.[35] *Nirguna Brahman* is the true religious ultimate, and personalistic representations of it must eventually give way, dispelled as instrumental illusion. The two categories of religious experience are reconciled, but by making one an imperfect form of the other, an imperfect form that can be eliminated completely with no religious loss. A classic parable likens enlightenment to a person who believes he sees a snake in the path and then realizes it is a piece of rope. In this realization the illusion of an animate agent evaporates, to leave only a true insight into impersonal reality in its place.

Personalistic theism, Gellman's example, provides a reconciliation of a different sort. Here experience of God as impersonal and experience of God as personal are combined, with neither being reducible to the other, any more than we can say of a human that they are a person but not a body. If the object on the path actually *is* a snake, it does not lose the substantive inanimate properties one presumed it to have in mistaking it for a rope. It still takes up space, has length and width, weight, and so on. Those perceptions remain valid perceptions. Similarly, a human person has impersonal dimensions (physiological and physical properties) and personal ones. We may experience one to the near exclusion of the other, but neither is simply an imperfect form of the other. We could say that the *saguna/nirguna* distinction puts a stronger emphasis on one true perception of the ultimate and narrows the complexity of the actual features of the divine ultimate. Personalistic theism affirms more thorough validity for both types of religious experience. If we accept Gellman's criterion that we should prefer an account which rationally

---

fying such reference as formal or indirect rather than substantive. And in practice he seems to take impersonality as a baseline. See Stephen Williams's criticism of Hick to this effect (Williams, 1997, p. 38). Williams contends that Hick deploys his "neutral" claim in a manner characteristic of a particular religious perspective, which sees a personal view of the divine as an optional and subordinate form for apprehending an impersonal reality.

35. Within Hindu tradition this hierarchical relation is maintained by Advaita Vedanta (whose great exponent was Sankara) but questioned by another stream of thought, Visistadvaita (whose great exponent was Ramanuja).

"saves" the greatest referential value for the largest number of religious experiences, this is clearly a strong recommendation for such theism.

Gellman's discussion of religious experience is very suggestive in a further respect. In discussions of religious pluralism, religious ends are often treated in a manner analogous to the treatment of religious experience. Ostensible diversity among religious fulfillments is viewed as a possible challenge to the reality of any religious fulfillment, just as differences among religious experiences might be thought to undercut the validity we can attribute to any religious experience. If people disagree about the religious ultimate they seek or experience, perhaps the notion of a religious ultimate is itself confused and none actually exists. If people disagree about religious ends, they cast doubt on the reality of any religious end. The problems are similar, and so are the responses.

For instance, Hick will say that nirvana and communion with God upon death are contradictory beliefs. If we grant that they are seriously proposed as alternatives, he contends we have only three options. All such faith in religious ends is nonsense; one end is real and all others illusory or unattainable; or the true content of religion, the true end, is some unknown positive condition on a plane far above such contradictions. Since, in their view, recourse to either of the first two options would render any idea of religious fulfillment implausible, pluralists like Hick opt for the third. They maintain that the varied accounts of religious ends are all conditioned and incoherent anticipations of a final human condition that is beyond description by any such account.

I believe that Gellman's basic principles for religious experience hold here as well: the best accounts of the varied reports of religious ends will be those that preserve the highest degree of concrete validity in the largest number of them. Religious fulfillments as human states can be viewed, after all, under the broad heading of religious experience. It is precipitous to conclude that because religious experiences are diverse, the only way to salvage their validity is to deny that *any* of their particulars are true and instead insist that they be packaged as unanimous evidence for a foggy ultimate beyond description. Likewise it is precipitous to conclude that because religious aims plainly differ, the only way to salvage plausibility for the attainment of any religious end at all is to imagine an end indeterminate enough to be the symbolic object of all these aims.

If we grant the reality of diverse religious ends, "conflicting" religious testimony need not be discounted. Instead, the testimony may be essentially valid in both cases, about different conditions of religious fulfillment. The fact that believers report accurately about varied religious ends does not undercut the trustworthiness of religious experience as evidence. Nor does it require that the varying religious traditions reject each other's accounts as false and baseless. Each tradition may have its own "inclusivist" means to assimilate and affirm the validity of most of the other's testimony. To use an analogy, two contending scientific theories or schools of thought may be in agreement about nearly all of the relevant experimental data, and yet at odds about the nature of the reality it reflects. This "contradiction" in accounts does not throw into doubt the validity of the evidence. The vast majority of the evidence may be rightly weighed as counting for both sides. It provides weighty reason to suppose that the right answer is to be found in one of the contending accounts and that where there is empirical agreement between the interpretations we have points of special interest. From this perspective, however, it is an obvious advantage for the religions to be able to find as much concrete truth in each other's affirmations as possible.

The supposed "incompatibility of religious experiences" provides no cogent logical objection to the existence of one religious ultimate, but illustrates a practical incompatibility, the impossibility for any one person or community to realize contrasting priorities in religious experience at the same time. Nirvana and communion with God are contradictory only if we assume that one or the other must be the sole fate for all human beings. They cannot both be the case at the same time for the same person. But for different people, or the same person at different times, they could both be true. Therefore there is no rational ground to conclude that mutually exclusive states cannot both be actual for different subjects and accurately reported by "conflicting" religious accounts.

III

Once we consider that there may in fact be multiple religious ends, diverse religious fulfillments, the whole question of pluralism is transformed. Clearly such a proposal requires some rethinking of traditional Christian theology.

Classical Christian inclusivist positions hold that adherents of other traditions may relate savingly to God either *apart* from their specific religious practices (through their observance of some natural moral law for instance) or *through* the concrete elements of their own tradition (assuming these are implicitly if not explicitly directed toward God and can be channels for the benefits of Christ's work). Such inclusivism grants that the same truth and benefits available in the Christian tradition can be made available within at least some other faiths. But the nature of these contacts is to lead people into relation with God through Christ. There is no *alternative* religious option in these traditions, just a different possible avenue to approach the same end. What is not directed to the full Christian aim is neither true nor real. It is just at this point that I propose a change. I suggest that Christians can consistently recognize that some traditions encompass religious fulfillments different from the salvation Christians seek. There are paths in varying religious traditions that, if consistently followed, prove effective in bringing adherents to alternative ends. The crucial question among the faiths is *not* "Which one works?" but "What counts as fulfillment?"

On the one hand this requires a revision of the traditional Christian outlook. Christians have historically recognized some grounding for other faiths in a general revelation in creation, while disagreeing whether this foundation could be practically effective apart from special revelation. But both sides of the disagreement have tended to assume that this common foundation could only serve attainment of the Christian end. That there could be a basis for achieving *other* ends was not considered in any terms except those of perdition. The fundamental challenge of my proposal for Christians is to consider the possibility of the providential provision of a diversity of religious ends for human beings, and the associated possibility that we recognize significant *distinctive* religious truths in other traditions, truths which in their peculiar purity and effect are not available in Christianity.

As Joseph DiNoia puts it, Christian theology can affirm "the distinctiveness of the aims fostered by other religions without prejudice to an affirmation of the unique valuation of the Christian community or of its doctrines about salvation. . . ."[36] Such distinctiveness raises the question of a providential role for the religions in the divine plan other than and in addition to serving as secondary channels for salvation as Christians understand it. These are roles "that are now only dimly perceived and that will be fully disclosed in the consummation of history for which Christians long."[37]

On the other hand, the true alternative character of these ends allows and even requires a judgment from the Christian perspective that subordinates them to salvation. To realize something other than communion with the triune God and with other creatures through Christ, in the continuing relationship of created being, is to achieve a lesser good. It is not the abundant life that Christians know and hope for in Christ. There is no reason to avoid this judgment, as long as we realize that other traditions make similar reciprocal judgments about the supremacy of their religious end.

36. (DiNoia, 1992, p. 91).
37. (DiNoia, 1992, p. 91).

The perspective I have outlined in this chapter raises a number of issues for Christian theology. In Part Two I take up some preliminary questions about Christian faith. The first, and most basic, asks what Christians mean by "salvation." If the discussion of pluralism shifts its focus from means to ends, we will have to devote attention to the Christian understanding of salvation and to its distinctive characteristics. This is the subject we will take up in the next chapter. A second, related question is what Christian scripture and tradition provide by way of instruction on the subject of diverse religious ends. In particular, this requires discussion of heaven and hell. That is the subject of Chapter Three.

Part Two

Religious Ends and Christian Tradition

Chapter Two

Salvation as Communion:
All the Fullness of God

A Christian theology of religious ends revolves around the Christian religious end: salvation. This chapter provides a basic overview of the nature of that end, lifting up certain features central to our later discussion. Salvation is a relation of communion with God and other creatures in Christ.
This simple definition has some far-reaching implications. After a brief review of some biblical perspectives, we will explore the implications of specific
facets of that definition. First, we will consider the significance of understanding the religious end as a relation, and the connection between Christ
and salvation. Second, we will explore the character imparted to this relation
by the one related to, the God who is Trinity. Third, we will review some of
the more concrete ways that salvation has been modeled in the Christian tradition. Finally, we will take a preliminary step back toward the issue of multiple religious ends by asking whether salvation, as Christians understand it, is
divisible into distinct parts.

I

We begin with a brief reflection on the perspectives on salvation found in
Scripture. There are two crucial emphases in the Old Testament's view of redemption. The first is its this-worldly character. Salvation is a historical reality of deliverance and fulfillment. It happens and is expected to happen

49

within the world as we know it. The language that describes redemption — a language of just rule, prosperity, and peace — is metaphorical primarily by extension and intensification of fragmentary historical achievements. The hope of salvation is the hope that God will bring perfected forms of earthly life. The second emphasis is the corporate or communal character of salvation. In Old Testament literature salvation is rarely conceived in purely individual terms. Participation in redemption comes through participation in a community which itself realizes this end. Paradigmatic past events of salvation, like the exodus or the giving of the Torah at Sinai, manifest both of these emphases. In these events, God has acted to save and constitute the people of Israel. The escape of slaves from bondage and the instigation of a new social order are events of "ordinary" history whose character as religious deliverance, participation in redemption, does not deny that fact but intensifies it. These events are not symbols of a salvation that takes place in some other realm or plane. They are representative realizations, the real presence of what salvation is on a more universal scale. The same two emphases are present in the visions of a future redeemed kingdom centered on Zion, very much a corporate reality with the distinct features of historical fulfillment.

At the heart of this understanding of salvation is the relationship of covenant faithfulness between Israel and God. Righteousness is the heart of this relation and the Torah is the soul of this righteousness. Torah-observance involves a broad pattern of cultic, social, and interpersonal practices. It is marked by obedience and justice, but it cannot be entirely reduced to these. The commandment to obey God goes hand in hand with a commandment to love God. God's distress at the breaking of the covenant extends not only to instances of behavior, but to the lament that the people's hearts are "far from me." God's relation to Israel is hardly limited to punishment and reward for actions. Emphasis also falls on a renewal or restoration of relationship, through images that liken God and Israel to spouses, or a parent and children. Salvation lies at an intersection of God's unconditional promises and Israel's faithfulness to covenant expectations. Since the hope of individual resurrection is a rather late and minor note in the Old Testament itself, participation in the realization of redemption depends on individual persons' participation in the coming kingdom through their solidarity with their ancestors and descendants, in one people.

In the New Testament a number of motifs are extended or added. There is increased emphasis on the cosmic setting of salvation, freedom from satanic powers, and the restoration of the entire created order — "a new heaven and a new earth." There is the extension of the communal aspect of salvation to include gentiles, in a "kingdom of God" which is corporate but universal.

There is a "new birth," that is, entry into a new level of existence through baptism and reception of the Holy Spirit, which leads to fruits of the Spirit. There is union with Christ and the reconstitution of the image of God in humanity. There is forgiveness of sins. There is the promise of resurrection and eternal life for the individual. There is expectation of an actual, proportionate participation in God's own life.

As we saw in the first chapter, the assumption that there is only one religious end directs all attention toward the effectiveness of various means to that end. In particular, it focuses Christian discussion on Christ as the unique and necessary instrument for religious fulfillment. In interfaith discussions, this contention that Jesus is the "only way" gives rise to a different sort of question: the only way to *what?* This is a very helpful development. Christ's place in Christian faith is subtly distorted if considered exclusively as a means or exclusively as an end. Christ figures as locus of unsurpassable *relation,* a fact that both in practice and theory escapes reduction to categories of means or ends.

In the New Testament, we find elements that stress Christ as the avenue to redemption and those that stress relation with Christ as the substance of redemption itself. When Christians argue among themselves about religious pluralism, they tend to pit these varied passages against each other. Was Christ's mission to give up everything, including his own importance, for the sake of the kingdom of God? Or was the kingdom of God the condition realized by those who took Jesus as their God and savior? Is Christ integral or instrumental to salvation? If one understands "salvation" as something which itself is detachable from relation with Christ, then the question is whether Christ must in every case be the conscious, explicit means used to attain that end. If relation with Christ is constitutive of what one *means* by "salvation," then argument over the instrumental means for getting there will hardly exhaust the issue. This consideration goes a long way to account for the fact that Christian views come in more complex varieties than simply "exclusivist," "inclusivist," or "pluralist." One who views Christ as constitutive of the reality of salvation itself may affirm that many other religious paths besides Christian ones may lead to that end, while still emphatically affirming Christ as uniquely necessary for salvation itself. Christ is more exclusive as end than means, in that case. And one who denies that Christ is constitutive of salvation may still affirm that relation to Christ is the superior and ordinary way to attain that end. Christ is more exclusive as a means than as an end, in that case.

As a thought experiment we could posit two ideal types on this point. At one end would be a contention that Christ was fundamentally constitutive of salvation, but that the *means* to that end themselves need have no specific reference to Christ at all. At the other end would be a contention that Christ plays no constitutive part in salvation itself, but that Christ is a *necessary* means that all must use on the way to that end. If we keep these two poles in mind, it clarifies our discussion. Views approximating the first pole do show up in many inclusivist theologies of religion. And views approximating the second show up sometimes in exclusivist theologies of religion. Pluralistic theologies of religion are notable for rejecting the premise of the first view (that Christ is constitutive of salvation) and the premise of the second (that Christ is a necessary instrument for achieving salvation).

I believe that Jesus Christ is in fact constitutive of salvation. Christ is constitutive of salvation (the Christian end) for all people who attain it. Christ is constitutive in this way not as some separate and additional actor *besides* God, but precisely as an expression of the triune life of God. Christ is one who comes *from* the triune life into human life but also one who brings human life into its fullest participation in the triune life. Christ is not extrinsic to the love of God, not only a representation of it, but also the working of it. Christ is in such unity with God that communion with God involves a fundamental relation with Christ.

Schubert Ogden has argued that salvation is constituted solely by God's everlasting love. Christ does not constitute salvation; Christ represents the God who does. Ordinary Christian sacraments and preaching can only symbolize God by representing Christ. Christ represents God by constituting these lesser representations. As Ogden puts it, "whereas they represent God's love by also representing him, he represents God's love by also constituting them."[1] Christ's special role is not to constitute salvation but to constitute the Christian symbols for it. Other religions may have their own representations.[2] The problem with this analysis is that it makes "God's everlasting love" an abstract quality and agent, some kind of prior decision in the mind of God, and downplays its personal nature. That love is precisely a feature of the personal communion that is the divine life, of which the second person of the Trinity is a constitutive member. Prior to being an idea or a decision, this love is an event. And Christ, the divine Word, is participant in that event, constitutive of that everlasting love. Likewise the extension of this love to humanity which constitutes salvation is not an abstract possibility. The path for human

1. (Ogden, 1992, p. 98).
2. And they may not. Ogden's answer to his own question "Is there only one true religion or are there many?" is that there necessarily may be more than one. He does not argue any specific cases.

participation in the triune communion is laid in the unity of God and humanity in Christ. Ogden's analysis makes good sense so long as Christ can be separated from any integral participation in the triune life. If Christ is definitively outside that life, then representation is the most profound relation that one can propose. But Christianity characteristically denies such separation. Likewise, Ogden's account works so long as salvation is a completely external relation between God and humans. But it does not fit well with salvation as communion with God, a proportionate participation in the triune life.

Though Christ is certainly "the way," in the Christian view, Christ is also "the life" and "the truth" in whom we rest and grow while on the way and at the end of the way. The proposition that Christ is the sole savior of the world is not adequately translated by saying that everyone must make use of Christ for at least one crucial moment, long enough to negotiate part of the passage to the promised land of "salvation," after which time Christ can be discarded or replaced. In inviting his followers into a relation with God like his own, Jesus presumed that those in such relation were one body, that they lived "in" him and he lived "in" them, just as Christ lived in God and God in him. Jesus did not counsel his followers to go out and independently approach God as Jesus did. Jesus invited them to *share* in that relationship by virtue of their connection with him. There is nothing purely instrumental about this: the images and substance are all organic. Communion is the way Christ saves, and it is the salvation that results.

II

At the beginning of this chapter I suggested a brief description of salvation as a relationship of communion through Christ with God and with other creatures. I would like to focus for a moment on the significant information that is already conveyed in one simple component of this description: the designation of the religious end as a relation. This tells us, for instance, that salvation is not the self-contained condition of a subject, a pure experience (like bliss or "pure consciousness"). A picture of a limitless line of individuals, each "perfect" in her/his own independent happiness, is not an image of salvation. Nor is salvation the clarification or resolution of diversity into a single absolute of some sort. Salvation is not the simple attainment by humans of some additional possession or capacity, a power or wisdom that exceeds the mundane. In comparison with these options, the Christian religious end shows an obvious lack of purity and simplicity. It is a composite reality, because it is relational.

This already distinguishes the end in question from those in Vedantic Hinduism or most Buddhism. Whatever the complexities of interpretation about the ends sought in those traditions, those ends plainly are not relationships. The prerequisites of such relation are emphatically denied and the religious end is designated as liberation or release from just such prerequisites, or from entanglement with mistaken belief in their reality. This view is confirmed by the consistent judgment offered by those within those religious traditions about Christian salvation. It is viewed as a spiritual mirage that must be seen through in the interests of religious fulfillment or, if real, ought to be left behind for another end. Salvation is an intensification and fulfillment of a dimension that in many religious visions is regarded as penultimate at best: relationship between distinct persons with distinct identities. From such perspectives, salvation is simply one of the things from which humans need to be delivered. From the Christian perspective, such deliverance is one of the things from which we may finally hope to be saved.

Creation and consummation are two ends of the Christian story, and traditionally they are seen to image each other. The establishment of relationship is the theme of creation, the story of God's relation as creator with all creatures and the multiplying relations of creatures to each other. Fulfillment of these relations is the theme of consummation. A single state of consciousness, a "one without a second," or an unrestricted release from every conditioned quality — insofar as all of these rule out relation, none can count as salvation from a biblical perspective. Christianity is captive to the reality of relationship and, coordinately, to the reality of distinct parties in relation. It requires "at least a second for the one."

Creation is the establishment and the extension of relation. Much of early Christian theology was developed in conflict with gnosticism. It was developed to defend relation, not just as an end but as a defensible beginning. The question was whether creation — the multiplication of beings other and less perfect than God, particularly materially embodied, distinct beings — was itself an evil and a mistake. Can relations other than those of pure identity or of formal analysis (part to whole) be regarded as good in any serious sense? Since distinct relations are by definition changeable and imply alteration in any party to them, gnostics viewed them as self-evidently corrupting and unfitting for the divine. Christians insisted that creation, with its relational nature, was good. They affirmed that *creating*, a definitive act of establishing relation, was a good act. It was an act particularly appropriate to the nature of divinity, and not an embarrassment to be attributed to some lesser or malevolent being. Relations with other persons and with other creatures are carried up into the consummation of creation, and remain a constitutive part of it. Though "made new," they do not drop away into nothingness. In this sense, creation is an irrevocable act by God, an act that constitutes not just a passing historical phase but the character of salvation itself. Creation is brought to consummation, but it is not closed out. Relation with God permeates the other relations humans have. The reverse is also true: relation with God cannot ever be completely "purified" of integral relations to other parts of God's creation.

In their defense of created relation, Christians often did compromise with the dominant nonbiblical ethos. That worldview presumed an unbridgeable contrast between an imperfect, changeable human sphere and a higher, unchanging perfection, a contrast now often negatively characterized as "dualism." At the very least, Christians held the realm of created relation was a positive, if transitory, good rather than an empire whose very nature was alien to God. But even supposed dualistic forms of Christianity were dramatically less so than the alternatives they developed to oppose. They acknowledged that the particular character of salvation was the fulfillment of relationship. The Christian religious end is one where relation and distinct parties to relation, asymmetries and interaction, give and take, persist. Salvation rests not in their elimination but in their intensification and glorification.

If salvation is a relation, we can understand the odd fact that Christians use that word to refer at the same time to a past accomplishment, a current reality, a process, and a future end. H. Richard Niebuhr is said to have responded to a street preacher's question "Are you saved?" with the statement "I was saved by what Christ did; I am being saved right now; I shall be saved when the Kingdom comes."[3] Relations exist over many points in time. They have beginnings and decisive moments of formation. They undergo growth, failings, and change. They can achieve fulfillments that involve neither termination nor fixed immutability. The end in view is a *living* realization. The Christian gospel has a narrative form and Christianity is a historical religion, hanging decisively on particular events and persons. Narrative and history are categories constituted by personal relation. Christianity's identification with them reflects the nature of the religious end it seeks.

The incarnation of Christ manifests this same reality. To suppose that incarnation is possible, that one can be human and divine at once, presumes an extraordinary commonality between God and humanity. The belief that humans are made in "the image of God" expresses that commonality. Capacity for relation with God, of the most intimate and powerful kind, must be an

3. (Fackre, 1978, p. 196).

integral feature of human nature for this unity to be possible. The mystery of the incarnation is that this possibility could be realized. And the oneness of humanity and divinity in Christ would seem to be a contradiction in terms on the divine side, if Christians did not also maintain — in the doctrine of the Trinity — that God's inner nature encompasses relation. The problem presented by Jesus Christ, who is claimed to be the communion of God and a human being in one person, would be an ontological conundrum if it did not go along with the belief that God's own nature is that of one being in a communion of persons. To say that Christ's person is a communion of two is in fact consistent with the belief that God's reality is a communion of three.[4] Therefore for God to truly be incarnate in Christ and yet to be truly relating *to* God as Christ is not impossible; it is the "exteriorization" of the same pattern of reality that exists in the divine itself. We will expand on this point at much greater length in chapters four and five.

The resurrection is crucial in this connection. The resurrection is an act of God, a vindication of Jesus, a promise of eternal life for humanity. But perhaps the key thing in the New Testament treatment of the resurrection is an assumption so simple it is often quickly passed over (by those who take it for granted and by those who dismiss it out of hand): relation with Christ is now a continuing possibility. The personal bonds humans form with each other are the repositories of the deepest fulfillment most of us know. Death undoubtedly crushes that fulfillment, breaks the interaction between the dead person and those who survive. These relations are partial and (to all appearances) intrinsically transitory. The strongest argument against the belief that relations are ultimately important or that the religious end itself could be constituted by relations is quite obvious. All relations end. But not in this case, the New Testament contends. The period between the resurrection and the ascension demonstrates this in such concrete terms as to make it unmistakable: the disciples see Jesus, talk with him, touch him. And when Jesus "goes away" this relation is not broken, though some of the concrete manifestations cease.

In the incarnation God forms an irrevocable relation with a human be-

---

4. The emphasis in christological doctrine on the two natures in Christ is in fact a point where Christians have "held the line" on the intrinsically relational character of salvation. If in Christ God and humanity were blurred or melded in some way, relation would have given way to an assimilation or a monism. Thus, in the face of metaphysical and psychological perplexities, the conviction remained that even at the point of deepest communion the human and the divine retain their own distinctness. Though God and Jesus are one incarnate person, yet they are one person by communion, not by fusion into a third entity.

ing at the deepest possible level. The personal character of the relation of God and humanity, of creator and creature, is realized and confirmed. And at the same time the situation is changed regarding historical relations among humans. The resurrection affirms that one relation, precisely of the sort that all humans know with each other and which they know to end completely with death, continues. The resurrection of Christ then creates a situation unique in human experience: it universalizes a normal human relation. The believer's relation with Christ has qualities of historical personal relation but unlike all such it is *not* transient. Nor is it now limited by the normal constraints of a historical person: it is open to all. In the resurrection of the particular person Jesus, particular relation itself is given a new lease on life. Eternal life, salvation, will have an interpersonal character. Against the contention that no relation can be anything but illusory or passing, Christians point to one counterexample, the first fruits of salvation itself. In the incarnation God irrevocably entered into relation under the very conditions God had set in creation, "personalizing" the creator/creation relation. In the resurrection, the mundane type of human relation in which Jesus participated is universalized. As creation gave the world its own irrevocable reality, so are the relations that creation generates now given an irrevocable meaning.

This is part of the reason Christians are "fixated" on this one relation, to this one person. It does not exclude other relations; it is the one instance that validates the suggestion that such relations (for all their apparent ephemeral nature) might in some way be our ultimate concern. Christians are obviously noted for their emphasis on relation with Christ. In interreligious discussion, it is often urged as desirable for religious believers to regard such attachments as entirely instrumental and temporary. The great virtue many see in certain Buddhist traditions lies in their perspective (in theory at least) on their own central religious figure, a perspective which denies that personal or particular relation with Buddha is itself an ultimate matter.

After the Buddha has pointed one to the true dharma or made one aware of one's own buddha nature, one can disregard and dispense with that relation. In itself, it has no enduring value. Once a teaching or person has pointed you in the right direction, once you attain the end of the path they describe, they should drop away. What is important is the moon, not the one pointing at the moon. Indeed, the helpers become obstacles if they are not put aside. "If you meet the Buddha on the road, kill him," is the intentionally startling way this principle is expressed in some branches of the tradition. And this is but the most dramatic instance of the consistent teaching about the insubstantiality of *means* in relation to the end itself.

From the Christian perspective, this "benefit" could not be less appealing. For relation with Christ manifests the fact that persons-in-relation are precisely not to be discarded after serving an instrumental purpose. Relations are constitutive of the religious end itself. They are thus ends as well as means. There is nothing more real on the other side of them. Relation with Christ is not the sole real relation, but the one that manifests in fact what in other relations is as yet visible or tangible only in very partial ways. Like the relation with Christ, these relations are not skillful means to be consumed and left, once their role as functional vehicle is fulfilled. They are, or can be, constituent elements of salvation. The continuing relation between Christians and the risen Christ embodies this. The refusal to "transcend" this particular one is also the basis for the conviction that a wider network of relations, of communion, is part of salvation. The resurrection of the particular person Jesus is an affirmation of particular relations.

Miroslav Volf points out that the dominant self-designations used by early Christians to describe their connection to others in the church were "sisters/brothers" and "friends."[5] Their *koinonia* or mutual participation in one another was described with sibling language (as something constituted by a prior, given relation) and with friendship language (pointing to a voluntary, associative freedom). God makes creatures with a certain autonomy in the freedom to choose, to condition their own relations. Yet God makes us with intrinsically relational natures, creatures who cannot be ourselves alone.

We have no choice but to be constituted by relations, those which are given, as well as those that are chosen. First there is our relation of creature to creator. This is organic and given. But this "external" constituting relationship connects us to one whose own nature is relational and whose external constituting act is to give us freedom. This is quite basic, but it does seem to rule out certain visions of the religious end that would not be consistent with such a starting point. It rules out a religious end that presumes that from the beginning creatures were never anything but God or a piece of God. It would also rule out a religious end that is a completely self-contained subjective condition of the individual.

Thus Christian salvation insists on an irreducible "more," in contrast with purely materialistic or naturalistic views, or in contrast with radically dualistic ones that see no bridge of relation between the human and the divine. At the same time, it can be seen as content with "less," in contrast with certain religious views that maintain the truly ultimate end must be a unity without variation, leaving behind the lesser world of distinction, relation, and interaction. Christian salvation looks negatively supernaturalist from

5. (Volf, 1998, p. 180).

the first kind of perspective and naively attached to nature and persons from the second.

III

Salvation is a relation of communion with God. We have seen that even the simple description of salvation as a relation actually distinguishes it from a number of possible religious ends. But this description remains quite limited, so long as "God" is an empty cipher. As soon as God takes on a determinate personal character, the nature of salvation becomes dramatically more concrete. The qualities of a particular person or a particular kind of person condition what relation with such a person would be like, what would be missing without such a relation. Salvation is colored at every point by the character of the one who encounters us.

This is different, we should note, from the definition of a religious end in terms of a certain generic type of relation. "Heaven is wherever love may be found" would be a greeting-card version of this idea. In that case, it doesn't matter who is having the relation or whom they are having it with. So long as the interaction itself has certain characteristics (loving care, self-denial, conformity of one to another's will) it is an example of the end so defined. But Christian salvation is very much shaped and constituted by the particular God who encounters us, the distinctive relation in which this God stands to us, the unique capacity this particular relation has to shape and permeate our other relations. This is why Christians understand salvation as communion with God in Christ. Relation with Christ is the decisive way of providing specific character to "God" and "communion." This leads us to the concrete Christian description of God as Trinity.

The first thing to note about Trinity is its thorough consistency with the character of salvation as we have discussed it so far. Salvation is an integrated set of relations. Relation with God is the heart of this network of interactions, "infecting" all of them. It is possible to conceive salvation as a connection with God that is, from God's side, completely extrinsic and contingent. But Christians affirm that the relation is a communion, in which there is some mutual participation between God and humans. For this to be true, the relation cannot be simply extrinsic on God's part. The fundamental Christian word about the "doctrine of God" is therefore that relation is intrinsic to God's character. Salvation as a relation of deep communion with God makes sense because God's nature itself has the character of communion. The kind of relation salvation is reflects the nature of the one with whom we relate.

If Christian theology has not often lingered long on the bare fact that salvation is a relation, it is because it usually hastens to specify that relation more fully. There is a striking unanimity in Christian tradition about the cumulative dimensions of this relation, although various confessional families have distinctive emphases. The unanimity lies in the recognition that salvation is an integrative relation, a relation that enhances and corrects other relations. "Salvation" refers comprehensively to the fulfillment of the entire interactive network of which we are a part in creation.

This network has three primary foci: the relation of human beings to God, the relation of humans with each other, and the relation of humanity with all of God's other creatures, the natural world. As the story of Eve and Adam in Genesis makes clear, these three are inextricably linked together. A change in one affects the others. In thinking diagnostically of the human situation, theology has named the disorders in these three relations sin, evil, and death. Sin is the estrangement between God and humans instigated by human defiance or abnegation. Evil is the disorder within humans individually and among them collectively. Death and despair are the disorders that enter the human relation to creation when that relation is constricted to a self-enclosed reality.

The tradition often associates each of the three persons of the Trinity with redemption in one of these dimensions. Right relation of persons with God, ruptured by sin and restored in Christ, is specially referred to the Son. Right relation among persons is specially referred to the work of the Holy Spirit, with emphasis on Pentecost and the community of the church. Creation in total is specially referred to the Father, and therefore restoration of right relation between humanity and nature is associated with the first person also. This view, which identifies each of the three persons with a particular set of God's actions toward the world, is called the "economic trinity." The three describe aspects of God's "economy" or external activity in the world.[6]

Just as Christians maintain that salvation cannot be limited exclusively to one axis (that of sin or evil or death), so they say that the saving bond with God cannot be restricted to one narrow band of relation. The long-standing theological affirmation that the Trinity is ontological as well as economic

---

6. The tradition also balances this economic language with a principle that the external acts of the Trinity are undivided. Therefore, despite the "association" of economic language, all three persons participate in any action referred to one. So, for instance, in Christology the "three offices" of Christ point to the participation of the Word incarnate in Jesus in all three of the "economic" redemptive tasks. As priest, Christ restores relation with God; as prophet, Christ restores relations among humans; as king, Christ restores relation with creation.

maintains that relation with God is not bound within the terms of God's external actions. If God's "economic" manifestations in the world are only extrinsic activities, then our connection with God through them is rather distant. If we know someone strictly through the function they perform as our doctor or accountant or car mechanic, we can always have legitimate questions or doubts about the real person. What is their character behind these roles? What might they prove to be like within a whole range of different or more intimate bonds with us (friend, family, spouse)? Christian belief that God is ontologically triune is belief that God's manifestation to us is shaped by God's true, deepest character. It is a conviction that our relation with God connects not just with God's purpose but with God's person.

Virtually all our analogies must give *temporal* priority to the oneness or the three persons of the Trinity. To think of one person who has three roles — mother, lover, friend — is to see a person who first existed and then took on these diverse roles. If we think of a "social trinity," and use analogies like a band of friends or the marriage relationship, we necessarily picture originally independent individuals who are drawn closer and closer into a unified life. In imagining divine Trinity we must remove this dimension of necessary sequence. The oneness and the threeness of God "arise" at once, not in succession. God is "composed" of relations, relations which at the very same time constitute the distinctness of the divine persons and the unity of the divine character.

We cannot say "in the beginning was the relation," and then later came the "things" that are related. Nor can we say "in the beginning were the persons," so that relations between them were subsequent and secondary events in the history of these persons. Beings and relations are two faces of a single complex, somewhat like "force" and "mass" in physics: two realities that are each implicated in the other's definition.[7] In our actual experience of beings and relations we virtually never see this perfect mutuality. All our actual instances are sequential in some way, whether a person who at some point adds roles or a wide range of individual links that at some point coalesce into a unified social movement. Examples suggestive of what we are saying about the Trinity are harder to come by. We might think of the birth of a child, who in the very moment of becoming a distinct individual also becomes a daughter, a sister, and a niece. But the relations here (to parents, siblings, uncle or aunt) are too external to make a good analogy.

Our interest in this brief exposition of trinitarian doctrine stems from

---

7. "Mass" is a measure of resistance to acceleration by application of force. "Force" is a measure of the energy required to accelerate a body. The law F=ma expresses this reciprocal relation.

our definition of salvation as communion (with God in Christ and with other creatures). Trinitarian doctrine affirms that the very nature of God itself is communion. The connection between the two is crucial. God's personal reality is complex: God is "made up" of personal communion-in-difference. Therefore any full communion with God will have to participate in that same complexity, just as in any close connection with another person our relation takes on a consonance with his or her (and our) distinctive qualities. Our communion will also have to be a communion in difference. To appreciate why this point is important, we should realize that communion with God can be (and often is) conceived in terms of possessing a divine substance or power or insight. So, for instance, to become immortal would be to share in a quality whose archetypal possessor is God, and this would constitute communion with God. We would occupy the same category, in some way. Our discussion of the Trinity points out that communion with the triune God must be a complex, interpersonal reality, not the acquisition of a divine quality or substance. This has obvious implications in Christology also, in whether we regard Jesus' divinity as a matter of "substance" or of communion.[8]

In our human experience, the link between persons is deeper if they touch comprehensively, across the range of their particular qualities. Communion occurs when more rather than less of the fullness of the other person is encountered. At the extreme, an awareness of the many features at play in another's life becomes a kind of second nature in ours. This can take such a lively form as to be almost another subjectivity within me. I do not so much know what my friend would do in a given situation, as I vicariously simulate in some measure the internal dynamics she might experience in that situation. This can be so even when the process is highly imaginative, when my own independent responses would be quite different (what would create joy or pain for her might not for me). I can share a kind of second-hand experience of those processes because I am so well aware of the aspects of the other's self that produce them. Through such relation to another person, and

---

8. Another interesting development of this same point in relation to another theological topic — ecclesiology — can be found in Miroslav Volf's contrast of the ecclesiologies of Cardinal Ratzinger and John Zizioulas. Volf shows how the different trinitarian assumptions we have outlined play out in different views of the nature of the church. The chapter on Ratzinger is called "Communion and the Whole," and stresses that for Ratzinger the true essence of the church lies in a universal quality or essence that permeates the specific parts. The universal church has priority over the local church. The chapter on Zizioulas is "Communion: One and Many," and stresses that there is a reciprocal relation between the local churches and the universal church. They constitute each other: the church too is a being in communion.

through such imaginative participation in that person's internal life, I may find myself changed. This participation becomes part of who I am, without my becoming that person or ceasing to be quite distinctively myself.[9]

Relation that is less than full is not necessarily empty. When we say we have a superficial relation to someone, it does not follow that this relation is unreal or based on error: we may be truly related to actual features of this person. We can also have very intense and deep but narrow relations with people, which are likewise very real. Such relations can arise in moments of crisis or they can obtain in important and long-term connections with people even when we touch each other only on one side, as it were. A professional mentor, a childhood friend, a political ally: any of these may be people with whom we have a profound relationship, one that undergoes its own process of development and maturity, while at the same time remaining quite segmented. The family life of my professional mentor, the professional work of my childhood friend, the religious convictions of my political ally: all of these may be complete blanks to me, a fact that I might note after many years with bemusement but no sense of loss. There is more to these people, but for the purposes of our relation it has never seemed necessary or relevant. It certainly would be so, if I sought to know them more completely, to be in full communion with them. But that is something perhaps neither of us desires.

If two different people know the same person "fully" they will not each have identical relations to that person. The nature of the relation and the knowing is in significant measure constituted by the communion of the two unique individuals involved. When we say that someone brings out certain aspects in us that may rarely figure in other circumstances, we are pointing to this dimension of relationship. A person is not a static content, a reservoir of information that is precisely the same for all people who access it. The person known in each new relationship is different, partly as a result of the relation itself, partly because of the peculiar pattern of their existing qualities evoked by that encounter.

Salvation is a relation of communion with the triune God. So far we have discussed the elements of that definition: relation, communion, and triune God. We should also briefly note that the Christian understanding of the church follows consistently from this basic conviction about salvation as a relation of communion, of *koinonia.* The church is a body called to live out this communion.[10] It is a community of people whose relations with

9. See (Volf, 1998, p. 211) for a development of this point. This "indwelling" of one person by another is an analogy for the much fuller indwelling of the trinitarian persons.
10. For an insightful exploration of the implications of this fact, see (Volf, 1998).

each other are shaped by their common participation in relation with God in Christ. For individuals to be "in Christ" is inextricably to be part of the church that is Christ's body. The church is a specification of the scriptural injunction that those who say they love God and hate their neighbors are liars.[11] Communion with God that does not at the same time encompass concrete communion with other human beings is a contradiction. That is why the common bond of the church is just such concrete communion with the human being Jesus, as constitutive of communion with God. A purely private Christian is impossible.

This is obscured for us in our cultural setting, where adherence to Christianity is often defined only by assent to certain beliefs. In much of Christian history (and today in many cultures) acts of belonging to the community of the church — the act of baptism, or participation in the eucharist — are more decisive indices of faith than verbal profession. This is certainly true in places where the church is persecuted and these acts of solidarity mark one for the same fate as other members. It is true in a different way in cultures like India where religious identity is crucially a communal identity, governing many fundamental features of life, including possible marriage partners, occupation, eating customs, and so on. The earliest Christian centuries were unacquainted with active members of the church who lacked faith in Christ or God, but were quite familiar with people who professed to have adopted Christian beliefs and yet held back from explicit entry into the church or participation in its concrete life. This posed the question of whether the faith could be a private commitment, the guiding norm of an essentially autonomous life. The consistent response to this question was that lived relation of community, the communion with others in the tangible and explicit acts of worship and mutual support, was not optional but essential.

Christianity agrees strongly with Judaism and Islam that the participation of all believers in one ongoing nexus of religious community is essential. Within this general agreement, Christianity comparatively appears to have a somewhat more "individualistic" emphasis and a somewhat thinner density of community life. From an Islamic point of view, Christianity appears to focus on private spirituality or inner ecclesial life more than the social dimensions of faith. From a Jewish perspective, Christianity is notable for its "conversionist" organization, for the fact that its community life is less stable, less tied to an ethnic and cultural tradition, more voluntaristic. From most Buddhist and Hindu perspectives, Christianity manifests a strong communal dimension and an excessive entanglement in social and historical relations.

11. 1 John 4:20.

To put the matter very simply, as a prelude to our further discussions, we might say that the trialogue among the three "Abrahamic" faiths generally presupposes relation with God and others as the focus of the religious end, and debates the nature of the relations in question. Conversation with Buddhism and Hinduism comes again and again to a question mark about relation itself as an end.

Finally, we note that the same watermark elements of salvation are characteristic of the Christian "scandal of particularity." Christian witness and mission are widely criticized on the grounds that any truly universal truth should not be subject to such particular and historical modes of propagation. It should be simultaneously and independently accessible in all quarters. The criticism finds offense in the suggestion that persons would need to wait upon those from other cultures, other classes, other religious traditions for anything essential to their human fulfillment. Christian missionary efforts are then *prima facia* violations of that doctrine of human spiritual autonomy. This argument depends on prior assumptions about both the nature of the divine and the nature of the religious end. It presumes that the divine is non-personal, at least in its mode of revelation. By contrast, it is reasonable that a personal God who wished to be known as personal would act through particular events and the narratives of specific lives: the distinctive modes of personal knowledge. The criticism also presumes that the religious end is a self-contained state. If the religious end is relational, the case is quite different.

Salvation is emphatically not a self-contained condition but one defined by the necessity of depending for it on others. There is no more powerful motto for this point than Mark 15:31, the entirely accurate observation by witnesses of the crucifixion: "He saved others; he cannot save himself." The bringer of salvation cannot deliver himself. In this, the person of Christ already encapsulates the transitive nature of redemption. Jesus Christ goes under the waves of death, not in an interim pause before reasserting his own intrinsic power, but in the genuine loss we all face in death: the complete end of our capacity to sustain ourselves. Christ is raised up by God, *receives* life and vindication at the hand of another, by virtue of the unparalleled depth of relation between them. So, too, disciples find communion with God through their reception of the risen Christ, who depends upon their faith for the realization of the church in history. The "wonderful exchange" of atonement exemplifies the same dynamic: God becomes as humans are so that humans may become as God is. God depends on the faithfulness of Mary and Jesus for the humanization of God, as humans depend on the condescension of the Word for the divinization of humanity. In all this, mutuality is the condition of salvation.

Salvation is not an autonomous achievement. Nor is it even an isolated relation between one individual and God, one that might satisfy the human request: "Cannot God deal with me directly without bringing another person, another religion, another culture into the business?"[12] This is a request that could only be met by a "relationship with God which is in principle accessible to everyone individually apart from any relationship with his neighbor."[13] Christians believe salvation is not of this nature. The point is actually encoded in the very basis of the tradition: the Hebrew scriptures are the foundation of the Christian Bible. Concretely, Christians receive everything at the source of redemption, including their savior, from Israel. Violently and perversely as we may have regularly tried to escape this dependence, that flight violates not only history but the living grammar of Christian faith. Only in acknowledging the election of others to be particular witnesses to us may we hope for any validity in our own witness.

Because salvation itself is communion and relation, the means to it are relational also. As Lesslie Newbigin puts it, "the means by which the good news of salvation is propagated must be congruous with the nature of the salvation itself."[14] This is the deep consistency in the conviction that God acts through particular historical events and persons on behalf of all, and the conviction that we connect with those acts through a web of concrete *human* relations and witness. The texture of that web is present in the religious end itself. The process of salvation is integral to the nature of salvation: communion can't be achieved alone. Everyone who would come to this end must stoop at the entrance, in reliance on and gratitude for the concrete bonds with others that make it possible and that endure as part of it. Only through the witness and continuing relation that link us with those others may we be drawn into this distinctive communion with God.

12. This formulation comes from George Hunsberger (Hunsberger, 1998, p. 55). Hunsberger's study takes Lesslie Newbigin's concept of election as the key to his theology of plurality and mission. In much of the next few paragraphs I am developing insights I have incorporated from Hunsberger's very perceptive work. In fact, I cannot help pointing out that my dependence on wisdom about salvation — which I receive from Hunsberger through his grateful dependence on Newbigin's insights into the meaning of Scripture (as well as others in a list that could be indefinitely extended) — is an apt if mundane illustration of the very point we are discussing.

13. (Newbigin, 1958, p. 79). Quoted by Hunsberger (Hunsberger, 1998, p. 55).

14. (Newbigin, 1954, p. 169).

IV

Our overview of the Christian religious end would not be complete without some reference to the coordinate negative possibilities it presumes. Salvation is a deliverance *from* certain conditions as well as a positive fulfillment. "Sin" is often the omnibus word for what salvation delivers us from. But this is unhelpful in many ways, since the word can be used as an umbrella term for all three types of broken or distorted relationships we described above (with God, with others, with nature more broadly). Confusingly, it is frequently employed also to designate one of these three in distinction from the others (estrangement from God). Or it may be used to refer to individual instances of brokenness of all three types: "sins" in the sense of discrete unfaithful, evil, or despairing acts. This overlap in reference is understandable in one respect, since these relationships are not entirely separable. The relationship of humans to God cannot be segregated from relations among people or relations to the rest of creation.

In a similar way, "salvation" functions as an umbrella term whose positive character is often articulated in categories corresponding to the three dimensions of estrangement: justification (righting relation with God), sanctification (righting human relations), and eternal life (restoring the relation with nature). Faith, love, and hope correspond as positive realities to the sin, evil, and death from which we are liberated. As each of these last three represent the degeneration or termination of relation, the first three represent fulfilled relations. This recapitulates the important point we have already noted. Creation has a certain permanence. Heaven and earth may pass away, but the *relations* that have come into existence through creation do not pass away. They endure and are fulfilled. The unification of these three fulfillments through communion with God in Christ is the religious end that Christians call salvation. The danger in this threefold schematic is that it might suggest that each can be pursued as a separate track, which is quite contrary to the principles we have developed in the previous section.

The three dimensions of relation involved in salvation have received somewhat different formulation in the Eastern Orthodox, Roman Catholic, and Protestant confessional traditions. The Eastern or "Greek" theological tradition has tended to emphasize one pair of factors: death as the root calamity of the human condition and eternal life or, more properly, participation in the divine life, as the primary fulfillment of that condition. We require deliverance from the destructive nexus of mortality, corruption, and death. The end result of the broken trust between Eve and Adam and God is mortality. Humanity loses its contingent possibility for unlimited life. For the first humans, the wages of sin are death. From our fall into mortality, other distortions of human life follow. After Adam and Eve, the effects of death are sin.

As is frequently noted, the Eastern church has nothing strictly comparable to the doctrine of original sin elaborated in the West. As described by Augustine and others in the West, original sin is an inherited moral guilt and an inherited negative moral bias, inevitably manifest in sinful behavior, which draws mortality upon those who bear it. The wages of sin continue to be death. In Eastern theology, by contrast, what is inherited from the first parents as a result of their fault is mortality itself, plain and simple. This is not first a moral taint, but an empirical condition that all our experimental knowledge of human nature verifies. We are liable to death and inevitably we die. In each generation, this fact and our awareness of it generate anew distortions in the divine-human and human-human relations. *Cf. Hebrews 2, 15*

As creatures made in the image of God, humans were suspended contingently over nonbeing by the slender but entirely sufficient umbilical cord of love and trust that linked us to God. Through that connection flowed the divine energy to sustain us indefinitely. Humans possessed no intrinsic immortality, but they were not subject to the necessity of death either, so long as the link held. The breaking of this link through sin cuts us loose and cuts us off. Unnourished by the divine energy, our existence fades into subjection to corruption and death. In such a state, our mortality becomes a source of anxiety. Futile attempts to defend ourselves from it lead us into active sin and estrange us from trust in God. Now sinfulness is more a result of mortality than mortality of sinfulness. To say that humans are "conceived in sin" does not mean that some guilt or evil inclination is passed on to them in the act of their conception, but that *what* they inherit is a mortal human nature, which became mortal as a result of sin. *Cf above*

This point is highlighted in the different attitudes toward baptism that developed in the Eastern and Western churches. In the West, the removal of the guilt of original sin became a primary function of baptism. But an Eastern contemporary of Augustine, Theodoret of Cyrrhus, denied that remission of sin was applicable to infant baptism. Though it was indeed a feature of adult baptisms, it was not the central feature of baptism itself. Baptism was primarily a "promise of greater and more perfect gifts."[15] As John Meyendorff says, the church baptizes children not to remit their sin "but in order to give them a new and immortal *life*, which their mortal parents are unable to communicate to them. The opposition between the two Adams is seen in terms *I think today Catholic Ch. I would agree*

15. (Meyendorff, 1974, pp. 145-46).

68

not of guilt and forgiveness but death and life."[16] Baptism is thus the reinstitution of the lost link, opening the flow of divine life into our mortal natures, a link that will be deepened through the sacramental life of the church.

The aim of this relation, already implicit in the first humanity, is full communion with God, participation in all of the divine nature that is communicable. The end is traditionally called *theosis* in the Eastern church: divinization. The relation between God and humanity could hardly be more intimate, for in this view what is sought is for humans to share all of God's own nature that can be shared while God remains God and we retain our created nature. This entire process centers in Christ, for it is in him that this link has been reestablished, "recapitulated," and opened permanently. The end of communion has been condensed, as it were, in one person. Through this person it can be unrestrictedly shared. Here God remains God and humanity remains humanity, but they are united in the deepest possible manner, a manner that has to do with relation more than substance. It is an ontological union, but only when one understands ontology itself in terms of personal communion.[17] By virtue of the communion, Christ's humanity is divinized and God is fully "humanized." The communion of God, in one trinitarian person, with a human person is not in the first place an example for imitation, but a *source* from which that communion spreads, a link through which divine energies pass to humanity and human love passes to God.

This is too brief and crude a summary of a rich tradition, but it provides a helpful outline of one dimension of salvation: *theosis*, participation in the divine life. Here human being receives the energies of God as an enrichment of its own nature and relates in communion with what is not communicated. This mutual flow of relationship reaches all persons, in some measure, by virtue of the unity of human nature. In the Eastern tradition, this commerce between the divine and the human is not limited to a spiritualization of humans. It is understood even in quite physicalistic terms: our body also is being nourished back into deathlessness through unity with God. This reflects the emphasis in this tradition on the restoration of the broken relation between human persons and created nature.

The Western church, in its Protestant and Catholic traditions, has developed different formulations. Differences between Catholics and Protestants loom so large in the history of both since the Reformation that their

16. (Meyendorff, 1974, p. 146).

17. On this point see the further discussion in Chapter Five below, especially in connection with (Zizioulas, 1985).

commonality is often lost to view until conversation with Orthodox Christians (or with other religious traditions) brings it dramatically back to sight. The West tended to see the root human failing in moral terms, rather than in mortality. In Augustine, this is particularly specified as a corruption of our wills. Though free to choose all their acts, humans are not free to control or choose the desires that direct their choices. In fact, there is a distorted bias in our moral decision-making that follows from a skewed perspective on the world. This leads us into sin and guilt, which prompt us to compound our situation through denial, defiance, and despair that lead us to yet further evil. Salvation is release from sin and guilt through forgiveness, leading to a new life characterized both by a reformed will and a reconciliation with God that overcomes our rebellion and sloth. If the East thinks of mortality and divinization, corruptibility and incorruptibility, the West thinks more of guilt and forgiveness, sin and righteousness, rebellion and trust.

Catholics and Protestants might agree to characterize the problem this way: How can creatures — who are by their own continual choice estranged from God, who distrust even God's aim for their good, whose actions against others merit judgment — be lovingly accepted by God, redeemed morally, and raised into intimate communion with God? They diverge in their further specification of the problem and its solution. For Catholics, the fundamental moral corruption of humanity is reversed by divine grace, which regenerates the will. This eventually produces sanctification, and therefore a person who is truly righteous and through grace fit for deep fellowship with God. The moral estrangement that divided humans from God is overcome by the gracious reconstruction of humanity that fits it for *koinonia* with a righteous God.

Protestants, on the other hand, believe that it is not so much moral failure that has created a personal estrangement between God and humanity but rather the reverse. Personal estrangement, a lack of trust and faith toward God, leads to moral corruption. The original sin humans share is not at base an inclination to specific evil acts, but a disposition to trust something else in place of God. Lack of attainment, actual sinning, stands between God and humanity only in a secondary way. "Sin" for Protestants means not primarily corruption of the will, but what Luther called a "want of fear, love and trust toward God." The first sin was not at root an act of disobedience, in eating the fruit that God had put off limits. It was the doubt and suspicion directed toward a God who had shown only love and generosity, the return of preemptive competition in the face of open gift.

For Protestants, this basic failing is not addressed primarily by sanctification, by a reform of behavior or even of will. Behind the right act and even the desire to do the right act, this estrangement may well persist, this want of love and trust toward God. It can only be addressed by justification, by an overcoming of the estrangement itself. If for Catholics God takes the initiative to regenerate the will and thus to make people who can commune with God, for Protestants God takes the initiative to restore people to communion and this leads to the regeneration of their wills. If for Catholics God saves sinners by making them righteous and then accepting them, for Protestants God saves sinners by accepting them into communion while they are still sinners, sinners who through faith in their acceptance become righteous. Both traditions affirm regeneration of the will and communion with God as aspects of salvation. They agree that Jesus Christ is integral to both aspects. They divide sharply over the sequence and relation of those two dimensions, and especially over the role played in each by human and divine action.

We saw the emphasis on *theosis* or divinization in the Eastern tradition, the move from mortality to eternal life in communion with the life of the triune God. On the Catholic side of the Western tradition we see an emphasis on the move from moral evil, disordered relationships, to love, the regeneration of the will. On the Protestant side we see an emphasis on the move from lack of trust to faith, to a full-hearted acceptance of God's promises to us. To return to the simplest form of our theme — salvation as a relation — we can see the nuance each perspective expresses. Protestants tend to stress the fiduciary character of this relationship: it is most of all a matter of God's freely chosen disposition toward us and our response, of trust or of distrust, toward God and the promises that express God's desire for our good. Catholics tend to stress the habituation to virtue that puts the relation with God on a new moral plane, and rescues relations among humans from violence and evil.

These contrasts can be exaggerated. "Regeneration of the will" may sound like the will is simply made strong and then set on its independent way to do the right thing. But this is a caricature of the Catholic view. "Justification" may sound as though one rests in God's unconditional reward, purity of faith in God's mercy substituting for the performance of God's will. That is a caricature also. Desire guides a regenerate will just as it does an unregenerate one. In deeper communion with God, both the habitual exercise of the will (a "Catholic" emphasis) and the desire or attitude that animates it (a "Protestant" emphasis) are transformed. And in neither case is sanctification or justification regarded as a gift that becomes the possession of the individual apart from their connection with God. Both are caught by communion and maintained through it.

The three different perspectives on salvation that I have sketched are rich with further questions. The distinct emphases they represent are important in Christian theological discussion.[18] But I offer them here only to further our pursuit of a clear picture of what salvation means in Christian terms. And for this purpose, it is very important to note that though I have outlined some differences, none of the traditions we considered excludes the dimensions that the others give greater pride of place. The differences arise in ordering the three dimensions. Protestants and Catholics hardly deny eternal life as an aspect of salvation. Protestants and Orthodox do not deny moral regeneration, nor do Orthodox and Catholics deny justification.

This ecumenical commonality has important implications. Various Christian confessions may use a different dimension as the primary framework integrating the other two. But they agree that a religious aim which definitively excludes even one of these aspects is not salvation. Salvation encompasses the dimension of love and justice, right and rich relations among humans. Yet a definitive limitation of salvation simply to "right relation among persons" would not be what Christians seek. Salvation encompasses relation with the rest of God's creation: harmony with nature and eternal life. But a definitive reduction of salvation simply to "ecological balance and personal resurrection" would not be what Christians seek. Salvation encompasses personal relation with God: faith and justification. But a definitive reduction of salvation to "spiritual experience of forgiveness and union" would not be what Christians seek.

Each of the three reductions we just noted affirms a real aspect of salvation. But it is limited, truncated. Segregated in such a way, and compared with the ecumenical constellation, these aspects of salvation appear as broken portions of a larger, integrated field of relationships. They are false not in their positive reality but in their isolation, like portions of an organism cut off from the circulatory system of the whole. In one sense the isolated portion is entirely correct and in order. Everything about it is right. On the other hand, because taken as a false totality it is entirely out of order. As a whole, it is comprehensively wrong. The eye is a perfectly good eye when it is the eye for the body. Entirely alone, its structural perfection remains unchanged in one sense. In a more profound sense, it is entirely lost.

The nature of Christian ecumenical discussion about salvation reflects

---

18. It goes beyond our primary focus to follow out the implications in Christology. Plainly, the presentation of the person and work of Christ is affected by these three different frameworks, with Orthodox stressing the incarnation and Christ's victory over death, Catholics stressing Christ's provision of grace for moral regeneration of the believer, and Protestants stressing the cross as overcoming guilt and estrangement from God. As is the case with salvation itself, all three traditions agree in recognizing the dimensions that others emphasize and agree that Christ's work is integral to each one.

this perception. A deep and increasing unity is possible among those who fully share these dimensions, though they frame them differently. The "convergence" of some ecumenical processes reflects this.[19] This convergence does not specify agreement on all details, but articulates an increasing confidence that each side can see in the other's position and practice the constellation of essential features, in living relation. But such convergence is not possible when one or more parties suspect a neighboring Christian tradition effectively excludes one of these dimensions in theory or practice. This dynamic, evident among Christians, certainly exists also in the relation between Christians and those of other religious traditions.

We began this chapter with the description of salvation as a relation of communion with God and other creatures in Christ. We tried to indicate how Christian tradition fills out this description. In this section I suggested that salvation is a communion with God that can be viewed in terms of three nested sets of relations which are mutually implicated in that communion: relation with God, relations among people (individuals and communities), and relations with creatures and our own created nature.

The description of salvation is obviously itself a piece of Christian theology, and is subject to argument among Christians. There are no doubt those who would contest what I have said about ecumenical commonality. Some might argue that salvation properly has to do only with the individual believer's relation with God and Christ after their death. And there are some who argue that right human relations within history constitute the sum total meaning of salvation. My summary takes an approach toward Christian tradition somewhat similar to that recommended toward the religions in Chapter One: I attempt to find the greatest extent of compatible truth in various concrete perspectives. In this case that approach has the additional virtue of being (so far as I can see) the most characteristic way the tradition reads itself. It also highlights the dynamic of unity and integration in the tradition, which in regard to salvation is summed up in the idea of communion.

It is true to say that salvation is justice, peace, justification, moral renewal, eternal life, mystical peace . . . the list could be extended. Each of these things is a *feature* associated with salvation. But salvation is not the cumulative total of a list of things. It is an integral relation that has these diverse faces. This is why Christianity has been insistent about personal language of relationship as irreplaceable in its thought, worship, and imagery. An exclu-

---

19. A recent example, for all its trials, is the Roman Catholic–Lutheran dialogue on justification. See the Lutheran World Federation/Roman Catholic Joint Declaration on Justification by Faith (1998).

sive focus on the attributes of the "condition of being saved" is fundamentally misguided, since it leaves out of account the others in relation to whom this condition is constituted and maintained. Likewise, an exclusive focus on God or some religious ultimate, as an exclusive all-encompassing reality, leaves out of account the ones in relation to whom God manifests the fullness of divine glory through the deepening of the relational qualities that are intrinsic to the divine nature.

V

This discussion of salvation serves as a good basis to ask another question. Is this religious end divisible? That is, can salvation be partial or vary in degree? This is a matter that has vexed the theological tradition, in various forms. It is clearly a very important question for our theological understanding of other religious traditions. With the relational character of salvation firmly in mind, we are in a better position to address the issue.

We mentioned earlier the way in which Christians have spoken of salvation as a past event, a current reality, and a future hope. If salvation is a relation, such language is not contradictory but quite appropriate. A relation spans time and is different at various moments. But can it be partial? Is it all or nothing? Plainly we speak at times in either way. We rarely say, of any but the most instrumental relations, that they are everything that they can be. My relation to a turnpike toll-taker may be, within certain functional limits, everything that it can be. He takes my ticket; I give him my money. The relation comes close to being a mathematical point. It takes place or it doesn't, but it is not susceptible to much elaboration. Any wider possibilities would require a change in the framework of the relationship itself. Within the terms set for it, it could hardly be richer than it is. The toll-taker relation might be seen as a near perfect — i.e., completely realized — instance of a certain type of relation. Or it could be viewed as a very partial relation, in comparison with entirely different types of possible interaction.

On the other hand, the most significant relationships in our lives are likely to be ones that encompass a very wide range of options for extension and development. This scope marks such bonds with a depth that contrasts with the narrow "purity" of the toll-taker relation. Ironically, our experience of this deeper relation at any given moment may strike us as dramatically partial and limited in comparison with the fullness of possibility open to us. Precisely because of the richness and the range open to this relation, any single moment (no matter how perfect of its kind) could be said to be fragmentary, representative of far less than the whole. Yet it is the most significant relations that, in another respect, we tend to think of as discrete realities. One is in love or not. You have a best friend or you do not. You have a religious faith or you do not. In other words, quite apart from the current state or latest turn of an important relation, we distinguish the separate fact of our participation in such a relation, its constitutive role in our lives. One can be in a troubled patch in a deeply loving, committed relation, just as one can have transient, intense interactions with someone where no serious or enduring relation exists.

These analogies are all relevant to our discussion, anticipating a similar range of nuances in our understanding of salvation. Christians can at times treat salvation as a quantum reality: one has a saving relation to God or one does not. At other times they may treat salvation as something that will be realized in the future and that is only partial or anticipatory here and now. Both perspectives are justified. A relationship may be decisively established as constitutive for a person, while it is still nothing like what it will become. That future may be implicit in the present, without being determined and automatic. In Scripture and tradition, salvation is viewed in just this way, in terms of an "already" and a "not yet."

The emphasis also varies according to whether focus falls on God's end of the relation or the human end. God's relation toward us is a settled matter of God's decision. It is the expression of love, of a universal salvific will. Insofar as Christians refer to this aspect of the relation, it is taken as certain, once for all, an accomplished event. There is a narrative to the working out of this relation of God to us, which is contingent upon human freedom, but there is no doubt of the relation itself. Our relation to God is not settled in the same way. There *is* doubt about the character we will give to that relation on our end. The way that God's redemptive aim is worked out in relation to us is shaped by us. And our relation to God is not and cannot be an isolated, independent determination. It is worked out in the midst of God's gracious acts toward us. God works in us, but not without us. And we in a faintly analogous manner work "in" God, that is, within God's providence, imparting to it a contingent quality that is ours but never without God's superintendence. In other words, God's attitude to us and our response to God condition each other, reciprocally if asymmetrically.

Let us close this chapter with a brief further reflection on one aspect of the view of salvation it outlines. Salvation is a relationship in three dimensions: with God, with other humans, and with the rest of creation. It is a relationship of communion with God, a communion that encompasses relation to others within that communion. Salvation presumes not only a person's participation in the divine life through relation with God, but anticipates that

* Does this scuttle predestination?

through that communion a person also participates in the unique realities of others' sharing with God as well.

If this is so, we can understand the universal salvific will of God as God's unconditional openness to all creatures. Every person has a relation to God, established in creation and realized in history. God's relation to each person is formally the same as God's relation to every person. That relation is both organic/familial/constitutive on the one hand and free/volitional/associative on the other. Both aspects are framed by God's will to bring the person into the fullest communion with God and all of God's creatures. This aim persists and is maintained through every possible twist or variation in the person's free relation toward God. The first aspect is identical for all (all are God's children) and the second is unique for each (no two people's relations with God are identical in pattern or sequence). This highlights a key point we will take up in the next chapter: salvation is not the same state for all who participate in it. In fact, it is not identical for *any*. This diversity within the Christian religious end itself has an echo in the multiplicity of religious ends, among which salvation is one. The nature of that "echo" will be explored more fully in Chapter Five.

God manifests an unalterably saving will toward all creation, an intent to ceaselessly seek and offer the widest possible range of communion to each creature. God acts in particular and decisive ways within the historical nexus of human life, reaching humanity *through* the web of interpersonal communion that is an enduring dimension of salvation. We have seen the deep congruity between this path toward salvation and the nature of salvation itself. Such particularity (of incarnation and special revelation) does not compromise God's impartiality to all unless it skews the availability of salvation for some in contrast to others. There is no need to assume that it does so. A wide range of Christian theologians, from virtually every period and tradition, have affirmed the impartiality of God in this respect, though they have offered differing accounts to support that view.[20]

The situation I have described is one where God's universal salvific will is the co-determiner of human religious ends. Because salvation is a free relation, God has taken absolute control only over God's end of the relation. Religious ends are co-determined by persons themselves in their relational activity. But it is also true that in a wider and prior way God has provided the terms, the relational context, for the constitution of all religious ends. Persons cannot entirely escape God's "Yes" to them. They are obliged to respond in

20. For examples of the varying kinds of theological rationale offered in different Christian traditions, see the material in (Heim, 1998).

some way to the saving offer of communion, even if their response is to constrict that relation to a vanishing point. We are free to persist in choices and formulations of our own identity that will finally constitute distinct religious ends, in contrast with the full communion God offers. Salvation is a communion that draws together various types of relation with God. *As* saving communion, it is not divisible. But humans have freedom to shape their response to these different types of relation, with results that could be seen as fragmenting distinct elements, and turning them toward different ends. This is the topic we will pursue in the next few chapters.

There is no point (set by the magnitude of our transgressions or the calendar of eschatological time) at which God's will toward us changes from a saving to a punitive will. Nor was God's will originally divided, predestining some to salvation and some to damnation. It remains constant, though the response to it is various. Does this mean that God's purpose and will are, finally, powerless to bring about what they seek? Can God be thwarted by human choice and the ultimate course of creation taken out of God's hands? We will return to this question in Chapter Seven. The short answer is that in its finest particulars God determines the world to be undetermined. It is out of God's hands, in the sense that God has freely forsaken the role of being the only decider. But the destiny of creation as a whole is not out of God's hands, for the universal salvific will remains a co-determiner of the ends of *all* creatures. This is a powerful boundary that sets limits to the course of the entire creation. There are real alternative futures, but in each of them all the religious ends of humanity will glorify God, and will be rooted in the same salvific purpose of God.

Chapter Three

The Glory of the Creature:
Religious Ends in Christian Theology

I n the last chapter we reviewed what Christians mean by salvation. In this chapter I want to raise a slightly different question. What, if anything, does Christian theology have to say about a diversity of human ends *apart* from salvation? This is not in the first instance a question about Christian assessment of specific religious traditions. It is an inquiry about whether theology has maps on which it might locate ends other than salvation. In Christian tradition such maps have largely been drawn with an orientation toward life after death, in terms of heaven and hell. That is the primary material we will explore. But, as we will see, the study also has a direct correlation with consideration of religious ends in historical and personal contexts.

In one sense these are very familiar subjects. But I come at them from a somewhat unfamiliar angle, asking what we can learn about how Christians have understood the various options. We will continue to develop our understanding of salvation. The primary purpose in this chapter, however, is to reverse our line of sight, to look away from the spotlight Christian sources throw on their religious end and look toward what lies outside that circle. In particular, I am interested to see what resources may be found in Scripture and tradition to help us understand alternative religious ends. Any thorough exploration of the subject would require a book in its own right. I intend to highlight a few historical points and to explore perhaps the most suggestive imaginative theological work that bears on our topic, Dante's *Divine Comedy*.

First we will consider the New Testament and some historical theological developments prior to Dante. Then we will focus on several motifs in his poem which are directly relevant to our discussion.

I

There are a number of excellent studies that sift biblical texts for their bearing on Christianity's relations with other religions.[1] Such treatments virtually always focus their attention on whether Scripture texts allow salvation, the Christian religious end, for those who practice other religions or do not explicitly follow Jesus. Whatever the answer to this question, it does not address the existence or nature of possible alternative religious fulfillments. These studies usually share the assumption we have already discussed and questioned in Chapter One, the assumption that there can be only one religious end. If we question that assumption, we explore the theological tradition in a somewhat different light.

It is often noted that in the New Testament there is nothing we could call an explicit and definitive statement on the fate of the unevangelized. Nowhere does Jesus, or even one of the New Testament writers, directly pose and clearly answer the question of the destiny of people in Jesus' time and after who never take him as their savior (who perhaps never know of him) and who diligently practice their own religions. To hypothesize a biblical answer to such a question, we must practice a kind of triangulation in which various texts on related issues are coordinated. The same holds even more emphatically for my inquiry about alternative religious ends. So it is very unlikely we could arrive at a clear teaching of Scripture in this area. This is doubly so because the whole area of eschatology and realized redemption is one in which we can claim to have guidance only in a few highly general principles and one particular instance (the risen Christ).

I might illustrate what I have just said by reference to two passages in the gospels with contrasting words from Jesus: "Whoever is not against us is for us" (Mark 9:40) and "Whoever is not with me is against me, and whoever does not gather with me, scatters" (Matthew 12:30). These are all the more striking because both statements occur in the context of a discussion about casting out demons, religious activity of the first order. The incident in Mark's gospel involves a person who does not belong to the followers of Jesus but is casting out demons in Jesus' name. This unknown exorcist is using Je-

---

1. These surveys, of course, are conducted from varying standpoints (Pinnock, 1992; Cracknell, 1986; Ariarajah, 1989).

sus' name religiously, but does not join him directly as a disciple. In Matthew's gospel, it is Jesus' own exorcism of demons that is challenged by people who claim that he does this work by the power of the devil.

It appears then that in a case where someone associates the true works of the Spirit with Jesus' name (though with no explicit contact with or authorization from Jesus), the principle is "whoever is not against us is for us." But in the case of someone who attributed the actual acts of Jesus and the presence of the Holy Spirit to Satan, the principle is "whoever is not for us is against us." We might suggest that what is most severely rejected is any claim that the Spirit and power of God are *not* associated with Christ. There is broad tolerance on the other hand for the unauthorized association of Jesus with real works of God's Spirit. In both cases, however, what is at issue is the way those of "other religions" treat Jesus. Neither text really addresses the question of religious practice that simply ignores Jesus, one way or another. What the passages do illustrate is the integrative trinitarian principle we have discussed earlier. In both cases, it is the *association* of Jesus with God and the Spirit that is the key issue. When this connection is made, even in an "unorthodox" way, it is accepted. The denial of such a connection is roundly condemned. Still, it seems we can hardly extract from such passages a distinct answer to our question.

The Christian theological tradition is correct in its common holding that the realm of eschatology is one where we tread with humility. We can search for the most adequate theological perspective by trying to align what we can find in the triangulation of the various scriptural sources with theological reference points regarding Christ, God, and humanity that seem more firmly established. My theological hypothesis is subject to all these qualifications. The most that I hope to suggest in this chapter is that this hypothesis has authentic roots in Christian sources. A stronger case for its validity will need to show how it fits into the wider web of fundamental Christian convictions, strengthening, enriching, and integrating the whole. That is a case I will try to provide in the subsequent chapters.

The issue I am raising may hardly appear to merit all this effort. The New Testament and Christian tradition seem to have a clear notion of alternative religious ends. There are two: salvation and damnation. What further study is needed? Matthew 25 presents a picture of judgment, where people will be separated "as a shepherd separates the sheep from the goats," with some going away "into eternal punishment, but the righteous into eternal life."[2] These alternative possibilities frame not only the future but the present.

---

2. Other passages: Matthew 13:42; Mark 9:43ff.; Luke 13:28; 2 Thessalonians 1:6-10; Romans 2:6-11; 2 Peter 2:4-10; Revelation 21:6-8.

To say that the kingdom of God has appeared in Jesus, that Jesus' healings and exorcisms and resurrection are first fruits of the eschatological age, is to say that the final reality of salvation has flowed back into history and begun to be present there. Salvation has "appeared," in an anticipatory, fragmentary, but real way.

In the view of the New Testament writers, this appearance has sharpened the contrast between salvation and other human options. In the course of their lives here and now, people set themselves on the path to one side or the other of this divide. This happens not through a cumulative scoring of someone's moral behavior, but through a person's free response to God's grace, which offers transformation of our created capacity for relation with God, with other persons, and with creation. These relations as such are open to all by nature. But our participation in these relations, and ultimately the shape of our ability to participate, is something fixed by our own constancy in patterns of desire and action.

The New Testament writers are concerned about one religious end, salvation, made available in and through Christ. At times they identify this end with the redemption promised to Israel. At other times they emphasize the intrinsic newness of this end, a relation with God beyond any even hoped for before. The first emphasis corresponds to Christ as fulfillment of traditional expectation. The second corresponds to Christ as pioneer or new revelation. Both intersect in a phrase like "new covenant," where the emphasis can fall either on the side of continuity or innovation. The New Testament writers are interested in what salvation is, and how we may participate in it. Specific, alternative religious ends are hardly considered at all.

The book of Revelation presents a sequence of plagues and varying judgments. These seem to have been one source for later depictions of diverse torments in hell. But in Revelation these are events of the end time and are not themselves ultimate ends. There is no explicit interest in any diversity among the lost. The little that the New Testament has to say on this score presents a rather undifferentiated picture of distress, as in a "lake of fire." The book of Revelation gives a slightly fuller glimpse of variation in the ranks of the blessed, where elders, martyrs, and myriad ranks of angels are distinguished.

It is actually more helpful to look at the emphasis on the diversity that marks the *community* of persons now beginning to participate in this "new life," the realization of salvation. Paul's description of the variety of gifts in the church (1 Corinthians 12:12-31) seems in part also a foreshadowing of the nature of redemption itself, as is the case with Pentecost. Both are eschatological signs. But there is no specification about the diversity of human conditions that might subsist in redemption or in damnation. The focus is on the specific character of salvation as communion with God, reconciliation with neighbors, and the overcoming of death.

The basic twofold distinction between salvation and its alternatives is a consistent feature of Scripture. Any consideration of alternative religious ends should be consonant with that pattern, not a substitute for it. However, later developments in theology arise from the attempt to coordinate the definite twofold division we have just noted with other elements in Scripture and the Christian life. We need to briefly indicate what these are.

There are a number of texts that stress God's universal and direct relation with creation. A range of images and ideas from the Bible come into play here: the image of God given to humanity in creation (Genesis 1:27), a universal covenant with all humanity through Noah (Genesis 9), a law written on human hearts (Romans 2:15). At many places in the Bible, such intrinsic or universal connections between humanity and God are presumed as grounds for the achievement of some religious fulfillment. A key text would be Peter's words in Acts 10:34-35: "I truly understand that God shows no partiality, but in every nation anyone who fears him and does what is right is acceptable to him." This is an interesting passage, since Peter is speaking to Cornelius (a Roman centurion) who is neither Jewish or Christian, but "upright and God-fearing." As a result of his virtue and desire to know God, the text says, God has sent an angel to direct Cornelius to Peter so that he may hear about and believe in Christ. Therefore we learn nothing about what would have been Cornelius's end if he had continued on his upright and God-fearing ways without faith in Christ.

Another relevant text would be Paul's words in Romans 2:6-11: "For he will repay according to each one's deeds: to those who by patiently doing good seek for glory and honor and immortality, he will give eternal life; while for those who are self-seeking and who obey not the truth but wickedness, there will be wrath and fury. There will be anguish and distress for everyone who does evil, the Jew first and also the Greek, but glory and honor and peace for everyone who does good, the Jew first and also the Greek. For God shows no partiality." It is unclear whether for Paul the possibility he describes is only theoretical, explaining why everyone is without excuse for sin, or whether "glory and honor and peace" might be granted by God to those who do good within various religious paths. Would this "glory and honor and peace" be the same thing as salvation in Christ, or is it something different? Passages such as we have just quoted indicate a firm conviction that upright people in other traditions are pleasing to God and that they will be judged in truth, with fairness. They will not go without reward. But *what* exactly such reward would be is not clear.

There is a universal God-human connection, given in creation, to which humans respond positively or negatively through their moral behavior and their spiritual search. Emphasis on this intrinsic law generally goes hand in hand with an expectation that people can be judged for their performance in meeting the obligations they apprehend. People can "do what is right," and God will honor their righteousness. But the biblical writers seem to suggest that insofar as this justice is insisted upon, humans must abide by the results, and accept the division of the righteous and unrighteous that results. This entire pattern is sometimes called the "covenant of Noah." In Jewish tradition this notion was developed as the framework for understanding the relations of gentiles with God.[3]

The Old Testament provides a number of examples that presume this relation. Jonah is a reluctant prophet sent by God to call for repentance from the Assyrian inhabitants of Nineveh, fierce enemies of Israel. They are not required to become Jews or to change their religious traditions, but only to recognize God's call to repent. It is striking to reflect that in the context of the book of Jonah, a people's collective prosperity or destruction is a near-literal equivalent to salvation and damnation as those terms were then understood. It is true that the prophets of Israel look forward to the definitive, final establishment of a secure, prosperous, and holy kingdom around Jerusalem, and do not regard individual historical victories or defeats as the final word. But it is also true that in sparing and blessing a gentile city or people, God was sharing with them in significant measure the religious fulfillment sought by Israel. This is precisely the source of Jonah's chagrin at God's behavior. We see a similar phenomenon with particular individuals as well. Abel, Enoch, Noah, Melchizedek, Abimilech, Job, and the Queen of Sheba are "pagan saints," whom Scripture holds up as just and godly persons.[4] The book of Hebrews takes one of these, the Canaanite king-priest Melchizedek, as a primary positive model in interpreting Christ and Christ's saving work.

From a Christian perspective, the great figures of the history of Israel offer yet another important case. Abraham is the one who is explicitly discussed by Paul in Romans. Abraham trusted God and this faith was counted as righteousness. He, and it seems other patriarchs and matriarchs of Israel, attained salvation by virtue of their complete trust in the revelation given to them by God. Paul appears to reject the idea that it was devout observance of discrete rites of an emergent Israelite "religion" that led to this religious end,

3. (Novak, 1989), chapter one. See also (Novak, 1983).
4. For a more extensive discussion see chapter two in (Pinnock, 1992).

that is, observance of the law. It was Abraham's ready trust in God's word that was saving for him and for those who kept the law out of such trust.

We can refer also to the prologue to the Gospel of John. There the Word of God who became incarnate in Christ is identified as co-eternal with God, and as active in creation itself. "All things came into being through him." This suggests that the same Logos encountered in the incarnate Christ also has played a distinctive part in the constitution of every part of creation. Whatever explicit relation one may have with the incarnate Logos, all creatures have an indirect relation. If the unity of Logos and humanity is "retroactive," this principle holds even more strongly. From the human, temporal point of view our intrinsic connection to the Word who participated in our creation is an indirect relation with Christ, united with the Word in incarnation.

Yet another important element is reflected in the resurrection appearances of Christ. A common feature in virtually all of these is the fact that the disciples do not initially recognize Jesus. The story of Jesus walking with two disciples on the road to Emmaus is a good example (Luke 24:13-35). The active presence of the risen Christ can be anonymous even for those with prior knowledge of Jesus. The appearance of the risen Christ to Paul on the road to Damascus is also at first ambiguous. The doubt is dispelled because Paul asks and is told directly "I am Jesus, whom you are persecuting" (Acts 9:1-9). After the ascension, when such bodily appearances cease, the question lingers whether Christ may be immediately present to people in various circumstances, with a similar lack of recognition, a kind of post-resurrection incognito.

Finally, the Holy Spirit plays a role in these reflections. Though generally in the New Testament the Holy Spirit "testifies of Christ" and is a seal of the life of Christian community, the Spirit may also be linked to the activity of God in the forms we have discussed above. Where explicit knowledge of the incarnation of the Word is lacking, the Holy Spirit as God's prophetic power and personal presence is nevertheless active in human life.

The interreligious meaning of all the factors I have just described is not worked out in Scripture. But the data are there and require serious attention. They have received that attention primarily from theologians dealing with a concern about means rather than ends. These texts figure as sources for "inclusivist" perspectives, which explain how those outside Christianity might be able to "cross over" to Christian faith and salvation, in this life or the life to come, even without direct knowledge of Christ or commitment to the church. This is a legitimate and important task and provides part of the picture. But the question remains whether these factors still have significance for those who do not cross over.

There is no doubt that the pattern set out in the New Testament is one where relationship with God is addressed in existential and decisive terms: yes/no. Gradations in this relationship are rarely in the picture. The disciples' disputes about who will be greatest in the kingdom of heaven are plainly rebuked by Jesus. Among those who do not respond openly to Jesus' preaching, little distinction is made between those who are already spiritual leaders and those who are social outcasts. The presence of Jesus, and response to him, moves people to one side or another of a line. This line is not between those with a relation to God and those with none. Even in encounters with gentiles, Jesus, as a Jew, presupposes the relation implicit in the image of God. Every human is connected to the God who created him or her. In most cases, dealing with fellow Jews, Jesus presupposes the much more concrete relation of persons who have collectively received special revelation and challenge from God, through Torah and prophets. Salvation is thus not the transition from no relation with God to some relation with God, nor from ignorance of such relation to recognition. Salvation is constituted by a particular set of distinctive relations. Our connection with God as creatures and our awareness of that connection provide the basis of some possible "upright" relation with God. But this is not necessarily the same thing as salvation. This basic connection clearly did not preclude damnation as Christians understood it and could, as Paul suggests, actually expose humans to more severe judgment. Historical Christianity faithfully maintained this basic twofold division, between salvation and damnation. But, as we shall discuss in a moment, the various biblical materials we have outlined, along with other factors, also stimulated some differentiation within this scheme.

But before turning to that issue, there is something to add. The initial, more urgent question in this area had to do not with additional differentiation of the two ends but with the continuity connecting them. The first theological question about religious ends in Christian history was over whether these two alternatives of salvation and damnation corresponded to a true dualism, of the manichaean or gnostic variety. The manichaean view saw evil and good as two co-equal powers contending for every piece of turf, with the universe split between them. The primary change possible was to go over from the control of one side to that of the other. The gnostic view saw a realm of supreme good and one of brutish ignorance and squalor, each unchangeable in its own nature, with the only change possible being the separation of elements of one from their entanglement with the other.

Christianity veered toward these views at times. One of the perennial, reasonable attractions of such views is the way in which they deal with evil. These perspectives also affirm two religious ends, but God is responsible only for one of the two.[5] Something else is responsible for the lesser or evil end. In the manichaean view it would be the evil power that is responsible. In the gnostic view it would be some lower, imperfect emanation from the divine. In the Christian tradition religious ends remained integrated in this sense: they were both referred ultimately to one God. This fundamental conviction set the stage for the incessant concern through the rest of the tradition with the question of theodicy. How could both ends relate to the same God?

It set the stage also for the fascinating history of the devil, whose relation to the Christian God was always confusing.[6] The devil offered a backdoor escape from the theodicy dilemma, by providing an informal vehicle for a manichaean or gnostic alternative to it. So the devil was sometimes tugged toward a manichaean status (a power equal and opposite to God, responsible for evil) or toward the gnostic status of a quasi-creator (a lower divinity responsible for the deficient character of material creation). This complexity was multiplied because of two different ways that the gnostic nuance could be worked out. In terms of gnostic cosmology the biblical creator God, as the source of the material world, could only be an imperfect and misguided power. Thus if taken as a negative figure, the devil might be *identified* with the biblical God. On the other hand, because of the traditional antagonism between the devil and the biblical God, the devil might be appropriated in esoteric spiritual traditions as a noble figure, a representative of true divinity and pure spirit. This last tack is represented in some gnostic treatments of the story of the Garden of Eden, where the serpent is the agent of true illumination. Satan initiates Eve and Adam into a higher spiritual knowledge and liberates them from bondage to the creator God who would block their escape from the material world. This complexity shows up in folk history in the fact that the devil is sometimes viewed as a creature whose dominion is gross materiality and sometimes one whose prime characteristic is an intense spiritual pride. These varied, even contradictory overtones remain in the background of the more orthodox Christian view of the devil as a fallen angel, a creature who has taken God's gift of freedom to its maximum negative extent.

Christianity rejected the notion that the two fundamental religious ends were rooted either in two equal opposing metaphysical powers or in two different *kinds* of creatures, intrinsically and irrevocably destined for different ends by their natures. Human creatures are truly open to both options. Their

---

5. In gnosticism it is a complex question as to where responsibility lies for matter and non-psychic souls. But at best these can be only indirectly connected to true divinity.

6. (Russell, 1981; Russell, 1984; Russell, 1986; Russell, 1987; Russell, 1988).

destiny unfolds in relation to only one ultimate reality, God. The "twoness" of Christian eschatological faith is thus adamantly opposed to a strict dualism in these two crucial respects.

In distinction from these dualisms there was of course another possibility, an "oceanic" one. Rather than struggle with the difficulties of a fundamental distinction between God and creation, one might simply deny the distinction. Though that distinction is a phenomenon of experience, perhaps it has no firm ground in reality, and will eventually flicker out. This too offers a number of rational and aesthetic benefits, which the Christian tradition early on declined. While, against the stricter dualisms, Christianity maintained that two religious ends were grounded in one God, it also resisted identifying these two ends as the same. God and God's creation are truly distinct because creatures have a real, if derived existence of their own. And Christians affirmed that this distinction between God and creatures was meant to endure.

The most concrete way that early Christianity encountered the question of multiple religious ends was in the pragmatic polytheism of the Roman world. So long as the emperor was politically supreme, there was no objection to various groups maintaining the reality and validity of their peculiar gods. These gods, like their adherents, might sometimes come into conflict. The more extensive or exclusive the claims of any individual divinity, the more likely those claims would create friction with others. But if each remained in a segregated niche, reigning effectively over distinct peoples and lands or having a special function (in connection with a certain trade, or particular life problems, for instance), a functional pluralism was possible. Your gods are real and deal with you; mine are real and deal with me. Or, we all can deal, sequentially and by occasion, with whichever power is most relevant to a given area. On such a view, certain features of the world are controlled by divinities that respond to one set of approaches, while other features of the world are animated by different divinities with different characteristics and preferences.

In the face of a variety of deities or nonhuman powers, one might attempt to form some integrated sense of the world by positing an order among them. This could be done through stories about the hierarchical rankings, familial relations, or conflicts and animosities of the gods. It could be done through consolidation of identities, assuming that the same gods went by various names in various locations. The philosophical search for wisdom and the good life threaded itself among these religious perspectives. It was notable for looking for more unity and universality than this view of the world allowed, seeking some analytical integration of these various sets of rules. As the early Christian apologists and writers reflected, Christianity felt a strong affinity with philosophy in this respect.[7]

In a true polytheism or a true dualism, different religious ends stem from relation to different realities. People serve different gods, or they belong to an evil power or a good power. For Christianity the possible religious ends for humanity (salvation and its alternatives) had to fall within a single structure, in relation to one God. Every religious end has God as its true context, exists within God's providence and power. This conviction has many implications. For instance, the religious destiny of an unknown people in a far off land is as directly a matter of God's concern as the destiny of any other persons. This is part of the universal character of Christian faith. It is a feature of virtually all "world" religions. Jews, Christians, and Muslims believe that one God is the God of all. Buddhists and Hindus believe there is one dharma, or order, which guides and determines all beings. What such approaches rule out is a true polytheism, the possibility that for some people, some cities, some societies, some parts of nature, there is a different set of ultimate rules than for another.

The major religions envision a universal structure. We regard this as virtually synonymous with what a religion is, but it need not be so and was not so historically. I might regard my god and my religion as explaining only some things (the origin of my tribe and the fertility of our crops, but not the origin of another tribe or of certain forest plants that figure in their lives but not ours). I might hold my religion to apply only in a specific area (having no relevance for people living on the far side of a sea that has never been crossed). We often forget that the universal principles of Christianity were quite concretely tested with the encounter with the "new world" and with the question whether its inhabitants perhaps belonged to a completely different order of both nature and redemption. Other religious traditions have faced

---

7. This same point was a key affinity between Christianity and modern science also. One of the key steps in the modern scientific revolution was the axiom that the same fundamental laws apply everywhere in the universe. This had particular application in maintaining, against philosophical tradition, that the same rules applied outside the orbit of the moon (in what had hitherto been regarded as an area where all was eternal and unchanging) as inside that orbit (where all was temporal and subject to decay). This was by no means obvious. Conditions vary dramatically from one part of the universe to another. It was long reasonable to suppose such different effects must have different causes. The stars have always been there; the leaves are gone each year. The laws of one must be different from the laws of the other. Today we would agree that they are in one sense different: the leaves follow biological rules that do not apply to stars. But at a more elementary level they both conform to and manifest identical rules of physics.

similar questions.[8] Today we can imagine analogous issues being raised by the discovery of extraterrestrial life.

The so-called "axial religions" understand difference *within* some wider, unifying principles. Purely local conditions may account for some things in human life, but the full flourishing of human existence, ultimate human destiny, and the causes of human evil and dissolution all depend on the same fundamental factors. The religions are all inclusive in this sense, recognizing differences and seeking a way to fit them within their own comprehensive vision, not content with blank variety, with an admission that the world works differently some places than others. For Christians, this universalizing principle is relation with the God revealed in Christ. On this, the conditions and destiny of all creatures turn. However many religious ends there may be, God is responsible for, implicated in them all.

II

We indicated earlier that Christian tradition presumed the salvation/damnation division we find in Scripture. But I also suggested that there were elements in the biblical material that would eventually stimulate further reflection on that pattern. Are there two simple, homogenous destinies that correspond to this division? We often presume that this is precisely what heaven and hell are. But if we survey Christian history, we find that the actual picture is rarely that tidy. Much of the Christian tradition's treatment of this topic has operated at a somewhat more unofficial level than is true of questions bearing on incarnation, creation, or Trinity. When we look closely at the ecumenical history of the church we find a developing geography of ends and of movement between ends, all pictured under the overarching distinction between salvation/damnation. More particularly, we can distinguish a pluralism of final religious ends and a diversity of more penultimate religious ends that may exist prior to them.

We can examine this topic in two main stages. One has to do explicitly with the concrete characteristics of heaven and hell. We will deal with that in the next section, where Dante will be our primary subject. But we will begin with the area where the questions of interest to us seem first to have been pressed: concern for the state of the dead prior to the final judgment or general resurrection.

---

8. Chinese culture and religion seriously considered the status of "barbarians," and Hindu tradition likewise faced the challenge of how to conceptually incorporate those not rooted in the Indian sub-continent.

The New Testament is quite clear that salvation is never fully or perfectly realized in this life, nor is estrangement ever absolutely definitive until death, at the earliest. Are religious ends actualized in full at the moment of death? The tradition generally said no: that awaited a final resurrection and eschatological judgment. What then of the state of persons in this interim? The Christian tradition has never been clear or consistent about the condition of persons between their deaths and the final consummation. Are they "asleep"? Do some go immediately to states of blessedness or of loss? Do some or all continue in intermediate conditions until a later judgment? As an early end to history failed to arrive, the question obviously came forward.

There has been extensive discussion in Christian tradition about the variety of possible destinies for persons in this period. Some supposed that all the deceased shared a shadowy and somewhat suspended condition, or "slept," until the eschatological resurrection and judgment. This was roughly comparable to Sheol, the general afterlife as it is pictured in Hebrew Scripture. But by the time of Jesus a distinction was arising in Judaism between this state and a more "infernal" place of punishment. The New Testament is aware of the same distinction.[9] But later Christians developed their own formulations. Drawing on Jesus' story of the rich man and Lazarus, it was common to identify the "bosom of Abraham" as a place of rest and happiness where the faithful would await the final judgment.[10] It is a muted, anticipatory heaven. Tertullian wrote: "This place, the bosom of Abraham, though not in heaven, and yet above hell, offers the souls of the righteous an interim refreshment until the end of all things brings about the general resurrection and the final reward."[11] Many Christians held that the souls of martyrs would bypass even this state and enter directly into the full bliss of paradise.

The title "bosom of Abraham" points us to a related issue. We noted that the New Testament (Paul in particular) presumes the redemption of the past faithful ones of Israel. What has been the fate of such persons as Abraham since his death until the time of Christ? The answer was what later came to be called the "limbo of the fathers," a condition distinct from the bosom of Abraham mentioned by Tertullian. This limbo was the "hell" to which Christ descended after his death and it was from this condition that he liberated the saints of the past to enter the same interim state that awaits Christians prior

---

9. See Revelation 20:13, "And the sea gave up the dead that were in it, Death and Hades gave up the dead that were in them, and all were judged according to what they had done." Here Hades appears to refer to a more neutral abode of the dead, while "Death" indicates a place of some torment.

10. Luke 16:19-31.

11. *Adversus Marcionem* 4.34, quoted by Le Goff (Le Goff, 1984, p. 47).

to the final judgment. The terminological curiosity that Abraham could enter "Abraham's bosom" only after Jesus descended into hell to lead him there is somewhat misleading. It suggests a confused system of the afterlife, when in fact there was no developed system at all. There was only a series of observations and terms in various early Christian writers. The attempt to organize and coordinate them came later.

As a reader will anticipate, the material we are considering also figures in the prehistory of purgatory. In simplest terms, we could say the idea of purgation relates to the difficulty in correlating the twofold scheme of salvation and damnation with the manifestly various lives humans live and the diverse moral/spiritual profiles they present. In the broad Christian tradition, purgatory is a shadowy topic. In a rather guarded form it was formally affirmed in the Roman Catholic tradition, but it belongs to the reaches of speculative theology.[12] Protestants and Eastern Orthodox have strongly criticized purgatory, or at least common formulations of it. Our interest in the subject has to do with the way in which the history of the development of purgatory has in fact also reflected thought about religious ends.

The word "purgatory" is often used loosely with several meanings, but its root theological meaning designates a time and means (and, later in the tradition, a place) of purification or preparation, leading on necessarily to redemption. Purgatory presupposes the broader principles that shape the view of salvation itself.[13] It presupposes life after death and resurrection. It presupposes (in contrast to reincarnation) that a single earthly life is sufficient prelude to eternal life. It presupposes that the dead will be judged; in fact it assumes two distinct "judgments," one at the time of a person's death and one at the general resurrection. It presupposes individual free will and responsibility. It presupposes human conditions that fall somewhere between complete moral and spiritual purity and complete depravity.

Purgatory is also directly linked to the relational character of salvation, since one of the questions driving the development of the doctrine was the relation between the dead and the living. An issue that clearly stimulated reflection was whether the prayers and activities of the living could aid those who had already died, and if so, in what way. Though at times these concerns were discouraged as a matter of superstition or as a kind of arrogance (the dead could be left to God without need of our administration) they followed

12. It was affirmed at the Second Council of Lyons (1274), the Council of Ferrara-Florence (1438-39), and the Council of Trent (1563). None of these statements defined purgatory as a specific place or offered any details beyond the affirmation that the taint and penance attaching to some sins could be purged after death.

13. The following suppositions are outlined in (Le Goff, 1984, p. 5).

rather naturally from an understanding that salvation is a relation of communion with God and with God's creatures. If no one can be saved alone in this life, so too in the life to come. If interpersonal ties are an integral part of Christian communion in this life and are expected to be so as well in the fullness of salvation, they link persons across the border of death as well.

The ideas that came to be associated with purgatory also crystallize around an observation firmly rooted in this life. It is obvious that people attain to quite varying religious/spiritual/moral conditions in the course of their lives. How do these correlate to ultimate ends? Can they be simply and immediately consolidated into two possibilities at the moment of death or (after a long period of suspended animation) at the moment of the final judgment? From a very early period Christian thinkers tended to argue that there must be at least some additional complexity to this picture, some transitional process.

Before any middle state was clearly imagined, some simply linked hell and heaven sequentially (for the saved): the purgative aspect of the next life involved a temporary and muted stay in hell. More specifically, there might be a state of trial or testing which, though severe, could serve as a prelude to heaven as well as hell. Origen and Clement of Alexandria inclined to this view. The Israelites passed through the Red Sea to freedom and Pharaoh's armies passed into it to destruction. Similarly, they believed, after death we pass through the fires of judgment, some to liberation and some to reprobation. Origen and Clement drew on Paul's First Letter to the Corinthians, pointing to what became the charter verse for purgatory: "The work of every builder will become visible, for the Day will disclose it, because it will be revealed with fire, and the fire will test what sort of work each has done. If what has been built on the foundation survives, the builder will receive a reward. If the work is burned up, the builder will suffer loss; the builder will be saved, but only as through fire" (3:13-15). For the redeemed the fire refines and purifies, while for the incorrigible the fire consumes and punishes.

Origen was unusual in holding that finally the fire of judgment is entirely a refining fire. All persons will eventually pass through it to redemption. The only difference is in duration. For Origen, hell *is* purgatory: it is not the middle way that is missing in his scheme, but the "bottom" option. Thinkers like Origen and Clement stressed that the varied conditions of humans spread them across a spectrum in relation to the final options of salvation and lostness. They translated this variety into trials of varying duration in the fires of hell, prior to the person's passage to ultimate communion with God.

Though Origen's belief in the emptying of hell was not typical, his understanding of the *character* of judgment was quite common. Ambrose of Milan, for instance, states that the blessed and the wicked will go directly to their ends at the final resurrection. Yet even they will pass through fire on the way. The fires of judgment seem tempered according to the state of the one who passes through them. Their nature and rationale is not to inflict pain and punishment *per se*, but rather to test, transform, and refine. Jacques LeGoff summarizes Ambrose's view this way:

> For the righteous, who are like pure silver, the fire is refreshing, like a cooling dew. For the wicked, who are like lead, the fire is punishment and torture. And for those sinners who are like a mixture of silver and lead, the fire is a purifying instrument, whose painful consequences will last only as long as their sins are heavy, as long as it takes to melt away the admixture of lead in their souls.[14]

Augustine, unlike Origen, has no doubts as to the eternal dimension of hell. Clearly recognizing the same data Origen sees — the various conditions humans reach in this life — Augustine moves in a different direction. Augustine does much more to suggest an intermediate purgatorial condition (and therefore to increase the emphasis on the privative and penal character of hell itself). Though heaven and hell may remain two ultimate destinations, Augustine posits three or perhaps four options for humans at death. The conditions of the truly righteous and of the truly godless are straightforward: each passes directly to heaven or hell. In either case, intercessions by the living are essentially irrelevant. But, says Augustine, "there is a manner of life which is neither so good as not to require these services after death, nor so bad that such services are of no avail after death."[15] For these people, the benefit of intercession "consists either in obtaining a full remission of sins, or at least in making the condemnation more tolerable."[16]

Between death and the final judgment, there seem to be four options, not two. Alongside the righteous and the godless is a third category of the "not so good and not so bad" who are further divided into those who may attain salvation through purgation and those whose maximal benefit is a lesser damnation. So we have intimations of three actual ultimate ends: salvation, and a lesser and a greater loss. Peter Lombard would later explicitly develop this interpretation of Augustine, stressing the four options after death, leading to three ultimate ends. Lombard added a suggestion that even in hell God might distinguish among the wicked, mitigating the conditions of some rela-

14. (Le Goff, 1984, p. 59).
15. (Augustine and Oates, 1980, vol. 1, p. 723).
16. (Augustine, 1980, #376, vol. 1, p. 723).

tive to others to recognize real variation in their sin.[17] Yet further diversity was introduced in the form of the "limbo of children." Unbaptized children who die with the burden of original sin, yet in innocence of actual sin, form one clearly named group that occupies a permanent and distinct end, a specific suburb of hell from which the application of any sensible punishment is absent. This notion was intimated by Augustine, and developed by others.

Christian theologians who reflected on the intermediate state of persons between death and final resurrection were intrigued with the "bosom of Abraham" noted in Luke 16:22-23. For some writers, it figures as a kind of pre-heaven, the abode particularly of the just who lived before Christ. It came to be identified with the "limbo of the fathers," the realm of hell to which Christ descended upon his death and from which he lifted the righteous pagans and the Jewish saints to salvation. This location shows an interesting ambiguity. It is an anteroom to heaven and an upper level of hell at the same time. One could put it another way and say that the limbo of the fathers *is* heaven prior to Christ. After Christ's resurrection, it is often depicted as empty and closed. That is, for many writers the bosom of Abraham, the intermediate state of the blessed who die after Christ, is distinct from the limbo of the fathers, which had served that role prior to Christ's death. If Origen's hell was eventually to be abandoned, we might say that the limbo of the fathers has the quality of a temporary heaven which is eventually closed in favor of an improved temporary heaven.

In this area, as in so many, Thomas Aquinas pulled various elements together into a single integrated outline. In his view there were five possible destinations for souls immediately following death: Heaven (for the righteous), purgatory (for those not yet ready for salvation because of personal defects), limbo of the fathers (for those not yet ready for salvation "from nature alone"), limbo of the children (for those with only original sin), and hell.[18] Of these, the limbo of the fathers is no longer open after Christ's resurrection, so there are four live options. And since purgatory has no permanent constituents, there are three final ends.[19] However, in line with Peter Lombard's view noted above, Aquinas adds that those in hell do not necessarily share identical conditions. Quoting Aristotle to the effect that there is one way to be good but many ways to be bad, Thomas says that God may differentiate the state of

17. Discussed in (Le Goff, 1984, p. 149).

18. See the discussion of Aquinas's views, drawn mostly from the *Supplement* to the *Summa*, prepared by disciples of Aquinas, in (Le Goff, 1984, pp. 266-78).

19. Key elements in Aquinas's understanding of the way that salvation might be open to those outside communion with the church, such as "implicit faith" and the "baptism of desire," are outside the scope of our conversation here.

those in hell, so that none are deprived of all good if there was any good in their lives.

Albertus Magnus used a distinction between punishment of the senses (pain) and damnation (separation from God, absence of communion in the divine life) in his discussion of ends other than salvation. In hell, both pain and loss are present. In the limbo of children, there is loss but no punishment of the senses. In purgatory there is both pain and separation, but only for a certain period, during which the soul has full knowledge of its deliverance. Above purgatory, according to Albertus, we find the limbo of the holy fathers, where there was separation from God but no punishment of the senses. Also called the bosom of Abraham, this is the place into which Christ descended to liberate inhabitants for salvation. For Albertus, like Augustine, this limbo of the fathers holds an important structural position, but after Christ it is no longer a possible destination.

We have glimpsed how reflection on the interim states between death and final judgment articulated a variety of intermediate human ends. This reflection even suggested ultimate ends in addition to simple blessedness and reprobation. We need to turn now to the other side of our question: the extent to which those two latter ends were not viewed as "simple" at all. What distinctions and internal variety marked the concepts of hell and heaven?

III

Dante's *Divine Comedy* will serve as the primary focus of our discussion. But before we turn to direct consideration of the poem, we need to consider elements in its background. Theologians, and especially Aquinas, provided Dante with the raw intellectual material for his imaginative vision. But the actual images themselves were drawn partly from Dante's genius and partly from a much more popular tradition of "vision literature." Until recently the antecedents for the hell, purgatory, and heaven of the *Comedy* were sought entirely in images of the next world in classical literature and in medieval theology. That is, scholars looked to the texts that a humanist like Dante would have known well, such as Virgil's *Aeneid*.

In a recent book Alison Morgan has pointed out that many specific elements were also ready at hand in popular traditions, which Dante inherited along with more classical texts.[20] There was a long tradition of vision literature, in which visits to hell and heaven were recounted. These ranged from

20. (Morgan, 1990).

the *Apocalypse of Peter* and the *Apocalypse of Paul* (from the second and third centuries) down to the *Vision of Tundale* and the *Vision of Thurkill* (from the twelfth and thirteenth centuries).[21] In such literature a protagonist is taken on a tour of heaven and hell during a dream or a vision or a "near death" experience. In these visions one often sees representative figures suffering representative torments or blessings. Over time a number of "geographical" features of the afterworld that will be used by Dante appear in these visions. The *Vision of Thurkill,* for instance, which is the last of the written visions prior to Dante, is the first to describe purgatory as a distinct third realm.

We can begin with Christian reflection on the ultimate state of blessedness. In the early Christian centuries the representation of heaven is drawn heavily from the two images that also shaped Jewish perspectives on salvation: the Garden of Eden and the city of Jerusalem. The word "paradise" means garden, and redemption could easily be viewed as restoration to the garden, a new Eden, an earthly paradise untroubled by sin. Salvation appears also as a heavenly Jerusalem, the perfect city of faithfulness to God. This is the image that pervades the book of Revelation, with its vivid description of a city where the lamb of God occupies the throne and there is no temple building because God's presence fills all.

Revelation is itself a piece of vision literature, and its images are reflected in early Christian writing like the *Vision of Paul* and *The Ascension of Isaiah.*[22] In the *Vision of Paul* the writer is taken up to the "third heaven" where he sees a great city of twelve ascending walls. Below this, in a second heaven, there is an earthly paradise where the blessed are grouped around four rivers, according to their different virtues. In *The Ascension of Isaiah* the prophet Isaiah is guided up through seven heavens of increasing glory. In these and later popular vision accounts down to the twelfth century the largest space is allocated to description of the states of the blessed. Images of a heavenly city of Zion are supplemented with descriptions of celestial spheres, a temple, a walled garden, an earthly paradise. By the high middle ages hell is receiving the lion's share of attention.[23] And by that time the iconography representing heaven draws increasingly not from the book of Revelation but from the last judgment in the Gospel of Matthew, a fact illustrated dramatically in the carvings on the portals of French cathedrals in this period.

In addition to popular vision literature and artistic representation,

---

21. Translations of many of these texts are conveniently gathered in (Gardiner, 1989).

22. See (Hennecke, Schneemelcher, et al., 1963).

23. See (Morgan, 1990, pp. 172-73).

there is extensive discussion of salvation in theological tradition, of which the discussion in Roman Catholicism of the "beatific vision" is but one prominent example. There are two significant ways that diversity within salvation is addressed. The first has to do with consideration of various paths and stages on the way to communion with God. From Augustine's *Confessions* to Bonaventure's *The Journey of the Mind to God,* from Julian of Norwich to Teresa of Avila, many Christian classics deal with the itinerary of the spirit. To take an example that was well known to Dante, Bonaventure's *Journey* sets out six steps of ascent toward God, which move from focus on aspects of the created world outside us through focus on the graduated powers of the soul within us to contemplation of the eternal God above us. Other spiritual geographies would organize the journey around various distinctive acts or characteristics of God. These different ways of approaching God were set out in either a progressive or cumulative sequence.

The enormously influential writings attributed to Dionysius the Areopagite highlight a second way that diversity within salvation was conceived. In these works of mystical or negative theology great emphasis is placed on a hierarchy among created beings. Dionysius's theology is "negative" in the sense that all reference to God based upon the qualities of such beings must be transcended as one comes closer to true communion with God. But from another perspective, these texts stress the fact that all of creation longs for God and strives toward communion, each rank of creatures with its own characteristic desire. Planets, plants, and animals all are animated by a "love" of God that draws them to act in harmony with God's will, a communion that manifests itself in quite different qualities in each specific case. There is a law of spiritual gravity which leads each level of being to "fall" toward its place and to find its fulfilled relation with God precisely in its unique position in the divine ecology. A planet moves in a circular astronomical orbit, for instance, because like all creatures it desires communion with God, and its particular created nature (its "planet" nature) dictates that a circular motion is the shortest path to that communion, the shape of its perfection. Today we say that gravity "bends" space, so that when light passes close to a large planet and seems to be deflected, it is actually following what amounts to a straight line but in a different geometry than we are used to. Dionysius has a somewhat similar idea in mind. The gravitational "attraction" of God alters the "space" of different creatures in different ways, making their natural straight lines to communion with God different from each other. This means that two different kinds of creatures, and at the extreme perhaps two individuals, could each be perfect in their blessedness while differing in their characteristics and having quite distinct, non-identical relations with God.

These two kinds of diversity — varying paths of approach to God and different kinds of communion with God — are distinct. Yet plainly they can overlap in some respects. In Christian tradition, this overlap often came through a shared hierarchical vision. For instance, Bonaventure commends to us the consideration of external created things, plants, and seasons. As we contemplate the qualities of these created realities, we can contemplate the one who is their maker. This is an early step on the path to knowledge of God, from which we must pass on to further knowledge of God through other creatures. According to their own natures, plants and seasons may be said to be "perfectly" related to God. But this perfect communion is of a type that corresponds to their nature, a nature that is different and more limited than the nature of humans or angels. The two types of diversity are superimposed when a hierarchy of being is taken at the same time as a "map" for human spiritual ascent toward communion with God.

Sources like these provided a vast reservoir of material for Dante to draw on in his creation of the *Divine Comedy*. But taken as a whole, there was nothing quite like the *Comedy* before. In saying this, I am not referring to the poetry or the literary qualities of the work. I am thinking only of its geography, the structure of what Dorothy Sayers called its "greater images."[24] The *Divine Comedy* is studied more as a great work of literature than a work of theology. And yet part of its unique power derives from its place at a theological intersection. Dante wrote at the beginning of the fourteenth century, a time of rediscovery and ferment not far removed from the world of Aquinas. The works of Greek science and literature that had been received back with amplification from Islam continued to pose a challenge. The influence of Aquinas on Dante is obvious. But there is a reverse flow as well. Dante does not simply illustrate Thomistic theology; he creatively interprets it. Dante faced a situation of contention between different and incommensurate worldviews, notably those of Greek philosophy, Islam, and Christianity. In the *Comedy*, he placed this material within one large, thoroughly Christian scheme. It is an extraordinarily complex pattern, interesting to us particularly for the diversity of human ends it presents to our view.

In the most general terms, there was ample precedent for the journey Dante and Virgil undertake in the *Comedy*. In Dante's time, purgatory was becoming differentiated as a "third place," rather than a limited stay in hell. In Pseudo-Dionysius and in Bonaventure, there already existed theological rationales for a variety of conditions among the blessed in paradise. In regard to hell, there was a vivid if unorganized tradition (in art perhaps even more

24. See (Alighieri, 1950, pp. 67-69).

strikingly than in literature) which graphically fit the punishment to the crime. In the visionary visits to the infernal regions one was apt to see fornicators tortured at their genitals, murderers drowning in blood, usurers crushed under piles of coins, and so on. Though such figures often appear merely as allegorical archetypes, there is precedent in this earlier literature for identification of actual historical individuals in various circumstances in the afterlife.

The genius of the *Comedy* is that Dante gathers all these pieces and more into a coherent picture. His vision not only exhibits a variety of possible human ends, but poetically expresses the inner logic of each one and of the interrelations among them. Previously Christian writers had provided disconnected reflections on topics like the bosom of Abraham, the limbo of the fathers, the limbo of children, the fate of Israel's patriarchs and matriarchs, and the fate of virtuous pagans. A few, like Aquinas, had provided a broader intellectual framework that suggested some order for these features. But Dante is unique in presenting a systematic and concrete Christian presentation of various religious ends.

The supreme example of this is found in the three protagonists of the *Comedy*: Virgil, Dante, and Beatrice. Dante is a soul still in the balance, so to speak. In contrast, Virgil and Beatrice have attained divergent human ends. Virgil is of special interest to us. He does not participate in salvation, and the poem is clear about the decisive loss this represents. But it would be false to say Virgil has attained no fulfillment. The honor and love which Dante (as both a character in the poem and the author of it) extends to Virgil and the regard which the reader gains for him are very real. Virgil is not an example of a literary character "getting out of hand," as would be the case with an author who against his every intention ends up making unbelief more attractive than faith. Virgil's status and our reaction to him are entirely consistent with Dante's intention, and with the structure of the *Comedy*. The goodness he has attained is real. What melancholy and shadow attend him have to do with an opportunity missed. They reflect goods he excluded, not evils he must bear.

This is one of the great features of the poem. Dante has taken up the proverbial challenge to make heaven more attractive (or more interesting) than its alternatives. And he has taken it up on the most difficult but most honest terms, those that let us feel the real attraction of the alternatives. Theology may affirm that hell subsists only by clinging to some thread of good. It is something else to let us taste some of that good, and then to face the challenge of depicting a deeper, wider good in heaven, something that might set us on fire with longing instead of offering escape from desperate torment.

Within the framework of dual destinies, redemption and loss, Dante has given us richly diversified visions of each. There are ten primary circles of hell, with other subdivisions. Paradise has ten spheres or heavens, though these are only rough representations of a communion in even more individual variation, represented by the vision of the celestial rose. Purgatory also has ten circles, though of course none of these are final ends. In Dante's universe there is no doubt that the distinction between the saved and the lost is still the organizing framework. In multiplying the diverse realities within each, in stressing the plenitude of possibilities, he does not remove the distinction. He intensifies its reality by representing it in ever more concrete ways.

Dante's universe in all its specificity can hardly be ours. But it communicates a supreme imaginative, theological vision, with a great deal of wisdom to contribute to our task. Without any pretense of an exhaustive discussion, I will draw out some of the features of this vision that are most suggestive to me on this count.[25]

First, God's presence and aim in every circle of hell, purgatory, or paradise is a gracious one. Each of these destinies has been realized in response to an original and continuing divine offer of good. God is truly angry at sin. And God is sometimes referred to by those in hell as if vengeful or punitive. But Dante does not attribute hatred or violence to God, even against the damned. Hell is a largely self-governed place, whose demons seem as much willing captives as do the other inhabitants. The famous inscription over the gate to hell combines the observation that hell's foundations were laid by "the primal love supernal" with the exhortation "Lay down all hope, you that go in by me."[26] The loss of hope, the absence of desire for something other than what hell provides is the precondition for entry to hell, not a punishment inflicted in it.

This leads to a second point. In the *Comedy*, everything happens by attraction, by free affinity and desire. No one is sent to hell or bound there by external force, just as no one is bored or uneasy in heaven. This is one of Dante's great achievements. Sounds of anguish echo from some circles of hell. But whenever Dante stops to talk with its inhabitants, he finds that God is not afflicting them. Rather it is the sin, to which they resolutely cling, that torments. There is bitter complaint, but not the slightest interest in change. God has not altered in attitude toward these persons. They are the ones who express their disposition as absolutely final, excluding any other option.

25. This necessarily leaves much aside. Dante's highly negative treatment of Islam, for instance, merits discussion. But the way that Dante himself dealt with that question does not rule out alternative developments of his vision.

26. Cf. (Alighieri, 1950, Canto III.1-9).

In visionary visits to the afterworld in texts that precede Dante, hell tends to be a rather flat place. It contains a variety of applied punishments, all of which exist more or less on the same level. Sometimes sins are ranked in some rough order, but the pains suffered are of the same generic type. The greatest interest seems to attach to the external application of specific punishment that fits the crime. In contrast, Dante has sketched portraits of attachment to sin or insistent limitation that constitute their own ends. This is what these people truly choose, and they have made themselves into persons whose ruling desire can be satisfied in no other way.[27]

The circles of Dante's hell are imaginative representations of internally coherent human conditions. In lower hell, for example, in the circle of thieves, Dante meets figures who cannot even retain their own shapes but continually transform into each other and into terrible monsters.[28] They refused to distinguish between what was their own and what belonged to others. Now, Dante suggests, they have *become* that disposition, unable to distinguish or maintain even the boundaries that define their own uniqueness or that of others. The "punishment that fits the sin" *is* the sin itself, having become integral to the person. God's love and will are constant. The various ends arise from people's use of their freedom as creatures to relate to that divine love and will in various ways.

An enormously important aspect of this change is the manner in which it connects this life and the afterlife. The visions of the next world which antedated Dante were largely oriented to the administration of just deserts. Such visions might be chastening inspirations to reform one's life. But with Dante the idea of externally applied punishments has faded. We can see this in the fact that earlier vision journeys often focused on the pilgrim's fear of being punished and even included episodes where the visitor is subjected to the penalties they observe. On a few occasions, Dante and Virgil seem to be menaced in this way, but the threat is turned away. The focus is not on changing one's behavior to avoid a brutal retribution, of which some vivid preview is now exhibited. The poem is consistently concerned with quite another issue, which gives it its character as a spiritual allegory: What kind of person shall we become?

At the higher levels of hell, particularly, Dante often responds to those

27. This is, we may note, a quite different matter than a karmic stream that is understood as a more cleanly "mathematical" issue; the karmic process can be run in any direction and any previous sequence can be reversed or erased. This vision is by contrast one of personal formation, in which we shape the wells of our own acts, our disposition and desire, to a point where they become our settled character.

28. (Alighieri, 1950, Canto XXV).

he meets by sliding subtly into their perspective. He is tempted in kind, as it were, either to sympathize with the other's outlook or to mirror it. In these encounters one cannot treat Dante's dialogue with the damned as conversation in which sin speaks only through the inhabitants of hell and the corrective comes from Dante. On the contrary, Dante often falls into the spirit of those he encounters, joining them or opposing them with their own means. The dangers presented are not future but present, and Dante is susceptible to them now. The threat is not punishment but negative transformation. It is often Virgil who draws Dante back from these temptations.

In this sense the afterlife is not an addendum to this life, but an unveiling and ratification of its actual character. In the next world, things are stripped of most of the ambiguity and uncertainty that may surround them in historical circumstances, when for instance someone's outward manners or accomplishments may make it hard to discern their inner life and motivations. But self-bondage of the sort laid bare in lower hell is every bit as "infernal" and punishing here and now as in the next life. What has changed in the afterworld is that the destructive power of such sin to hurt others than those captive to it has been removed. The incidental success or pleasures that might be compatible with it in earthly life (or even aided by it) fall away. But the misery is not new; it is only a concentration or distillation of what was always there.

We may say a similar thing about the very real goods of limbo in upper hell. The justice, moral strength, and love of truth and beauty manifest there were already the characteristics of the lives of these non-Christian philosophers and sages. From this perspective, the *Comedy* can be read with equal profit as a story entirely about diverse human paths and fulfillments here and now. Indeed, this is one level at which Dante clearly intends the poem to be read. The various ends laid out in an eternal geography are realized in various forms in history. In the poem, these various circles are both real final ends and "stages" or realities that a human pilgrim may taste in life.

The same dynamic holds in different ways for purgatory and paradise. Their inhabitants are not perfect. The frequent examples Dante took directly from his own time make this clear. It is often far from obvious that their earthly behavior stood head and shoulders above that of the lost. The crucial difference is the way these people's desires face outward, rather than being narrowed or self-enclosed, even if to begin with they are not supremely focused on God.

This leads us to the third point. The *Comedy* thoroughly reflects the relational nature of salvation as we have described it in Chapter Two. This is nowhere better illustrated than in the distinction between hell and purgatory.

103

There is tremendous similarity in the two. It appears that the sins dealt with in lower purgatory are largely identical with those that characterize lower hell. In hell these are called malice and fraud, while in purgatory they are called love of harm to neighbors. They both involve harm to others. In Dante's structure the difference between the same sin in purgatory and hell is that in hell it has truly and definitively cut one off from relation with others. The love of a neighbor's harm which is purged in purgatory is no different in "kind" from the sin of malice (evil or violence toward others) in a circle of hell. The difference is not necessarily evident in the act but in the relation. Purgatory is not possible without contrition, without some enduring sense of the significance of one's acts for others and some concern for that significance. The same principle holds for excessive attachment to limited goods in purgatory and hell. The question is whether such attachment has irretrievably deformed a person in the direction of isolation or whether that attachment retains a spark of desire for the good of communion with others.

It is thoroughly consistent with this principle that Dante ranks most sexual sin in the highest circles of hell and purgatory, as least hateful. "Lust is a type of *shared* sin; at its best, and so long as it remains a sin of incontinence only, there is mutuality in it and exchange."[29] The bottom circles of hell are occupied by those enamored of fraud, betrayal, and treason, ranked according to the depth of the trust and faith they have betrayed. In general, as we travel downward in hell we move from sins of disordered attachment toward those that systematically destroy relation itself. The pride that puts self first in relations with others is not so lost as that disposition which no longer simply seeks its own pleasure from relations (without sufficient concern for the other) but in fact desires the corruption or end of relation itself.

In upper hell we see the sad pairing of the adulterous lovers Francesca and Paolo, united by shared sin. But in the colder depths we meet Count Ugolino and Archbishop Roger, who are linked only by their conspiracy against a common enemy, which was then followed by the archbishop's betrayal and murder of Ugolino. Roger shut up Ugolino in a tower with his children and grandchildren, to die of starvation. Here we fall even below the hot-blooded violence of middle circles of hell. The heat of relation has frozen into a solitary consideration of advantage.

At the bottom of hell Satan stands half-encased in ice, the coolest, most solitary "I" of all. For Dante, Satan is Lucifer, the fallen angel, whose rebellion against God was to reject the relation inherent in creaturely nature, even that of the most exalted creature, and to strive to the limit of the extreme to be a

---

29. (Alighieri, 1950, p. 101).

call Karen
Broglie
||

talk re $/

here The 130
PM

he older suburbs and from exurbia. Although
ds of society and never meet, these children
rhoods as our churches.

the Red Clay District, are building a program of
els, primary, middle and high school.
not have parental support for his learning, for
ducation and face a troubled adulthood.

an help a young person to see himself in a new
ry, if the individual student lacks this
we make in our educational system may never

ate in this mentoring program by inviting your
perintendent of Red Clay District, Mr. Dorrell
help.

alk over how your members can take part.

Pearl Johnson, Pastor
son United Methodist Church

purely autonomous being. Lucifer and the fallen angels reject the relation of dependence inherent in being derived beings. In fact they reject relation itself, the need to be constituted by relation, and instead assert pure self-sufficiency. The irony is that this defiance — the insistence on striving to be "like God," by renouncing dependence on relation — is a thorough misunderstanding of the nature of God. As Trinity, God *is* communion in relation and is "dependent" on relation as the very constitution of the divine being. The error of evil is actually less the desire to be "like God" than the misdirection of the effort, imitating the wrong thing. Incarnation in Christ speaks directly to this, for if Christ is divine, self-sufficiency on Lucifer's model can't be right as the path to "equality" with God. Lucifer's attempt at autonomy then necessarily results in a being divided against itself, for relation is what constitutes creatures. In this sense, Satan is a fraud and the father of fraud. The first one he deceives is himself, and there is no more fervent believer in the fraud he perpetrates.

Fourth, we note that although Dante honors the clear division of redemption and loss, and although the *Comedy* is organized in three realms, he still has introduced more eternal variety than any prior theologian. There is a region called the vestibule of hell, where souls swirl about aimlessly and endlessly. As heaven and hell are places where choice is eternally fixed, this vestibule is a place where "the refusal of choice itself is fixed."[30] It is a place of permanent indecision, shadowy, insubstantial, not unlike the biblical Sheol. This is a destination that does not quite fit into a traditional heaven/hell division.

Even more interesting is the next circle: limbo. This is Virgil's home. Here the "virtuous pagans" enjoy the afterlife that they had hoped would await the righteous and the wise. There is no pain and no suffering, only at worst a kind of noble melancholy. Indeed, when Dante is led into a beautiful green meadow before the graceful castle of the place, he seems nearly overcome with excitement to see great poets and philosophers ranged about him. In all respects, this seems a much more blessed place than the vestibule of indecision. In going one circle "down" its inhabitants seem to have come a long way "up." In fact, the geography, the inhabitants, and Dante's reaction to them are all very much like our popular image of heaven. For instance, if we think of heaven as a place where we look up great figures from the past and find them exactly as they were in life, limbo fits the bill better than Dante's paradise. In paradise Dante does meet great figures from history, who are very much themselves. But they are also significantly, if subtly, changed.

Limbo is an eternal destination. Virgil tells Dante that this is the place to

30. (Alighieri, 1950, p. 89).

which Christ descended after the crucifixion and from which he led out the mothers and fathers of Israel into paradise. The physical resemblance of limbo to the "Elysian fields" of pagan myth and expectation is not accidental. Even though it is the top circle in hell, limbo does not appear much different from the earthly paradise (the original Garden of Eden) which is found at the summit of purgatory. We might say the only difference is that the earthly paradise looks *toward* paradise (for all those who reach it now pass beyond), while the "limbo of the fathers" does not. Here those like Virgil who chose human virtue and wisdom have their reward, the fullness of the greatest good they imagined. Their loss was only in not hoping for more.

The "limbo of the fathers" was traditionally a resting place for the faithful and virtuous who lived before Christ, and was completely emptied and/or closed to further entry after the resurrection. But for Dante it was not emptied. Those who were firmly settled in their great but limited good proved unresponsive even to Christ's descent. Like Virgil, they remain. This is a crucial feature of Dante's entire conception of the *Comedy*. In Dante's vision the glory of salvation can be lost not only by the most hardened depravity but it can also be deferred for a lesser gain. There is a fixation in limited virtue, in a great and real nobility, that can hold us from full communion with God. Actual goods can be taken with such completeness or resignation that they close our spirits against any openness to what "eye hath not seen."

With one small touch Dante suggests a dramatic new dimension to limbo. Among many notables, Dante records that "I saw great Saladin, aloof, alone," and Averroes "who made the commentary" on Aristotle.[31] Limbo not only houses those who have remained after the harrowing of hell. It remains an open destination for those living after Christ but with no direct knowledge of him. And it is an earthly paradise in accord with the heavenly visions even of those like the great Muslims Saladin and Averroes who "though living in touch with Christianity and practicing all the moral virtues, find themselves sincerely unable to accept the Christian revelation."[32] These great figures, and all in limbo, have attained the end they aimed for.

The vestibule of indecision and the limbo of the virtuous non-Christians are two eternal human ends, neither identical with hell in the normal sense. There is no savor of punishment about either of them, and limbo is a gracious and idyllic place in every respect save in comparison with paradise. We have several examples in the *Comedy* of the cordial and respectful relations that obtain between its inhabitants (like Virgil) and those of paradise

31. (Alighieri, 1950, Canto IV.129 and IV.144, pp. 94-95).
32. (Alighieri, 1950, p. 96).

(like Beatrice). And yet these two ends are clearly distinct from salvation, formed by commitment to their own goods.

Dante's hell is quite a complex place. The initial entrance gate leads to the vestibule of the permanently indecisive. There is then a river Acheron that must be crossed, as a kind of second entrance, and this leads to limbo. At the threshold of the next circle below limbo, Dante and Virgil find the station of Minos, the judge of hell. Perhaps we should say he is the administrator of hell, since Dante tells us that each soul which comes before Minos freely pours out a perfect confession of its history and state. They are then assigned the appropriate place. Here we seem to be crossing yet another threshold, to a distinctly different destiny. The self-knowledge expressed in the soul's confession before Minos is a chilling dimension of hell. It is the settled desire of persons that draws them to a particular end. They are entirely clear about the choice and what it means. This rules out any change that might come from enlightenment. It is not that those in hell no longer have ignorance of themselves or of the consequences of their choices as an excuse. They no longer have ignorance as a hope. A particular sin is seen plainly for what it is, and chosen nonetheless. It is reaching this point that brings people to hell. Minos hears their testimony and marks them for the level they already belong to.

Still further down, past the circles of incontinence that deal with the sins of lust, gluttony, miserliness or extravagance with money, and anger, there is another river. This is the Styx, the traditional border of hell in much myth. It is also a kind of moat before the walls of the great "city of Dis," or lower hell proper. Here is yet another entrance, a gate at which Dante and Virgil must wait for admittance. As this brief review indicates, in Dante's telling "upper hell" has in fact become a set of discrete religious ends which have an intermediate character.

The fifth and last point I want to make is that in the *Comedy,* short of the bottom circle of negation itself, there is *some* relation with God manifest in every level. It may be an unbalanced obsession with a limited good that God has given. It may simply be God's upholding of the free desire that clings to its sin. In hell's upper circles of incontinence there are real positive goods affirmed. In limbo there is much more than this. Moral goodness and truth are not only affirmed but lived out as of divine origin. There is a real and effective relation to the true, the good, and the beautiful as expressions of the divine.

But the entire poem is an eloquent answer to anyone who would suppose or propose that "so long as everyone has some relation with God, then that's all that matters." There are many different kinds of relation one can have with God and with others, and the differences are constitutive of different patterns of life. One of the dramatic things about paradise as Dante describes it is the overflowing variety there. The blessed plainly recognize these differences among themselves and yet the distinctions are no occasion for distress. They are causes for joy and delight.

What then is the difference between the variety in relation to God that exists in heaven and the variety in relation manifest in the existence of heaven *and* hell, the existence of the ambiguous intermediate circles of hell and the variety within hell proper? The simplest way I can put it, consistent with Dante's vision, is to say that the relation with God that characterizes heaven is one that is unhesitatingly open to others' relation with God and to the various dimensions of God's relation with creation. What is not complete or ideal in one individual is not filled out to bring them into conformity with some single mold. The deficiency is supplied through participation in communion with others who each have their own unique grasp of aspects of God. It is each one's relation with God that makes possible and sustains this intercommunion among them, through which in turn their individual experiences and capacities are multiplied to allow the fullest communion with God. By contrast, the kind of relation that characterizes hell is one that constricts and limits this mutuality of communion (with others and God) to some level beneath what is possible for creatures. There are many possible levels of such limitation, and the diversity in Dante's hell reflects this.

There is a difference between "finding one's level" in heaven, and doing so in hell. Both involve real variety. The first involves very distinct diversity in the modes and levels of appropriation of God's goodness and the goodness of creation. But this is a variation within a communion of love, where others' appropriation is shared. The variety in the lower reaches of hell is that among distinct negative ways that relation can be limited or simply negated. The variety in the upper reaches of hell is that among ways that attachment to *some* good can also function as an exclusion of further goods in relation.[33] The key dividing line between salvation and other alternatives lies between relation with God and with others in a communion that allows you participation in the dimensions beyond your individual grasp, on one side, and on the other side relation with others and God (even relations that fix on real goods and make real connections) which seal you off from communion with goods that are not your own. In heaven, the limitations of anyone's good are real and uniquely personal. But on the other hand they are cause for joy, because they are the occasion to lean on and delight in others' special gifts through com-

33. Here Dante seems to feel that the great failing of those in limbo was a failure to hope more comprehensively, based on what they did know of God's truth and nature.

[handwritten margin note, left:] in heaven total communion

[handwritten margin note, left:] in hell no Communion

[handwritten note at bottom:] * my delight in the young men who jacked my car out of the hole that Sunday in Nuevo Amanecer

munion with them. In hell, these limitations become walls and wounds, endless causes for isolation and resentment.

So, for example, in the circle of the angry or wrathful in hell, God himself is perceived by the inhabitants as wrathful. This is because, though God is present to them in the same way as to all people, they have so narrowed themselves that they perceive God's presence and relation to them solely in this mode. We might call it projection. Having narrowed their mode of relation to this one channel, they restrict their free connection with God to these terms and no others. The only reality about God that passes their screens of perception is God's opposition to evil. They are not in error in thinking they have apprehended truth. But they have so globalized this truth that they can conceive of God's relation to them only as one of wrath, which they return in kind. And their anger blocks them from true communion with any other humans by which they might participate in some wider knowledge of God and so be freed from their bondage.

To say that someone in hell has a partial relation to God and one in heaven a "fuller" relation does not primarily mean to indicate that the saints in heaven have personal, private, intrinsic capacities to know God that far outstrip those of others. The fullness comes through mutual participation. Though the relation is real in both cases, in hell it is made captive by the person, forced to remain only within certain constraints, which then become the constraints of the person's world. In heaven, the blessed are given over to relations that are the means to open their destiny, beyond virtually all constraints.

When Dante enters the realm of paradise, he ascends through nine circles or "heavens," each associated with one of the astronomical spheres. And in each circle he meets different citizens of paradise. In the first circle, the sphere of the moon, Beatrice explains something to Dante that is crucial for understanding the rest of the journey. All the redeemed and all the angels, whatever their differences, reside in one and the same heaven, the empyrean or "highest heaven." Dante encounters them in the various circles, under the sign of the sphere and its associated virtues that most characterized them during their earthly lives.

> But each in the First Circle glittereth,
>   And all share one sweet life, diversified
>   As each feels more or less the eternal breath.
>
> They're shown thee here, not that they here reside,
>   Allotted to this sphere; their heavenly mansion,
>   Being least exalted, is thus signified.

This way of speech best suits your apprehension,
  Which knows but to receive reports from sense
  And fit them for the intellect's attention.[34]

When Dante reaches the tenth heaven of which Beatrice speaks, there is another vision: the celestial rose. This image, in which all the blessed are gathered like individual petals in a vast, layered flower, is a recapitulation of what Dante has already seen in paradise. Rising sequentially from "lower" to "higher" circles has allowed Dante to grasp the differences among the saints. But in the celestial rose they are all seen again, one dimension further in as it were, and this time in terms of their unity and relationship in variety. Angels flit between the petals of the rose like bees in a garden, signs of the intense communion among all.

This is the prelude to Dante's final vision, that of God the divine Trinity. Here we find the definitive contrast with Dante's hell. In hell there is no communication between the circles. And once we pass below the higher levels, there are none but the coldest and most external interactions between those who share the same circle. By contrast, in the empyrean, Dante finds that communication takes place by a kind of gentle mind-reading, so close is each to the other. Knowing each other as God does draws all into a shared life.

Dorothy Sayers summarizes the ambiance of paradise this way: "The derived self is the glory of the creature and the multiplicity and otherness of the universe is its joy. The true end of the creature is that it should reflect, each in its own way and to its capacity great or small, some tiny facet of the infinite variety comprised within the unity of the One."[35] She goes on to say that the nearer the created being is to God, "the more utterly it is itself and the more it differs from its fellow creatures."[36] Some medieval theologians, she notes, could contend on this principle that each angel was itself a separate species. *genus?*

Everything is made perfect according to its capacities. And capacities differ. Since humans share the same basic capacities, in varied proportions, the perfections of paradise differ according to the ways that persons have shaped life around those capacities. Perhaps it would be better to say the perfections differ according to the interplay of free choice and the unchosen circumstances of one's life. Though all are knit in one communion, there are those of greater and lesser capacity: all cups are full, but some cups hold more or different contents than others. And Dante is quite clear that all the parties

---

34. (Alighieri, 1962, Canto IV.34-42, p. 82).
35. (Sayers, 1969, p. 48).
36. (Sayers, 1969, p. 48).

in paradise are quite aware of this. Being in such close communion with each other, they could hardly fail to be so. This is the focus of Dante's famous interchange with Piccarda. Does she not desire a higher place in heaven? asks Dante. She begins:

> Brother, our love has laid our wills to rest,
>   Making us long only for what is ours,
>   And by no other thirst to be possessed.[37]

And she ends with one of the most famous phrases in the *Comedy*, "His will is our peace."

In the sphere of Venus, the third heaven, Dante meets Cunizza. Sister of a brutal tyrant, she was of an ardent nature, having had two lovers and four husbands over a life marked by compassion and works of mercy. Her brother has been seen earlier in the poem, in hell. She says,

> One root with him had I, and was by name
>   Cunizza; and I glitter here because
>   I was o'er mastered by this planet's flame;
>
> Yet gaily I forgive myself the cause
>   Of this my lot, for here (though minds of clay
>   May think this strange) 'tis gain to me, not loss.[38]

Sayers points out that a Muslim author, Ibn Arabi, whose writing on the afterworld might have been known indirectly by Dante, made a point of saying of the grades in heaven that each person "loves his own grade passionately and cannot conceive that a higher could exist. If it were not so, heaven would not be heaven but a mansion of grief and bitter disillusion."[39] In other words, there should be a veil of ignorance to shield any from envy or shame. But in Dante's paradise awareness of this variety is a deep delight to all, the very substance of their love and communion with each other. "The blessed creatures know one another and delight in one another."[40] He uses the image of fish in a clear, still pool who all draw toward anything dropped to the surface as it might be food. Just so, Dante says the blessed ones draw toward him on his approach, saying "Lo, one who shall increase our loves."[41] It is not Dante's ex-

---

37. (Alighieri, 1962, Canto III.70-72, p. 75).
38. (Alighieri, 1962, Canto IX.31-36, p. 126).
39. Quoted in (Sayers, 1969, p. 58).
40. (Sayers, 1969, p. 59).
41. (Alighieri, 1962, Canto IV.106).

traordinary powers or holiness that stimulate this interest. It is the characteristic of this communion that it desires ever greater breadth and delights in every new, distinctive member.

In Dante's paradise, as is often noted, there is much concern about events on earth and much distress and anger about sin. But this coexists with a striking lack of anguish about either the circumstances of the lost or the past sins of the saved. This points us to the question of whether the blessed may be said to "enjoy" the condition of those in hell. Awareness of those in hell, let alone any enjoyment, would seem to be a radical break in the communion that otherwise is the very heart of salvation, a contradiction. But in fact this is another side of the coin we just described. Those in paradise are not jealous of any, don't mind if someone has "more" in the sense that their full gallon jug might be "fuller" than my full quart jug. They are no less joyful because of others' joy. Nor are they less joyful for others' deficiencies. How is this?

It is not that those in paradise simply acquiesce that all must be for the best if God wills it so. It is knowledge of the consonance of God's will with the wills of all creatures that gives them peace. Like God, the saints accept the freedom of others, who have made their desires completely their own and who now receive perfectly what they desire. We saw above that this is precisely the structure of hell, as well as of heaven. Those in hell have achieved the fulfillment of their desires. It is not a matter of external punishment (if I knew and felt then what I do now, I would have behaved and thought differently and so avoided this retribution). It is not even simply a matter of an intrinsic consequence (I overate and so now have a stomachache which is entirely my own fault). In that case my situation is entirely the product of my own choice, and the distress follows directly from the choice, rather than being "enforced" by someone else. Paradoxical as it is, I wanted the overindulgence but not the suffering. But Dante's hell is yet a third situation. It is more like someone who, with a stomachache, does not for a moment regret the behavior. The person chooses *both* the act and the consequence, desiring both. The stomachache itself becomes part of the end sought. If there is any regret it is decisively focused elsewhere. It becomes, for instance, a reason to reproach God for mixing this vexing concomitant with my pleasure, and the reproach itself becomes a pleasure I do not wish to give up.

Those in hell insist on not substituting any others' lives or wills for their own. In striking symmetry, those in paradise have no desire to substitute others' lives or wills for their own (even if that might be on some scale "better"), nor do they have any desire to substitute their will for others' wills. It is in this respect that their purposes harmonize with God's will. It is not passive acceptance of God's autocratic decree, but a free concurrence with God's decision to give and honor freedom in creatures. To take away that freedom from the lost would be the last, absolute destruction of their selves. What makes them uniquely themselves may have been diminished to a vanishing point, as is certainly the case in the lower circles of hell. But it endures at least in the free and continuing choice of their circumstance. There is a good of self-determination. It is, tellingly, a good frequently and emphatically affirmed in hell. It is honored in heaven.

In his eschatological allegory *The Great Divorce,* C. S. Lewis points out the way in which a certain attitude (in our current jargon we might call it "co-dependency") evaporates in the air of heaven. He illustrates through an account of a bus excursion which brings residents of hell to the outer limits of heaven, where they visit with people they had known in their earthly lives. The visitors deflect invitations to stay longer with suspicion. They insist on the superiority of their current accommodations and cast aspersions on the little-mindedness or cruelty of those who extend the offer. They observe, correctly, that walking closer to heaven is difficult and painful for them (even the grass hurts their feet). Most take the bus back.[42]

The person in hell who has no wish to be elsewhere, but wants others to feel guilty or anguished on their account, gets no cooperation from their acquaintances in heaven. Any who manifest even the slightest wavering in their desires, some openness to a different life or relation, always find the most profound care and responsiveness from God and the saints. The relationship is honored under the terms set by the one who insists on narrower limits. Those in Dante's paradise accept this, with joy for the good reflected in the freedom of the choice itself, but with no tears for the person's fulfilled desire. But toward those who have perfected their religious ends, there is no patronizing and coercive insistence that they acknowledge *they* are the mistaken and miserable ones. This, after all, is hell's attitude toward heaven.

The repellent picture of the blessed in heaven looking down with joy on the torments of the damned presumes first that the damned are tormented and second that the blessed delight in the infliction of pain. Neither is true in the *Comedy.* Dante's vision pays special attention to the fact that the gaze goes in both directions. The inhabitants of hell look to heaven with a spectrum of attitudes. In lower hell these range from contempt to disdain to rage and in

42. Lewis's protagonist in this piece of vision literature is told the bus runs regularly between hell and heaven and any who wish can take it at any time. "There are only two kinds of people in the end: those who say to God 'Thy will be done' and those to whom God says, in the end, '*Thy* will be done'" (Lewis, 1946, p. 72). This is a pithy summary very much in keeping with Dante, whose work Lewis had clearly in mind.

upper hell from accusing dismissal to the grave and gracious preference for another good. In none of these cases is there any desire to exchange places. From heaven there is no delight at pain. There is a spectrum of attitudes toward the diverse conditions in hell. Those in heaven evidence almost no knowledge of or interest in the condition of lower hell. This is not because of a lack of compassion but because of a lack of purchase for compassion.

It would indeed be terrible to look with serenity on what takes place in a crude picture of hell, to look upon a consciousness, a spirit (however twisted) unwillingly bearing punishments that sear its senses with pain, writhing in search of escape. But it is this divided consciousness or divided sense that is absent in hell. If the traitors in lowest hell are tormenting each other, the pain they feel is only the frustration of imperfectly betraying the other. There is not a trace or wisp of desire left to be free of the condition of malice. The only pain that is here rises not from the suffering of punishment but from a blocked capacity to inflict it. To pity such pain would be blasphemy, like pitying the sadist their lack of victims. At the other end of hell, matters are quite different. Toward the inhabitants of limbo, as we have seen, the residents of heaven show respect, honor for their virtue, even a kind of courteous deference. If the blessed delight in the prospect of limbo it is because of its good, not because of its suffering, of which there is none.

In heaven, the powerful passions are directed toward earthly human life, because there people's choices still have the power to wound, crush, and deform their neighbors and there people's desires are still in the making. Our analogies are all drawn from situations where it is quite otherwise. In the earthly frame, as Dante makes very clear, it is never the case that desire and choice are irrevocable. Therefore active concern for others' spiritual and physical well-being is always in order. There is always something to be done (give some food, heal the disease, comfort the suffering) and real possibility of change to hope for. But in Dante's afterworld the situation is stripped of those elements. The only element that remains is the persons themselves, their spirit and choice, their chosen relations. They may be fixed in their desires. If so, the person is "loved and accepted just as they are," a phrase we are wont to use without an ear for its terrible overtones as well as its comfort.

However, Dante strikes another note as well. In the sixth heaven of the just, he is surprised to find the Trojan Rhipeus and the Roman emperor Trajan. The first lived before Christ, the second after Christ, and neither were Christians or Jews. Regarding Trajan, there is a legend that through St. Gregory's prayers he was restored to life long enough to be converted. But regarding Rhipeus, Dante's angelic counselor acknowledges that the "how" of his salvation may escape Dante's sight. Rhipeus

by a grace from such deep ground
   Gushing that no created eye can plumb
   Its hidden well-springs where they run profound,

On righteousness spent all his earthly sum
   Of love; whence God from grace to grace unsealed
   His eyes to the redemption yet to come.[43]

"Ardent love and living hope" meet grace and come to God. Here Dante takes a step beyond what we saw in the Elysian fields of limbo, the home of Virgil, Averroes, and Saladin. He learns in paradise that it is not only the forerunners in Israel, who believed in Christ through "types," who have come up from the limbo of the fathers, but also some of those who belonged to other religious contexts altogether.

We must say a word about Dante's third realm, purgatory. The classical basis for purgatory is twofold. Sinners have entrance to such "preparation" for heaven only because the guilt and punishment for sin are freely removed by grace. What takes place in purgatory is the rehabilitation of the person's own nature from the deforming effects of sin. Purgation is to make us strong enough for joy we can't bear yet. It is about getting used to glory. "The only way in which the soul can injure or 'grieve' God is by injuring itself, and the only thing it can restore to God is itself."[44] Whereas through much of the tradition before him purgatory had been pictured as a subdivision of hell, Dante's purgatory is a true middle earth. There is nothing dark or closed about it. It is a mountain rising from the sea, high in the wind, surrounded by stars and crowned with an earthly paradise. There is a price to be paid here, but it is like the strain of rigorous physical therapy in recovery from injury or disease, with the difference that one can see the benefit at each step and is certain of the end. This accounts for the fact that those Dante meets in purgatory are reluctant to spare him much time from their labors.

The levels of purgatory are a mirror of those in hell.[45] The bottom half of purgatory deals with love of the wrong object, which amounts to love of the negation of created realities. So pride is not so much love of self as attachment to contempt for others. Envy is not so much desiring goods our neighbors have as it is enjoyment of seeing them deprived of them. The common link is the love of another's harm. In the top half of purgatory it is misdirected

43. (Alighieri, 1962, Canto XX.118-23, p. 235).
44. (Sayers, 1969, p. 81).
45. This paragraph draws heavily on insights from Dorothy Sayers (1955, pp. 61-68).

love that is addressed, moving from excessive love for money and power through excessive love for pleasure to excessive love for persons. This last, highest level points to the fact that excessive love of persons is the misdirection that needs the least reform and which can carry humans farthest toward the highest good. In fact, Dante's relations with Virgil and with Beatrice as the guiding spirits of his journey are one long illustration of this fact.

On the corresponding levels in hell we find persons settled in their choices, exercising their desire only to continually confirm the nature they have shaped for themselves. The difference in purgatory is that in each circle Dante encounters people who are changing and reconstituting their character, the very instrument by which they desire. Their longing is to become more fully the people who will be capable of communion with God and others. Aimlessness is the hallmark of the circles of hell, but purpose marks every step of purgatory. In each circle the pilgrims combine the same elements: experience of the effects of this particular sin (the closest similarity to hell), examples and experience of the opposing virtue, prayer and worship. This last element reminds us that those in purgatory have a lively sense of connection with others who through those connections are supporting their passage. They seem to delight in praising and encouraging each other, and the prayers of the living and the grace of the blessed are constantly with them. As communion is the end, so also is it the means. When a person leaves one rung of purgatory for the next or takes leave for paradise, the whole mountain shakes and great shouts of common joy erupt from all its members.

At the summit of purgatory stands an Eden and it is from here that purgatory's graduates embark for heaven. They depart not because a term is served or because enough petitions on their behalf have accumulated. As soon as they are ready and able, they go:

> But when some spirit, feeling purged and sound,
> > Leaps up or moves to seek a loftier station,
> > The whole mount quakes and the great shouts resound,
>
> The will itself attests its own purgation;
> > Amazed, the soul that's free to change its inn
> > Finds its mere will suffice for liberation. . . .[46]

When Dante and Virgil arrive here, Virgil says he has led his pupil this far by discernment and skill. But now Dante should take his own pleasure for his guide. Those who reach this point can follow with perfect freedom where

46. (Alighieri, 1955, Canto XXI.58-63, p. 236).

their loves direct them. They belong to heaven not because they have purged and beaten down their desires, but because their desires have finally "grown up" to be satisfied with nothing less than everything: communion with the full scope and glory of God and God's creation. The only rule now is that you should do whatever you want:

> No word from me, no further sign expect;
>   Free, upright, whole, thy will itself lays down
>   Guidance that it were error to neglect,
> Whence o'er thyself I mitre thee and crown.[47]

This incandescent moment is also an ironic one. The freedom to set my own course, by my own will, is of course the law of hell as well. It is not the capacity of our desires to realize the ends they seek that has changed, but the end that is sought. The only path by which we can form and enlarge our desire to the shape that can "fit" full communion with God, is one that accepts communion with others, in relationships of love and trust. This is the openness we see in Dante's journey, animated by the interplay between his love for Virgil and Beatrice and his love for Christ and God. Constituted by such communion, the heart can "do what it likes, for it cannot but like what it ought."[48]

When we have read the whole poem, we are suddenly struck with the dramatic realization that suffering — if by suffering we mean brute, meaningless pain — is actually completely absent from all three of Dante's realms. There is none in paradise. In hell, where pain of sense exists, it has been appropriated as part of the end most deeply and truly desired. It is not something one is willing to give up, even if it could be subtracted from the current experience. And in purgatory whatever pain is involved is hardly suffering, for it is full of hope and meaning, suffused with the joy of one's own birth.

IV

Our survey of Dante's *Comedy* has been necessarily brief and thin. We could profitably look much longer. But we have seen the way in which Dante knits several elements in one comprehensive vision. We have seen that the *Comedy* in fact presents us with a variety of ultimate ends. There is great diversity within hell, purgatory, and paradise. In particular, we noted in upper hell the existence of at least two ends that have a distinctly intermediate character.

47. (Alighieri, 1955, Canto XXVII.139-42, p. 285).
48. (Sayers, 1969, p. 93).

Despite this growing and fascinating complexity, Dante emphatically maintains the scriptural twofold division between salvation and loss as the overarching structure. He locates the root of that division in relation to Christ and the triune God. Although the landscape has been elaborated, the dividing line between these two is expressed with greater intensity and clarity because its inner logic is revealed. On one side of the line is a settled desire for openness to and participation in communion with the triune God and in the communion with others that is characteristic of that God. On the other side there are settled desires that reject or permanently limit such communion. On either side of this line we find a variety of specific human possibilities and on either side the variations have deep significance. In fact, the line marks two very different ways of dealing with that diversity: communion and self-sufficiency.

The pursuit of justice, truth, and love can each lead to their own rewards. But in Dante's structure salvation hinges on the three theological virtues — faith, hope, and charity. Faith goes beyond justice to the acknowledgment of the need and gratitude for divine grace. Hope dares to imagine a greater bliss than can be demonstrated or known in advance. Charity advances not only to the irrationality of love for enemies but to the desire for love-by-participation with the triune God. Wherever and however these "supernatural" desires are born, they are always met with grace and the way to salvation is open.

It seems that much of the energy that has gone into the discussion of religious ends in Christian tradition has been lavished on the issue of "unification." This is often identified with the question of universalism, but it is in fact broader. Christian eschatological expectation looked for an *apokatastasis,* or "universal restoration."[49] As we have seen, Christians did recognize some variety in religious ends, but primary emphasis was directed toward some future resolution of this variety into the two ends of salvation/damnation, and even perhaps toward some resolution of that distinction itself. *Apokatastasis* is the conviction that God brings the entire creation, the entire work of creation, to a good and fitting consummation.

Universalism is one way to formulate this fulfillment of God's purpose. This is Origen's vision of a hell eventually emptied, everyone gone home to heaven and God's aim for each creature realized. From this perspective, there is a limit to how long creaturely freedom can resist God's love. That freedom is never compromised, but God outlasts it in every case. Another way to deal with the question is to affirm that alienation from God eventually leads to an-

49. From Acts 3:21, which says that Jesus must "remain in heaven until the time of universal restoration that God announced long ago through his holy prophets."

nihilation. Hell is finally emptied not because all go home to heaven but because the inevitable outcome of a truly settled negation of our relation with God is the end of our existence itself. As it is possible to starve one's self to death physically, so it is possible ontologically. The final state of creation is a "restoration of all things" because whatever is not restored long ago stopped being a "thing" at all.

Yet another way to deal with the question is to affirm that the consummation of creation as a whole is consistent with the fact that creatures within it realize a number of different ends. Dante's poem presents a powerful version of this view. Taken together, heaven and hell and the diverse ends that they encompass *are* a fulfillment of creation's promise, a "pluralistic perfection."

In the Christian tradition the debate among these various ultimate eschatological visions has not led to clear-cut decision but to caution against closure. Thus universalism has been regularly rejected as a dogma, but allowed as a hope. Annihilationism is not beyond doctrinal consideration, but it has been explicitly affirmed by only a few Christian groups. These two possibilities hover in the background of the "two destinies" so amply suggested in Scripture.[50] By contrast, we would have to say that Dante's vision stands in the center of the Christian tradition. Yet it is a center which has been oddly unarticulated in theology, at least in regard to the variety of distinct ends it suggests.

This is the clue which I believe points us toward a new understanding of Christianity and religious pluralism, toward a theology of religious ends. Dante suggests a variety of ultimate human ends, each with its own internal coherence. And he freely acknowledges that there is profound good in some such ends other than salvation. He does not define alternatives to salvation simply as conditions of external punishment. Instead he draws out the positive, internal logic by which each end is constituted. Dante provides a clue, not the answer to our question. But if we can develop these elements for our task with a wisdom and insight comparable to his, we will have achieved a great deal. In the next chapters we will venture some steps on that way.

50. I will argue more extensively in Chapter Six that a consummation of creation which involves a diversity of religious ends need not for that reason be defective or contrary to God's purposes. But in principle my hypothesis of multiple religious ends is not intended to resolve the debate over universalism, for instance.

Part Three

Trinity and the Religions

Chapter Four

The Depth of the Riches: Trinity as the Framework for Religious Diversity

I n the previous chapter we explored Christian tradition, asking whether within the fundamental distinction between salvation and its absence we might find any recognition of multiple religious ends. Our aim now is to connect that discussion with our understanding of God as Trinity. In Chapter One I indicated that theologies of religion rarely consider religious ends in the plural, and that to do so might deliver us from the impasse our current categories encourage. We can add to this the observation that "it is surprising that the Trinity, with its unique solution to the problem of the one and the many, is not more regularly invoked in the theology of religions."[1] This is all the more peculiar, since the trinitarian doctrine was developed in a context that raised many issues similar to those faced by the theology of religions. A few writers have begun to redress the strange absence of the Trinity from these conversations.[2] The heart of my project in this book is to connect these two missing links — religious ends and Trinity — and to outline one perspective on religious pluralism that results.

Before we go on to do this in some detail in the next chapter, we must say something about the Trinity itself as the general framework for under-

1. (Vanhoozer, 1997, p. 57).
2. These writers (D'Costa, 1990; D'Costa, 2000; Williams, 1990; Williams, 1997), along with those discussed more fully in the last part of this chapter, have contributed much to my thinking.

standing religious diversity. After discussing that general framework, we will indicate some of its implications for Christianity's internal life. Then we will review two significant contemporary attempts to develop a trinitarian theology of religions, creative explorations that provide much of the material for our constructive argument.

I

Christians believe God is intrinsically relational. Salvation is communion with the triune God. Chapter Two sketched the way this communion presupposes and integrates enduring relations among persons and relations between humans and creation. As we saw, this very basic description tells us quite a bit. Salvation is not a realization of pure identity, the unity of one absolute Self, a one without a second. That religious end would be relationless, because there is nothing outside the One with which to relate. Any relation of the One to something outside it could only be a diminishment or contamination of the divine perfection.[3] Salvation is also not emptiness, the dissipation of any continuing consciousness of being at all. This too is a relationless end. In the first case there was one absolute with nothing/no one to relate with. In this case it is not the absence of an other that rules out relation, but the radical insubstantiality even of one. Instead of one without a second to relate with, we might regard this end as pure relation, with no "ones" — distinct persons or entities — to have the relation. These religious ends differ from salvation because they exclude relation itself, seeing it as extrinsic to religious fulfillment. In that light, salvation appears too interactive, too wedded to difference.

There are obviously other religious options that do conceive of the religious end as a relation, but differ with Christianity in their understanding of that relation. Islam is a notable example. It seeks a profound relation with God, characterized by obedience, devotion, love, and awe. Islamic criticisms

---

3. Taking this perspective, an Advaita Vedanta view tends to regard the Trinity as a cipher of the single consciousness of the absolute One. The three persons could not possibly be co-constitutive of Brahman as three permanent subsisting distinctions, but would have to be seen as some kind of "play" on the surface of that unitary consciousness, "persons" who continually realize their "selflessness" and complete identity with the One. One might even call this *kenosis*, with of course the dramatic difference that what is "set aside" is regarded as not real in the first place and there is no reason for it to be taken up again. Likewise there is no reason this "play" should always take a triune form. "Trinity" is simply one of numberless patterns or forms that play across the surface of the One.

of Christian beliefs in incarnation and Trinity are well known. In Muslim perspective, the first is an impious association of the human with the divine, and the second plainly compromises the unity of God. At base, these objections caution that what Christians seek as salvation is too intimate a relation, an actual participation in the divine life. Such an aim is beyond human capacity and impious to imagine or attempt: it is impractical at best, blasphemous at worst. The unity of God is a supreme religious value, and a God of perfect unity relates to creation with complete external simplicity. From the Muslim perspective, the Christian religious end veers too much in the direction of the kind of unitive end discussed above, and threatens to blur the distinction between creatures and creator. In contrast with some religious ends, communion veers too close to union. In contrast with others, communion requires too much individuality.

Christians believe that the understanding of God as Trinity, the understanding whose catalyst is the incarnation of Christ, allows us to grasp key features of God's character and God's relation with us. If relationship itself is an impossible, unnecessary, or counterproductive religious aim, then this belief is in error. But if relation is truly an irreducible component of the religious end, then characterizations of God are not only passing tools. They are in some measure constitutive of that end. Salvation is shaped by a particular vision of the God with whom we are in relation. Here we glimpse the way in which Christ is integral to salvation, both embodying the relation with God that constitutes salvation and distinctively representing to us the nature of the God with whom we have communion in salvation.

Distinctions of some sort are a necessary feature of salvation, as a condition for the fullness of relation. Communion involves awareness of the others with whom we participate and of their particular identities. If the ultimate religious end is a relation with God, then God has a determinate character in that relation. Therefore there must be a dialectic between instrumental distinctions or representations of God which can fall away in the journey toward communion, and enduring ones which are themselves integral to the nature of salvation.[4] The doctrine of the Trinity has addressed this dialectic in the language of the "economic" Trinity and the "ontological" Trinity. All of God's

---

4. The position that all representations of God are arbitrary and must give way ultimately to no representation at all, would seem to imply no relation at all. Even then, we have the odd situation that this contention that all such representations are empty in an ultimate sense is typically combined with a claim that some experts or masters know how to prescribe which kind of representation is appropriate for various stages of religious advance. This seems to presuppose some representation of the ultimate as a means of reference.

manifestation in the world is economic in the sense of being an outward expression of God's purpose. Some of the ways we might describe or represent that activity could quite easily be otherwise, or could be dropped completely. The affirmation that the economic Trinity (an understanding of the triune persons as varying external faces of God's action in the world) is grounded in the ontological Trinity (the actual triune persons whose communion in God is the divine life itself) implies that not all representations of God are mere projections. Relational images of God express something of God's true nature.

The fact that such images are partly projected out of the essentially relational character of our own nature does not disqualify them. For that nature is itself a "projection" of God's intrinsically relational character. In salvation, Christians believe that what makes one person different from another, and what makes creatures different from God, will all be the occasions for inestimable joy and glory. They are the basis for mutual participation, just as the differences that distinguish the Word from the Spirit or the Father from the Word are occasions for love and coinherence in the life of the Trinity itself. Salvation is communion with God, whose very nature itself is communion. The faith that the religious end is a relation that brings us into the divine life is coordinate with the faith that the divine life is itself relational.

In claiming communion with the triune God as their religious end, Christians make Trinity central to their understanding of religious diversity. Despite the real and permanent differences between the divine and the human, the saving relation between them is one of profound consonance. Because God's own nature is a communion-nature (Trinity) and human nature is a reflection of this (we are persons only in relation) the two can meet at a point of extraordinary similarity. In the divine-human communion that is salvation, the *difference* between humanity and God is not the primary obstacle to religious fulfillment, but a necessary prerequisite to the deepest relation with God, one that recapitulates God's own mode of relation. The specific differences between the divine persons, differences integral to the communion that constitutes God, are not the same as the specific differences between humans and God. But communion-in-personal-difference is the shared pattern. In God's relation with the world, "peace and harmony are gained not by excluding the Other, but by God's covenant promise to be for the creature *precisely in its difference* from its Creator. Difference — internal and external to the trinitarian life — is the condition for fidelity and fellowship."[5] The very fact that our being is constituted in relation with others, relation with what is

5. (Vanhoozer, 1997, p. 67).

unlike (and this includes most basically of all the fact that we are different from God who made us), is the most fundamental way that we are like God. It is the deepest thing we have in common.

The Trinity represents the Christian context for interpreting religious pluralism. Gavin D'Costa outlines this in five concise theses.[6] His first thesis is that "a trinitarian Christology guards against exclusivism and pluralism by dialectically relating the universal and the particular."[7] The second thesis is that the Holy Spirit "allows the particularity of Christ to be related to the universal activity of God in the history of humankind."[8] This leads to another thesis: if the Holy Spirit is active in the world religions and the church stands under the judgment of the Spirit, then attention to the religions is vital for Christian faithfulness.[9] These three theses set the normativity of Christ within the context of the wider work of God. The other two theses indicate how that particular standard itself points toward respect for the other. One states that Christocentric trinitarianism "discloses loving relationship as the proper mode of being," and so love of the religious neighbor is imperative for Christians.[10] Another states, "The normativity of Christ implies the normativity of crucified self-giving love," and this prescribes the *mode* of relationship with those of other traditions.[11] That relationship must be one of dialogue and of common work for the good of God's reign. In addition, the pattern of self-giving love is a standard that can validate witness to Christians from other traditions. In recognizing the reality of such practice in others, Christians realize that these neighbors must have contact with God.

Trinity provides a particular ground for affirming the truth and reality of what is different. Trinitarian conviction rules out the view that among all the possible claimed manifestations of God, one narrow strand alone is authentic. Trinitarian conviction would rule out as well the view that all or most of these manifestations could be reduced to a single pure type underlying them. A simple exclusivism and a simple pluralism are untenable. There is an irreducible variety in what is ultimately true or of greatest significance. Christians can find validity in other religions because of the conviction that the Trinity represents a universal truth about the way the world and God actually are.

Trinitarian perspectives combine the recognition of this diversity with the contention that there is one way (or a limited set of ways) of correctly

6. (D'Costa, 1990).
7. (D'Costa, 1990, p. 18).
8. (D'Costa, 1990, p. 19).
9. (D'Costa, 1990, p. 22).
10. (D'Costa, 1990, p. 19).
11. (D'Costa, 1990, p. 20).

grasping that variety. The trinitarian model tells us that the simple fact of difference does not automatically imply either a forced choice between truth and falsehood or a hierarchical division between higher and lower being. Everything depends on whether or how this difference functions in communion. Therefore, for Christians, the simple facts of religious difference do not automatically require flat judgments of rejection or acceptance. However, a particular, universal claim is very much at issue. The claim is that the trinitarian mode of integration allows for the greatest level of communion. This claim may be contested by those who maintain there are better ways to attain communion or who deny that communion is possible. Alternatively, the claim might be granted, but the Christian path still avoided, because communion with God and others is not valued or desired as the ultimate religious end. From within a trinitarian perspective, specific differences need not be condemned, but alternative ways of integrating difference are regarded as penultimate at best in comparison with the trinitarian option.

The plausibility of this claim hinges on the capacity of trinitarian approaches to comprehend or integrate other religious truth within their vision of reality. In this sense, the claim cedes a tremendous amount of authority to the self-description and witness of other traditions. Christianity is not alone in this structural characteristic, for virtually all traditions claim to explain the character of other religions. This is an inevitable, but possibly fruitful form of "competition" among the faiths: seeing which can most adequately take account of the distinctive testimony of others.[12] To put it another way, the question is whether one faith's sense of the ultimate is such as to allow it to recognize that real (if limited or less than full) relation to that ultimate exists in another tradition, *in terms largely consistent with the distinctive testimony from that tradition itself.* The faith that proves able to do this for the widest possible range of compelling elements from other traditions will not only be enriched itself, but will offer strong warrants for its own truth.[13] I say the "widest pos-

12. John Cobb provides an interesting commendation of such "competition" (Cobb, 1990).

13. In this connection, it does not count for much to affirm that the faith/convictions of another tradition are "true" in the very limited sense that, though false in all particulars and failing to designate any distinctive religious end, they can be seen as veiled and crude representations of the reality accurately understood by the home tradition. Nor does it count for much to add the belief that those convictions can serve as stepping stones toward better forms of faith. These affirmations are important for all inclusivist perspectives and have great value in that connection. But such affirmations can be made in largely identical formal terms by all traditions. A more discriminating test is the capacity of one tradition to recognize another's *distinctive* religious content.

sible" range of such data, because not everything that one tradition holds as true must be accepted as so by another in the process I describe. A primary task for the Christian theologies of religion is to "translate" other religious elements into Christian perspective while keeping them as clearly as possible themselves. This would not be necessary unless one believed that these elements contained real truth as they stand, and that the ability to register and honor that truth is in fact one good internal check on the validity of our own theology.[14]

The truth in any religion must stem from some actual relation to God, in one or more of the possible modes for such relation. I want to focus on that truth, leaving aside for the moment consideration that there may also be simple error in other traditions, as in Christianity. If substantive religious differences (as opposed to entirely cultural or circumstantial ones) exist between valid Christian convictions and valid convictions of another religion, these differences must have to do either with differences in the scope and range of the relation with God and other creatures sought in the two traditions, or with differing expectations about how the variety of such relations are to be integrated. This latter point is important. We cannot assume that other religious traditions are "monophone," allowing for one and only one mode of relation to God, any more than Christianity is. They may differ from Christianity not by lacking something that is present in Christianity or maintaining something lacking in Christianity, but by integrating similar elements differently. This returns us precisely to the question of the Trinity, as the distinctive Christian pattern of integration.

It is common today to hear religious assertions that claim to be based on data from all religious traditions, weighed without favor for any. Admitting the implausibility of the practical execution of such a project, many still endorse the principle that only through some quest for the *sum* of the insights of all traditions can we gain the best, if still limited, grasp of the religious ultimate. My point is simply that the religions themselves *are* just such efforts at integration. It is mistaken to believe that we can assume some perspective above all the religions or some perspective that belongs simultaneously and equally to them all. It is rare for religious traditions to exalt one extremely narrow aspect of divine encounter and to totally ignore the existence of any other religious phenomena. Typically the great traditions draw together a wide variety of elements (including those that are featured in other

---

14. I have argued elsewhere (Heim, 1995, introduction) for the importance of distinctive particularity in religious traditions and the need of theories of religion that can value these particularities.

religions as well) into what they regard as the single most comprehensive and valid perspective. Usually this is done through some hierarchical ordering, which makes one type of contact with the divine the basis and source of other more derivative ones.

"Neutral" accounts of the religious ultimate, wishing to vindicate the religions generally without taking sides among them, tend simply to become variations on existing religious options, unless they retreat to extraordinary levels of abstraction. For instance, to claim that the religious ultimate is equally represented by its characterizations in all the religions, we will have to take scrupulous care to describe it in terms equidistant from the specifics of the individual religious traditions. In that case, it seems all we can say is that there is a reality beyond these descriptions: not one they all describe, but one to which they are all responding. John Hick calls this "the Real," and denies it any attributes that might define it as either personal or impersonal. As Jacques Dupuis notes, for Hick it is "the Real" that is the true referent of the Christian "God" or the Hindu *"Brahman."* Dupuis agrees that there is one true referent for all such religious (and non-religious) references to the ultimate. Hick is wrong only in the particular that it is the triune God who is behind "the Real" (and the other referents) rather than the other way around.[15]

Our concern is to consider what difference it makes if the triune God is taken to be the reference *from which* to understand religious diversity. More particularly, I am interested in the implications of the Trinity for the understanding of religious traditions themselves. People in one faith commonly hold that those in other traditions can be "saved" through some approximation to the practices and beliefs of the home tradition. That is, others may reach religious fulfillment *in spite* of the distinctive religious features of their own tradition, because of some superimposed use of those features for the sake of another end than they ostensibly seek. The validity and truth value of the other religions, considered as paths to distinct religious ends in their own right, is rarely addressed. It is this question, and the possible relevance of the Trinity for it, that concerns us.

By "Trinity" I do not mean to refer to a generic and symbolic scheme of abstract threeness. With such a minimalist pattern, one can run merrily through the religions gathering "trinities," from the *Brahma-Shiva-Vishnu* triumvirate of Hinduism to the *trikay* or "three bodies" doctrine of Buddhism.[16] I am speaking of the reality of God as presented in the doctrine of the Christian church, which presupposes the incarnation of the Word as crucial revelation

15. (Dupuis S.J., 1997, pp. 402-3).
16. This point is made effectively by Williams (1997, pp. 28-29).

and act of God. Although of necessity I will refer often to trinitarian doctrine, I do not mean to imply that the reality is absent where theological formulation is absent. The doctrine tells us something true about God and also embodies the pattern of Christian conviction and experience. But Christians may be thoroughly trinitarian without using any technical language.

By affirming the closest possible unity of Christ with God, in the specific context of Jewish monotheism, Christian faith created a problem absent in more monistic or polytheistic traditions. For God to be distinctively connected with historical particularity in this way, while also remaining the sole, transcendent creator, obviously required diversity in the means, the *economy*, by which God related to the world. And if this economic activity of God was to be at the same time true revelation of God's very self, then that variety of manifestation had to be rooted in a complexity of relation intrinsic to God's self. In other words, the means and ways in which God related to creation were not accidental or artificial but expressions of God's intrinsic character.

The development of the doctrine is itself instructive. Without the constitutive role attributed to Jesus, there would have been no reason for Christians to evolve this understanding of the mystery of God. Yet, though the divinity and saving decisiveness of Jesus are the preconditions for such an understanding, the doctrine of the Trinity in turn rules out the strongest "exclusivist" reading of those qualities in Jesus. Thus, as Gavin D'Costa says, "The Trinity safeguards against an exclusivist particularism (Christomonism) and a pluralist universalism (theocentrism) in that it stipulates against an *exclusive identification* of God and Jesus, as well as against a *non-identification* of God and Jesus."[17] To make sense of the fact that God was as decisively in Christ as Christians believed, it was necessary to hold that God was elsewhere than Christ also. This is perhaps the key pivot point of the Christian theology of religions. It balances the tensions such a theology must maintain: without high Christology, no Trinity; with Trinity, no Christology so high that it cannot fit within a wider economy of God's action. The reality of God's active relation to creation in ways distinct from the event of the historical Jesus is coded into the trinitarian basis of Christian faith. So too is the intrinsic connection of all of God's action with that historical event.

Among other things, the Trinity unifies patterns of religious experience. Some patterns might easily be viewed as completely different from each other, relating to entirely different realities, and thus as constituents of different religions or types of religion. For instance, there are experiences of mystery, of a numinous power or powers that encounter us in nature, which dwarf our

3 ways of experiencing God

17. (D'Costa, 1990, p. 18).

perspective and hint at a mysterious transcendence in contrast with our contingency. This could be a storm at sea, a starry night, or the birth of a child. Second, there are experiences of transformation in historical process, which grow from revelatory persons or events that become the ground of individual and community life. An example might be the deliverance and new life that comes to a person who throws himself on the hope of a savior or divine name in the midst of a desperate depression or addiction. It might be the liberation that comes to people who together transform their social condition by active commitment to a norm that exists only in a shared vision. Third, there are experiences of unity, of mystical communion and self-transcendence, that overflow the normal divisions between isolated persons. These might be ecstatic prayer or meditation, an altered state of consciousness whose reality casts into doubt the conventions of ordinary life.

Those who are convinced they have touched or heard the divine likely refer to one of these occasions: God above us, God alongside and among us, God within us. The Trinity is an account of God that says these are experiences of the same reality, not different ones, and yet each has its own irreducible integrity. They ought not to be separated and pitted against each other (as for instance in a religion of nature over against a religion of history or one of spirit). Nor should they be reduced to some generic reality underlying them all or hierarchically ranked so that only one is the definitive truth behind the other two. God is known in the midst of these different patterns. "Only such a 'pluralist' doctrine of God can allow for the equal validity of finding God as the fundamental and indescribable ground of all, as a partner in personal dialogue, and as the energy of one's own deepest selfhood — and only such a doctrine can present these elements as united with each other, requiring each other to make full human sense."[18]

The Trinity is not about *levels* of divine being (the Neoplatonic temptation) but about *dimensions* of God. Height, length, and width are features of a whole body and of every part of it, and yet the three are not the same. If emanations from God or acts of God are put on a ladder of being, then humans, who are farther "down" the ladder of creation, can relate only to the rungs immediately above or below them. Ultimate divinity lies further above and beyond. If the three divine persons of the Trinity are treated in this way, they become levels of being. But in fact no person of the Trinity is a lower or earlier step, and none is "less far in" to God. For the Christian, salvation is not passing beyond the Spirit to the Son or the Son to the Father. Salvation is participation in the divine life that is the communion among the three persons.

18. (Williams, 1990, p. 4).

The Trinity is Christianity's "pluralistic theology." Its basis was set by the disciples' conviction that their encounter with Jesus could be correlated with the encounter with Israel's one God and with the new life they experienced within and among themselves as a result of Jesus. These were not identical experiences, but they were encounters with the same God. Of course there are innumerable ways that God may be manifest in relation with humanity. These three encounters — with the God of Israel who is not to be named or imaged, with the concrete humanity of Jesus, with the indwelling of the Spirit — were not simply three acts or manifestations among numberless others. They were revelations of the constitutive pattern of God's relation to humanity and of God's own relational nature.

Christology is plainly the key to this. Christians' belief in the incarnation affirms that in Jesus the internal relations which constitute God's divinity (inner trinitarian relation) and the external relations between God and humans (creator-creature relation) participate in each other. God's relation with Christ is at once an inner-trinitarian relation (of the first and third persons with the second) and an external relation of creator with creature.[19] That is not yet a full map of the intersection, however. The intimate overlap of the inner divine life and the God-human relation also participates, via Jesus, in the interpersonal human social nexus and in the relation between humanity and created nature. Through the web of communion from this single human point, God becomes a participant on the creature side of the creator/ creature relation. This means, for instance, that God also has communion with the characteristic forms of alienation in these relations. Christ experiences the sense of alienation from and abandonment by God; the reality of betrayal, malice, and indifference in his dealings with other persons; the loss of consciousness, control, and identity in death that comes at the collapse of the self-sufficiency of created nature.

If people object that one incarnation is too few, they may miss the point that the Christian doctrine of God does not limit the going out of God into creation to just one instance. God's living presence in the world has a complex variety. Some dimensions of that presence are static, like a force field of the same strength in place always and everywhere, sustaining creation. Access to such presence does not depend upon developed solidarity with others. There is a way in which God is "in" all of creation, always and all at once, by virtue of God's continual, sustaining power.

---

19. The long and convoluted theological discussions of the hypostatic union of God and Jesus attempt to explicate this relation. At the moment we are only concerned to see what prompts such discussion.

There is also a narrative dimension of God's presence, revelation from the personal to the personal. This is a "going out" which proceeds by unique acts precisely to meet humanity under the conditions of creation and, just as important, to meet humanity in a way that can only be grasped through communion and community. Particularity and limitation are crucial necessities for this work. Incarnation premises access to the full personal dimensions of God on willingness to participate in a web of interpersonal witness, life, and service. Because of incarnation's particular location, none of us can connect with it except through a web of relations with others. There is no way that we can go around communion with others, no way we can dispense with it. If we complain that the "problem" of access to a particular person makes us dependent on this communion, requires our participation in a network of others, we are objecting not just to the means but to the end that Christianity offers. In this case the two are exquisitely congruent.

The Trinity teaches us that Jesus Christ cannot be an exhaustive or exclusive source for knowledge of God nor the exhaustive and exclusive act of God to save us. Yet the Trinity is unavoidably Christocentric in at least two senses. It is Christocentric in the empirical sense that the doctrine, the representation of God's triune nature, arose historically from faith in Jesus Christ. And it is so in the systemic sense that the personal character of God requires particularity as its deepest mode of revelation. The fullness of God's mystery is never grasped by us. It is hidden in the divine source (Father), overflows in Christ beyond the measure of our means to receive it, and is continually active in all of creation through the Spirit. "*All* history, both past and to come, is potentially a particularity by which God's self-revelation is mediated."[20] Christ is the concrete particularity *by* which Christians know this about the potential in all history and *in* whom, in the unity with the divine Word, this self-revelation decisively takes place. The scope of divine activity in all of religious history widens in proportion to the decisiveness of God's self-revelation in Christ, not the reverse. Christ is normative, not absolute, and so is the ground by which we can be open to other faiths.[21]

There are many avenues for the interpretation of religions. The distinctively Christian way passes through the trinitarian dynamic we have been describing, the heart of a Christian theology of religions. Implicitly or explicitly, Trinity has been the framework within which Christians have reflected on the salvation of those in other religious traditions. This was so whether people stressed a general revelation through creation (focusing on

20. (D'Costa, 1995, p. 19).
21. M. M. Thomas provides a thoughtful exposition of this theme (Thomas, 1987).

imagery of God the Father), a universal, active presence of God (stressing the Holy Spirit), or the "incognito" activity of the Word that was incarnate in Jesus. When expressing a wider hope, the conviction that salvation is available to those beyond the bounds of the church or explicit confession of Christ, Christians have inevitably turned to variations on these three themes. Likewise, in developing theologies of religion, Christians "mine" the same three themes, often emphasizing one to the detriment of the other two. Many of the divisions among Christians over how to understand religious pluralism stem from the divergent theologies of religion that grow out of those differences in emphasis.[22]

One approach to religious pluralism delves into the implications of trust in God as the source of a unitary creation. Religious diversity is addressed in terms of a universal fit between humanity and its maker, the imprint of the divine nature in all that is and the capacity for all persons to perceive that imprint. A range of ideas comes into play here: the image of God in human beings, general revelation, the light of reason or conscience, covenants with Adam and Eve, with Noah. There is a universal revelation of God in the things that God has made, and this can be activated through the religions. So a typical advocate of this approach might argue that persons can relate to God apart from special revelation through this natural moral religion: "what the law requires is written on their hearts, to which their own conscience also bears witness."[23]

A second theological vein runs through the depths of christological confession. Questions about the pluralism of faiths are explored through what we might call preincarnate, incarnate, and postresurrection modalities. An example of the first would be reflections concerning the ways in which the *logos,* the Word of God, is already active in the world by virtue of participation in creation and therefore can be known in some measure apart from the gospel. The second involves consideration of the ways in which various faiths might providentially prefigure or reflect the concrete historical reality of Jesus Christ, ways in which the messiah is truly expected, to use Reinhold Niebuhr's phrase. The third modality concerns the active presence of the risen and living Christ to those in various religions, perhaps "incognito," on the model of Jesus' resurrection appearances, where he is unrecognized either briefly (Mary in the garden) or for long periods (the road to Emmaus). Christ is actively present, and directly responded to, though not identified or named.

22. See, for instance, a collection that lays out the patterns of theological thought characteristic of a number of Christian traditions in (Heim, 1998).

23. Romans 2:15.

SPIRIT

The third vein of theological reflection turns to the work of the Spirit and focuses on the continued freedom and providence of God's action. The continual striving of all created beings toward their source is a sign of God's immanence with creation, stimulating that desire for communion and reaching out to fulfill it. The Spirit blows where it will, and the religions can be viewed as sites for this direct, spontaneous action of God. Whenever the religions are instruments for creation to fulfill some portion of its ordained beauty, justice, and love, that presence of God is realized.

Christian theologies of religion affirm what is valid in other religions by identifying it either with God's revelation in creation, with the implicit presence of the Word, or with the direct action of the Spirit. Insofar as they are trinitarian, Christians recognize the validity of all three of these approaches, and at least nominally affirm that the three are integrally related. Still, as it has been difficult to maintain a full and unified trinitarian perspective within the "internal" work of Christian theology, so it has been doubly hard to do so in the consideration of religious pluralism.

II

In the third section of this chapter we will consider two recent, creative trinitarian theologies of religion. But first we will pause to explore the way that the dynamics discussed above *internally* impel Christian faith into engagement with other traditions and cultures. Belief in Christ leads to an understanding of God as Trinity. Such an understanding of God rules out a view of Christ as an isolated source of relation to God or knowledge of God. And yet trinitarian logic further indicates that this "expansion" of God beyond what could be expressed in a simple, historical, Christomonistic way is always integrally connected with that incarnate Word.

One way to put this is to say that what was revealed in the particularity of Jesus Christ has in fact not yet been fully specified. Even the historical Jesus has not yet been fully revealed to us. That is, although Christians rightly hold to the universal particularity of the incarnation, the history of the Christian church indicates that the *meaning* of this revelation was not received whole. The presence and action of God in Christ encompassed elements that remain latent and unrealized. Until the full work of the incarnate Word is put in the full context of the participation of the Spirit and the Father in that work, and in the context of God's other work in the world, the understanding of the incarnation will be partial at best. The grammar of Christ's work is the action of one on behalf of all. The reflexive side of *development of doctrine / but much more*

that equation is that this decisive act of God's communion with humanity can only be fully appropriated when it is grasped through the responses of the "all." The communion Christ came to instigate is itself the fundamental instrument for understanding who Christ is.

The missionary history of the church demonstrates this. The maxim that "mission is the mother of theology" conveys a crucial truth. To say that the Christian gospel has been translated into varied cultures and contexts can be taken in three ways. The first would be to think of mission as the translation of a fixed and finished message from its original form into some lesser approximation in another language or culture. The copy would never quite equal the original. A second interpretation would be to see the mission translation resulting in an alternative form of the original gospel, one just as adequate for the receiving culture as the original is in the sending culture. The third possibility suggests that translation into new contexts brings out new and additional aspects of the gospel. Some of these may not apply only to the new cultural context: they carry universal value and need to be assimilated and received by the whole church. That is, the "translated" gospel has to be carried in mission back to the churches that sent it. This third option is the operative reality for Christian theology. Even when denied in theory, it has been the practice in fact.

Translation continues to be the primary means to discover the depth and extent of the gospel. This is no cosmetic adjustment of Christianity's external expression. The life, the thought, and the witness of the church become new in new contexts. This newness often has a universal character. It expands and transforms the common faith by discovering aspects of revelation that had not been received before. The paradigm example of this, beginning within the New Testament itself, is the encounter of early Christianity with hellenistic culture. In taking the Nicene creed or trinitarian doctrine itself as crucial standards, Christianity affirmed the dynamic I have just described. New contexts occasion "translation" and discovery of elements of faith that now are seen as part of the common reality of Christ, part of the "given" that had not been grasped before.

Dialogue is a key element in this process. Western Christians have probably been more conscious of this recently in terms of the long-term dialogue with enlightenment thought and secularism than in relation to world religions. But historically it has been the diverse religious-cultural complexes Christianity has encountered that have been the primary contexts for theological development. Though dialogue is necessary, it cannot replace conversion and the existence of living churches in different cultures. It is one thing to be told how Christian faith appears from a particular religious vantage point. It is another thing to see what comes to light in living out the Christian path authentically on different spiritual soil.

This offers an important but little-discussed light on missionary activity. Conversion is an integral element in the nature of such activity. But quite apart from any conversion, the missionary who crosses religious/cultural boundaries to identify with people in a new environment is already contributing to the catholicity of the church's life. The missionary's first task is to become a converted member of the new culture, even of its religious heritage insofar as that is consistent with Christ, in order to know more of Christ through this extended human communion. The missionary's conviction that she brings a transforming message to the new context is or should be balanced by the recognition that the transforming of that message itself is a new gift that is returned from the context. It is a gift that can be given only from that particular place.

Those Christians most avid for world evangelization hope for the planting of a church within every "people group," for the purpose of bringing each individual within effective range of Christian witness. However, the priority of saving souls can argue for diverting attention and effort to locations or subcultures where people's response to Christianity is most positive. Missionary history is full of such prudential judgments. But the complementary side of the call for Christian mission is the search for the realization of the fullness of Christ. This view values the existence of Christian communities in varied cultures for the greater light that breaks forth on God's word and work from each new translation. That mission can succeed even without great numbers.

The fact that the church exists now in so many parts of the world provides the basis for an important mission task that is little appreciated, though it is of vast scope. This is the task of assimilating and bringing to unity the fruit of these many transpositions of Christianity that exist within the Christian family. The urgency of this work is obvious, now that Christianity is a predominantly non-western religion and becoming ever more so. "While what we call third-world theology is too much an 'echo' of western theologies, there is another kind, 'namely, that which is being continuously produced in the languages of the churches of the Third World — in the form of preaching, catechesis, song, story, and drama.'"[24] This ecumenical challenge is an integral part of mission, a part that depends on the nurture of Christian communities in the largest possible number of distinct contexts.

These characteristics distinguish Christianity from many other traditions, for better or worse. Some religions see little or no intrinsic need for

24. (Hunsberger, 1998, quoting Lesslie Newbigin).

such missionary activity, and would typically prefer to see their adherents in highly homogenous, consolidated social or national communities. Picture, as a thought experiment, a world in which all religious communities maintained their current population of adherents, but the distribution of the adherents was changed. Members of each faith were scattered into every social/political/cultural grouping, with no one religion being a majority in any such grouping. We can see that this picture would be more troubling for religious traditions that integrate their tradition most closely with an ethnic or cultural or political unity.

That same picture presents an interesting self-test for Christians' readings of the nature of mission. Do we find the situation it describes distasteful, because Christianity would achieve greater success by fully permeating a few populous cultures? Or do we incline to celebrate such a vision for the unprecedented richness and catholicity it would bring to Christian life, and for the explicit Christian witness it would place at hand for nearly all people? This is a telling question, particularly as the global interchange among cultures and religions accelerates in our time. Such "mosaicization" of the religions is much more congenial to some traditions than to others, and to some versions of each tradition than to others. For this reason, closer approximation to such a situation may heighten tensions among the religions rather than lessen them.

The catholicity which has figured so much in theological discussion in Christian history is not just head counting, measuring whether some idea or practice has been widespread enough among Christians to be validated. It has to do equally with multiplicity of contexts. The more languages, the more races, the more nations and geographies, the more religious contexts within which the faith of the church has been embodied, the more closely that faith can approximate a true understanding of what was given to it "once for all." The fullness of Christ awaits unveiling. This is a conviction embodied in Christian beliefs about the Holy Spirit, the presence of the risen Christ, and the eschatological return of Christ.

Development of doctrine is a subject usually reserved for systematic theology. Even there it often takes on a very rarefied quality, as if development were an entirely intellectual process in which continued analysis of Christian sources draws out new implications, hidden before. Yet surely the most important vehicle for the development of revelation has not been the succession of philosophical enthusiasms from one generation to the next but rather the larger cultural and religious diversity which Christianity has actively engaged. Andrew Walls makes a useful distinction between a proselyte and a convert.[25] "Proselytism" is

25. (Walls, 1996).

often used as a pejorative term for illegitimate types of evangelism, but this is not the subject in view. Walls's reference point is the first century, and he contrasts gentile proselytes to Judaism (who adopted its practices entirely as they found them) with gentile converts to Christianity (who brought transforming cultural and religious elements). Proselytes conform completely to the existing model of the community they join. Converts do not.

Though both missionaries and new adherents often incline toward a proselyte model, Christianity is distinguished in Walls's view by its commitment to the conversion model.

> The divine Word was expressed under the conditions of a particular human society: the divine Word was, as it were, *translated*. And since the divine Word is for all humanity, he is translated again in terms of every culture where he finds acceptance among its people. The unchanging nature of the Prophetic Word of the Qur'an, fixed in heaven forever in Arabic, produces a single Islamic civilization recognizable, despite all the local variations, from Indonesia to Morocco. There can be no single Christian civilization; the Christian scriptures are not, like the Qur'an, the Word of God only when delivered in the original languages. In Christian understanding the Word of God can be spoken in any language under heaven. The divine Son did not become humanity in general, but a specific man in a specific place and culture; he is, as it were, made flesh again in other places and cultures as he is received there by faith. . . .
>
> Christian faith, then, rests on a massive divine act of translation, and proceeds by successive lesser acts of translation into the complexes of experiences and relationships that form our social identities in different parts of the world. . . .[26]

An internal imperative in Christian faith draws it across cultural boundaries. One form that imperative takes is a concern for the eternal destinies of unreached individuals. That concern can readily be structured as the need to pass on to others what those in the church already have. But there is an imperative at least as deeply rooted which relates to the very substance of what the church has received, and to the fact that the church does not "have" it at all. There is a very real sense in which the church does not know what it is talking about, does not begin to fathom the one in whom it puts its trust, except as the gospel is re-translated back to it through the full range of human diversity.

I do not understand/appreciate what it means to be a Christian/Catholic unless I go out every day to meet whom God sends me — what

26. (Walls, 1996, p. 47). This point is powerfully presented at greater depth in (Sanneh, 1989).

140

Raimundo Panikkar wrote a significant book, *The Unknown Christ of Hinduism*.[27] The book plays on the traditional Christian idea that Christ as the *logos* may be present incognito in places where the name of Jesus Christ is not recognized. But Panikkar presumes that the "Christ of Hinduism" is unknown to Christians as well, and that their own relation with Christ will be richer for this expansion. There is an "unknown Christ" for Christianity, a Christ whose full dimensions and character are hidden from Christians and await the further particularization that can only come from additional contexts. Christians have truly encountered Christ as savior. We do not begin to fully know the one to whom we have given ourselves.

A common criticism of Christianity in the modern period has been to point to the historical particularity of the Christ event and to infer that because it took place in a specific context and is interpreted through conditioned categories it cannot carry universal and decisive significance. Christians can go astray in their legitimate rejection of this modernist dogma if they lose sight of the fact that the imperative is not simply to defend that single set of singularities, but to appropriate the continuing truth that they generate through new encounters with *other* particularities.

Scripture and the earliest Christian witnesses retain a necessary normativity not because one culture is exalted above others but for the same reason that translators, if they have a choice, will not work only from a text which is itself a translation of a translation of a translation. They will go back to the earliest texts and the first translations. But it would likewise be a mistake to think that we are perfectly well served with only an original text and our own contemporary cultural situation. *All* translations are relevant, indeed crucial data. In the ideal case, knowing what Christ can mean in a specifically Hindu religious and cultural context should be a valuable resource for a Christian trying to live faithfully in any culture. Such insight widens and specifies even more richly the substance of the faith in Christ we hope to embody in our own place. The true, operative "translations" are always the actual lives of persons and communities.

For example, the Chalcedonian formula that confesses Christ as "fully human, fully divine," expresses the distinctiveness of Jesus in terms of categories familiar in the Hellenistic world. Within that context and its understanding of "divine" and "human," it is necessary to speak and think of Jesus in this way in order to be faithful to who he is and what he means. This recognition was not a passing insight. It remains of universal significance in two respects. First, it is a paradigm instance of how the translation we are discussing takes

27. (Panikkar, 1981).

place. As such it always bears reflection for other instances of translation. Second, it was received by the church in its experience of life, worship, and thought as a faithful translation, one that fruitfully guided other transpositions of faith. When a context poses essentially the same question that was posed in the fourth century, *this* continues to be a universal answer. It is normative both as a methodological example and in its substance.[28]

However, the formula leaves an enormous amount unsaid. The door is open to do what Chalcedon did *again*, differently but not incompatibly. Indeed, given the Christian dynamic, this is required. A similar point was made by Kosuke Koyama when he wrote of his experience in communicating the gospel in the Buddhist culture of Thailand.[29] People readily responded to certain aspects of Jesus' teaching and person that harmonized with their own religious tradition. That heritage taught them to respect "coolness," nonattachment. It is passion, attachment, craving, desire — all "hot" — that lead to suffering. It is the cessation of desire and craving — "coolness" — that leads to release. So, Koyama said, when Jesus counseled his followers not to take thought for tomorrow, not to lay up treasure on earth where moth and rust consume and thieves break in to steal, the Thai hearers nodded. This was very "cool" and wise. But when Jesus talked of an agitated and passionate God, spoke of loving enemies, hungering and thirsting after righteousness, when he wept and groaned before the cross, this was too "hot." The crucial doctrinal rule in this case, Koyama suggested, was not "Jesus Christ, divine and human" but "Jesus Christ, cool and hot." Jesus' attachment to God and neighbor is the avenue to a characteristic detachment from selfish craving: he is cooled by love. This proclamation, as paradoxical as Chalcedon, is an equally valid witness to the same Lord.

"Divine and human" and "cool yet hot" are not contradictory doctrinal statements. Nor is one a simple translation of the other. They stand on equal ground. The equality is based on the faithfulness with which each, as a "grammatical" rule, reflects the deep structure of the communion embodied and

---

28. In its study program "Towards Common Confession of the Apostolic Faith," the Faith and Order Commission of the World Council of Churches has produced and stimulated much fruitful work that illuminates this point. See (World Council of Churches. Commission on Faith and Order, 1987; Link, World Council of Churches. Commission on Faith and Order et al., 1988; World Council of Churches, 1991). Also of interest are (Song, World Council of Churches. Commission on Faith and Order et al., 1980; Link, Houtepen, et al., 1983; Link, Tamez, et al., 1984; Link, Castro, et al., 1985) and (Heim, National Council of the Churches of Christ in the United States of America. Commission on Faith and Order et al., 1991).

29. (Koyama, 1971).

received in Christ. Neither one is entirely dependent on the other, but together they give a fuller grasp of the reality of Christ than either does apart. Both are normative and can apply beyond the context in which they were formulated, though the circumstances in which one of them would come to the fore may be different from those in which the other would.[30]

I remember traveling with a group of Christian students on an evangelistic tour through some rural villages in South India. The lyrics of one of the songs they sang went like this:

> Jesus Christ, a real human person;
> Jesus Christ, he left his father's trade;
> Jesus Christ, not all who followed him were fishermen;
> Jesus Christ, he doesn't have to come again and again:
>   He's already here.

If you asked me the essential things to tell people who were not familiar with Jesus, these are not what I would have come up with! But with some reflection I realized the wisdom in these formulations.

In our culture we are used to skepticism about Jesus' divine nature. In India this has rarely been a problem: it is Christianity's insistence on Jesus' historical humanity that has been puzzling. In a culture where birth and caste determined one's occupation as well as most other social relations, it is a significant fact that Jesus did not remain a carpenter like his father. The first converts to Christianity in India came from the coast and from among castes of people who lived by fishing (like some of Jesus' original disciples). For Indians, a ready conclusion followed that Christianity was the caste religion of that particular group. Finally, the avatar doctrine, according to which gods from time to time manifest themselves under the appearance of humans, provides a ready category into which to place Jesus. The song uses each of these particular features of this religious and cultural context to witness to Christ. In the process, it lifts up elements that are plainly part of the scriptural record and Christian tradition but whose significance had not been grasped in this

---

30. We could distinguish this from *upaya* or "skillful means," which in Buddhism refers to using whatever terms or ideas are necessary to the stage of development of the hearer to lead on to enlightenment. All such terms are in principle unrealistic and can be disregarded once they are used to go on to the next spiritual level. The Christian view is much more a matter of expansion, accumulation, and complementarity. Since in salvation the creaturely is not abolished, revealed as illusion, or totally transcended, the varying insights and realizations gained through different human contexts remain part of the concrete relation to God.

way by the western churches of which I was a part. I cannot be sure how many of the villagers found this witness revelatory. I know that I did.

Such perspective is crucial for our theological work. We need to avoid the notion on one hand that we simply plug our received traditions into other cultural situations and the notion on the other hand that contextual theologies are in fact ghetto theologies, of interest and significance only for the group within which they were developed. We sometimes assume (to continue the linguistic analogy) that those in the church are "Christian speakers." Assuming we are fluent in this language, the task that remains is to translate what has already been said into another form. It is more accurate to say that all of us in the various parts of the church are only partially "Christian speaking" (or living). We are at best rather pidgin practitioners.

The whole language as yet escapes us all. Someone learning a language, whether a child in their native culture or an adult in a new one, learns how words are used in one situation, then in another. And so they finally gain a tacit grasp of the ways in which particular words relate to various situations. Given only a few instances, it is possible to venture a supposition as to how to apply the words in entirely new situations, a venture that may also turn out to be wrong![31] So we learn the form of life that is Christianity by an accumulation of the personal, cultural, and social contexts in which we see it embodied. As Christian faith rediscovers itself in various environments, all of its communities are in principle enriched.[32]

All that we have said has particular application to the question of religions. Religions express the most comprehensive and the most regulative visions of the world that humans know. Whatever the varying degree in which any given religion specifies a particular blueprint for metaphysics, morality, social structures, interpersonal relationships, or individual development, religions are visions *within* which such particulars are formulated, evaluated, and implemented. Religions and other worldviews constitute the primary contexts in which the Christian Word must be articulated if we are to grasp its full range of meaning, apply it in new situations, and live it out.

We could interpret this exclusively in terms of Christian mission as evangelism. The translation we have discussed could be focused entirely on witness to non-Christians and on the new churches and converts that arise in

---

31. I am aware of the argument that language acquisition does not proceed in such a simple inductive manner as I may seem to suggest, that there is a "metagrammar" in the human neurological make-up that guides or supercharges the response to inductive clues. This does not affect my limited point that *instances*, language modeling and practice, are needed in any event for a sense of grammatical meaning to develop.

32. For further discussion see (Heim, 1987).

response. This modality has an intrinsic place in Christian faith. It could hardly be otherwise for a tradition that is both incarnational and missionary in nature. The "translation" seeks in its very nature to be an embodied one: not just an abstract formula of words, but a tangible, organic community that lives out of the Word.

I believe that our discussion points up another focus as well. The purpose of translation is not limited to an approach to individuals or to the transformation of cultures. It aims also at the transformation and enlightenment of the existing church and of Christians. It is an indispensable part of their struggle to be faithful, to *know* the one in whom they have believed and to conform better to that likeness. For this, they need what only their Buddhist, and Hindu, and Muslim neighbors can provide: insights into the breadth and depth of God in Christ that are unrevealed until those contexts have been fully explored. If there is something in God's revelation in Christ that we will not receive until persons have lived it *through* the contexts of these other religions, then there must be something intrinsically valid about those religions themselves, some providential role for them.

This might not appear to follow. Some hold that the only thing Christians learn about Jesus in new religious contexts is another kind of error he dispels. This view is represented in some missionary circles past and present: the religions are only different ways to be simply wrong. But if we sincerely and consistently held to this, the entire history of the church, including its most vital missionary expansions, would be deeply suspect because of the way in which the gospel was steadily transposed to diverse, specifically religious contexts. We need only mention the regular practice of Bible translators of taking over a culture's common word for its sole or primary deity and using it as the biblical noun for God.

There are two further points to make here. The first has to do with seeing "anticipations of Christ" in other religious traditions. There is an understandable inclination for Christians to focus on those aspects of other faiths that seem most similar to Christian convictions: pointers that are "fulfilled" in Christ. We will speak more about this in the next chapter. But in terms of our discussion at the moment we should note that our special emphasis is precisely on that in other traditions which is *not* familiar or similar. It is this that provides the opportunity for a unique and additional dimension of God's work and life to be opened to us. The Christian conviction is that through these we may find some of the "more truth" that Jesus promised to his disciples, and that this truth will testify to, deepen, the decisive nature of the Christ we already knew dimly and in part.

Second, the planting of new churches is not the only way in which this comes about. Dialogue with and study of other religions is a key part of the process. When people become Christians on a strict proselyte model (adopting in entirety another's particular cultural form of Christianity), lives may be transformed and the church expanded. There may be valid reasons for individuals and groups to *choose* a proselyte model, as for instance if they believe their existing cultural context is largely oppressive for them. But that particular type of church growth may not contribute so much toward this other task of mission, seeking out the full stature of Christ and our relation with God in Christ for the enrichment of the whole church.

We see an example of this contrast in India. Many lower caste persons converted to Christianity and at the same time rejected their traditional place in Hindu social structure. There was (and often is) little interest in maintaining cultural traditions that were among the primary things from which they hoped Christianity would liberate them.[33] Therefore this Christianity often has a strong proselyte character, with extensive Western trappings in architecture, liturgy, and theology. It would be wrong to denigrate these choices because they may not provide novel data for Western Christian reflection. On the other hand, within the renewal of Hindu thought and Indian tradition called the "Hindu renaissance" there was an intensive dialogue with Christianity and a special interest in the figure of Jesus on the part of Hindus interested in remaining within and revitalizing Hinduism.[34] This offered much suggestive light on Jesus for Christians in India and elsewhere, and stimulated a good deal of reflection on Christian theology and Christian spiritual and social practice. In this sense, it was a signal contribution to Christian mission.

Perhaps this situation is not so paradoxical as it appears, but in fact illustrates the dynamic we have been describing. Many Christians in the West experience a fundamental challenge to disengage their faith from captivity to a pervasive secular and modern cultural tradition. They therefore look with hope and interest to churches that demonstrate in their lives dimensions of relation with Christ that may have been filtered out in Western Christianity or never fully received. On the other hand, some Christians in parts of Asia are drawn particularly to dimensions of Christian faith that are lifted up in its Western developments, while taking for granted certain elements that they bring into their own Christianity from their cultural background. Both are finding something new and transformative to expand their existing practice of Christianity. The ecumenical challenge is to seek the unity in such expansion.

33. It is a similar story for the mass conversions to Buddhism in India in this century, under the influence of Ambedkar.
34. See (Thomas, 1970).

We should also point out that this trinitarian dynamic has a profound ethical and moral dimension. A number of theologians have highlighted this point.[35] There is a trinitarian practice as well as trinitarian doctrine. That practice focuses intensely on the nature and quality of relationships, personal and social. The triune communion in the divine life and the human communion which responds to it provide the distinctive Christian sources for ethics. "Reconciliation" is sometimes used as a virtual synonym for salvation, indicating that a peaceful resolution of conflict which respects and maintains human differences is an integral part of trinitarian practice.[36]

Whatever valid generic values interreligious dialogue may serve — reducing tensions, dispelling stereotypes, fostering friendship — there are specific Christian dynamics that commend it. Some of these are generic in a Christian way: love of neighbor, avoiding false witness, seeking reconciliation. These are ways Christians are called to live out their faith with all, and religious neighbors are particular examples of those to whom this love and respect is due. But I am pointing to something very specific about religions themselves and about the Christian need to encounter them in order to be faithful in "internal" Christian life, in order to grow into the full stature of Christ.

The Christ who is already present in all cultures, who has "gone before" the church's witness (as so many missionaries testify), is not there only for the salvation of others. Christ is there with more truth to be revealed to the church itself. The church cannot forget that it has a mission to the world. Nor should it forget that the world has a mission to the church and, specifically, that Christ has a mission to the church out of and through the world religions. These are all features of the divine economy, in which God strives to bring humans into communion with that diverse fullness of relation that characterizes God's nature.

We have stressed that an incarnational view of Jesus Christ, which is the catalyst for the doctrine of Trinity itself, leads via the Trinity to a recognition of the need to "fill up" the incarnational revelation of the Word through its appropriation in various cultural and religious contexts. This process presumes the presence and experience of God within these contexts. The Christian mission thus involves a "piecing together" of the unified action of the triune God. Although the ultimate framework for Christians always involves bringing all these elements into unity with Christ as the incarnate Word, this

---

35. (Moltmann, 1981; Boff, 1988; Cunningham, 1998).

36. See the interesting discussion of trinitarian practice in (Cunningham, 1998, Part Three).

cannot proceed without respect for, and in a certain sense submission to, the knowledge of God expressed in non-Christian traditions.

In this section we have emphasized what might be viewed as a selfish Christian interest in religions for the role they play in the path of Christian faith. The religions are more than a context for Christian confession. But it is important to remember that this engagement is lodged in the heart of Christian practice itself. Religious pluralism is not an esoteric and optional concern. Our review has also helped to clarify the continuity between the trinitarian shape of Christian mission and life and the trinitarian template which frames our theology of religions.

III

We will turn now to some contemporary Christian theologians who have built on this trinitarian framework to develop their own creative perspectives on religious diversity. The first of these is Raimundo Panikkar, the Roman Catholic theologian and cultural polymath, who has offered probably the most thought-provoking recent attempt to interpret the religions in trinitarian terms.[37] Deeply immersed in Hindu tradition, he writes out of a profound knowledge of India's religious history and with special concern for spiritual practice. His writing is allusive, thick with ideas and linguistic echoes of the many traditions he has studied.

Panikkar distinguishes three spiritualities which he observes in human religion. The first is what he calls "iconolatry" or the path of karma. In such spirituality, some image, icon, or concept serves as the focus and norm for religious practice, attracting, inspiring, and above all, directing the faithful. The characteristic elements of this approach are moral aspiration and a stimulus toward action to transform the world and the self. Desire to give religious practice a concrete worldly form is integral to iconolatry. Its temptation is idolatry, the adoration of false images. The second spirituality is personalism, a path of loving devotion. Relation to the divine is realized only in an intimate personal commitment. The characteristic features of such faith are experiences of mercy, joy, and ecstasy, an emphasis on worship as an act of passionate devotion. It thirsts for love, and its great temptation is anthropomorphism. The third spirituality is mysticism, a path of unitive knowledge. Its characteristic focus is forgetfulness of self, a realization of the divine that comes not through relation but identification. Its

---

37. See especially (Panikkar, 1973; Panikkar, 1987).

thirst is for a "not-two-ness," and its temptation is an indifference to the phenomenal world.

These three spiritualities are described in terms such that they may be recognized in many various religious contexts. Panikkar claims that only a trinitarian concept of reality permits a synthesis of the three spiritualities, a reconciliation of their apparently irreducible concepts of the Absolute.[38] "The Trinity, then, may be considered as a junction where authentic spiritual dimensions of all religions meet."[39] And Panikkar is clear that the trinitarian "concept" has these qualities because it rightly describes a divine trinitarian reality. The Trinity "is the acme of a truth that permeates all realms of being and consciousness. . . ."[40] At the same time, however, Panikkar denies that the Trinity is the unique property of Christianity. "It simply is an unwarranted overstatement to affirm that the trinitarian concept of the Ultimate, and with it the whole of reality, is an exclusive Christian insight or revelation."[41]

This approach is marked on one hand by the insistence that the Trinity, a feature of Christian faith, is the context in which religious diversity must be understood. On the other hand, Panikkar maintains that this Trinity is hardly understood by Christianity, and that a real appreciation of it impels Christians constantly out beyond what has constituted "Christian religion" historically or has been the exclusive Christian religious experience. So he says, "the faith I wish to call christian, though others may prefer to call it simply human, leads to the *plenitude* and hence to the *conversion* of all religion, even though to date it has only succeeded from a Judaic substructure in converting to some extent helleno-latin-gothic-celtic 'paganism.'"[42] And he says that the distinctive Christian perspectives are in the end "humanity's common good and that Christianity simply incarnates the primordial and original traditions of humankind."[43] In short, Christianity is not wrong to think of the triune God and the Christ it worships as the fulfillment and culmination of all religion. But it is wrong to think that Christianity has any privileged relation to them. To put it the other way around, the divine reality and truth that Christians know is also authentically grasped in other religions, but Christians rightly witness to the particularly Christian revelation of it.

In Panikkar's view Christians are right to understand all religious truth through the prism of the unique revelation in Christ. But precisely because

---

38. (Panikkar, 1973, p. 41).
39. (Panikkar, 1973, p. 42).
40. (Panikkar, 1973, p. xi).
41. (Panikkar, 1973, p. viii).
42. (Panikkar, 1973, p. 4).
43. (Panikkar, 1987, p. 102).

this universal claim is *true*, the very universality of the "christic principle" it confesses means that all concrete, particular "Christianness" stands in need of radical expansion and supplementation to approach the fullness of what it confesses. Exclusivism is a collapse into an absolutization of the inadequate forms that have *so far* been the most revelatory for us. Popular pluralisms (contending all religions are equivalent) are dilutions that remove the saving properties from each faith. We must seek to include the valid truth in all religions within our particular religion's defining framework, a framework which we must confess remains itself largely mysterious to us. In this process, what is particular will become increasingly universal.

Panikkar's own use of "Trinity" in his entire project is the supreme illustration of the dynamic we have just described. He uses the Christian understanding of Trinity as the fundamental organizing, ontological description of all reality. As Rowan Williams has written, "his stance is paradoxical at first sight. It involves a clear commitment to a distinctive vision of what unifies reality, and a clear option about the nature of God; but the more deeply we enter into that vision, the more we are able to see it as the ground for a nonexclusive dialogue with other visions."[44] He is sometimes criticized from a "pluralistic" side for the Christian particularity of his framework. And he is often accused from the more conservative Christian side of making of "Trinity" something that comes unmoored from its specific formulations in Christian tradition, its specific roots in the historical Christ. Panikkar believes that theological reflection and spiritual life can be stretched to cover this distance, remaining authentically rooted in concrete particularity at one end and touching true universality at the other.

He is further convinced that there are a number of ways this can be done. But each of them is "further on and deeper in," that is, further along the path and further into the life of a *specific* religious tradition. So, for example, Panikkar says that "in the Trinity a place is found for whatever in religion is not simply the particular deposit of a given age or culture."[45] This is at once an extraordinary totalizing and inclusive Christian claim *and* an agenda that promises to remake the existing particular expressions of Christianity beyond ready recognition. A radically evangelical, mission-oriented Christian may propose that we will hardly recognize the church once it has been rooted and has flourished in all the diverse "unreached" cultures of the world. And a radically pluralistic, dialogue-oriented Christian may propose that we will hardly recognize the church once it has recognized and honored the validity in other

44. (Williams, 1990, p. 12).
45. (Panikkar, 1973, p. 43).

religious traditions. Panikkar seems to suggest that they may both be quite right, and about the same church!

To follow this one step further, we must consider Panikkar's treatment of the persons of the Trinity. A key is Panikkar's distinctive treatment of the person of the "Father." As the uncreated, unoriginated source, the first person of the Trinity is defined by a relation to the second person, and this relation is one of *kenosis*. The Father or source gives and transmits everything to the Son or Word. The Father "is not," for even the being of the Father has been transmitted to the Son as gift. This is what Panikkar calls the "cross in the Trinity" or the "integral immolation of God of which the Cross of Christ and his immolation are only the images and revelations."[46] Nothing, literally, can be said of the Father "in himself," for in begetting the Son the Father gives up everything, "even the possibility of being expressed in a name that names him alone."[47]

Early trinitarian formulae speak of "God, Christ, and Spirit." Panikkar points out that this is to speak of the same God three times: God, Son of God, Spirit of God. But in fact, we can speak the "first time" only in terms of the next two. If we have seen the Son, we have seen the Father. No one can come to the Father but through the Son in the Spirit. Panikkar pushes this point very hard. The first way to speak of God is, literally, silence. The Father cannot be spoken of except through the Son, as the Son cannot be "begotten" apart from the Father. To say that the two mutually imply each other is to say what trinitarian orthodoxy has always held. Likewise, to say that each implies the other in a way unique to itself (the Father is not the Son and the Son not the Father; the relation between them is asymmetrical, one begetting and one begotten) is also very traditional doctrine.

Panikkar strikes a new note by affirming that whenever we speak of the Father we are actually talking about the Son. The Son is what we concretely mean when we use the word "God" to refer to the divine. We cannot know the Father and the Son side by side, as it were, but only as two sides of a single coin: the Son as the making visible of the Father, the Father as the invisibility of the Son. Panikkar supports his argument by appeal to much traditional language about the incarnation of the divine Word making visible the invisible God. On the other hand, Panikkar's thesis would seem to imply that the incarnate Son's talk about God was in fact simply self-reference, which appears to be something of a trinitarian short circuit.

Panikkar says humans can have a personal relation only with the Son, and

46. (Panikkar, 1973, p. 46).
47. (Panikkar, 1973, p. 46).

that therefore in fact the God of theism *is* the Son. It seems Panikkar is saying that the Father is God "without qualities" and the Son is God "with qualities," and it is the Son who is manifest in Christ. However, "Christ" fundamentally means the link, the mediator between created and uncreated. This link and mediator, this sole "Lord," may be called by other names in other religions: isvara, tathagata, Allah, or even Yahweh.[48] Panikkar does not presuppose that Christ must always be identified with Jesus of Nazareth. Christ, who links God and the world, does this linking in many places without association with Jesus of Nazareth. And yet Panikkar does seem to claim that though the linking need not be done in the guise of Jesus, yet the one who does the linking is himself most fully revealed in Jesus. Panikkar says "the claim of the church is not that she is *the* religion for the whole of mankind but that she is the place where Christ is fully revealed, the end and plenitude of every religion."[49]

For Panikkar true transcendence (the Father) cannot be revealed, for then it would not be transcendent. It is revealed only as the invisibility above the revealer, the depth of emptiness behind God. This aspect of his thought is very similar to the apophatic emphasis of Eastern Orthodoxy. Likewise, true immanence cannot be revealed: if we could separate out what is immanent, it would no longer be so. To be immanent is to be truly united, present within another: an invisibility of identity. For Panikkar, this is the case with the Spirit. The Holy Spirit is the "we," the bond of unity between Father and Son, the bond between the spirituality of emptiness and the spirituality of images.

The only connection we can have with the Spirit is that of non-relational union. We don't pray to the Spirit; we are *in* the Spirit. When the *Upanishads* say that *atman* is identical with *Brahman*, they mean by *atman* what Panikkar means by Spirit. It is a consciousness of identity with supreme reality. This consciousness cannot be cloaked with the categories of person or relation. The only connection we can have with the Father is an indirect one. Like Kant's thing-in-itself, we never directly know the Father, but only some icon representing the Father. The mediator (the Son, the Logos, God with qualities) connects these two: the divine transcendence we can "know" only as emptiness and the divine immanence we can know only by identity. Since we can know the mediator by direct devotion, by relation or perception, this offers a third way to know the one divine reality.

This means that the Trinity offers a "dazzling, almost blinding revelation of the fullness of the divine mystery."[50] Panikkar believes world religions

48. (Panikkar, 1973, p. 54).
49. (Panikkar, 1973, p. 55).
50. (Panikkar, 1973, p. 55).

have not taken enough notice of Trinity, as the full elucidation of the divine mystery. Therefore he builds his whole theology of religions around it. Yet the differentiation provided by the trinitarian schema has its drawbacks. He says religious traditions lacking such a schema have preserved "in their experience of the Absolute a kind of trinitarian indiscrimination. But is it not precisely this that has allowed them to maintain sometimes a perhaps more satisfactory equilibrium between these three essential dimensions of every spirituality that we have described above and that we may sum up as apophatism, personalism, and divine immanence?"[51] In other words, Panikkar implies that by *not* distinguishing the three persons as sharply as Christians do, other traditions may be less likely to fixate on one. Yet some clarity about the distinctions is crucial for true unity of the religions.

So Panikkar concludes that

> it is in the trinitarian possibilities of the world religions, in the striving of each in its own fashion towards the synthesis of these spiritual attitudes, that the meeting of religions — the kairos of our time — finds its deepest inspiration and most certain hope.[52]

All the religions are striving (or should be) for a trinitarian synthesis. This synthesis would link a spirituality of the silent, empty God behind God (the Father who has given all to the Son, in Panikkar's terms), a spirituality of a personal deity (the Son who manifests God), and a spirituality of mystical union, forgetful of all distinction (the Spirit as the bond between the two). Panikkar can describe this synthesis poetically and at dazzling (if rather cloudy) length.[53]

Panikkar is suggestive and concise in his description of the limitations (he calls them the characteristic heresies) of each of these spiritualities taken alone. He says contemporary atheists who reject the "god-idol" are advocates of a spirituality directed toward the Father, but "severed from the living trinity."[54] Looking behind the icons of God, atheists bear witness that there is nothing there to see. Panikkar sees some Buddhists as representing a similar insight: the ultimate mystery is empty, and talk or thought of it is nonsense. The characteristic heresy of the spirituality of the Father is nihilism. This is a thirst for the absolute that is itself so absolute that it rejects all intermediates, all forms which might yet be surpassed. It has the virtue of

51. (Panikkar, 1973, p. 55).
52. (Panikkar, 1973, p. 55).
53. See (Panikkar and Eastham, 1993).
54. (Panikkar, 1973, p. 78).

critiquing idols. The truly transcendent is not anything we can conceive. No one can see the Father. Nihilism moves from the truth that nothing we can fully grasp can be absolute, to the false conclusion that the absolute is literally nothing. To Panikkar, nihilism is the mistake that comes from reading the "emptiness" of the first person of the Trinity in a literal and isolated way. In fact this emptiness is not a static absence of being, but a dynamic, relational fact: the emptiness exists because being has been poured out from the first person to the second.

The spirituality of the Son can fall into mere anthropocentrism, in which some historical manifestation of God is taken as identical with God. This characteristic heresy Panikkar calls "humanism." The absolute has been poured out into concrete being, even human being, even the physical and historical dimensions of human being. This staggering, incarnational truth can be isolated in an anthropocentric way, and so result in simple naturalism. If nihilism smashes all possible idols, including finally our own humanity, humanism insists our idols are all there is. If nihilism insists that transcendent being is simply unreal, ignoring the fact that it has "gone out" in relation with the world, then humanism ignores the fact that concrete being has come from beyond itself and is rooted in transcendence. Nihilism insists there must be something higher than any entity that could be an idol. And finally it appears that the only category that will fill this bill is "nothing." Humanism insists that our concrete idols must be the height of reality. The occasional practical convergence of the two outlooks should not, in Panikkar's view, obscure the different paths they represent.

The third characteristic heresy is "angelism," the distortion of the spirituality of the Spirit. This is a rejection of everything creaturely or of any self that is subject to historical contingency. Such a spirituality identifies the self with pure spirit. The interiority and unitive consciousness of such spirituality shields it from the two pitfalls we have just mentioned. The tension between icon and absolute is collapsed not by one eclipsing the other but by a unification of the two. The result, Panikkar says, is the error of pantheism, which assumes a static identification of our being with divine being. The immanence of the Spirit becomes a flat fact rather than an active indwelling. In trinitarian terms, the Spirit relates and connects two persons that are truly distinct. It is a real bridge of love, because there is a real history and future of relation. Even for the trinitarian persons, this unity is a continually reenacted relation, not an inert fact that is repeatedly discerned. Angelism views even the distinction of creator and creation itself as a distraction from a permanent and perfect identity. Panikkar says that the claim to such an identity will always have to proceed through a disdain for the body, a truth reflected in the common connotation of "spirituality" as a word that refers to a path of perfection that forgets the body.

As we have seen, Panikkar's distinctive way of treating these questions is to stress the dynamic of self-giving among the triune persons. The Father gives away everything, even being and name, to the Son. This makes the first person of the Trinity the ground of apophatic transcendence, a well of emptiness. Except through the Son, there is literally no Father to know. The divinity that the Father "gives up" is manifested concretely in the Son. The Spirit is the divine immanence, by which this divinity dwells in the Son and is returned completely to the Father. The Spirit abides in both. Panikkar says the Father has no name of his own because he is beyond every name. There is only the Son, or "God" as the name of the manifestation of this "beyond." And the Spirit has no name of its own because it is fully immanent in the mutual giving of the other two persons.

Humans can contact the divine as the radical emptiness of the Father or the radical immanence of the Spirit, as well as the personal "other" who is the Word. Relation to God as the first person of the Trinity can only authentically be a plunge into an apophatic emptiness. Relation with the Spirit is realized only in a kind of atman/Brahman identification. Relation with the Word is realized in a number of various "icons" of God, of which Jesus Christ is the paradigmatic instance. In Panikkar's scheme it seems that human beings can have only impersonal relations with the first and third persons of the Trinity; personal relation is reserved for contact with the incarnational Word. This might seem to imply that a direct personal relation with Father and Spirit was out of the question even for the historical Jesus, the incarnate Word, despite all the New Testament indications to the contrary.

Panikkar's approach is similar to that of some other Indian Christian theologians who correlate God the Father with *nirguna Brahman* (Brahman without qualities) and God the Son with *saguna Brahman* (Brahman with qualities).[55] He firmly resists the traditional Hindu priority for *nirguna Brahman*, and instead argues in favor of co-equality. Panikkar's treatment of the Trinity is notable for its refusal to regard the personal and the relational as secondary, as only "economic," as is so natural for Advaita Vedanta to do, for instance. But it is interesting to consider the differences between the Trinity as Panikkar views it and as many recent theologians view it.[56] The simplest way

55. For a very sophisticated and detailed exposition of this approach see (von Bruck, 1991).

56. Notably (Zizioulas, 1985; LaCugna, 1991). This will be pursued further in the next chapter.

to put this is to say that for Panikkar person and personal relation are one feature of the Trinity, but are not strictly to be applied to more than one of the three divine persons. For these other theologians the most basic key to the Trinity is the "ontology of personhood," the personal character of each of the three and of their relations with each other, all of which are mutually implied. The Trinity is a communion of persons whose personhood is constituted by their communion with each other.

Though the richness of Panikkar's exposition makes it hard to simplify, there is clearly a tendency for him to associate different types of religion, different "spiritualities," with the different persons of the Trinity.[57] Apophatism is the spirituality of the Father, monism the spirituality of the Spirit, and theism is the spirituality of the Son. Christianity has a unique, universal witness to the religions in its testimony that Trinity is the only way in which these spiritualities can all be validated and integrated. On the other hand, Christianity itself is helpless to realize that integration apart from the religions, whose contributions to this ultimate synthesis will explode any form of Christianity as we have known it. In Panikkar's work these two go hand in hand. One of the many virtues of his thought is the way in which he seamlessly integrates the "internal" theological dynamic we discussed in the last section (mission to other religions as a necessary condition for Christians' fuller understanding of the particular revelation in Christ) with the concern for the religions themselves (their witness to their own particularity will increasingly "convert" Christianity into something less alien to them and less bound by the Christian past).

Ninian Smart and Steven Konstantine offer a different approach to a trinitarian theology of religions in their book *Christian Systematic Theology in a World Context*.[58] Smart is an Anglican and a distinguished scholar of world religions. Konstantine is a Greek Orthodox theologian. Konstantine and Smart (hereafter KS) are ardent advocates for the "social Trinity," stressing the distinctive individual qualities of the three divine persons and the way the communion of the three persons constitutes the divine nature.

One of the distinctive and helpful features of KS's thought is their argument that this active communion among the three persons is expressed in three aspects of the divine life. These aspects are not divided, one to a person.

57. It is interesting that one set of spiritualities Panikkar describes (iconolatry, personalism, mysticism) does not correspond exactly with the set he provides in his discussion of the trinitarian persons: apophatism (Father), theism (Son) and monism (Spirit). To some extent these can be mixed (there is a mystical type of monism and a mystical type of apophatism, for instance).

58. (Smart and Konstantine, 1991).

It is very important to grasp that KS are not, as Panikkar was, associating different spiritualities with different persons of the Trinity. Instead, KS are talking about three dimensions of the divine life that exist *because* God is triune, but that do not belong to one person as opposed to another. These dimensions are generated by the shared life of the three persons together. The first dimension is what they call the infinity of the divine life as it circulates through the three persons. This is something like the life processes within an organism, the circulation of blood, the network of the nervous system. There is a constant mutual exchange, giving and receiving. One cannot say of any living being that the "life process" is specifically isolated here or there. It is active in all parts of the organism. KS prefer this image of the oneness of the Trinity to the notion of a single divine substance, which seems to imply a material, uniform "stuff" distributed among the three persons. The second aspect of the triune life they describe is the plurality of the three persons themselves, and their relations with each other. KS are unequivocally in favor of viewing the triune persons as three distinct centers of consciousness, despite the opposition of many theologians and charges of tritheism.[59] God has a dimension that can rightly be viewed as "social." The third dimension is the common will or the collective "I" of the Trinity, according to which God acts with perfect unity of purpose. This corresponds to the classic theological principle that holds all the external acts of the Trinity are undivided.

The first and third aspects may be grasped by partial analogy to a human being, where there is a "physiological" unity at the organic level (of the circulatory system, for instance), and an integrative unity of a different sort in the individual's personal consciousness. This analogy raises an obvious problem with the second aspect of the divine life that KS describe. The three divine persons are much more distinct relational foci within the divine life than any analogy with a single human person can suggest. With humans, we could only speak of relations among cells or organs or psychological faculties as constitutive. We have to move to the interpersonal or community level to find analogy for the second aspect of the divine life, and it is this social analogy that leads to the title "social Trinity" for those formulations that stress this aspect.

These three aspects of divine life indicate three different kinds of unity in the Trinity. The first dimension is a somewhat impersonal unity of process. The second is an interpersonal unity, a "social" unity of distinct different persons. The third dimension is the internal unity of a single center of consciousness. The relation between the second and the third dimen-

59. (Smart and Konstantine, 1991, pp. 168-69).

sions can be viewed from two sides. On one side, we might think of the single "I" of the godhead as a kind of super-consciousness that arises from the three persons being "of one mind." On the other side we could think of the three persons as distinct "organs" within one consciousness, rather like one software program running on a network of three linked processors. KS may incline toward the first approach, but trinitarian doctrine holds both types of analogy in tension.

KS stress that the first dimension is non-relational, while the other two are relational in distinctly different ways: one focused on relations *within* the Trinity among the three persons and the other focused on relations of the Trinity as one God with creation. The Trinity thus encompasses impersonal as well as personal aspects. Taken by itself, the first aspect, the infinite divine life, can be encountered as an impersonal reality. It is an infinite transcendence, an ordered if mysterious flux, just as the organic processes of a human body might appear to us if were we infinitesimal specks within it. All of the exchange and "give and take" have the character of a dynamic and transcendent structure far above us. Externally apprehended, this infinite can be given "rather impersonal descriptions, such as Tao, *Dharmakaya*, Emptiness."[60] Such external apprehension can give rise to an experience characteristic of Taoism and Zen Buddhism.

Internally apprehended, in forms of meditation and contemplation, this divine infinity can be experienced as a simple unity, a non-dual absolute. Since the divine life sustains all creatures through immanence, including immanence in us, this aspect of the triune life can be perceived at the "bottom" of our own subjective consciousness. This discovery can have the quality of an illumination, breaking through the illusion of the world's outward appearance. This fundamental aspect of the divine life is "in, with, and under" all aspects of the world, since God sustains the world. Whether the apprehension is external or internal, there is no sense of relation to a particular divine entity. There is no sense of a personal encounter at all, since this aspect of the triune life is not itself personal.

KS note that this reality and its experience can be given rather different religious interpretations. A more minimalist interpretation of this transcendence appears in *Theravada* Buddhism. Here perfect internal apprehension of this divine infinity in a permanent state of non-dual consciousness is simply the final state of liberation, requiring no further reference. The Hindu Advaita Vedanta tradition can regard this experience as realization of oneness with an impersonal Brahman. *Mahayana* Buddhists have still different characteriza-

60. (Smart and Konstantine, 1991, p. 174).

tions.[61] In the dominant nonpersonal Buddhist interpretations and in Advaita Vedanta the contemplative experience contains affective states of bliss and peace. KS write, "We suggest these are also experiences of the Holy Spirit who ... is characterized by such states."[62] They suggest that the sense of timelessness and permanence in these experiences, giving rise to the notion there is an unchanging transcendent state beyond the flux of events in this world, derives from the inexhaustibility and stability of the divine life processes in the Trinity.

KS say that "our account enables us to show how the *Theravadins* can experience the transcendent (or an aspect of the Trinity from our perspective), but without having to characterize it in terms foreign to their own understanding."[63] They point out that some Christians have argued that what Buddhists actually experience is the unity of their own souls, while some Hindus argue that Buddhists come to experience the absolute Self, Brahman. Such interpretations are deeply contrary to Buddhist tradition, since "souls" and "Self" are precisely what that tradition teaches is not involved. KS suggest that it is an advantage that "our more complex view of the transcendent (as the Trinity) contains an element which taken by itself can quite reasonably be interpreted in the Buddhist minimalist manner."[64] This is a crucial point, and it exhibits one of the great strengths of KS's vision. Their exposition of trinitarian doctrine makes it clear that they can regard this *Theravadin* religious claim as substantively true, and true in the very categories that it is advanced. They are not compelled to deny that claim or (much the same thing) to affirm it in a form reinterpreted past all recognition by those who make the claim. But they also do not give up their own distinctively different understanding of the divine, and the claim that this vision is ultimately more accurate. From Chapter One onward, I have suggested that these are precisely some of the qualities we should seek in a theology of religions. KS have taken a dramatic step toward meeting that job description.

KS contrast the Trinity with two Hindu analogues. The first is *Satcitananda,* a designation for the divine very common in the Advaita Vedanta tradition. The trio of qualities it summarizes — being, consciousness, and bliss — characterize the single ultimately undefinable entity, Brahman. The second analogue is the triumvirate of deities, *Brahma, Shiva,*

---

61. In *Mahayana* Buddhism the internal *dhyanic* experience is subject to different interpretations. The more common Buddhist view takes the ultimate as nonpersonal ("emptiness"). But in traditions such as Pure Land and *Shingon* there is a turn toward a view of the ultimate as personal in some arguably non-reductive sense.

62. (Smart and Konstantine, 1991, p. 175).

63. (Smart and Konstantine, 1991, p. 175).

64. (Smart and Konstantine, 1991, p. 175).

Vishnu. From an Advaita Vedantan perspective, these both are only conventional and surpassable symbols for the great oneness behind them. The three deities are a cruder representation, appropriate to the practices of theistic devotion. They express three modes of action, not three "members" of an abiding trinity. And even "action" itself is problematic, as associated with the absolute. The three qualities of *sat, cit,* and *ananda* are more refined representations, appropriate to contemplative insight. But they too are only external forms cast on the absolute, which in its simplicity and unity is beyond them. There are three levels then, moving from the One as it is, to an instrumental representation as *Satcitananda,* to the yet cruder and more personalized deities with their diverse characteristics.

In a similar way, KS contrast Trinity with the later *Mahayana Trikaya* or "Three Aspect Doctrine." This doctrine distinguishes the truth aspect of the Buddha as an impersonal ultimate which at lower levels is manifest in visions in the form of celestial Buddhas (an enjoyment aspect) and at still lower levels is manifest in the historical Buddha (the transformation aspect). Clearly, KS say, this is a hierarchical order, which regards the personal aspects as more imperfect or clouded representations of reality. By contrast, they say, "We do not accept this kind of priority in the Trinity doctrine, which we see as synthesizing both personal and non-personal aspects all at the one level."[65]

We have been discussing the first of the three dimensions of the Trinity that KS identify, the "infinity of the divine life as it circulates through the selfless spirits" of the three persons.[66] For KS, this infinity of the divine life is one source of unity in the Trinity. Western theology has referred to this impersonal principle of unity as the divine substance, or essence. KS's third dimension provides another principle of unity. This is the single, common divine consciousness, the divine "I." The unity among the three persons constitutes a true common will and identity, so that the acts of God in creation and with creatures are actually of one piece. KS say that this single divine consciousness is the personal "God," the pure "thou" encountered through relational devotion within various religions, from *bhakti* Hinduism to Pure Land Buddhism to Hasidism to Sikhism to Methodism.[67] It lies at the base of the numinous experiences of prophets and shamans. "Contact with the Trinity in its unity accounts for these events: even if those who have such experience may not know that they are also in contact with the divine three-foldness."[68]

---

65. (Smart and Konstantine, 1991, p. 176).
66. (Smart and Konstantine, 1991, p. 174).
67. (Smart and Konstantine, 1991, p. 176).
68. (Smart and Konstantine, 1991, p. 176).

This brings us to KS's second dimension of the Trinity's life, the interactions among the three distinct persons. This dimension presupposes an ontological as well as economic Trinity. KS do not provide a concentrated and clear explanation of what direct encounter with this dimension of the Trinity looks like in religious experience, though we will say more about that in a moment. They make two very clear arguments for the ontological and social Trinity. The first is that only such a complex divine nature, which generates these diverse dimensions, can account inclusively for varieties of valid religious experience. It is the real diversity of divine persons that allows us to "embrace the phenomenology of religious experience worldwide and so give an account of other religious traditions which sees them too as containing apprehension of the same Transcendent we have depicted in this discussion."[69] On this basis we can say "The other world religions have apprehension of differing facets of the Trinity."[70] The second argument, to which we will return below, maintains that only real relations among the persons makes possible God's great venture to come into creation under the conditions set for all other creatures.

KS think it naïve to believe "that all traditions and subtraditions have an equally valid (or invalid) version of the nature of the one reality."[71] They affirm that the social Trinity is the true divine reality at the center of the world's religions, able to "fulfill both non-personal and personal aspirations among adherents of other faiths."[72] It is precisely the desire to recognize truth in the widest variety of religious claims that points toward the specific characterization of God which Trinity provides. It meets the need more effectively and plausibly than a great, hazy, and unknown reality beyond any description. In their view, this definitive and exclusive claim has no necessary implications for salvation. Those who do not share the trinitarian vision may be closer to God than those who do. KS believe in a universal salvation in any event. They affirm that in some way the variety of religions stem from a divine plan for mutual criticism and correction.

Let us return to the connection between the second dimension of the Trinity and Christian belief and experience. KS say that this dimension explains why Christians believe Jesus transcends the categories other traditions naturally apply to him. A trinitarian God creates creatures for enduring relationship, in reflection of the eternal relations of the divine life. This means

69. (Smart and Konstantine, 1991, pp. 177-78).
70. (Smart and Konstantine, 1991, p. 290).
71. (Smart and Konstantine, 1991, p. 297).
72. (Smart and Konstantine, 1991, p. 296).

that the humanity of Christ has a permanent character. In Hinduism there is no clear dividing line between human and divine. Not only avatars, but gurus are seen as divine. And in the vision of transmigration, different bodies temporarily manifest the same karmic stream of action and effect. Identity, historicity, relation, and personhood are thus all secondary and inessential categories for understanding Jesus. He is easily comprehensible as one who realized perfect consciousness of his identity with the absolute Brahman. From such a perspective, there can be no place in Jesus' life for a *bhakti* relation with God, for suffering, for historical and physical human particularity, except as part of an external pedagogical façade for the benefit of those at lower spiritual stages.[73] Real relation-in-true-difference has no place in the divine reality, nor in any consciousness that is in true union with that reality. Christians affirm just the opposite on these points, because they believe Christ is rooted in a triune God.

KS explain that similar considerations set Christ apart from the multiplicity of *bodhisattvas* or from the transformation body of an earthly Buddha.[74] The manifestation of a celestial being like the great Buddha *Amitabha*, accessible to humanity in visions and meditation, is surely real enough to the eye of a faithful beholder. But it fades into vacuity when one has higher knowledge of universal emptiness. Earthly Buddhas preach and exemplify the *dharma*. But once the *dharma* is grasped, the Buddhas may be left aside. There is a tendency in these traditions to take states of consciousness as central, and to view the worth of ideas, beings, and relations in terms of their capacity to affect consciousness. Thus many regard celestial Buddhas and *bodhisattvas* essentially as objects of meditation. Their existence or nonexistence is neither here nor there. This is often urged as a great advantage for Buddhism, since the "non-reality" of such figures removes them from the messiness of history and preserves devotees from all the distractions endemic to relation with historical figures or to relations of any sort. A vast range of epistemological and historical questions simply become irrelevant. There are similarities in the self-sacrificial love of *bodhisattvas* and the selfless love of Christ, but KS suggest they are embedded in different schemes and cannot be equated. This difference has a positive side, for if *avatars* and *bodhisattvas* are profound figments of the meditating religious imagination on its way to enlightenment, then KS suggest that they do not represent alternatives to the historical Christ. The two may coexist, with distinctively different roles.

73. For a thorough and sensitive exploration of this issue see (Thangaraj and Kaufman, 1994).

74. (Smart and Konstantine, 1991, p. 257).

KS argue that in the activity of creation, the triune God practices a threefold *kenosis*.[75] First, God "contracts" by restricting the totally free use of omnipotence in order to create a stable background for creation's freedom. Providing a universe of impersonal natural law, God enacts what we might call a kenosis of the Father. Second, God leaves individuals the freedom to learn and struggle through to their own identities, gives up the ability to directly determine individual consciousness. This we might call a kenosis of the Holy Spirit. This forms a complement to the first "contraction." If God puts aside the option of acting with total freedom as an *external* agent to determine events in the world, God also puts aside the power to be an absolute determinative *internal* agent, controlling individual's choices and desires. Finally, in Christ, God puts aside the privilege of living "outside" the conditions established by the first two acts of kenosis and becomes a creature under those conditions. This is the kenosis of the Word. God practices full communion with the creature.

KS note that some think Christianity is the most problematic of the monotheisms, because we can logically defend a unitary first mover of some sort more easily than a triune God. But they argue that Trinity proves more cogent.[76] If God is almighty but wishes free creatures, it seems some kind of kenosis is required to make space for them. And if that freedom involves suffering, then God ought to be willing to share the burden of the conditions God has created. But this is impossible unless there is complexity or "division" in God. A simple God would be barred from this depth of communion. The threefold kenosis KS describe requires a triune God. As a division of persons is necessary for incarnation, so a third person is necessary for the divine bond of love that holds the divine unity in place even through such kenosis. Thus, they maintain, the Trinity is in fact the simplest possible condition for resolving this problem. Were it merely a contrived solution, it would not be a fully authentic expression of God's own character and being. Therefore they claim that the "solution" is intrinsic to God, and that creation itself reflects and prefigures it.

Such kenosis also explains why perfect clarity of revelation is precluded. Under the conditions of God's "contraction," a pure and obvious manifestation of God, one that makes humans plainly culpable for their lack of full knowledge, is impossible. The space that God opens between God and creation assures creation's own freedom. But it necessarily serves also as a screen through which God can communicate with the world only in terms that leave

---

75. (Smart and Konstantine, 1991, see pp. 244f.).
76. (Smart and Konstantine, 1991, p. 244).

that freedom in place, and therefore in terms that cannot be indisputable. As a result, the diversity of claimed religious truth is something implied in the nature of creation itself.

In sum, KS hold that non-Christian world religions "have apprehension of differing facets of the Trinity."[77] Bhakti or devotional theism apprehends the "divine I" of the Trinity. The infinite divine life which "circulates" among the three persons can be apprehended at the base of our own existence, through meditation that leads to forms of non-dual, impersonal consciousness. It is thus divine *process* and not the divine "I" that is apprehended. This perception can be taken in two different ways, either as an insight into the emptiness of all being (which privileges apprehension of the divine kenosis) or as an insight into identity with the divine (since the divine process incorporates me). The pattern of Christian religious experience, centered on Christ, reflects the divine acts of kenosis that require three distinct persons. The social Trinity known in Christian revelation, KS contend, proves able to "fulfill both non-personal and personal aspirations among adherents of other faiths."[78] KS do not expand on this last phrase. They unequivocally affirm universal salvation, but they do not directly address the nature of salvation in terms of other proposed religious ends. They explain that the Trinity allows for a variety of valid religious experiences, but seem to assume that it allows for only one religious end.

These brief reviews do not do full justice to Panikkar or to Smart and Konstantine. But they give us a glimpse of two creative contemporary attempts to apply trinitarian thought to the religions. Both demonstrate that the Trinity provides a matrix within which Christians can recognize distinctively different religious practice as relation with God. Though there are many similarities in the two approaches, they diverge in at least two notable ways. Panikkar, as I noted, tends to identify various religious options with specific persons of the Trinity. KS move in a different and I think even more fruitful direction. They outline dimensions of the life of God that stem from the triune nature but which are not identified exclusively with individual persons. God has these dimensions by virtue of being triune, by virtue of the communion among the persons. The dimensions are not parceled out one to a person. On the other hand, Panikkar gives more attention and weight to the separate and distinct spiritualities within the trinitarian framework. Consistent with the whole tenor of his thought, his outlook at this point is more pluralistic than KS. Panikkar sights down the path of each of these spiritualities

77. (Smart and Konstantine, 1991, p. 290).
78. (Smart and Konstantine, 1991, p. 296).

as far as one can see, and stresses that they remain unique. They have their own integrity. At least by implication, Panikkar contemplates the religions as parallel paths, leading to distinct ends. KS assume universalism. They see that various religions may tune themselves to different aspects of the Trinity, but they hold that religions all lead to a single end.

I have highlighted features in these writers that are very suggestive for our project, and left aside others.[79] I believe that some of the insights they develop can be extended and deepened if we add explicit consideration of varied religious fulfillments. In the next chapter, we will build on their work to fill out our own trinitarian theology of religious ends.

79. So, for instance, I do not accept the large gap Panikkar introduces between Jesus Christ and a Christic principle of which he is an exemplification (perhaps *the* exemplification). Nor do I agree with KS's conclusions that the religions can enrich each other but that they do not offer substantive alternatives to each other.

Chapter Five

The Riches of the Glory:
Trinity and Religious Ends

The last chapter surveyed Trinity as the general Christian framework for understanding religious diversity and reviewed two trinitarian theologies of religion. We saw that Trinity is a non-reductive religious ultimate, in whom the three persons and their unique relations subsist as co-equal dimensions of a single communion. This is like a musical polyphony, a simultaneous, non-excluding harmony of difference that constitutes one unique reality. Each voice has its own distinctive character by virtue of its relation with the others. We can equally well say that each receives its special voice by participation in the oneness of the whole musical work.

Since Trinity is constituted by an enduring set of relations, the divine life has varied dimensions. So human interaction with the triune God may take different forms. It is impossible to believe in the Trinity *instead* of the distinctive religious claims of all other religions. If Trinity is real, then many of these *specific* religious claims and ends must be real also. If they were all false, then Christianity could not be true. The universal and exclusive quality of Christian confession is the claim to allow the fullest assimilation of permanently co-existing truths. The Trinity is a map that finds room for, indeed requires, concrete truth in other religions.

In this chapter I will develop some fuller specification of the trinitarian framework and the way it provides for the recognition of multiple religious ends. The distinctive religious ends of various traditions correspond to relations with God constituted by limitation or intensification within a particular dimension of the trinitarian life.[1] This provides the basis both to affirm the reality of these religious ends and to distinguish them from salvation. Salvation, as communion with the triune God, is multidimensional. This fact is crucial to Christian desire for this religious end, and to the disinterest and critique it elicits from other religious perspectives.

I

In recent years Western theology has seen a dramatic renewal of trinitarian theology.[2] This rich mix of retrieval and reflection provides crucial resources for our project. I would like to draw on one contribution that is particularly relevant to our topics, the work of John Zizioulas.[3] An Eastern Orthodox theologian, Zizioulas presents a view of the Trinity that emphasizes elements typically thought to reflect that tradition's divergence from common Western treatment of the doctrine. Some current scholarship suggests that this divergence is more presumed than real.[4] In any event, so-called "Eastern" motifs are in fact widely reclaimed in much of the current rethinking of the Trinity in Western theology.[5] Though I focus on Zizioulas, the primary features in our discussion are not peculiar to him or even to the Orthodox tradition but are common aspects of trinitarian theology, despite variations in terminology.[6]

Early Christian theologians were not primarily concerned with philosophy. But Zizioulas maintains that the doctrine of the Trinity introduced an extraordinary philosophical transformation. He makes two striking claims. The first is that the very vision of the human person we take for granted is bound up with the development of trinitarian doctrine. "The person both as

---

1. As we will see below, this may not be a matter of strict limitation to one dimension, with no recognition of others. It may also be an integration of dimensions in which one or more lose their co-equality and ultimately "collapse" the trinitarian dynamic.

2. See, for instance, (LaCugna, 1991; Schwobel and King's College. Research Institute in Systematic Theology, 1995). Significant recent works on Trinity include (Jungel, 1976; Hill, 1982; Jenson, 1982; Kasper, 1984; Boff, 1988; Moltmann, 1991; Lash, 1992; Gunton, 1993; Peters, 1993; Torrance, 1996; Cunningham, 1998).

3. (Zizioulas, 1985).

4. See (Barnes, 1995; Barnes, 1995). I am grateful to Sarah Coakley for alerting me to Barnes's work through her essay "'Persons' in the 'Social' Doctrine of the Trinity" (forthcoming in a volume from Oxford University Press edited by Gerald O'Collins), which also questions these categories.

5. See (LaCugna, 1991) for an approach from a Roman Catholic theologian which is very consistent with Zizioulas.

6. For convergence from a Reformed perspective, see (Torrance, 1985).

concept and as a living reality is purely the product of patristic thought. Without this, the deepest meaning of personhood can neither be grasped nor justified."[7] The second claim is that the Trinity introduces a genuinely new option in the severely limited list of possible ontologies or accounts of reality.

Those who study the history of the doctrine of the Trinity are familiar with a warning that appears regularly in the literature. They are cautioned that "person" (or the Greek word *hypostasis*), which early Christian writers chose to apply to the three divisions in the Trinity, did not at that time carry with it all the meaning we would now associate with it. Perhaps few stop to consider the significance of a related fact: there was then no notion of "person," as applied to a human being, which carried our common associations either. The important distinction is that while we think of a person by definition as a unique individual, constituted by difference, pre-trinitarian usage took *hypostasis* (as applied to humans) to refer precisely to what is common in human nature, the substantial underlying reality. To say I am *a* person is to say that I belong to a class of beings with the same qualities. The word does not imply (as later notions of "person" do) a unique, separate personality. What is particular about an individual is accidental to that identity-by-sameness. The differences between individuals amount to fringe variations like hair color (essentially irrelevant) or to defects, a failure to match the single normative mold (as with a speech impediment or a missing limb). The type of variation that seemed most meaningful to classical thinkers was a variation in *kinds* or ranks of persons, rather than between individuals. In short, what we now think of as intrinsic to personhood — personality and individuality — was in some ways the opposite of the meaning that *hypostasis* suggested.[8]

The Latin term *persona* expressed something more like concrete individuality, though this had to do primarily with social or legal roles that some-

---

7. (Zizioulas, 1985, p. 27). Peter Geach expresses the same idea this way: "The concept of a person, which we find so familiar in its application to human beings, cannot be clearly and sharply expressed by any word in the vocabulary of Plato and Aristotle; it was wrought with the hammer and anvil of theological disputes about the Trinity and the Person of Christ" (Geach, 1977, p. 75).

8. Historically this story is profoundly complicated by the fact that the Greek *hypostasis* was directly translated into the Latin *substantia*, with the result that those in both the Western and Eastern churches readily equated the two. But the Eastern church used *hypostasis* to refer to the three and *ousia* to refer to the one in God, while the Western church used *substantia* to refer to the one, and *persona* to refer to the three. Though this confusion contributed much to the controversy at the time, the tension between the pre-trinitarian connotations that came with the word *hypostasis* and those that came with the word *persona* fits Zizioulas's argument very neatly. The developed trinitarian notion of "person" combines both.

one assumes.[9] It is similar to what we mean by individuality in the external sense. It refers to features that characterize one (or a few) people in distinction from others. These distinctive features are manifest in outward relations with others, added on like a mask over pre-existing human nature. *Persona* has to do with individual differences, but entirely with those that are social in nature. In Roman law, a slave did not have "personhood." This did not imply a slave was excluded from the category "human," but that they could not contract social relationships. They could not function as agents in the public sphere. They lacked a civil *persona,* though through emancipation they might acquire such personhood. If one wished to refer to a universal or essential humanity shared by the slave and others, it is not the language of personhood that would be used but the language of a fixed nature. What is real about someone, in the sense of the most quintessentially human, is not "personal."[10]

To say that God is three *hypostases* sounded like saying God is three different substances or realities (a possibility early Christians consistently rejected). Or it sounded like saying that God is three instances of the same thing (three people would be three "human natures," three examples of one substance). On the other hand, to say that God is three persons sounded like saying God plays three different external, relational roles (such as cook, governor, and teacher).[11] According to Zizioulas, the unusual accomplishment of the theologians (especially the Cappadocian theologians) who refined trinitarian thought was to slowly bend this language to another meaning. The key step was the identification of *hypostasis* with "person," a blending of their different meanings and the addition of new elements. It would take centuries to consummate this development. But trinitarian confession eventually made clear that the three divine persons were each constituted in their personhood by their distinctively different relations with each other. The variation of one from the other was not a superficial "add on" placed over a pre-existing, self-sufficient nature. Their differences constituted their personhood and their personhood was their nature.

At the point of departure, "person" expressed many features of what we would call an individual, but few in the Hellenistic world would suppose that what "person" described had anything to do with the true being or essence of humanity. By contrast, *hypostasis* was a name for the true substance or es-

9. Greek has a parallel term, *prosopon,* which could be contrasted with *hypostasis* just as in Latin *persona* could be contrasted with *substantia.*

10. For an interesting counterpart to Zizioulas's discussion see (Brown, 1989, p. 241).

11. The terminological argument can become very complex indeed. A good treatment can be found in (LaCugna, 1991, chapter two).

sence of human nature, but it would not be associated with anything that was accidental or merely individual. In crossing the two, trinitarian thought in fact developed a new meaning of "person," pushing the sense of human "substance" in a more social direction and deepening exterior social roles with a dimension of inner life. The result is that a person's true being or nature is more deeply identified with free, distinctive, unrepeatable individuality.[12] According to Zizioulas, there is an irony in the way we read the early trinitarian controversies. We remind ourselves that participants in those controversies who used the word "person" did not (yet) have the connotations we give it. But it is what they were doing with the term in those controversies that eventually gave it much of the meaning we now assume and readily project retrospectively.

God's substance does not precede the three divine persons, as if they are "made up" of the divine essence or are divisions of it. Being is not prior to personhood in God. To put it another way, personality is not a quality added to being. The qualities of a "person," as they were then understood, would have been considered a failing in true divinity. Aristotle's God or Plotinus's God is not a person, almost by definition. The triune God is not just such a generic divinity with personhood added on, meaning by personhood those external relations and interactions that classical philosophers found so problematic for God. Instead, in the Christian understanding person becomes the most basic category of the triune God, whose divinity is constituted by the relation of the persons.

Zizioulas says the significance of this breakthrough can hardly be overestimated. In the Trinity, person becomes the primary ontological category: "God exists on account of a person, not a substance."[13] This vision eventually transforms both the understanding of God and our notion of "person" in other connections. God is not one, on the basis of some pre-existing divine substance, and then only later becomes persons. Instead, the principle of God's existence is found in the persons themselves. "Person" is the most basic category of divinity, and not one person or three in isolation, but person as constituted by relation with others. The nature of God's *being* is the communion of persons. God's nature is to be a person constituted by the communion of persons. This is a social view of the Trinity, which does not so much stress threeness as it does the one communion among the three. It highlights

---

12. However, this development apparently took place in these early centuries without focus on the question so prominent in later discussion, the question of self-consciousness in the trinitarian persons.

13. (Zizioulas, 1985, p. 42).

three mutually implied dimensions in the divine life: person as premise of communion, communion between persons, communion as constituting persons.[14]

There is no more basic source of the divine being than person and communion. On such a view, the unity of the Trinity is not to be understood in terms of the persons all being composed of the same "stuff." It became common in the West to locate the principle of unity in a single divine substance or essence. But in Eastern Christianity the principle of unity was associated with the first person, the Father. This is the reason that the Eastern church has insisted that the order of the Trinity must proceed from the first person, from the Father: the original ontological principle lies in a person. And it is the same reason the Eastern church critiques treatments of the Trinity in Western Christianity which deal first with the divine essence as basic, and then with the three persons. This is reflected in Western theological texts which tend to talk first of the one God, and then of Trinity as a quality or characterization of the one God, while Eastern theological texts tend to take Trinity as the departure point in naming or discussing God.[15]

Purged of all temporal priority or domination of power, the Father is the principle of unity as the *arche,* or point of reference of the whole. The first person is the "origin," a word like "father," which in this context is wrenched from its ordinary temporal associations. In Zizioulas's view, personal communion can only be derived from personhood, and the person of the Father is this designated formal starting point for the co-equal, co-eternal persons.[16]

14. The notion of persons as relational, so prominent in Zizioulas and many other contemporary treatments of the Trinity, has been criticized (Harris, 1998). Though valid at least against incautious or hyperbolic statements of "relationality," this criticism does not seem applicable to Zizioulas's formulation of being as communion, where it is the *mutual implication* of person and relation that is key and not the priority of relation over persons. In fact, as seen below, Zizioulas might even be argued to make person more basic than relation, in his treatment of the first person of the Trinity.

15. As much contemporary scholarship points out, this contrast has been overblown, since one can find classical Eastern theologians as well who expound the doctrine sometimes from the "one" rather than the "three." This indicates it is not just a matter of starting point.

16. Catherine LaCugna emphasizes the influence of this development on the idea of "monarchy," which the Trinity makes the property of a person, the Father, shared with the other co-equal persons. Monarchy is the Father's in that it *comes* from the Father to the other persons, but it is fully theirs by virtue of communion. She quotes Gregory of Nazianzus: "Monarchy is that which we honor, not a monarchy limited to a single person, but a monarchy constituted by equal dignity of nature, accord of will, identity of movement and the return to unity of those who come from it." This, she says, was a radical departure from prevailing views of divine monarchy (LaCugna, 1991, p. 390).

This explains the intense resistance of the Eastern church to the Western church's teaching that the Holy Spirit proceeds from the Father and the Son together, rather than from the Father alone.[17] But we can see that even in this often bitter argument, the two sides each saw their approach as the better way to defend the same conviction Zizioulas describes: God's nature as person-in-communion. The East saw this best preserved through emphasis on the first person as the unique personal source. The West saw it preserved best through the vision of the Holy Spirit proceeding from the communion of the first two persons, and even as being the bond of love between the Father and the Son. That is, communion or relation itself has the power to "generate" person. The Western preference can lead us astray by seeming to make that communion the special work or feature of one person among the three, rather than constitutive of each and of God. The Eastern preference, stressing the first person as the principle of origin and unity, has its own dangers. It suggests in images a hierarchy that it denies in fact.

The idea of personhood as the very foundation of human reality is quite entrenched in our culture now. But this belief, let alone the conviction that distinctive individuality and relation lies at the basis of *all* being, appears to be one that requires a thought experiment like trinitarian doctrine. It hardly seems to be an inductive hypothesis. It is rather difficult to formulate such an idea logically if we confine ourselves strictly to human references.[18] Empirically, human nature always precedes person.[19] A whole species stretches behind us, including the two parents from which our humanity is immediately derived. No one person or few persons can be said to bear in themselves the sum total of human nature, making the nature and that set of persons co-

17. The Western church interpolated this view into the Nicene-Constantinopolitan Creed with the Latin word *filioque*.

18. For our purposes at the moment we are simply ignoring later developments in the understanding of "person," most notably the enlightenment emphasis upon absolute autonomy, which tended to make individualism rather than individuality a hallmark of the person. This connotation is now also very powerful in our culture, and introduces its own confusions into attempts to understand the three persons of the Trinity.

19. Our contemporary discussions of abortion are a fascinating confirmation of this. No one denies a fetus human nature, but many deny it the status of person. Our discussions are complicated because (unlike the Greeks or early Christians) we are aware that the embryo's genetic "nature" already encodes many of the unique individual features we associate with personhood. The notion of person as an ontologically basic category seems to fuel thorough opposition to abortion, while acceptance of abortion tends to take "person" as an emergent reality. A creature viewed to have the generic substance of human nature does not elicit the same protection as one viewed as a unique human person, which is in fact the legal unit to which we attach "rights."

extensive. The situation with the triune God is quite different. There the three persons do not share or derive from a pre-existing nature. The "nature" is the coincidence of the persons. The multiplicity of the three persons does not imply a division of the divine nature, as the multiplicity of humans implies a division of human nature, because the three divine persons coinhere. The entirety of divine nature is in them.

A traditional trinitarian paradox asserts that the sum of divinity is in each person as well as in all: there is no more of God in the Father and the Son together than in one of them alone. One can say that two infinities are not larger than one, but this paradox makes more concrete sense if we understand the divine nature as communion. Thus it is true that all of the persons are present in each one, by communion, but the whole of divinity is present in a distinctively different pattern in each case.[20] It is the same wholeness, taken three different times, through three different persons. This somewhat esoteric discussion indicates the counterintuitive flavor of the idea that person is an ontologically basic category.

The most important point for our discussion lies in the next phase of Zizioulas's argument. If "person" is basic in the way just suggested, then the notion of a more fundamental substance or a prior being must give way to some other understanding. What is the divine nature, the "same substance" by virtue of which the three persons are one God? That nature is communion. The communion of the three is something distinct from each of them, something shared fully by all, something "made up" of nothing but the persons and their relations. Nor are the divine persons prior to their communion with each other, for their character as persons not only includes the capacity for relation but this capacity has always been realized. To be and to be in relation are the same thing for the divine life. As the title of Zizioulas's book indicates, God's being is communion. Therefore if Trinity is our guide, the most fundamental definition of being we can give is person-in-communion.

This has far-reaching implications. An old conundrum in Western thought (and in philosophy generally) has to do with otherness, or the one and the many. Philosophy seeks for some foundational explanation of reality, of being itself. But to the extent that such an account can be provided, it seems to leave no categories for ontological difference except those of defect and loss. If, for instance, the one true kind of being or substance is found in God, then whatever is different from God is defective insofar as it is not the

20. This same idea shows up in ecclesiology in Miroslav Volf's development of a free church argument that the catholicity of the whole church is present in each concrete local church (Volf, 1998, pp. 270-76).

same being. This line of thought was well represented in the Greek philosophical tradition. Since it understood true being to be eternal and unchanging, it understood both the divine and the world (insofar as it was truly real) as eternal. All that did not have this quality of being was deficient: difference equals defect. As applied to humanity, this meant that the true being of humanity must be some common and unchanging nature. Personal variations and relations (which Greeks plainly recognized as actual) were external, accidental, ultimately less real.

In articulating Trinity as the character of ultimate being, Christians affirmed an ontology in which the differences of the persons are basic and integral. There is no being without both difference and communion. In God the two are coincident. The being of the one divine nature is the communion of the irreducibly different persons; the being of the individual persons is constituted by their relations with each other. Consistent with their embryonic trinitarianism, and unlike Greek-minded contemporaries, Christians denied that either the world or humanity itself were eternal (they affirmed creation and did not believe that humans had intrinsically immortal souls). From the Greek perspective, this could only look like a disparagement of the world and humanity, attributing defects to them. On the other hand, Christians affirmed the goodness of the most contingent, changeable, and "personal" dimensions of both creation and human beings, affirming their capacity to participate even in the divine life itself. From the Greek perspective, this could only look like an irrational exaltation of the manifestly imperfect and earthly. This situation was reflected in the church's conflict both with those who held the world was eternal (and thus divine) and with gnostics who denied that the world was eternal (and therefore concluded it was bad). Christians affirmed that the world was different from God, had a separate kind of existence, and yet the world was good. It was good because its very distinctive individuality fit it to participate in the divine life by communion. This is the trinitarian dynamic. The mode by which creatures can participate most fully in the divine life, communion, is consistent with the very nature of God, which is itself communion.

The differences among the divine persons imply no inequality between them. But Christians perceived the relation between God and creation as intrinsically unequal, relating two different levels of being. Christians did not transpose the equality-in-difference of the divine communion to every sphere where differences exist among human beings, for instance. Though insisting that personhood implied an ultimate equality of human beings before God, the church did not apply this universally to human social relations. Nevertheless, the shift in the way the question was posed was crucial. The difference in level between God and creatures has to do with God's character as the source of communion and as the deepest embodiment of it. This is an understanding of God's nature that is not a zero-sum game. In sharing such a nature with creatures, God does not have less of it. On the social front, the church generally accepted spiritual equality between persons as compatible with socially hierarchical relations.[21] But the expectation was planted that as persons are drawn into the life of the Trinity their relations with each other should increasingly approximate the triune ones, where asymmetry coexists with equality.

After all, the precipitating occasion of the whole trinitarian development was the overcoming of the most extreme inequality of all, that between God and humanity. Christ's incarnation might be unique, but it was the case that proved the rule. Despite the obvious hierarchical character of the disparity between God and humans, even this radical asymmetry could be assimilated or transposed to the key of trinitarian communion. The fact that the fundamental nature of both is being-in-communion (and more specifically, being as communion of the distinctly different) means that they can have true communion with each other while remaining distinct. Christians can thus understand salvation as *theosis*, divinization, or sharing in the divine nature. By this they did not mean that humans acquire all the specific properties of God (like omnipotence). The trinitarian discussion we have just reviewed shows that to share in the divine nature (in quite literal terms) is to share in the triune communion. The participation is not the same as that of the triune persons themselves (that would be to *be* one of them), but it is a communion appropriate to our personhood.

Trinitarian doctrine was even more explicit about this. In the relations between the three divine persons there are incommunicable properties. To say the persons share everything with each other is to say they share all that can be shared while still remaining uniquely themselves. The identity of the first person is incommunicable to the others, and so on for each person. So when, in the relation between God and humanity, it is said that humans may become by grace what God is by nature, a similar reservation applies. There are human properties that are not communicable to God as there are divine properties not communicable to humans. This does not compromise the oneness of God and humanity (in Christ) any more than it compromises the oneness of God (in the Trinity). To suppose that the existence of any difference at all between Jesus and God rules out the true unity of Jesus with God

---

21. This is not to deny that in the early church, and periodically throughout Christian history, people drew egalitarian social conclusions from these premises.

simply ignores this trinitarian grammar. If a human and God are to be truly one person — and the most profound standard for this would be the way that God is one — then difference is not only possible, it is necessary.

In the Eastern Orthodox tradition the "energies" of God were distinguished as communicable aspects of God's nature. This recalls those portions of Scripture that treat God's holiness and glory as somewhat impersonal qualities. The divine energies are certainly personal in that their communication to humans enhances and deepens human personhood, relation with God and others. Perhaps they might be called "interpersonal." They can be communicated from one to another. The divinity of the Word, who is already God, is incommunicable, but the energies are transferable. They flow out to humans and in no way diminish the source from which they come. God is no less God for sharing the divine energies. The primary image the tradition uses to describe these energies is light, the light which illumines Christ and Moses and Elijah on the Mount of Transfiguration, for instance. This light of glory or divine energy is thoroughly personal in the sense that it is intrinsically associated with the triune persons. When received, it becomes part of the person, a visible expression of communion with the divine. Abstracted or isolated, it is impersonal. It is the glory of persons, but by itself it is not a person. Taken by itself, it leads only in an apophatic direction.[22]

Humans can receive the communicable life of God, what the Eastern church called the uncreated energies of God. But humans cannot in any sense possess or incorporate the incommunicable properties (which are both the distinctive identities of the persons and also certain qualities like omnipotence) in the same way. These are realities creatures can only commune with while they remain the unique properties of the divine persons. If it is objected that the human communion with God is not really complete, because some aspects of the divine life are not transferred to humans, the answer is that such "reservations" exist in the communion of the divine life itself. In communion some things may be transmitted from one to another, but there are always aspects that remain the unique property of one and cannot be given away. In that case communion is not a bridge over which gifts are passed, but an intimate relation that gives you the benefit of and access to qualities that remain an integral part of the person with whom you are in communion.

Therefore the divine life which humans participate in by grace has exactly the formal characteristics of the divine life which is God's by nature. Because God's being is communion-in-difference, humans truly and partially

---

22. This is reflected in the argument within the Eastern tradition over whether the light of the divine energies could be seen by physical eyes.

participate in that divine nature through a communion with God that is also a communion-in-difference, even though the differences in the two cases are different! God's nature is intrinsically open to relation. Therefore the debate about whether relationship to others is necessarily a defect in the divine (as it would be for Plotinus's Neoplatonic God or the gnostic God) is quite moot. Humans, though finite and mortal and radically other than God, are persons whose nature is also communion-in-difference. Therefore they have a point of contact with God. They are in the pattern or image of the divine being. And their very difference from God is part of that image they share with God.

In Chapter Two we reviewed the Christian understanding of salvation as communion or *koinonia*. Traditionally, Christians have seen three dimensions of saving relation in this communion: relation of the person with God (faith), relation with others (love), and relation with creation (hope). The first dimension of salvation is often called justification, the second sanctification, and the third eternal life. Salvation is one reality, a personal communion in which these three dimensions (the existential, the moral, and the eschatological) are all present. Participation in the divine life is manifest as communion, in a kind of commutative law. It is a recursive process which sees the same pattern of mutual participation repeated and extended. We become members of each other by being in Christ; and through that *koinonia* we become partakers of the triune life of God.

God is a mystery that we cannot break down into smaller ontological units. Though often regarded as obscure, the doctrine of the Trinity gives two quite clear directions. First, the right ontological category for God is person-in-communion. Second, other kinds of being must be understood in relation to this, rather than the reverse. Trinity is not ambiguous about the nature of the religious ultimate. It specifies a particular coordination of personal and impersonal elements. An essentially impersonal absolute has no personal side. Any personal descriptions could only be projections cast upon the absolute in ignorance or a mistaken perception appropriate to a lower stage of insight. Such description is a mask that may be useful for certain purposes but it must finally be dispelled.

By contrast, a personal absolute can have a real impersonal dimension that is not at all extrinsic in that way. We need not leave behind the notion that persons have bodies that follow physical laws, for instance, in order to believe persons are not only physiological. If one person falls from a balcony to land on another person, we can understand this event in a completely "impersonal" way, described strictly in terms of mass and acceleration. This in no way rules out personhood in either party, nor a further personal explanation of how the fall came to happen. If the religious ultimate and the human religious end are themselves both impersonal, then the personal is excluded in a definitive way.[23] A trinitarian view of God does not require such rigid exclusion. The impersonal dimension of God is real. It is not dispelled by insight and it need not be exiled from God's nature. It is always an aspect of the divine persons and their communion.

We have pressed this exploration of trinitarian thought, and particularly of the meaning of "person," for a specific purpose. The complex nature of God holds out the possibility of a variety of distinct relations with God. That variety is the basis for truly different religious ends. Alternative religious ends represent an intensified realization of one dimension of God's offered relation with us. This intensification comes through limitation, in that a dimension (or some subset of dimensions) is taken to be God's *sole* true relation with us. The distinctive Christian claim is that salvation is participation in divine life, encompassing many dimensions on a level of equality and mutuality, and sharing in the "inner life" of God that only makes sense if God is triune, i.e., that there is meaning to "inner life." Because that life is a communion of persons in relation, salvation is also such a communion. This does not mean that Christians claim to understand the inner life of God. The fact of this trinitarian life is more, not less mysterious than a "simple" deity, as witnessed by the fact that it obliges Christians to encompass other religious ends in their affirmation of relation with God.

God is related to us in complex and distinct ways. The channels between God and humanity are open on several frequencies. Salvation consists in a particular enrichment, intensification, and harmonization of all of these, in interrelations that allow each its own scope. There is a "hierarchy" between full communion with the triune God and lesser, restricted participations. But all the types of relation with God are grounded in God, in the coexisting relations in God's own nature. In the strict sense there can be no question of a real relation to the triune God, no matter how penultimate or incomplete, being simply replaced by another. It can only be a matter of expansion or deeper communion. The key characteristic of the interrelation of these dimensions is the fact that none need be relegated to the status of a mere imperfect form of another.[24] Therefore the difference between some real relation and full com-

---

23. See, for instance, Stephen Williams's argument to this effect (Williams, 1997, p. 38).

24. In other words, none of these relations can be taken simply as instrumental, as a representation adapted to some people's psychological and cultural condition which need have no constitutive place in the religious end and no constant role in characterizing the religious ultimate.

munion is not a matter merely of linear increments: different types of relation and different dimensions of communion have quantum effects.

Traditionally, Christian theology stressed that the external acts of the Trinity were indivisible. In relation to creation, it is the trinity-in-unity that acts. Creatures can never rightly say that they are in contact or relation with one person to the exclusion of the others: where one is, the others are by virtue of their unity. But this always raises the question of what purpose the trinitarian distinctions serve. The primary purpose of trinitarian theology is not to identify God's action in the world with one divine person or another, though that theology has served as a vehicle for expressing the divine economy. A schema of the trinitarian "missions" of the three persons narrates the various ways God acts in the world, and the various ways we experience God's presence. Trinitarian theology does not primarily aim to provide a detailed, objective description of God when God is "home alone."

The primary spiritual and theological point of the doctrine is focused precisely between these two poles of pure economy and pure ontology. It affirms that the one God we encounter in any one way at a particular moment is — at that same moment and always — richer and more various in certain specific ways than that single encounter would indicate. This richness is both phenomenal and objective. It includes both other ways God can seem and other dimensions of what (and who) God is. Trinity affirms that any conception of God in se or "alone" which leaves aside the dimensions of communion is inadequate. The doctrine's primary benefit for us is to sensitize us to the communion-nature of God, and hence to the various dimensions or frequencies through which God can simultaneously connect with us. Trinity draws us steadily out of isolation in limited (though real) relations with God that can be absolutized as screens that block richer communion.

With all its complexity, Trinity does say what it appears to say at first glance: the Christian idea of God is somewhere between our idea of a person and our idea of a community. To picture God as a simple person makes the three too much like organs or faculties within a human being, makes them too sub-personal. To picture God as a community of individual persons makes the one too much like an abstraction or a contract, makes the godhead too impersonal or trans-personal. We have to cross our ideas of person and community as the early Christian theologians crossed their ideas of *hypostasis* and *persona*. If "person" is our model for God, then we have to transform it to the point that each of the three constituent parts of the person seem analogous to the whole. If "community" is our model for God, then we have to transform it so that the whole seems truly analogous to each of the three that constitute it. Trinity is a pattern from which these two concrete realities we know best are derived and diverge. In salvation, persons (and their communion with others) will converge more toward that pattern, without losing their distinct identity as creatures.

The Christian theological tradition suggests that mistakes about the Trinity affect Christian life. God's own nature does not change according to our ideas of it. But without a living sense of the Trinity, we contract the range in which God can share that nature with us, and the scope of our relation to God diminishes. This is so in connection to our prayer life, for instance, which is partial if limited to the approach to a generic "God" or to Jesus alone. If the trinitarian confession is sound, prayer is actually entry into the ongoing "conversation" of the triune life, as well as the communion of the saints. The doctrine of the Trinity is about knowing God, participating in the divine life by communion. This knowing is critical: it leads to steady transformation of our ideas about God. But it is also pervasively constructive for life and practice. "Knowing" God as Trinity is a way of life, a nurturing and growth into closer communion with God across a range of relations that fully encompasses our lives.[25] There is a trinitarian praxis without which it is hard to make sense of trinitarian doctrine. But without at least an implicit trinitarian confession, that complex of practices, especially in its communal character, is often truncated.

II

We can now see the connection between the Trinity and varied religious aims. The actual ends that various religious traditions offer as alternative human fulfillments diverge because they realize different relations with God. It is God's reality as Trinity that generates the multiplicity of dimensions that allow for that variety of relations. God's threefoldness means that salvation necessarily is a characteristic communion in diversity. It also permits human responses to God to limit themselves within the terms of one dimension. Trinity requires that salvation be communion. It makes possible, but not necessary, the realization of religious ends other than salvation.

Humans can concentrate their response to the divine in a particular dimension of the divine life, and if this channel of relation is maintained in isolation from others it can lead to a distinct religious end. A trinitarian perspective can affirm diverse religious ends as real, and the traditions that offer

25. For a discussion of theology in this context as "sapiential wisdom" see (Charry, 1997).

them as valid ways to relation with God. *Any* of these is preferable to no realized relation with God. At the same time, a trinitarian framework recognizes that these contacts with God are not identical in their meaning or result. *A relation with God is not the same thing as salvation.* Insofar as alternative religious ends lack or rule out real dimensions of communion with the triune God, they embody some measure of what the Christian tradition regards as loss or damnation.

This possibility of loss and the human freedom involved in it stem from God's "withdrawal" from us in creation to provide the space for our existence and self-determination.[26] This has particular relevance for the first dimension of the divine life that we discussed briefly above, the more impersonal dimension or what KS call the infinite life of the three persons. Creation establishes a distance between God and creation for the sake of the freedom of creation. Calling the universe into being, God also provides space to let it be. This is not only a veil from God's immediate presence and power, but a foundation of what we call natural law and order, a ground for human freedom and development. Though this is a creative act of God, the substance of the action involves a certain apparent absence of God.

The distance between God and creatures which allows them the freedom for relationship is also an occasion for sin and loss. This freedom, and the fact that God's economy of relation with us involves self-limitation, opens up the possibility for a variety of relations with God. As a part of the "letting be" which is integral to God's creating, there is a withdrawal of God from direct presence to human knowledge. Immediate, sensible presence of God would be incompatible with human self-determination. God puts humans in a situation from which there can be varied, defensible conclusions about God's existence, a situation therefore in which humans are free to choose to believe in God and love God or not. But this also means that who and what God is becomes uncertain and God's actions of revelation themselves take place within the frame of this epistemic distance.[27] The varied religions and their varied religious ends exist in this space, a space which is itself an intrinsic part of the good creation.

The Christian perspective on other religions thus deploys a rather complex map within which to locate and recognize a variety of distinctive paths and ends. One of the most notable aspects of this map is that it leaves areas to be further specified by the details of other religious traditions. Take, for in-

---

26. The kabbalistic doctrine of *zimsum* or self-limitation expresses a similar notion.

27. "Epistemic distance" is a term John Hick uses to describe God's withdrawal from our immediate apprehension (Rowe, 1991 and Hick's reply in the same volume).

stance, the extraordinarily complicated and nuanced analyses of consciousness and mental events that are found in Buddhist tradition. This insight to the very roots of emptiness fills out the apophatic side of the Trinity's impersonal dimension, reflected in our created nature. It does so in a way Christianity alone never has or could. This specification greatly enriches the trinitarian map, though on that map there are other, co-equal domains as well.

There are different ways the complexity of the Trinity and its relations with the world may break down, to varying religious effects. One way of fragmenting the Trinity would be to effectively take only one of the three persons as real, and treat the others as purely economic or secondary representations of that reality. So, for instance, one might hold to some kind of first mover, a transcendent agency of some sort, but deny any incarnational dimension or any personal immanence. This would correspond to certain kinds of deism, for instance. One might instead deny both a creator and particular incarnation but affirm an immanent pantheistic "Spirit." Or one might affirm a historical *logos* or pattern for human life, without either creation or immanence. This broad "map" is helpful in some ways, with its tendency to classify religions according their focus on creative transcendence, historical incarnation, or spiritual immanence.

But as we have stressed, the Trinity suggests another complexity that is of even greater relevance for the religions. In truth, the world religions are beyond any simple treatment as unitarianisms of one divine person (religions of the Father or the Word or the Spirit). In their sophistication and wisdom, the traditions integrate a wide variety of religious phenomena. They generally show a keen appreciation of at least the economic elements of trinitarian expression.[28] Rather than focusing on unitarianisms of various sorts, it is more helpful to inquire about the principle or principles *by* which that integration takes place in particular traditions. This often involves concentration and refinement of a particular dimension of the shared life of the Trinity to the exclusion or limitation of one or more of the others. This is not the isolation of the Father or the Word or the Spirit *per se,* but rather the elevation of a single dimension of the relations among them and a single dimension of their complex relations with the world. For instance, one perspective might orient itself to the impersonal, infinite life shared among the three persons. Another might focus on what KS call the common "I" of the three persons, the indivisible acts of the one God in relation to the world.

In the last section we described some of the ways the development of

---

28. This leads Panikkar, for instance, to his firm confidence that Trinity is the true matrix of all religion and that the religions themselves implicitly manifest this.

trinitarian theology employed and stretched existing notions about human nature, and in turn helped to reshape our notion of the human person. We can develop our discussion further by considering certain kinds of human interaction as analogies for encounter with God. One human person can connect with another in at least three dimensions. It is important to remember that we are not analogizing this relation between two people with the relation of one human or community to one of the triune persons. Instead, we are drawing an analogy between three avenues of human interpersonal relation and contact with three aspects of the shared triune life as a whole, three aspects that exist by virtue of the divine communion among the three.

First, two people can have an "impersonal" relation, a connection that does not require personhood. This is the case with a purely functional interaction that could just as well be achieved by a machine (one person stamps another's ticket). It is the case when we interact on a purely biological level (one person receives a blood transfusion from another). This last example is a particularly good one. We are literally in contact with the life processes within another, but the contact takes place (or may) entirely without the exchange or engagement of any "personal" qualities.

A second dimension of relationship between persons involves an encounter with the unitary agency of the other. We directly meet the distinctive products of personality: words, thoughts, intentions, aesthetic expressions, feelings. These are sent by one and received by another. This may be a face to face event, emphasizing bodily and vocal communication. But the outward personal expression can also precipitate in a medium (like writing or art) that opens this dimension of relation even between those who never physically meet. This dimension is personal in a profound way, raising the full range of moral and social questions that mark human culture. It covers a wide range of interactions of varying intensity, from asking a stranger for directions to working together as student and teacher in a math class to living as friendly neighbors for the better part of a lifetime, to studying the work of a poet from another century.

A third dimension of relation is that of communion. Here one not only encounters another *as* a person but in some measure *shares* in the life of the other person. Empathy and familiarity with the way that the other's emotions and responses are formed eventually give us the vicarious capacity to experience the same responses in some measure. These arise in us not instead of our own reactions, but alongside them, though in some cases this line too may blur. Two people who share the experience of listening to a great musical performance exemplify this. The effect of this sharing might range from the simple awareness that another's responses are virtually identical to your own (a knowledge which has its own distinctive impact on the nature of your experience) to a rather complex phenomenon in which you appreciate someone else's appreciation for elements that do not speak to you in the same way.[29]

Intimate contact with someone's life consciously and unconsciously shapes our own, and this process is steadily nurtured by exchange and open communication. Relationships of deep love, close family connection, intimate friendship, are examples of this. In such relations we certainly contact the unitary outward expression of the person's will and thought. But in addition we have some participation in the constitutive process that is behind such expression. We are in contact with the non-unitary features of their personality, with the tensions or unique separate dynamics that are at play in their experience and life.

My contention is that the life of the Trinity manifests three dimensions analogous to the three I have described, and that relation with God can be tuned or concentrated in one of these channels, with distinctive religious results. Let us consider the three in much greater detail.[30]

Consider the first, more impersonal dimension. KS speak about the "infinity of the divine life," referring to the process of exchange among the triune persons, the life processes of the shared nature. This is the radical immanence and the radical emptiness, by which the divine persons indwell each other and make way for the others to indwell them. The question of self-consciousness in the divine persons is a complicated one, but we can simply note that there is a difference between personal activities that proceed with awareness, though with no deliberation or self-interrogation, and those that are self-conscious in a deliberative sense. Persons who are very close may maintain a steady flow of "unconscious" exchange, where each registers what is happening to the other. This takes place at a level that is almost physiological as much as psychological. KS are pointing to a dimension like this in the divine life.

In the biblical tradition, we find clear indications of relation with God tuned to this wavelength. There is a very real note in Scripture that highlights an impersonal side of the divine. In the Old Testament the holiness of God and the direct presence of God frequently have this character, like a fire in the presence of which everything mortal is consumed. Theophanies, or even the

29. I am developing an example suggested by William P. Alston (Alston, 1988, pp. 142-43).

30. As will be clear in much of what follows, my thinking parallels and develops suggestions present in KS's theology of religion, which we reviewed in the last chapter. I do not imply, of course, that they would necessarily agree with the way I have used those ideas.

continuing presence of God that rests in the ark of the tabernacle as it travels with the people of Israel, have this quality. Humans exposed to this presence are in great danger, in a purely "chemical" and impersonal sense, quite apart from any specific intention on God's part. It is as if a creature stepped into a circuit where unimaginable current was being exchanged. The raw divine life is a "consuming fire," and accounts of those who encounter it (Moses or Job, for instance) trade strongly on the language of impersonal forces like fire and wind. This divine power or force might be viewed as something like an electrical charge or field, generated by the constant interchange of the three divine persons with each other. Just as living organisms have a variation in electrical potential in the body, a living exchange, so does the divine life have its own generative process.

We made the point in our discussion of Trinity that there is no uniform divine substance or essence. What there is one of in God is not a "stuff" but a communion. This means that in relating with God we are encountering dimensions of shared life. One such dimension is precisely this infinite exchange among them. In a rigidly empirical way, if we look beyond the three divine persons toward some substance or essence of the divine, what we encounter is the flux of relation among the persons. It is as if we searched within a human body for its life, trying to find in what specific place or function it resided. Or it is as if we tried to isolate the "life of a community" in one individual or event. In either case, the living fullness of the whole would escape us. We could come up with process, or structure, a set of dynamics that underlie the life we are trying to explain. What we find would be quite real and we would be right, at least in certain senses, to believe that this flux lies underneath the larger-scale phenomena of a human body, a community, or God. We might even jump to the conclusion that this "life" is nothing but the processes we isolate in our investigation.

God is not static, nor simple, and the divine life underlies every aspect of the created order. One dimension of the presence of God in the world is precisely the manifestation of this aspect of the triune life, its presence "in, with, and under" all creatures. Whether by science or meditation, a profound empirical effort to distinguish what is at the bottom of natural world processes, or of our own mind, can attain an awareness of this sustaining or creative interaction. But that awareness will be limited to the phenomenal character of that process. Just as our personhood is not discernible at the level of the molecular interactions that take place in our bodies, so God is "impersonal" when encountered in this dimension of the divine immanence.

This divine impersonality can be perceived in two different ways, with their own integrity. The first apprehends the exchange among the divine per-

sons, the flux itself, as most basic. The nature of all is changing and impermanent: all is arising. And behind the arising there is nothing more substantial
than that process itself. The only thing that could be more fundamental
would be the cessation of such arising: something like what Buddhism calls
nirvana. Contact with the impersonality of the divine can suggest the unreal-
ity of the self or the individual as we normally understand it.

If creation is examined rigorously in this dimension, it can rightly be
found to have "emptiness" at its base. A striking contemporary analogy for
this fact comes out in physics. Quantum mechanics provides a consistent and
highly effective account of the most basic constituents of our physical world,
an account in which matter itself seems to dissolve into something else: energy, or fields of mathematical probability. The occurrences that make up the
regularities of our world, from subatomic particles on up, take place according to quite concrete mathematical schemes. But why (and how) these equa-
tions are taking the trouble to actualize themselves, if I may put it that way, is
as unclear to physicists as to the uninitiated. If the quantum world represents
an "edge" of reality, as the cosmological origin in time of the universe is another such edge, then it appears so far to be neatly turned back upon itself,
leaving us quite self-enclosed. What's "there" is no fixed thing but rather a
flux which, when smoothed out at higher levels, has a quite hard and regular
tangibility. If looking into the constituent make-up of matter in fact is a
glimpse toward the heart of reality, then reality manifests an "emptiness," in
the sense of the lack of substance or the dissolving of entities with enduring
distinct identities.

It appears to me that this insight is far more developed and its particular implications more intensely understood in Buddhism than in any facet of
Christian tradition. It is rather common for Christians to concede that Buddhist teachings are an impressive analysis of a godless world. This obviously
implies that they are an accurate analysis of a world that does not exist, since
God does. I am suggesting instead that this Buddhist vision of emptiness is an
accurate picture of an aspect of the real world and an accurate, if limited, description of God's relation with the world.

The "emptiness" described *is* one of God's relations to creation, a fundamental dimension of distance given in the creative act itself. Nor is emptiness an entirely economic feature of God, one that God has only by virtue
of creation and in relation to creation. As a "making space for the other," we
can say such emptiness is a feature of the inner-trinitarian relations of the
divine persons. We saw a reference to this in Panikkar's talk of the kenosis in
which the Father makes way for the Son. Therefore the discussions between
Buddhists and Christians which consider whether emptiness is a name for

God (and vice versa) have a point.[31] It is interesting that Buddhism typically regards Trinity, incarnation, and virtually all positive Christian representations of God as passing, instrumental representations, suitable to the spiritually undeveloped, while regarding "emptiness" as belonging to a different and more ultimate plane of reality. For them emptiness is not merely an economic representation of the ultimate, and it cannot be made co-equal with other characterizations of the ultimate. Christians on the other hand are obliged to coordinate the dimension of emptiness with others in the trinitarian view of God.

Apophatic theology, that branch of Christian theology that has focused particularly on the emptiness of references to God and on the negative spiritual path toward God, reflects a particular texture in the emptiness it finds in the divine life. This texture is "personal emptiness." We can distinguish three sides to this negativity. The first side is contingency. God acts out of a divine and sovereign freedom and God's actions are not necessitated. They are "empty" in that there is no causal determinism, no prior set of circumstances that strictly requires them. They flow freely from God's character and will. The second side of the divine emptiness we can call reservation.[32] God is truly revealed but never fully or exhaustively revealed. There is a depth of God that remains unknown to creatures. In our contact with the divine nature there are always parts of the map that remain blank. The character of personhood is such that it cannot be captured entirely and permanently by an external understanding. The third side is what we have already discussed as God's withdrawal, the self-contraction that allows creation its space and integrity. This is not the emptiness of the great "beyond" in God, which must always exceed our finite grasp. It is a purposeful absence or a divine secret, in which God shields us from the blinding divine presence that would overwhelm us with such totality and certainty as to leave us immobile. God actively transcends the range of our finite faculties.

All of these, and especially the third, give a point of purchase for the Buddhist insight regarding emptiness. However, from a Christian perspective the category of "person" qualifies that of emptiness without displacing it. We can see how this works out in each of the three cases I have just described. In the first case the emptiness is the freedom, the lack of prior constraint, in a contingent, personal act. In the second case it is the quality of unrevealed depth intrin-

---

31. But attempts to understand God as Trinity *entirely* in terms of emptiness are not very plausible. See, for instance, the essay by Michael von Bruck and the response by Paul Ingram (Corless and Knitter, 1990).

32. This corresponds to the point made by Jerome Gellman, discussed in Chapter One, regarding a dimension of inexhaustible fullness in religious experiences.

sic to a person, the "more" present beyond the bounds of any particular encounter. In the third case it is a personal act of self-limitation to leave space for another. In all these instances, emptiness is not regarded as transitory or less than real. It is a permanent dimension of personal reality and relation. It is an interpersonal reality of the divine life as well as of human life. But it is not the sole ultimate. If this avenue of relation is regarded, and actualized, as the sole ultimate, the Buddhist religious end becomes a real option.

This is one mode of perceiving the impersonal dimension of the divine life. A second mode reads this impersonality as that of a self without relation, a "person" of radically different definition.[33] If there were but one absolute self, then the flux and impermanence humans perceive as a dimension of the divine presence could be taken as the natural inner reality of that self. This is analogous to the constant biological and chemical and physical flux characteristic of any individual's physiological or even psychic processes. From this perspective, it is a category mistake to take the emptiness of the flux as the real story. That illusion arises from fixation on one level, the impermanence of the constituent parts, that blinds you to the larger reality they compose. Once you realize the identity of all with this single self, this impermanent activity falls into place as ephemeral expressions playing across one deeper consciousness. That consciousness itself is perfectly complete, for there is no "other" to which it relates.

The act of creation involves the divine contraction we spoke of above. It is also true that at the same time God is present to creation at every moment, as the sustainer without whom it could not exist. There is a relation of utter dependence between creatures and God, for their very life processes depend on God's life, are supported by God's presence. The connection of creator to creature cannot be effaced. The other side of the divine withdrawal from sensible, cognitive, or spiritual dominance of creation is the anonymous immanence by which God upholds each creature. There is a sense in which God is in us "by nature." This is not a relation of identity. It is not that creation *is* God, or that God's sustaining immanence is the *same* as our life and self. But there is an unbreakable link between them.

As a result, we can look deeply into ourselves or nature and find not only an emptiness of substance (because of God's withdrawal) but also a positive matrix that sustains us. Quantum mechanics can be viewed from one perspective as the running out of matter into "no thing." From another it can

---

33. This is a "self" or a person much more like the enlightenment view of the autonomous self, one that exists independent of others. Of course in this case it is a matter not of an autonomous self among other autonomous selves, but of a *total* of one.

be viewed as an indication that the material world is upheld by an active process, a highly ordered structure whose mathematical signature is one of startling elegance and compactness. Christians regard this as the immanent, sustaining activity of God. But taken alone it is liable to characterizations like "matrix" or "force." If the insight regarding emptiness can point toward a conclusion about the insubstantiality of all things, the view of a sustaining power at the base of all things can lead toward a more positive image of an underlying reality, present alike in all that is. Nowhere is this perception more powerfully manifest than in the Advaita Vedanta tradition of Hinduism. Brahman, the one unshakable reality, sustains all things by pervading all things, by identity with all things.

Either apprehension — insight into a basic emptiness or insight into a total immanence — can lead reasonably to the conclusion "I am that." The boundaries that mark off any persons or creatures from others are only apparent. All things are empty, or all things are instances of divine immanence. This applies to us as humans: *my* being also is an instance of emptiness or immanence. The conviction that *samsara* is *nirvana* or that *atman* is *Brahman* are two distinctive religious conclusions born of such insight, and they point to two distinct religious ends. Relation to God derived from our meditation on or investigation into the ground of nature and our own being may very well take the two forms we have described. Insofar as we concentrate on this insight and on revelation restricted to this particular vein, those two religious ends are viable options.

Such ends are tuned to the dimension of the divine life we have been discussing, with its two faces: the "distance" established by God's withdrawal and the simple divine immanence which upholds our existence. We can reasonably take the first face as emptiness, since all that is left behind in this withdrawal of God (what Panikkar calls the silence of the Father) is the flux of the divine life and its connection with us. All is impermanence, arising and passing. This can be taken as the lack of enduring substance or self. But, as the second face, it can also reasonably be taken as the eternal, ongoing life of a single subject. In that case, the fact that we find it at the base of all being does not lead to a conclusion that being as such is empty. Instead it leads to the conclusion that there is one reality alone whose life is immanent in all being and identical with it. In either of these perceptions, a real encounter with the impersonal dimension of the divine is honored. No-self and self-without-another are both construals of that encounter that provide true witness about the nature of this relation. Within these terms, Trinity itself is viewed as a misleading confusion, because of its attachment to the notion of person or its attachment to relationship between persons or both.

Although both of these convictions are represented within great religious traditions, the first in major strands of Buddhism and the second in the Advaita Vedanta strand of Hinduism, they also appear in less traditionally religious forms. For instance, there are a number of works that rightly draw extensive comparisons between modern science and certain strands of Buddhist and Hindu thought.[34] The most common contemporary forms of spiritualized science reflect the same two options. There is a spiritualized form of reductionistic science. It concludes that on the cosmological and quantum mechanical fronts the more we understand the way the world works, the less sense it makes, in terms of having any transcendent or substantial meaning. At the root of the universe we find intellectual and even causal emptiness. The human task is to grasp this emptiness with an existential authenticity. On the other hand, there is a spiritualized form of what we might call "ecological" science. It concludes from essentially the same data that the flux of one continuous world process is itself divine. We, and all other beings, are simply parts or moments in this unity and meaning comes in recognizing this identity. Our world ("Gaia") or perhaps our whole universe is a divine being, and we are one with it. From a trinitarian point of view, these two options veer either toward understanding the divine as pure relations, pure process, or toward understanding the divine as an absolute with no need of relations (since it is already in perfect identity with all that is). In either case the "impersonal" dimension of the divine life is isolated as an absolute and cut off from its integral place in the relation of the divine persons.

God's immanence in creation is consonant with the withdrawal or kenosis that goes with God's act of creation. Both might be regarded as impersonal faces of God. Insight into either, and the religious practice built around such insight, constitutes a relation with God within the band of only one dimension of the triune life. In encountering the emptiness of the world or the sustaining activity that upholds the world, we are meeting God in a particular phase of God's relation to us as creator. This is a real and valid relation, but it is isolated from other features of the triune communion. Each of the divine persons "makes space" for the others (as God makes space for creation). But each person also lives by coinherence with the others. From the Christian point of view, any impersonality in their shared life is always the product of the creative withdrawal (kenosis) of a person and the mutual immanence (communion) of persons.

To encounter God as an impersonal reality touches in depth a dimension of the divine life, the ceaseless exchange among the persons. There is an

34. (Zukav, 1980; Capra, 1991).

interesting corollary with this dimension in the history of Christian theology. Awareness of the dimension has been nourished in Eastern Christianity, where apophatic theology has remained a living tradition, in conjunction with a trinitarian theology. In Western Christianity the same strand is present in a minor key through some mystical and devotional traditions. But Western theology has shown a great interest in a divine substance or essence as the principle of unity in God. Particularly after the enlightenment, attempts to think about or relate with this divine essence (the "ground" of the Trinity) in a direct and pure way show a tendency to move toward the same insights into an impersonal dimension of the divine life that we have been discussing.[35] In fact, at least some varieties of modern atheism, as well as the "death of God" movement, can be seen as a certain reassertion of this dimension, a return of the theologically repressed.[36]

But against the background we have sketched, and under its conditions, God also relates in a direct way with the world. In addition to the dimension of God's self-limitation or withdrawal in all creation and the dimension of God's universal immanence (two relations of God with creation which can be viewed in impersonal terms), there are ways that God relates as a character or agent. In fact, it is the first kind of relation, providing the freedom and separate sphere of creation itself, which makes this second one possible. It is God's "absence" and background immanence which allow for a free and historical encounter of humans with God as a single "Thou" on the stage of creation. If the first type of relation is one that can often be equated to insight or realization (of emptiness or of oneness with a single impersonal ultimate) then this second type is one that has clear interactive and interpersonal marks.

This dimension has the quality of an encounter between persons, a relation of active agents. The communion of the Trinity and the indivisibility of the Trinity's external acts mean that God is truly one. God encounters us as a free and consistent individual. God's activity, God's character as a personal agent, is the predominant theme of Scripture. God acts, covenants, commands, punishes, loves, and redeems. Humans seek God's presence, hear God's word, see God's acts, obey or disobey God's commandments, and offer

---

35. Tillich's "ground of being" might be proposed as an example of this dynamic.

36. This is reflected, for instance, in the background of a number of death-of-God theologians in Barthian theology. Coordinate with his emphasis on the free Word of God, Barth revitalized a sense of the apophatic dimension of God, the withdrawal and transcendence that are only bridged by God's act and promise. Without an equally revitalized trinitarian theology, which Barth himself sought, this insight could readily move in the direction the "secular" theologians took it. On the enlightenment reconfigurations of Christian theism and the modern atheisms that corresponded to them, see (Buckley, 1987).

praise or petition. KS call this kind of interaction a meeting with the ego or the common "I" of the Trinity. When we use "God" to refer to a simple personal deity, we are reflecting this relation.

The focus of this encounter is the outward communication of the will, purpose, thoughts, and feelings of one to the other, on the analogy of external interpersonal relations. Obviously, this is a vision Christianity shares with most other theisms, certainly with Judaism and Islam.[37] This relationship exists *between* God and humanity. It is characterized by events and by mediating forms, like Scripture itself. From this perspective, it is possible to treat Trinity as a name for successive kinds of possible personal encounter in this mode. We may engage God the Father as creator, Christ the Word as redeemer, or the Holy Spirit as sanctifier.

Panikkar offers an important insight when he chooses to characterize this class of relations with the divine by using the word "iconolatry."[38] Iconolatry is a representation of the divine under some particular form, mental or material.[39] This form could be that of a personal deity, "God." But it need not be. It could be a law, a teaching, or a narrative. Any definite image that represents the ultimate, and resists reduction to merely one limited expression among others serves as an icon. An icon marks the divine and relationship with it off from other possibilities. The first type of relation we discussed above involved insight into conditions that are always and everywhere the case. The realization of these conditions is marked with the motto "thou art that." Iconolatry by contrast demarcates some specific kind of relation that must be realized from among options.

We may most readily think of this as a connection between God and humans as individuals. This is an external, social encounter. It focuses on interactions like gratitude, obligation, and worship, relations that expect persons on either end. God appears as one with whom persons can have personal encounter. This is the God of the biblical and Qur'anic traditions. KS speak of the divine "I" of the Trinity, and Panikkar speaks of the Son as the "God" we know. This relationship with the divine is marked not by the silence characteristic of the emptiness or immanence we just treated, but by acts and speech. God is an agent, who speaks and acts with humanity. Humanity

---

37. I say "most," because if one takes Aristotle or Plotinus as theists, for instance, then there are instances where God is defined as impersonal. This is also the case on some understandings of ultimate Brahman as impersonal (if believers in such a Brahman are taken to be theists) or with some contemporaries who may define "god" as some impersonal or cybernetic force.

38. (Panikkar 1973, p. 10).

39. (Panikkar, 1973, p. 15).

speaks and acts in return. Insight and knowledge are less to the fore than attentiveness, obedience, and faith.

But (and this is Panikkar's point) although we may commonly think of icons as the medium for a personal divinity, this need not be the case. Under the influence of the biblical tradition, we tend to think of icons as outward expressions of God's personal nature. Through an icon, like the law given at Sinai, we encounter an external crystallization of the will or purpose of a personal deity. But it is possible to have a specific transcendent order or "law" without any personal will of which it is the expression. The "Tao" of Taoism or the *logos* in Stoicism, or the Kantian moral law would be examples. The Buddhist *dharma* might be another, depending upon whether it is taken as an eternal structure or order, or is itself simply the most important tool or skillful means used on the way to enlightenment. Even in the latter case, it comes close to iconic status. Thus at one end of the range of this iconic dimension there is some transcendent, impersonal structure or rule (like the Tao) which has iconic representations, and at the other end there is the personal God of monotheism whose expressions of will and purpose take iconic form.

The key point that distinguishes this dimension as a whole from the impersonal one we discussed first, is not personality in the divine, although that becomes a crucial feature of much "iconolatry." The key point is that an iconic view of the divine allows for contrast and tension. The icon points to the fact that the divine is not empty nor is all being already in perfect identity with it. There is a distance between us and the divine, between us and our religious end, which must be traveled. Iconolatry typically manifests an ethical or moral emphasis, a drive toward transformation. Icons lie between us and the transcendent, pointing the way for change. It is not an existing condition that must be recognized (though that step is a valuable one), but a new condition or transformation that must be attained. It is not being, or the emptiness of being, that must be known. It is a change that must happen. The motto of iconolatry is not "thou art that" but "become what you are called/structured to be."

Islam is an excellent illustration. Here there is complete clarity about God as a free, transcendent, and personal creator over against whom humans stand as responsible individuals and communities. The great icon of this relationship is the Qur'an, for here the nature of that relation and the plan for it are clearly, divinely set forth. God and humanity do not meet as equals, but they do meet as free individuals. The important categories of relation reflect this. Commandment, covenant, obedience, sin, faithfulness, trust, mercy, repentance, guilt, love, anger: all these come into play. We relate to God as to a unitary center of consciousness, a person who manifests will, purpose, decision, emotion. God communicates with us. God commands us to live in certain ways. God responds to our response. God loves righteousness, cares for the poor, condemns injustice, shows mercy to the repentant. This is a narrative and historical interaction.

Relation with God is limited if it remains entirely in the impersonal end of the iconic range. When it encompasses personal encounter as a mode for relation with God, it can stumble by treating God (on strict analogy to human relations) as simply one agent or character among others. This is an error against which Islamic tradition is particularly vigilant. Personal encounter can also go astray by taking the analogy of God as a single "I" too far, and so obscuring the complexity of the divine life. This can lead to exclusion of that first dimension we discussed (emptiness and immanence), and of others as well. But these iconic relations, as elaborated in different ways in traditions like Taoism or Islam, are very real relations with God. Maintained with devotion they can achieve distinctive religious ends, constituted by our human conformity to and enjoyment of the divine order that is offered to us.

A trinitarian perspective suggests that what is apprehended in these cases is the external unity of the Trinity, its cooperative unity in willing the good for creation. Human "reception" may focus specially on the *content* of what is willed by the Trinity (and this is consistent with impersonal icons of the divine) or may on the other hand closely connect what is called for with the personal character of the one who calls. In relating to God as personal in this way, as a single "I," Christians are on common ground with other monotheists. Christianity characteristically qualifies this common faith in two ways. The first is the conviction that the icon for this personal God is believed also to be a living person: Jesus Christ. The second, as we have described at some length, is the understanding of God as Trinity, which finds this single divine "I" grounded in a communion of persons.

We have just referred to encounter with God as a distinct personal being or through a particular icon. This can be a largely external encounter. It is a different matter when some further complexity is presumed in the divine itself. This complexity can be thought of minimally as a necessary need for a variety of specific icons (in contrast to just one). Or it can be seen as rooted in greater intrinsic personal depth and complexity (as is the case in the Trinity). This suggests participation in a third dimension of the triune life, that of personal communion. We have already said a great deal about this (in Chapter Two, for instance), and so we need only to summarize a few points.

The third dimension of relation with God is personal not only in the sense of interaction between persons, but in the sense of communion among them. To encounter each other as persons is not the same thing as to have personal communion with each other. In Scripture there is a longing for the external relation to become also internal, with a law "written on our hearts." The New Testament puts special stress on this, both in the case of Jesus' unique relation with God and in terms of the relation with God possible for believers through their communion in Christ and the Holy Spirit. This *koinonia* or participation has to do with a sharing of inner personal lives, with human sharing in the divine life.

Personal encounter is a relation that focuses on the responsiveness of one to another. Communion is a mutual indwelling, in which the distinct persons are not confused or identified but are enriched by their participation in each other's inner life. If the first dimension of relation we discussed tends toward identity of humans and the ultimate in impersonal terms, and the second type tends toward encounter in difference, this third dimension emphasizes communion of persons in their distinctive personhood. This is the participation in the divine life that is spoken of by Jesus in the Gospel of John and by Paul in his letters. By being in Christ we are able in some measure to be "in God." When Paul says "not I, but Christ in me" he does not mean "not me, but instead Christ who has now replaced me." Nor is he talking of a sudden insight that my self and Christ's self have always been the same, identical self.

He means a communion so close and full that not only external acts and effects are exchanged between persons, but also features of their inner lives. It is a communion so real that a person can rightly say of certain aspects of her own willing, longing, or loving that they seem to arise more from the indwelling of the other person than from any purely isolated individuality of her own. It is a telling part of the description of this communion that its most characteristic manifestation is in relation to yet a third person. Communion between two who love each other can often lead to the metaphorical situation of not knowing where one stops and the other begins. This can also be confused with a *loss* of person or a fusion. The ecstatic forgetfulness of sexual union, for instance, can be taken as an image of undifferentiated oneness. The more typical feature of communion as I mean it is the discovery in ourselves of an openness or response to a third person which we can hardly credit as coming from us, except by virtue of the indwelling of a second in us. No one can love God and hate their neighbor. It is not an accident, of course, that this reflects the classic trinitarian formula that sees in the communion of any two of the triune persons the implied communion of each with the third. It is the same pattern that marks God's action in the world, the "economy" of redemption, as moving from the Father, through the Son, in the Spirit. The motto of this dimension is "transformation through communion."

The image of salvation is not complete identification with God (oneness), nor perfect agreement of wills (obedience, faith) between a human and God as a pair in external relation, but the personal communion of self and God which flows into communion with other creatures. Salvation is participation in the divine life precisely in this sense of communion. If the divine life were not triune, did not embody in itself just this communion of two that requires communion with a third, then salvation would be a more extrinsic relation with God than Christianity assumes, and hopes, it is.

III

We have outlined a variety of relations touching aspects of three particular dimensions of the triune life of God. It might appear at first that these stand in a roughly linear order, moving from the impersonal (emptiness and immanence) to the iconic (whether a transcendent order or a transcendent person) to personal communion. But they might better be pictured in a triangular or circular order, making impersonal relation and personal communion border each other instead of standing as polar opposites. This is so because there is a tendency for personal communion to be interpreted by some at the extreme as the same as pure union. If followed out fully, this can lead back to an impersonal identification, not unlike that characteristic of the first type of relation. For instance, it is not surprising that the most hopeful reports of the essential convergence of Buddhism and Christianity come from those who correlate the insight into the essential emptiness of things on the Buddhist side with a strand of Christian mysticism that takes achieved communion with God closest to a union in which relation itself is erased. The most personal thus becomes the impersonal, or the impersonal becomes the suprapersonal.

If God is Trinity, these dimensions of the divine life are a seamless unity in the communion of the three persons. The various relations with God we have outlined are themselves irreducible. If God is Trinity, then no one of these need be or can be eliminated in favor of the others. And anyone who clings to the truth of one of the relations can never be forced from it by pure negation, but only possibly by enhancement. All three dimensions of relation connect with the Trinity's own reality, though not to the same cumulative extent. The three triune persons share an interpersonal communion, they relate to each other with the freedom and asymmetry of agents, and they participate in a common, infinite divine life of exchange and process. All three are a feature of the triune God's integral reality. No one is a lower expression of the others, for all are integral to what "person" means. The three kinds of relation we have outlined deal with aspects of this shared life. Christians hold that the richest human end is a communion with God that encompasses all these dimensions.

The validity of human responses to each of these dimensions of the complex divine life provides the power of religious pluralism, grounds the worthy claims of alternative traditions. This poses another question. If at least several religious ends are not simply illusions or errors, the problem appears even more vexing as to how they might be maintained together. The fact that validity and truth are distributed across a number of relations reveals to us the need for some grounding that unites them. Trinity provides that grounding.

Christians can understand the distinctive religious truth of other religions as rooted in the triune God's real, specific relations with people in those traditions. On the one hand this provides a rationale for the Christian inclusive hope that such truths might lead people toward salvation, since the ends sought through such relations have an intrinsic ground in the triune God. But on the other hand, this perspective also provides the basis to affirm the separate reality of those religious ends in their own terms. In particular veins of relation, the distinctive religious paths and truths of other traditions exhibit greater purity and power than are usually manifest in Christianity. Limit can lead to such intensification.

This does not mean that the differences among the religious ends simply have to do with degree of intensity of the same thing. We have sketched several dimensions of relation with the divine life. An intensification of one such dimension, when coupled with exclusion of others or their relegation to an instrumental, secondary status, in fact can lead to a distinct religious end. For instance, the end sought (and I believe achieved) in Theravada Buddhism is based on a human relation with God "tuned" entirely to the frequency of God's emptiness or withdrawal to leave creatures to their contingent freedom. Human relation with God is intensified and purified to fit completely within this one channel of God's relation with us. An analysis of the self carried out in this dimension will find selves themselves empty. Since a crucial element that gives selves their "substance" is their relations with others, the attempt to find a "remnant self" after subtracting all relation will lead only to emptiness. The person has no intrinsic ground for self-sufficient being. I am convinced that the Theravadan end is in fact, as that tradition claims, a cessation of suffering. In that concrete respect, it is similar to salvation. But the realization of this end relinquishes (as unreal) a whole range of possible relations with God and others whose presence is essential to the end Christians seek. In that respect it is much more similar ultimately to what Christians mean by loss.

198

It is important to make the point that relations with God in *all* three dimensions we have described are real relations with God. They are not relations with something else (idols) or with false gods. What humans find in such relations is truly there. These are all relations with the God who is triune, though some may refine and restrict their relationship with the triunity of God. They are not relations to only one divine person rather than to others, since given God's nature and the communion of the persons that is not possible. An isolated relation with one person of the Trinity is something that exists only in abstraction. In each case it is God in God's triune nature we meet.

By virtue of the constraints that we as humans put on our approach and relation to God, various aspects of the shared divine life are received in these relations. Human relations with God lead to alternative religious ends for two reasons. The first is that human conditions are in a measure constituted by the images and understandings persons bring to them. The second reason, closely connected, is that the relations between God and humans largely follow the logic of personal relations: mutual openness is required for persons to have true contact with certain actual features of the other. Unless we establish the channels to apprehend and connect with certain aspects of another person, those will remain a closed book to us and our shared life will lack that dimension. Religious ends differ in some measure because our own "conditioning" shapes our experience, but also because objective dimensions of relation with God are realized (or not) depending on whether we respond to the particular channels God has opened for that relation. For this reason, the fact that it may be the same ultimate reality which is behind distinct religious experiences and traditions does not by any means require that they result in the same religious end.

This points up a problem with two common attitudes. From the Christian side we might recognize that the aims sought within other traditions touch on specific aspects of the triune life, aspects of salvation. We may then conclude that since that aim is included as an aspect of the Christian end, those who pursue the other path necessarily attain that Christian end. This does not follow. From within another religious tradition, someone might observe that aspects of the Christian aim are "included" in that tradition's path, as a preliminary or instrumental stage toward the true religious fulfillment. She might then conclude that this means Christians will necessarily attain that end, rather than the one they ostensibly seek. This does not follow either.

We can pause for a moment to consider the three dimensions we have outlined in terms of their embodiment in Christ. We can see that as a human being, Christ lived under the conditions of the withdrawal that is part and parcel of creation itself. Jesus therefore experienced the emptiness of reality in its "suchness." He knew this dimension of the absence and/or total imma-nence of God. At the same time, as the Word of God, the second person of the Trinity, Christ directly knew the archetype of that relation between God and creation: the "kenosis of the Father" in which the first person makes space and shares life with the second person. And the general sustaining relation of God with all creation, God's immanence, upholds the humanity of Jesus no less than that of any other creature. Like other created persons, Jesus thus has access to experiences of emptiness or immanence. This is made possible by the unique kenosis of the Word. As God withdrew from all creation to allow its integrity, the second person specifically withdraws from the prerogatives of divine power, in order to be incarnated as a creature living under the con-ditions of that first withdrawal.

This all provides the condition for relation with God in the second di-mension. As a particular, historical person, Christ can also relate with God in direct personal encounter. They encounter each other as distinct individuals, such that Jesus can truly pray "not my will, but thy will be done." This is a real dimension of incarnation, along with the third dimension, that of inner com-munion with God, which takes place both through the relations of the Word to the other triune persons and through the communion of the human Jesus with the divine Word.

The three dimensions of the triune life which we have discussed, and the corresponding types of human relation with God in these dimensions, are each embodied in Christ. If we were to point to representative moments for each of these we might point to Christ's cry from the cross "My God, my God, why have you forsaken me?" as an instance of the first dimension: a concrete encounter with the distance and the kenosis of God in relation to creation. And the external personal relation with God is evident in Jesus' address to God in prayer (as *abba*), his participation in worship, the occasions when he deflects simple identification of himself with God ("Why do you call me good? No one is good but God alone.").[40] The personal communion with God, the unity of Christ and the Word, is reflected in any of those moments when Jesus assumes divine authority, as in forgiving the sins of others. The communion of the triune life, with its various dimensions, is reflected in Christ who manifests relation with God in all of those dimensions. In Christ the isolation or separation of these different dimensions is overcome. We tend to foster such isolation, once we have received some contact with the di-

40. Luke 18:19.

vine. For us it is always possible to abstract dimensions of the divine life and relation with them, to fragment communion. In Christ, this fragmentation is overcome. Christ not only reconciles us with God, but reconciles our varied ways of relating to God.[41]

This throws some light on Christology proper. One of the most common criticisms of the Christian view of Christ is that it involves contradictory statements about Christ's status. Jesus can't at the same time be externally related to God and also share the divine nature. The objection presumes a view of incarnation where being is a stuff of a certain sort or a homogenous status. As our review of Trinity has made clear, if we understand being as communion the situation is quite different. To say Jesus is divine by virtue of communion may sound like a "low" Christology, calling up pictures of Jesus as a human being who was specially sensitive to God, pursuing the same purpose, and so on. Some may reject this as not *real* divinity, real oneness with God. So long as we operate with the substance categories, this might be true. But if we take seriously the notion that God's "substance" is the communion of the triune persons, then to say that Jesus is divine by virtue of participation in that communion is to speak of the most profound unity and identity possible. It is God's free choice to extend the inner communion of the triune life to a human being through the Word (the unique divine act) and Jesus' free participation in that communion that makes Christ divine.

Christ as a human has an "external" relation of communion with the Trinity as well as an "internal" relation of communion through the Word who is one of the divine persons.[42] It is the nature of both relations as communion that makes them compatible. There is an external distinction among the divine persons in respect to each other which is a condition of their communion with each other in the godhead. As the uniqueness of that communion within God is yet open to the possibility of the further communion realized in the incarnation, so the uniqueness of Christ's relation with God is open to participation by other people in that communion.

This is the premise of the extraordinary Christian claim that other humans can participate in the inner divine communion in a proportionate way. The human Jesus does not become the second person of the Trinity, but becomes one with that person, a communion as perfect as is possible without

41. This is the work of reconciliation or atonement in its broadest terms, and is not limited to the cross.

42. This is the issue treated in discussion of the enhypostatic union, which holds that Christ's entire humanity enters into the communion with the Word.

confusion, without the dissolution of the two "natures," human and divine. God became what we are in order that we might become as God is. We become by grace what God is by nature. We have communion with God by having communion with Christ, for the "inner" divine life is otherwise inaccessible to us. Christ participates in the triune life by nature *and* by grace — by the nature of the divine Word and the grace of the incarnation — and opens the path for others to join in that communion. This is only to say, in different terms, what can be said in more familiar trinitarian language. God meets us in three characteristic dimensions, dimensions that have to do not only with the way we perceive God but with God's own character. God is the creator who is above and under us, the personal source who transcends us. God is the Word and redeemer who is with us to overcome the sin that breaks our relationship with God, to make right our relationships with each other and to deliver us from death. God is the Spirit in us and among us, who transforms our inner life and maintains our communion with others.

Early Christian writers often depicted the Christian journey as a recapitulation, a return. This was not a literal return to the garden of Eden, nor the literal gnostic view in which actual particles of the divine nature migrated out of the material world to reunite with their source. Instead, this "return" was a growing up into the image in which we are made, a realization of the divine pattern. The idea that humans could become by grace what God is by nature says a great deal about how early Christians thought of God's nature. If that nature was preeminently omnipotence, or aseity, or infinity, then the idea of humans taking it on was patently incoherent. If that nature was a literal substance, then the only way in which it makes sense for humans to share it would be the gnostic idea that some humans have a small, separate piece of this substance hidden in them.

But if that nature is understood crucially as a certain life-in-relation, then the possibility of taking it on is already present in humans because they are created in the image of that divine nature. Humans *are* that image, for their being also is constituted by relation. Humans are able to realize this nature only by grace.[43] We are so constituted that we can realize our nature only through relation with God and others. But those concrete relations themselves are not ours. They are not given to us as part of our autonomous "na-

43. This is on the face of it a distinction between God and humanity. Humans require grace to realize their own nature, and God does not. This is true in the sense that God does not need external gifts to realize the divine nature. But since the relations of the triune persons involve the free gift of each to the other, there is another sense in which grace — this grace of the free gift of each person to the others — is also necessary for "realization" of the divine nature, and is integral to it.

ture," but depend on the free choice of others. They must come as the gift and grace of others relating with us or not come at all. Being created as human is a gift, the gift of God's relation with us which is unshakable and establishes us as persons. But fulfillment of our humanity, growing up into the image we bear, is also a gift. The second is given as a possibility in the first but cannot follow automatically from it.

Of course God and humans are different, and different in some constant ways. The non-identity of God and creation precludes absorption of one into the other. But even this difference is not simply a generic one, in which it is only the same general distinction of creator/creature that marks every specific relation of communion with God. There is in addition an individual difference, where the nature of one person's communion with God has its own unique texture, distinguishing it not just from monism or separation generally but from any other person's communion with God. The salvation Christians anticipate is a personal communion of distinct creatures with God their maker.

The crucial precedent for this in the trinitarian life of God is not the equality, co-eternality, "same substance" of the persons but precisely the *asymmetrical* character of these relations of love and equality. The divine persons are fully one, fully mutual, even though they are not and will not become identical, even though what each one does out of a unique personhood is irreplaceably something the others do not do. In this specific sense there is a model in the Trinity for full communion between those who are not the same. The communion of creatures with creator is such a communion, though it involves kinds of difference that are not in question within the trinitarian life.

We can pause here for a moment to consider the somewhat complicated topics we have been discussing from another perspective. The Christian view is in many ways a metaphysically pedestrian one. Christianity resolutely affirms and accepts attachment to "middle" realities of ordinary life: persons, relations, community, communion. Our human instantiation of these things may be frail and distorted but, as our consideration of Trinity has indicated, this *kind* of thing partakes of the deepest level of reality. These features carry over into salvation and are fundamental constituents of it. Persons, relations, communion: Christians desire for these to be transformed or renewed. They do not hope to get over them.

For this reason Christianity is frequently viewed as somewhat naïve in contrast with supposedly more sophisticated perspectives. Many religious and secular worldviews purport to see through these middle-level realities, to understand them as transitory epiphenomena of something more basic. For these worldviews it follows that the prominence given persons and relations in our everyday experience of life results from a distorted perception in some way. Truth and liberation would stem from insight that reveals these things as secondary, insubstantial, passing. Christianity's peculiar middleness places it between the appeal of esoteric analyses that tell us the ultimate, the true religious end, is nothing like what things appear to be and the opposite insistence that there is "nothing but" our historical human experience, without deeper transcendent grounding.

The Christian vision of salvation looks toward a condition in which relation with God is realized (in all three of the dimensions we have discussed) and in which one shares that realization with others. Salvation is a *complex* state, for in it a person is open to each of the dimensions of the divine life that we have described. It is also crucially dependent on intersecting communions. There is no uniform plan for every person's relation with God in each of the dimensions we have outlined. Each instance will have its own unique features. No individual realizes the complete fullness of possible relation with God in any of these dimensions in a self-contained way. But we *do* approach that fullness through communion with other persons and creatures, each of whom in relation with God and with others fills out aspects that would be lacking for any one individual. Salvation is actually much more than the sum of any individual perfection.

The way that we can most deeply participate in a divine fullness, which literally overflows our finite capacities, is through mutual indwelling with other persons. This is rather like a set of parallel computers or processors that together can solve a problem that is beyond any one alone, or that can together produce a graphic image of depth and resolution otherwise impossible. To take another analogy, the body of Christ is like the array of multiple sensors in sophisticated radio telescopes or sonar systems.[44] Humans' communion with each other is also an instrument of the fuller communion with God. Our finite receptions of the triune self-giving multiply each other, in a kind of spiritual calculus that deepens each one's participation in the communion of the triune life itself. The key is openness for communion through the whole range of the divine dimensions, and openness to communion with other persons and with their unique relations with God. We saw this vision embodied in Dante's paradise as described in the *Divine Comedy*. Such a vision embodies a profound imperative for justice, since every wound in the so-

44. We might say that the divine nature is so great that even God cannot encompass it except through sharing, in the dynamic of trinitarian communion. It is an important point that in the analogies I use, the sensors and arrays contribute data to a "big picture" that is viewed or consumed elsewhere. But in the communion of the body of Christ each of the members or "sensors" is also enjoying the benefits of the "big picture."

cial fabric of human relation is likewise a rupture in the raw material of salvation. Broken bonds of human solidarity violate God's commands, but they
also close the very circuits of communion which are the nervous system of
the redeemed life. A number of recent writers on the Trinity, notably Jürgen
Moltmann and Leonardo Boff, have lifted up this perspective and drawn out
its implications.[45]

When we discussed salvation in Chapter Two, we talked particularly of
three kinds of relation: humans with God, humans with each other, and humans with creation. I hope it has become increasingly clear that a serious
consideration of alternative religious ends has the benefit of raising our appreciation for the specific character of salvation, the religious end Christians
seek. All that we have been discussing, about tuning ourselves to the diverse
"frequencies" or dimensions of the divine life, might be seen as an attempt to
specify the first, the relation of humans with God. But we can now see clearly
how the other two elements are necessarily included. Sin, evil, and death can
be effectively described as the empirical dilemmas of human life. But from
the trinitarian perspective we have outlined, we can also see why estrangement from God would take these specific forms. The doctrine of the Trinity
understands God as intrinsically relational. Since salvation is constituted by a
communion that encompasses our relations with God, with other persons,
and with the rest of creation, it follows that disruption in our capacity for
communion with others (God, persons, or nature) blocks realization of salvation. All of these are enduring and crucial components of the religious end.

These dimensions retain their own distinctness and authenticity. The
reality of one is not compromised by its inclusion with others. This is not
only true for the broad dimensions of relation I have described. It applies as
well to the specific way they are realized in individual cases. Every person who
enters into communion with God in Christ does not have an identically formulated inner and outer life, in which some identical proportion or intensity
of the different dimensions of relation we described is maintained at all
times. According to Christian scripture and tradition, such a thing is not desirable, even were it possible. There is an extraordinary range in the relative
power with which these dimensions may show up. Paul's discussion in his
First Letter to the Corinthians (chapter 12) about the varied gifts among the
saints makes this clear. In any event, an individual person can only realize a
very tiny portion of the possibilities in *any* of these dimensions, isolated or
not. This is why communion is the fundamental shape of salvation. Participation to the fullest in all these dimensions of relation with God is dependent

45. (Moltmann, 1981; Boff, 1988).

also upon communion with others, so that both variety and depth can be enhanced and expanded.

"Saints," from this perspective, are as much those who have learned to participate by communion in others' communion with God as they are those who have developed to perfection their individual faculties for private unity with God. This is precisely what the "communion of the saints" is about.[46] Mutual participation, communion-in-difference, is integral to salvation, as it is to the triune life itself. This is also why in Christian tradition community, the actual concrete body of the church, has been regarded as fundamental to the Christian life, even to salvation itself.[47] Fuller communion with God and fuller communion with other persons go together. One is impossible without the other, for one person's total communion with God can plumb only a portion of the possibilities that the triune God offers. We have tended to stress the full array of human communion as a constituent element of the fullness of salvation. But there is another side to the picture that is also important. The multiple connections are crucial, but entry into this communion at the extreme only requires one point. A person can be drawn into this extraordinary, cosmic communion through initial attachment of the most humble and basic sort to one other person. In Dante's *Divine Comedy* this is exemplified

46. It is interesting that the official requirements for canonization in the Roman Catholic Church include authentication of a minimum number of miracles performed by the saint or through appeal to the saint. Characteristically, these are miracles of healing, pointing to the fact that even the most contemplative or solitary of the saints must be seen to demonstrate the transfer of spiritual benefits to another. It must be demonstrated that others can participate in the effects of the saint's relation with God. Sanctity must be communicable, in at least some ways. Christian faith is clear that our communion with Christ is the key gate to wider communion with God in all the triune dimensions. *Based* on that relation, salvation is marked by webs of communion. As we saw, this fact is dramatically illustrated in Dante's vision of paradise and the celestial rose. In the West the Roman Catholic tradition may have stressed too much that it is through communion with a saint that deeper communion with God is possible, leaving aside the equally important fact that it is through communion with others that the heavenly bliss of the saint is actually multiplied to its full extent.

47. "Outside the Church there is no salvation" is a phrase that expresses this conviction, though it has often been interpreted in terms that focus more on extrinsic than intrinsic boundaries to communion. For an excellent review of the history of both the phrase and the idea see (Sullivan, 1992). In a different connection, we can also note that some contemporary liberal Christian theologies effectively claim that "salvation" can be identified without remainder with the creation of a just and participatory human community. The error in the exclusive narrowness of such a reduction should not cloud the legitimate basis from which it proceeds. Salvation does have an intrinsic communal and participatory character.

in Dante's relation with Virgil and, above all, with Beatrice. Loving attachment even to one person, if that love has the character not of closed possession but of further openness *through* that person, can finally draw someone to the very heart of the celestial rose.

In this chapter we have tried to describe the way that distinctive religious ends could be understood in relation to Trinity. It remains for us to address the question of how the existence of such ends fits or does not fit with the conviction that God brings creation to an eschatological consummation. That is the topic we will take up in Chapter Seven. But first, in the next chapter, we will take the principles outlined so far and explore what they might mean more concretely in relation to specific religious traditions.

Chapter Six

True Relations: The Integrity
of Other Religious Ends

We have been exploring the distinct dimensions of God that Christians believe are constituted by God's triune nature, as well as the various relations with God these dimensions make possible. Seen from one side, these relations compose the substance of salvation. Salvation is precisely communion with God across the breadth of these complex dimensions of God's nature, a communion whose fullness requires participation in relation with other persons and with creation. Humanity realizes its deepest encounter with the plenitude and diversity of the divine nature through this web of communion, this shared relation with God.

From another view, these same dimensions frame the Christian perspective on alternative religious ends. Communion, whether the communion of the triune God or the communion that constitutes salvation, is an ontology of freedom. It is a unity sustained by love and mutual participation. It cannot be forced. To encounter God through a single dimension of the divine life is to encounter the one God who exists in all these dimensions. But such an encounter does not require a person to enter into those other dimensions of relation. That can only come by free choice. If pursued consistently and exclusively, relation through any one of these dimensions results in its own distinctive religious end or fulfillment. The "one way" to salvation, and the "many ways" to religious ends are alike rooted in the Trinity.

In this chapter we will review and extend our general account of the way the Trinity grounds a variety of religious ends. Then we will briefly illustrate that view through consideration of the religious end in two concrete religious traditions: the Advaita Vedanta tradition of Hinduism and the Islamic tradition.

I

In the last chapter I described three types of relation with God, one marked by impersonal identity, one marked by iconographic encounter, and one marked by personal communion. Within the first relation, we distinguished two possible variations, each rooted in aspects of the triune life itself. The first (more apophatic), is grounded in the emptiness by which each of the divine persons makes space for the others. Each is constantly making way for the others and going out to them, in an exchange that transcends rigid, autonomous boundaries. The second variation (more unitive) is grounded in the coinherence or complete immanence of each of the divine persons in the others. From the trinitarian perspective, these are two views of the same constant interaction and flow of relation among the three persons. One view grasps the ceaseless process itself. The other grasps the unity of spirit it sustains.

When "externalized," in terms of economic interaction between God and creatures, the first of these possibilities has to do with God's active contraction from creation. This withdrawal allows creation a real and distinct, if derived reality. It makes possible a valid human insight into the insubstantiality of all being and the "emptiness" of God. Such insight, and rigorous practice based on it, make contact with a very real aspect of the divine, with the kenotic process that is always taking place within the triune communion and is lived out in God's relation with creation. Characterization of the divine in these terms leads to a profound realization of relation with the divine in this dimension. Maintained in all its purity, this results in a religious fulfillment essentially as described in the Buddhist *nirvana*. This religious end is quite distinct from salvation, in its clear exclusion of relation or personal communion, in its firm bar against any enduring participation in the other dimensions of relation with the triune God.

The second side of this dimension of the divine life is economically expressed through God's sustaining presence in creation, in, with, and under the natural order. This constant divine activity reveals a universal immanence of God in every creature. It reflects the impersonal mutual indwelling of the three triune persons. In apprehending God's immanence in creation, humans meet a true aspect of God's own nature and of God's connection with us. In one sense, we are nothing but an extension of the power of God, an expression of God's will and purpose. If pursued intensely and separately, this insight suggests a pantheistic end in which the small "I" of the particular creature resolves into a perfect identity with the one existing "I" of the absolute being. This end is plainly different from salvation, for it relinquishes the distinct identity and reality God has granted the creature. Deep as Christians hold that loss to be, this pantheistic end is an actual possibility, constituted through exclusive cultivation of relation with God in these terms. The creature can realize the impersonal immanence of the divine as its sole being, and yield back all unique identity and relations.

We called the second dimension of the triune life "iconographic" (borrowing Panikkar's language). Within the Trinity, each of the three persons encounters the others as a unique character. The triune God as a whole also has a determinate character in relation with humanity. We encounter God as a distinct other, over and against us, with one divine nature and purpose. There are two variations on this encounter. The first focuses on encounter with the divine life under an authoritative but not explicitly personal "icon": a law, an order or structure. The Buddhist *dharma* or the *Tao* of Taoism are examples. From a Christian perspective, it is the common purpose or will of the triune God that is apprehended under such an image.[1] Faithful efforts to conform to this transcendent order, to live in accord with its pattern, can lead to distinct religious fulfillments. Such ends are distinct from the personal relation that constitutes salvation, but they realize connection with an authentic dimension of God.

The second variation focuses on God as a personal being, and on personal encounter with the divine. Law and morality figure strongly here also, but in the context of command, promise, trust, and faith. The encounter with God is primarily interpersonal and external, an "I-thou" relation. The religious end in view is faithfulness and obedience. Though distinct from the communion character of salvation, this personal faithfulness is a profound relation with God, one that may also integrate dimensions we have discussed above. I noted Islam as an excellent example of such an aim, with its emphatic emphasis on the otherness of God and its concern to avoid God's association with creatures in any manner that would confuse this distinction.

The third dimension of the triune life derives from the *perichoresis* or mutual communion of the three divine persons. This unity is such as to leave

---

1. Deism is an interesting view that partly straddles the two variations on iconography I am suggesting. Insofar as deism effectively focuses on the self-sufficient order that a first-mover God simply kicked off, it tends toward the more impersonal iconography. Insofar as deism emphasizes some personal encounter with its God (say by rational means) it swings toward the more personal iconography.

each one's unique particularity intact. Because God's nature is constituted by the communion of three persons, that nature maintains within it distinct and irreducible dimensions. The correlative to this dimension of triune life would be a relation between creatures and God in which the dimensions we have discussed so far each maintain their own integrity and achieve a co-equality. Now it seems there are two ways to imagine this. The first possibility would simply put these different "frequencies" of relation side by side, emphasizing the pure independence of each one as parallel and non-converging absolutes. Traditional polytheism and some postmodern theological perspectives reflect this approach. They agree in maintaining that there are many discrete ways of relating with divine reality. That reality itself is seen to have a number of in-commensurable forms, and no intrinsic principle of unity. More than one dimension of divine life is recognized, but there is no way to understand them as dimensions of *one* divine life. There is association, but no communion. In principle, such a perspective adds no new religious end to those constituted in the ways we have just reviewed. It simply affirms them separately and rules out any normative integration of these disparate possibilities. The divine diversity underwrites a pluralism of autonomous relations with roughly autonomous divine realities.

The second vision proceeds through an explicit trinitarianism, a particular vision of the inner complexity in the life of the one personal God. The conviction that this complexity takes the form of a communion of persons offers a pattern that can maintain a unity-in-distinction of the dimensions we have outlined. The variety of human relations with God then in principle may find integration, communion-in-difference being the very means, the necessary means, to fully relate with a God who is a communion of distinct persons. This is the trinitarian path, whose distinctive feature is not simple pluralism but communion, as we outlined more fully in the last chapter.

Christian faith holds that salvation, as a unique religious fulfillment, is constituted by a communion with Christ that opens an integrated communion with the divine life in the various dimensions we have outlined. Salvation is a relation with God in which humans connect with these varied dimensions of the divine life in a unified way. The fact that these dimensions have an integral unity in God does not mean that any contact with God in a single dimension compels one to participate directly in all dimensions. Expansion or change in relationship is something that cannot be, should not be forced entirely from one side. A particular type of relationship can have its own reality and stability. This is the light in which Christians may view religious ends other than salvation.

These dimensions of the divine life and the varied possible relations with

God they make possible together provide a map within Christian theology for locating diverse religious ends. The possibilities we outlined are not strictly linear or cumulative. We might think of the impersonal dimension as basic, with the personal as a further addition, and trinitarian complexity as a culmination. But this is somewhat misleading. It is possible to have a firm hold on the personal dimension of the divine life and to be wanting in an adequate grasp of its impersonal dimension, for instance. The second does not follow automatically with the first in practice, even though the first implies the second. Nor does the fact that the aim of Christian faith is a communion with God through these various dimensions assure by any means that Christianity in practice naturally subsumes any one of these dimensions in its fullness. On this score, Christians need humble apprenticeship to other religions in regard to dimensions of the triune life that those faiths grasp with profound depth. *We can learn from a Muslim.*

Typically, a religious tradition takes one dimension or one aspect of one dimension as the root divine reality. Christianity does a similar thing, in that it takes one aspect, communion, as the key to its understanding of the others. Its peculiar way of including the other dimensions is to include them *as* other.[2] Christians see trinitarian communion as the key to the coordination of all of these dimensions, as an additional dimension that assures the continuing integrity of each of the others. They are to be interpreted from the trinitarian basis and not the other way around. This means that each of the dimensions is granted co-equality with the others.

This does not mean that the dimension of communion lacks its own characteristic dangers and limitations. Christians believe it is the only way to the mutual coinherence of the varied valid religious aims. But communion loses its character if it loses touch with the distinctive relations that make it up. The only truly unique component of the Christian identity is communion in Christ. That uniqueness is the decisive key. But we should not frame this uniqueness as simply one separate kind of relation with God over against any other mode of relation with God. If its distinguishing feature is precisely a relation that reconciles, brings to communion, these various dimensions of relation with God, then it must embrace these dimensions as they may be found concretely in other religions. Communion cannot function effectively as an identity of pure contradiction.[3] When Christians incline in that direction, they short-circuit the special witness they have to share.

2. This is the point that John Milbank develops specifically in its social aspect. Milbank sees Trinity and the Christian vision of salvation as a unique source for the aim of a community composed of diverse others who remain distinctly other *as* members of the same body (Milbank, 1993).

3. Communion in Christ is the distinctive Christian mode of relation with God, the

The composite character of salvation as communion throws light on the relation of Christianity with other religious traditions in dialogue and mission. Belief in the unity of various dimensions of divine life means that Christians are obliged to recognize validity in the unique claims of many religions, obliged even to recognize a ground for their distinctive criticisms of Christianity. On the other side of the equation, Christians will bear witness to their own universal vision of communion in Christ. This witness is a distinctive affirmation *that* these varied dimensions with God can cohere in co-equality and mutuality. It is also a distinctive confession as to *how* that communion comes about.

The particular shape of this witness will be different in different settings. Christian response to religious traditions will vary depending upon which dimensions are mutually recognized. Although the church has a common faith, its articulation of that faith will appropriately vary in different contexts and conversations. Different aspects of the Christian religious end will come to the fore, both by commonality and contrast, depending on the specific end in view for another specific religious tradition.

For instance, throughout history Christians have often been in contact with traditional or primal religions. Such traditions usually recognize many divine beings with personal or quasi-personal qualities. Such divinities or spirits are often marked by a whimsical or variable quality of personal character, and the interactions among them result in a spiritual and natural environment that is highly unpredictable or requires extensive ritual control. In such settings, Christians have often emphasized that the personal qualities of God do not imply arbitrariness. They have stressed unvarying order in God's relation with creation. That is, they have stressed the "impersonal" dimension

---

only thing that Christians can claim as truly distinctive of their tradition. But communion is an obviously tricky basis for a claim of unique identity. It can't be entirely self-sufficient, as it depends on others. Christianity then on one hand is impelled to be among the most "syncretistic" of religions and on the other hand is nervous about syncretism, both out of fear of losing its own distinctive identity and because the nature of the communion it seeks (on the trinitarian model) requires the different relations with God to retain their distinctive qualities. Christianity cannot fall back on a simple identity, for its identity is complex in nature. To put it another way, Christianity aims so intently to include various modes of relation with God in their varying uniqueness that it necessarily sometimes will run the risk of *becoming* what it intends to incorporate. Its own churches and theologians regularly, and purposely, produce "Buddhist" forms of Christianity, or secular forms of Christianity, or Hindu forms. It is this border area to which Panikkar points so effectively in his work. The ecumenical internal challenge to coordinate various enculturated forms of Christianity is precisely the challenge which ought to exist, according to the pattern of Christian faith.

of the divine life, both in its universal, sustaining immanence and in the divine withdrawal to provide for a world with its own freedom for human initiative and understanding. God's personal will and freedom are expressed significantly in a settled order. Christ is not only a source of spiritual power but also the universal *logos* present in the consistent structures of creation. This is an aspect of the encounter of "monotheism" with "polytheism" that takes it beyond the level of dueling divination. These issues have been much discussed in regard to Christianity's role in the rise of modern science, and the development of the creative mix of expected intelligibility and contingency necessary for science.[4]

In other contexts, Christians have been in contact with religions that have a clear and sophisticated sense of transcendent order, of constant, impersonal process. The Christian witness then characteristically emphasized personal encounter with a personal God. Topics of special interest might include revelation as a personal and historical reality or the role of God as creator. Focus falls on the necessity for personal reconciliation, not only moral justice. Christ is a personal revelation of God's character and will.

In yet other contexts, in interaction with those who have a strong sense of personal relation with a unitary divine, Christian witness has shifted more explicitly toward communion and participation in the divine life, toward issues of divine complexity and its meaning for coordination of various dimensions of human relation with God. The result is an emphasis on communion with God that may seem to push the envelope of the "personal," and also an emphasis on a certain vicarious communion among persons as a condition of deeper unity with God. Christ has entered into communion with us, so that we can enter into communion with God.

I have tried to sketch the way in which various religious ends might be related to the triune God. It is clear that in some measure individuals or subgroups within a non-Christian religious tradition may navigate *through* that tradition *toward* the salvation Christians seek. It is likewise true that some within Christian tradition can navigate toward the different religious end sought by another religion. Religions may be used more or less against their grain as stepping stones toward alternative aims. Inclusivists in all traditions grant that other religions contain this measure of validity: they have good elements, rays of light, that can be put to use by persons who sooner or later will leave that religion and its goal behind in favor of something better. Thinkers within various world religions have viewed Christianity in this light, as Chris-

---

4. (Butterfield, 1965; Jaki, 1978; Klaaren, 1984; Jaki, 1988; Cohen, Duffin, et al., 1990; Kaiser, 1991).

tian theologies of religions have largely focused on how those in other traditions might journey from them toward salvation. These are inevitable and appropriate forms of mutual religious interpretation.

not anonymous Christians

But the insistent question rightly lingering over such work asks: How are we to understand these distinct religions themselves? How are we to understand devout adherents who do not pass beyond those traditions on their way toward the Christian end, but who in fact achieve their own? What do we make of the religions when they are not secondary means of being Christian? Some Christian theologians have maintained that the various world religions ordinarily serve as the means for their adherents' salvation (i.e., attainment of the Christian end). Christianity would be (for those adherents) simply an extraordinary means of doing the same thing.[5] Would it not make more sense to regard these traditions as ordinary and primary means of attaining their own unique ends, in contrast with the Christian aim? This recognition does not deny that these religions could secondarily, at the same time, serve those so inclined as the path to "anonymous" (and necessarily, finally explicit) Christian faith. Where this process takes place, it involves not only a conversion to Christ as God's Word but a conversion to communion in Christ as the nature of the end desired. The two go together.

The interaction between traditions does not commonly present itself in flat and simple terms. As I have said, Christianity is not alone in registering the various dimensions we have outlined. Other religions have their own distinctive ways of interpreting this diversity, their own claims to unify it. Usually this involves an explanation that one of these dimensions is ultimately real and the others represent prefigurations or cruder approximations on the path from misunderstanding toward that truth. The issues between the religions usually have to do with the manner in which the various dimensions are coordinated in theory and practice, how much basic reality is attributed to each dimension, and what the *means* of integration among them is to be. The religious traditions provide alternative normative ways of resolving this diversity of relation with the divine. Different configurations of the constellation of relations lead to different cumulative religious ends.

The distinctive Christian feature is not simply recognition of these dimensions. It is trinitarian communion as the pattern of their integration. The particular claim is that these dimensions can be coordinated with co-equality. When brought together through communion, each of these relationships is

---

5. This view was articulated by Hans Küng, drawing on the thought of Karl Rahner and H. R. Schlette. See the discussion of this view and its sources by Jacques Dupuis (Dupuis S.J., 1997, pp. 153ff.).

not only affirmed as valid, but maintained as rooted in a real dimension of the divine life itself, with its own particularity. They become one, but each remains itself. This is the trinitarian pattern, encompassing the various relations as all grounded in the divine nature, as all real, without recourse to reduction or dissolution.

From this perspective, the peculiar thing about the Trinity is not that it adds or multiplies types of relation with God beyond those that might be found individually somewhere in other religions. The Trinity is striking in its stubborn refusal to subtract from these relations, its refusal to unify by reduction or absorption. If there is a unique added relation — communion — its hallmark is its peculiar recognition of the individual particularity of the others. This is reflected in the collective criticisms of Christianity from other religious perspectives. Islam, for instance, objects that both internal, personal complexity in the divine nature and the possibility of human participation in the inner life of God (let alone incarnation) are illusory, unreal. These relations do not exist. Christianity's error is in not excluding them. Language about them, if legitimate at all, must refer to another dimension of relation. It is Christian conviction about the irreducible character of these relations that is unacceptable to Muslims. It would be rather different, perhaps, if Christians were willing to collapse this whole dimension by treating it as a matter purely of extravagant metaphorical expression for the external personal encounter between God and humans. But it is this subordination of some dimensions of relation as less real than others that the Trinity is structured to avoid.

On the other hand, most Buddhists and much of Hinduism object that it is this personal encounter of distinct beings (the dimension that would be emphasized by the Muslim) that is secondary or less ultimate. These critics reject Christian belief that this relation also has ultimate validity. The divergence might be overcome if Christians could agree that this dimension of interpersonal personal encounter were itself only a rough metaphor to lead spiritual novices toward recognition of impersonal emptiness or absolute identity. Yet this would only truncate the Trinity in a different direction.

Those most thoroughly committed to naturalistic beliefs object that the notion of a universal divine immanence (veering in a pantheistic direction) or the idea of a transcendent "emptiness" is without foundation, mere metaphysical superstition. Even if Christian beliefs in communion and personal encounter with God were subtracted, Christian affirmation of an impersonal, universal divine immanence and divine "withdrawal" at the base of the natural world would be unacceptable to positivistic secular reason. This is a practical example of the way Christianity sides concretely with Islam, with Buddhism, with Advaita Vedanta, and with other traditions by affirming as real the specific dimensions of divine relation with the world that each affirms.[6]

To expand on one example, Buddhism certainly regards the "emptiness" discerned in impersonal insight as ultimate. It generally regards various icons (such as the teaching of the dharma) and personal images or relations (deities, heavenly buddhas, bodhisattvas) as instrumental aids toward that end, as "lower" representations of truth.[7] If the religious ultimate truly *is* exclusively impersonal, then the Buddhist inclination to treat personal religious relations as secondary and dispensable is hardly a loss. In that case, Christianity is burdened with a profound superfluity. It elevates what are only instrumental metaphors or erroneous perceptions to a level of importance they cannot support.

On the other hand, if the ultimate is personal, or is such as to uphold enduring human personal relations, then the Buddhist approach has a profound failing. Yet, even were Buddhism in error on the nature of the ultimate, it might certainly have a core of truth in other respects. So too Christianity, if wrong about the personhood of the ultimate, does not lack recognition of the reality of the impersonal dimensions of emptiness and immanence. There is an asymmetry in the two faith commitments. The Christian terms affirm the impersonal as real, an integral and irreducible dimension of the personal, not as an imperfect perception whose final role is to be superseded. Most Buddhist affirmations of the personal are much more equivocal, granting it only an apparent truth that is dispelled through insight into the impersonal.

Christianity characteristically risks in the direction of including more relational possibilities at the level of irreducible reality. Christian tradition holds that the nature of the religious ultimate actually is being-as-communion. And it maintains that this is the greatest fullness we can imagine as true. Other religious perspectives may deny one or both of these contentions. That is, even if it were true that personal relation could be enduring and ultimate, for some it still might be viewed as a fate they hope to escape in favor of some alternative end.

6. Like John Hick, I see a common cause of the religions over against naturalism. This is not because each religion makes the same confession about an ultimate and undefined "Real," but rather because they separately affirm specific testimony to concrete aspects of the triune God. See also (Clooney S.J., 1999, particularly chapter two) for a fascinating picture of shared rationality in arguments for God's existence in the Hindu and Christian traditions.

7. I am of course aware that in some *Mahayana* traditions "personal" entities may be given more significant status than is suggested here. For our purposes at the moment it makes no difference if my characterization is limited to *Theravada* Buddhism.

This case is of special interest in the interreligious discussion, for it illustrates that it is not only matters of fact but of evaluation and judgment that bear on the realization of religious ends. That an end is truly real and available does not mean that humans are compelled to value it.

The purity of the particular Buddhist religious end fosters sensitivity to what cannot be articulated. It encourages analytical sophistication, a skepticism about language, a critique of anthropomorphism, and an existential focus, all of which Buddhism generally finds lacking or deficient in Christian thought and practice. In dialogue, it is common for Christians to argue either that these qualities are unimportant, or else that they can be found to the same extent in Christian sources. The perspective I have outlined suggests that these Buddhist insights are truly grounded in relation with a dimension of the divine life. It also suggests that on the whole we should not expect to find their intensity and purity equaled or surpassed in Christian tradition. It is true that this dimension of the divine life is recognized in the Christian trinitarian pattern. But that observation in no way deflects the truth that a different kind of depth is found through the exclusivity with which Buddhist understanding grasps this dimension. Christians need to engage Buddhist confession as rooted in a reality that Christians must also affirm, or lose touch with their own trinitarian ground. Divergence stems from the Christian affirmation and Buddhist denial that a communion is possible that unites this dimension with other equally valid dimensions.

What I have said so far reflects my conviction that Christian theology may locate various religious ends within a trinitarian framework. We must keep three things in mind, however. The first is that those in various religious traditions reasonably make analogous types of judgment, characterizing Christian salvation in terms of their own frameworks. This keeps before us the very important fact that these religions can and do interpret Christian tradition as a fragmentary resource and our adherence to it as at best an intermediate step toward something different and better than we imagine. I believe any framework for diversity ought to recognize this inevitable and legitimate aspect of religious encounter. Traditions rightly "impose" their evaluative standards on others. The question is not *whether* this is done, but which tradition or traditions prove able to assimilate the widest range of concrete truth from the others in the process.

Secondly, our analysis should have made it clear that the Christian attempt to understand religious ends in a trinitarian framework requires a detailed knowledge of religions in their own terms. Few individuals are in a position to do this adequately with respect to even one tradition. This provides a plain rationale for the importance of community study, in the congregations, schools, and seminaries of the church as well as in the secular academy. It indicates especially why study of the particular and unique features of religious traditions is valuable, study that takes seriously their concrete practices and truth claims.

This leads to a third point. The study of a religious tradition will rarely yield a simple profile, in which all the features of a tradition can be categorized as belonging to one dimension of relation with God. This is where the complexity of the issues and the need for careful study come most to the fore. The theological task will require patient attention to the unique way that the religious tradition in question manifests its awareness and sensitivity to the various dimensions we have described. The complexity of religious traditions, and the empirical insight reflected in that complexity, are what make inclusivist claims and accounts by each tradition plausible. Though the religions differ in what they take to be the basic nature of the religious ultimate and the corresponding religious end, they each provide some purchase for persons to pursue an end and an understanding divergent from the one dominant in that tradition.

It is plain that this comparative theological enterprise can hardly be carried out by a single scholar. Though this book tries to specify a Christian theological map that orients and justifies participation in this enterprise, it certainly does not exemplify what this would mean in relation to any single religion. In the balance of this chapter, I will give two brief examples of how my perspective might be deployed in interpreting religious ends in one variety of Hinduism and in Islam. In line with the thesis I have advanced, I will give primary attention to theological understanding of the unique, the irreducibly distinct qualities that separate these traditions from Christianity. The aim is to indicate how what makes these faiths different from Christianity can be understood as valid in its own terms, and yet how Christians may view those differences as deficits, open to Christian witness, as well as realized relation with God.

I am not an expert in either of these traditions. The topics we touch on here merit more fine-grained treatment. Yet the primary issue is not whether my accounts are definitive ones, but whether this *kind* of perspective holds promise for an engagement of religions in which both our own distinctive Christian witness and the validity of the other religions' witness can be credited in concrete terms. My perspective gives Christians strong grounds on which to *defend* the truth and validity of the specific self-descriptions of a number of other religious traditions. We can defend these accounts against secular, reductive criticisms (or against criticism from other religious views, for that matter), while at the same time maintaining the validity of Christian witness *to* these traditions.

220

The approach I have outlined does not prescribe one way in which the Christian theological interpretation of concrete faith traditions must be carried out. Since this book does not offer an extended concrete reading of any single tradition, it may be helpful to point for illustration to a few authors whose work richly exemplifies such reading. I believe their work fits well with the framework I have outlined, though I do not mean to suggest that these writers themselves necessarily agree with all the arguments I have advanced.

A key element of such approaches is what we might call alternating perspectives, in which the priority is to view the two traditions each in terms of the other, as opposed to setting both within a supposed neutral or third framework. This does not deny that there are modes of reasoning, for instance, that can make sense across traditions. But it asserts the legitimacy, in fact the necessity, of theological interpretation (or tradition-specific interpretation). Although the title "comparative theology" is susceptible to many definitions, this is the meaning I would give to it.[8]

This process always begins with study to appreciate the distinctive, actual features of alternative religious traditions and subtraditions. At this stage, it is crucial that priority be given to the internal voices of the religious tradition itself, its original texts, its great spirits, its prominent interpreters. But comparative theology uses this learning to ask further how one's own faith tradition might be construed within these terms, as well as what place those concrete religious elements might find within one's own faith. Thus sometimes one might "read" some aspects of Christianity through the terms in which they could be construed by another tradition, to explore what illumination this provides. An example would be a Buddhist reading of the notions of incarnation and Trinity.[9] Sometimes one might "read" some aspect of Buddhism to see how it might be understood from a Christian perspective. An example would be a trinitarian understanding of emptiness. I would emphasize that in either case, the primary aim is never to find a reading in either direction where nothing is left out, nothing remains at odds. The aim is not to read into unity or identity, though unity of some sorts is readily discovered. It is the tension, the distinctiveness, the recalcitrance of the reading in both directions that is the continuing source of light and fascination.

An outstanding example in regard to Hindu tradition would be the work of Francis X. Clooney S.J.[10] Clooney is notable both for the clarity with

8. See (Clooney S.J., 1993, esp. chapter one; Clooney S.J., 1995).

9. For such a project carried out by a Christian, see (Keenan, 1989; Keenan, 1995). For an example of a Buddhist scholar doing the same thing, see (Yagi, 1987).

10. See particularly (Clooney S.J., 1990; Clooney S.J., 1993; Clooney S.J., 1996; Clooney S.J., 1999). In relation to Buddhism, I would point to the work of Paul Griffiths as

which he states the theological dimension of his comparative work and for the concreteness of that work. He describes his inquiry as a kind of "cross reading" of Hindu texts and Christian scripture. On the one hand, Clooney affirms the commitment from which he works as a Christian in reading Hindu texts. On the other, he affirms that in return his own understanding of Christian texts is continually transformed, as those texts are for him inevitably also read from Hindu perspectives, through the lens of Hindu wisdom. He advocates a form of comparative theology which "remains close to the particularities of the traditions studied, which maintains the prominent position of the practical issues of faith and commitment which characterize theological investigations, and which generalizes in the sense that as a member of a larger community, the comparativist as theologian is required to recount for that community both the details and implications of the comparative project in order to engage the community in the practice or its results."[11] Other fine examples of scholars who embody a similar ideal would be Thomas Thangaraj, a south Indian theologian now teaching in the U.S., and John Carman, past director of the Harvard Center for the Study of World Religions.[12] In regard to Islam I would point to the ground-breaking work of Kenneth Cragg.[13] Cragg calls his work a theology of "cross reference," a theme that strikes many of the same notes as Clooney's approach.[14] In Cragg's case, an entire pioneering career has been devoted to deepening the reciprocal interpretations Islam and Christianity give of each other. Especially striking, for my interest, is the way in which Cragg maintains a firm respect for the concrete distinctive character of Islam over against Christianity as a focus of his comparative task.

Happily, scholars like these are not as rare as they were at the time Cragg began to write. Theology will be increasingly dependent on them in the decades ahead.

---

very consistent with my theological framework. Griffiths is somewhat more apologetic than Clooney in his writing, but he proceeds with the same admirable focus on the specificity of Buddhism and the same seriousness about its unique character (Griffiths, 1991; Griffiths, 1994).

11. (Clooney S.J., 1993, p. 14).

12. See particularly (Thangaraj, 1983; Thangaraj and Kaufman, 1994; Clooney S.J., 1993; Carman, 1994).

13. See particularly (Cragg, 1977; Cragg, 1984; Cragg, 1985; Cragg, 1986; Cragg, 1986; Cragg, 1992; Clooney S.J., 1993).

14. (Cragg, 1986, pp. 4-5).

II

Hinduism is a daunting or even, some argue, a misleading subject heading. For the sake of clarity, we will focus on one great tradition within Indian religion, that of Advaita Vedanta. "Vedanta" generally covers a number of schools of thought in Indian tradition that take a group of Sanskrit texts, the *Upanishads,* as their primary religious authority and as the interpretive key to the wider body of Vedic scriptures or texts. This tradition devoted special emphasis to clarifying and resolving the meaning of certain key (and controverted) terms in the *Upanishads,* notably the nature of the cosmic principle *Brahman.* The religious aim of this tradition is *moksha,* liberation or enlightenment. If we ask about the specific nature of this religious end, traditional Advaita might respond that the best description we can give of this goal is that it is the condition attained by one who becomes a competent reader and practitioner of the great Advaita texts, either by direct reading or through the instruction of a teacher or through both.[15] The end is the enactment or realization of the wisdom of the texts regarding *Brahman.* An outside observer or an Advaitan interpreter might provide a "short cut" description of that condition in philosophical terms, referring to it as "monistic unity" for instance. But this could only be a subordinate and insufficient summary compared to the reality itself or to the text's approach to it. This is particularly true, since the texts themselves (notably the *Upanishads* and the commentaries on them) contain a variety of often contrasting descriptions of the nature of *Brahman.* Achievement of the Advaitan end is contingent on the insight that allows one to rightly interpret these various descriptions into one truth. The conviction of the tradition is that this knowledge is contained and conveyed in the texts to the highest degree that is possible in such a medium. A secondary summary of this teaching — if it proved to be a better explanation of the substance of the text — would be a "higher revelation." Since such a thing is ruled out, a summary can only be assumed to do less well what the text is already doing. So it is at best only a lower-level preliminary, not a short cut to the text's meaning.[16]

15. A good deal of this discussion of Advaita as a commentarial tradition draws heavily on (Clooney S.J., 1993). Along with the *Gita* and the *Upanishads* themselves, the other sources seen as deserving of commentary are the sutras of Badarayana, sometimes called the *Uttara Mimamsa Sutras.* Badarayana can be regarded as the first to formulate Vedanta, although Shankara's later commentaries on Badarayana (and through him on the *Upanishads* and *Gita*) are perhaps more definitive of the later tradition.

16. This leaves aside for the moment the special role of a teacher or guru, whose teaching about the text may in fact be given extraordinary authority, but only as, so to

Virtually all religious traditions, it appears, offer us some variation of a similar response to questions about their ends. The point of similarity is the assertion that if one is to understand the nature of the end, one must embark on the path that attains this end. Descriptions from a distance cannot be adequate accounts. Advaita's version of this conviction is notable (like the Buddhist version) because it stresses the necessity for its adherents to learn the inadequacy even of descriptions given within the textual tradition of Advaita itself. The religious end, *moksha,* is a condition of insight attained by those who have undergone a particular path of training and who have grasped a certain set of teachings. Perhaps the best account of the end would be to say that it is the goal that you reach by beginning to do *these* things, and then doing *these* things, and then contemplating *this* problem, and so on. It can be described as a program of practice that realizes the end.

For the sake of argument, let us assume that we regard swimming as a capacity that is natural to all human beings, part of their true intrinsic reality. "Not knowing how to swim" is a state induced in us by fear and ignorance, and it may require certain disciplines or practices to dispel this obstacle. "Swimming" is what you will be doing when you have completed the process of insight and training that begins right now by lowering your face to the water and blowing bubbles. Description of this sort will of course shift. For someone who has long been blowing bubbles, we might say swimming is what you will be doing when you have completed the process of insight and training that continues right now by practicing the "dead man's float." These two descriptions are both identical and different. They describe the same end, but with practical variations.

What such descriptions resist is either an "essentialist" definition of the religious end by reference to certain fundamental qualities of a human state or a "transformationalist" definition of the religious end that presumes a fundamental change of nature or being in one who has attained the end in contrast with one who has not. This is completely consistent with Advaita's outlook. The state of religious liberation is the actual human state that always obtains, and it can be a misleading deception to focus on getting "there" from "here." Human beings cannot make themselves other than they are: the one thing needful is that they should fully comprehend what they are. In such

speak, the living voice of the text itself, commentary from the condition of one who has realized what the text describes. All speech about the ultimate is inadequate, but Advaita distinguishes the inadequacy of perfect speech (as found in the *Upanishads* themselves and even in the enlightened discourse of a Badarayana or Shankara) and the inadequacy of ordinary erroneous speech (as in the gross errors of competing schools of thought or crude popular literalism).

comprehension lies liberation from all the conflict, uncertainty, and pain that follow from illusion. Mere information is not the same thing as liberation. I may be taught that I am immortal. I may even say and believe that this is so. That is not the same thing as *realizing* that it is so. To speak of a religious end in which I realize my oneness with *Brahman* may be a correct form of speech, even at times a useful one. But it is more an instrument of that end than an adequate description of it, since between the name and the truth there is a vast gap.

The importance of this gap cannot be overestimated. For Advaita, in the attainment of the religious goal nothing changes except the understanding. The world does not need to be different. I do not need to be different. Even (and here is one of the most profound sides of Advaita) our varied descriptions of the world do not need to change (such variety, as we already noted, is present in the Advaitan texts themselves). It is awareness that must change. This points up the great difficulty in applying a label like "world affirming" or "world denying" to this tradition. The religious end, full liberation, is achieved in and through the world just as it is. There is a tremendously world-affirming side of such a tradition. This liberation comes through seeing into an underlying unity that relativizes or dispels all apparent distinctions and divisions in the world, and there is thus a tremendous world-transcending dimension to the tradition as well. Advaita, and Hinduism generally, are marked by the specific way they coordinate these dimensions.

[margin annotation: High praise of Advaita]

We can approach this issue from another angle. Like Hindu traditions generally, Advaita presumes a cycle of reincarnation, birth and rebirth — *samsara* — that is governed by the rules of *karma*. From this perspective, the religious end is clear. It is release from this cycle itself, an end to rebirth, an extinction of karmic entailment. The path of spiritual progress is thus an ascent of rebirths from lower beings and castes to higher ones. But at the same time we must recall the fundamental oneness of being that underlies all these "separate" beings and the different "levels" of being. As one changes places to go up higher on the chain, one comes closer to the insight of the undifferentiated oneness of all these places and to the realization of that oneness.

In the cycle of birth and rebirth an individual person's death brings an end only to the self's "gross body" which is sloughed off and consumed. The "subtle body" is the accumulated traits of the individual, the karmic "capital" of actions carried out over a life. It is this that transmigrates for rebirth into another physical body. Only with the release from rebirth itself is one freed from the subtle body. The gross body and the subtle body can both be called "self" in a certain, qualified way. But when they are gone, something still remains. This is the *atman*, the self that is also *Brahman*, the one Self. The teaching from the *Upanishads* which became so significant for Advaita, the injunction to recognize "thou art that," applies at this point. Plainly a dog is not a tree and a human being is not the universe's sole cosmic absolute, so long as we are thinking of the gross or subtle bodies of these entities. But if we understand the non-transient reality, the true self of each, we see that the teaching is true: that is I, and I am that. *Atman* is *Brahman.* This is admittedly (as we suggested earlier) simply an abstract and attractively philosophical summary. Grasping it cannot be confused with the insight which is itself the enlightenment it describes. Still, if crude, it is essentially the description the tradition itself offers to those who are invited to seek the real thing.

On the whole, the Advaita tradition is very conservative, enjoining people to observe the distinctions of different caste status and to observe the religious rituals and practices that texts and traditions prescribe for various groups. On the other hand, the tradition is quite clear that the religious end is not to be identified with such observance. Liberation lies on the far side of these practices, as it lies on the far side of meditative practice and textual study. True liberation encompasses an insight that reveals the emptiness of these distinctions themselves, and a liberated person passes beyond them. While this insight sees through these distinctions, so to speak, it also typically affirms the wisdom of leaving them in place. Though from a higher perspective they may not be real, they have a necessary role to play in people's ascent to reality. The realization of the unity of all being need not disturb those appearances not obviously consistent with that realization. This reflects the complex relation between *dharma* and *moksha,* between the order or structure of the world and the religious end or liberation.

Dharma is essential for the religious end, but the religious end involves an understanding of *dharma* that breaks through to the oneness, the seamless unity that underlies it. Therefore Advaita, like Hinduism more generally, can articulate and order several distinct religious ends. It is a religious goal to fulfill the worldly duties defined by one's place as father, mother, daughter, son, husband, wife, member of a caste or religious group. These duties themselves may go through different phases depending on the stage of life.[17] Consistent with one's fulfillment of these obligations, the goal of worldly success in material terms and the goals of love and pleasure are not only allowed but endowed with a religious character, being in part also spiritual disciplines. Finally, *moksha* is the most fundamental and inclusive goal. The achievement of the other three goals is transitory. Only *moksha* is a permanent end.

Advaita presents us not only with a very sophisticated vision of the ulti-

---

17. The *ashramas* of student, householder, hermit, and ascetic.

mate religious end, but in fact articulates a series or hierarchy of religious ends. It is not a question of having to show the relevance of the final end for life here and now (though that can certainly be done) but rather of specifying concrete, penultimate religious goals that are a part of every person's daily life. In this respect, Hinduism's claim to be a total way of life is certainly validated.

Brief though this sketch has been, it indicates the way in which Advaita deals with dynamics we have identified in our Christian theological discussion. For instance, some elements of personhood and personal relation which are integral to the Christian end, salvation, are recognized, and certain penultimate religious ends are in fact organized around them. Such would be the duties that I as a son owe to my father, according to the *dharma*. At certain times and for certain people, these are the nearest religious summit that must be reached, the highest point on the present spiritual horizon. But equally and eventually for all, they are foothills that must be left behind. The final end does not participate in them nor they in it, for that end is itself the realization of their illusory and transitory character. At most, we might say they remain a kind of dreaming in the consciousness of the one *Brahman*, the consciousness which is our *atman*. Devotion to a personal deity, for instance, is a strand of religious life recognized by Advaita. The grammar of personal encounter, of love and obedience, is given extensive play. This strand is at home in the tradition, so long as it is clearly acknowledged that this "twoness" is provisional. It is a stage of perception that one passes through on the spiritual journey, to give way to better understanding. From another perspective, it is a "play" within the one infinite consciousness of *Brahman* itself. Its reality is either "emptiness" in the first case, or complete immanence in the second case.

The dimensions of God and relation with God which Christianity, through the Trinity, understands to be "coinherent" in salvation are not absent in Advaita. They are instead serialized or telescoped. From an Advaitan perspective, Christians make ultimate what is penultimate and so entrench their resistance to "seeing through" the transitory play of relations and distinctions to a deeper oneness. For all their talk of participating in the divine life, Christians draw back from "thou art that." They long for communion but balk at total identity.

At least some of its adherents argue that Advaita Vedanta is not monistic in the strict sense. The word *advaita* means "not two." Vedanta is non-dual because it rejects the icon relation of encounter between distinct entities (God with world, self with other selves), in favor of their ultimate identity. The oneness or "monism" of Vedanta then follows secondarily from this insight into the "not-twoness" of things. The insight is primary, the monism inferential. We might say that Christianity is a "not three, not one" religion. It insists that the three dimensions of relation with God, grounded in the Trinity, cannot be isolated or exclusive alternatives to each other. These three are not three ultimates. It is not right simply to say in sequence: there is no God, there is an impersonal God, there is a God of personal encounter, and there is a God of personal communion. Each of these is true in the sense we have described in our earlier analysis: there is one God about whom they can each be said truthfully, under the special trinitarian grammar. That is, each one alone as an exhaustive statement is false. No one of these reduces to simple identity with the others. The Trinity is "not one" and "not two" as well as "not three." "Three in one" is the tradition's shorthand way to express this, the co-eternal coinherence of the unique persons.

Advaita clearly emphasizes what we described as the first dimension of the divine life. This is the infinite interchange among the divine persons, the "emptiness" in which each makes way for the other and the immanence by which each shares perfectly in the life of the other. The divine persons of the Trinity could come close to saying to and of each other "thou art that," for each one "has" all that the others have, by virtue of constant giving and self-giving, except for the distinctive, asymmetrical features that make each one unique. Taken impersonally, if we might put it that way, the three persons of the Trinity do share everything. They are identical in "substance," to use the language Western theology took to express this fact. But the three are not impersonal, and they are never just "substance" and not person. For Advaita, even the teaching or the thought "thou art that," with its tensive, connective form, must dissolve at the moment it is actually realized. If you truly were that, and knew it, there would be no separate "you" and "that." But the triune God and the life of the triune God glory in the eternality of the distinction, in the non-identity that allows communion, in the three that are one. "Three in one" is not, then, like "thou art that," a truth that must dissolve in its own realization. It is a pattern of diversity and communion repeated wherever the divine life is shared.

From the Christian, trinitarian viewpoint this does not mean that the fundamental positive affirmation of Advaita is wrong, or that it is not possible to attain to the religious end Advaita seeks. In discussing the Trinity, we stressed that one dimension of the divine life was the constant exchange between the three persons, their mutual immanence. We indicated that this could be abstracted in an impersonal way. It is not mistaken to affirm impersonal features of a human being — from physics to biology — but it is partial. So too, the Christian holds, it is not mistaken to identify impersonal qualities of God, but it is not complete. God's immanence with every creature can be taken as a ground of being, as the impersonal condition of the creature's existence. If one seeks to look to the very bottom of every finite being, past everything apparently transient and particular, and to find where its true source of being lies, one can truly discover just one divine life beneath it all, one divine process of immanence. Indeed, if God is known in this way alone, the result is identification. Precisely in looking past bodies, personalities, and individuality, one arrives at a point of contact with the source of our being. If this point is taken to be the individual's real self, because it is the origin of the self, then in a way it can rightly be said to be the same as the divine Self who is that ultimate origin. If God is taken neither as the three divine persons nor as the collective "I" of the Trinity but as the process, the communion itself, then at the root of our own existence we find that divine "play" as the most basic reality we can identify. We can identify ourselves with it. In a very real sense we are that.

Thus, I as a Christian do not deny that a Hindu may actually realize identity with the divine, with absolute *Brahman*. I regard this as in fact identity with the underlying immanence of the triune God. Real though a relation of immanence may be between the creator and creature, this kind of identification in such pure form is achieved through a constriction, a limitation of both human reality and of God. The identity rests finally only on the contact between an aspect of the human and an aspect of the divine. "Absorption" into God can take place only at a level beneath the personhood of God and of humans. If perfect unity were to be realized at the level of the personhood of both, it would not be absorption but instead communion. And this is precisely the salvation for which Christians long. What is striking, and important, is that what from a Christian view is loss and limitation is quite the reverse from an Advaitan view. Leaving "person" and relation behind is not loss but gain. In the Advaitan view, it is Christians' attachment to such penultimate categories of understanding that restricts them to lower levels of spiritual attainment. Communion with a personal God and with other persons cannot be constitutive of the final end, but represents at best a preparatory stage.[18]

Here we have quite distinct religious ends. From a Christian perspective, there is no need to assume that only one of these ends is real. We have sketched a Christian understanding of the reality of the Advaitan end, and its root in the divine nature. The question is not which one of the two is telling

18. Modern Advaitins, like Vivekananda, have criticized Christianity particularly for the machinery of relation that grows up around the premise of distinction between humans and God or between one person and another: issues like sin and reconciliation, faithfulness, obedience, and righteousness. In their view, the effort to close a gap that does not exist is dysfunctional and destructive.

the truth. They both are. Instead there are two crucial questions. Which of these truths do we desire to realize? Which one, if either, encompasses or can recognize the fullest measure of truth in the other? I believe these questions are fruitful ones for study and dialogue, and have the advantage of corresponding not only to the interest of the scholar but the concerns of the seeker.

Advaita Vedanta is of course only one Hindu tradition, however it may have come to dominate many modern presentations of Hinduism. Within Indian tradition itself the nature of the end is contested. To the "non-dualism" or Advaita tradition one may add the "qualified non-dualism" or Vishistadvaita tradition.[19] In very simple terms we may say that this view agrees that the end is identity with *Brahman,* but holds that there is some real distinction in *Brahman* itself, so that difference is not abolished completely even in *moksha.* There is also a school of explicit "dualism," that holds to the distinct and enduring reality of individual souls, separate from *Brahman* and from each other.[20] Both Vishistadvaita and dualism provide more room for personal devotion to God as constitutive of the final religious end. Christianity has historically often taken a somewhat positive view toward these two traditions, seeing in Vishistadvaita some intimations of God's trinitarian reality and in dualism some recognition of the reality of creation.[21]

These features of Hindu tradition indicate that there are ample resources for someone within that tradition to pursue a path that converges significantly toward the Christian religious end. This accounts for the special attention Christian inclusivists are prone to give to these traditions. Our concern, however, has been to consider the way in which Christian theology may recognize and understand the reality of a religious end that is not salvation.

III

Islam is a tradition that emphasizes relation with what we described as the second dimension of the divine life: the collective "I" of the Trinity, the agent-God who reveals truth, ordains the course of the world's life, and calls humans to obedience. In its emphasis on a personal God, Islam clearly includes some consideration of impersonal qualities of divine life as subsumed in this personal nature. The emphasis in respect to these qualities falls on the tran-

19. See (Carman, 1974; Carman, 1994).
20. The great figure of the Advaita tradition is Shankara (8th century), of the Vishistadvaita, Ramanuja (11th century), and of dualism Madhva (13th century).
21. (Carman, 1974) and (Otto and Foster, 1930).

scendence and otherness of God. The immanence of God, the dimension given pride of place in Advaita Vedanta, is definitely given restricted scope. Sufism, that strand of Islamic tradition which has turned to this dimension with the most spiritual ardor, has found a permanent acceptance within the tradition through a clear acknowledgment that outward personal obedience to God's stated direction is the core of common Islam. The spiritual love of God may set this obedience aglow from inside, as it were, but it must not in any way challenge its primacy.

Despite the extensive similarities between Islam and Christianity as monotheistic faiths within a common scriptural tradition, they provide an interesting illustration of the difficulty in looking at religious ends comparatively. One cannot readily identify a word or set of terms in Islam that are cognate with "salvation" in Christianity. Words like "reconciliation," "communion," "justification," and "regeneration," which figure centrally in a Christian view of salvation, are not prominent in the Qur'an or in Muslim tradition. In part this follows directly from the two traditions' divergent readings of the human situation, and particularly of what must be overcome in order for humans to reach the religious end. For Christians it is an estrangement from God, an inner distortion of our desire and will, and of our communion with each other and creation that must be overcome. This is a diagnosis that connects with the need and meaning of Christ's incarnation, atoning death, and resurrection to new life. It is hardly surprising that Islam, which denies the reality of these three, would also see no crucial need for them. This points us to the whole texture of difference in the two traditions. But our interest at the moment is not to pursue this global question but rather to focus on Islam's positive conception of the religious end, a conception which makes the whole Christian complex appear somewhat superfluous or blasphemous.

In common with Christianity, Islam sees the religious end as a transformation of the human person that leaves the self still distinct, still in a relation with God the creator. Through Muhammad, in the Qur'an, God has given the guidance and direction for this end. In general terms, this end is the realization of humanity's true condition, the practice of the proper recognition of God and the right fulfillment of human duties. "Islam" is a comprehensive word for this, a term for both the goal and the religion which is the way to the goal. "Surrender" or "submission" identifies obedience as the key feature of this condition. This submission is specified in three fundamental aspects of Islamic tradition: faith (the confession of belief in the one God), acts of worship (including the five pillars of Islam and observance of the more extensive law or shariah), and the practice of virtue or excellence. Although Islam looks forward to a final judgment and to heavenly reward, it seems fair to say that its religious end itself is not strongly eschatological. Though the rewards and happiness of heaven may be unparalleled on earth, the religious condition attained there is of a piece with the aim in this life: gratitude and upright obedience to God.

If we ask about the nature of the human transformation such gratitude and obedience require, the "how" of the religious end, there would seem to be three points of emphasis.[22] The first is habituation, reflected in the "pillars" of Islamic practice: confession of belief in the one God, the five daily prayers, the payment of alms, the yearly fast in the month of Ramadan, and the pilgrimage to Mecca. Regular fulfillment of these religious duties is personal participation in the Islamic way of life. They are not just obligations to be fulfilled as conditions of some further reward. In a real way they are constitutive of the religious end itself. They *are* conformity with the will of God and to practice them is to be in right relation with God.

The second emphasis is solidarity. Islam is an intensely communal faith and all of the five basic practices mentioned above, as well as many others, are carried out together with other Muslims or in intense consciousness of such corporate unity. The timing of the five prayers, the common orientation to Mecca, the solidarity of simultaneous observance of the Ramadan fast, the simple, identical garb of all pilgrims on the Hajj: all of these reflect this solidarity. There is a collective as well as an individual conformity to the will of God. Belonging to the *Ummah* or Muslim community is crucial for this reason.

This brings us to the third emphasis on social and political structure. The will of God is to be realized not only in individual practice or in the life of a religious community, but throughout the entire political and social order. The Muslim religious end is to live in full submission to God's reign, within a community and society also in such obedience. Therefore it plainly cannot be realized fully by a single individual or even a sectarian religious community. If there is a "messianic" strain in Islam it pertains not so much to a person as to the appearance of a Muslim society where the submission to God of the truly righteous person would find perfect consistency with a culture and state also perfectly obedient, each reinforcing and perfecting the other. Christians in centuries past criticized the Muslim picture of heaven as too "worldly" in nature. The same data might be read equally well to indicate the proximity and the relevance of the Muslim view of religious fulfillment, as something quite conceivable and relevant here and now as well as in the life to come.

The Muslim conception of the religious end is intensely personal, relational, and communal. These are all features in common with Christian sal-

22. The following points are taken from (Cragg, 1980, pp. 156-57).

vation and distinct from the Buddhist religious end, for instance. In light of our discussions earlier about various dimensions of the divine life, we can see that the divergence of Christianity and Islam is of another order. The personal character of the Muslim religious end is very much a "face to face" encounter with God, mediated by behavior and carefully observing the difference between creator and creature. The personal character of Christian salvation encompasses further dimensions that are specific offenses to Islam.

First, the notion that God's nature is a communion of persons, mutual indwelling, is viewed by Muslims as introducing division into God, compromising the divine unity, and perhaps even casting doubt on whether God relates to the world with a single will. For this reason, Trinity has been rejected by Islam. Second, belief in incarnation only compounds the offense of diversity in God by adding the intimate association of a creature, a human being, with the divine nature. To Muslims, this compromises the innate transcendence of God and blurs the distinction of creator and creature. These are well-known points of Christian-Muslim difference. My interest is in the way both points condition salvation for the Christian tradition and their absence conditions the Muslim religious end. Salvation is a state of religious fulfillment primarily constituted through both incarnation and Trinity. As communion with God in Christ, salvation is a communion whose possibility rests on the reality of these two more fundamental forms of communion. If God's nature is not itself a communion of persons, and if God has not taken on incarnational communion with humanity, then salvation is incoherent and cannot be real as Christians describe it in phrases like "communion with God," "participation in the divine life," or "life in Christ." It is this dimension of relational communion that is excluded in Muslim rejection of Trinity, incarnation, and human "association" with the divine life. The three hang together. It is reasonable that Christians maintain them together and Muslims reject them together.

In terms of our discussion of the various dimensions of the triune life, we already mentioned that the Muslim religious end focuses on the personal "I" of the Trinity. The triune God acts with one purpose, one will, and one economy in relation to creation. Human well-being rests in taking up the proper position, by act and will, as a created agent in fidelity to the one, transcendent creator-agent. In isolating and intensifying this dimension of the divine life, Islam defines a distinctive religious end. As we have seen, the communion/participation dimension of the divine life is in many cases actively excluded. The emptiness/immanence dimension of the triune life falls somewhat into the background. The result is a religious end of unsurpassed concreteness and practicality. It is constituted, not by subjective states, inner regeneration, gnostic insight, or intimate mutuality between the creaturely and divine natures, but by the consistent implementation of divinely revealed patterns for human behavior.

It is clear then that Islam prioritizes and consolidates the dimensions of divine life in a particular way. This is in line with our earlier observation that religions do not ignore this diversity, but offer distinctive ways of resolving it. Perhaps the strongest example of this dynamic in Islam is the case of Sufism. There is argument between those who regard Sufism as a minority tradition within Islam (akin to a sect or school) and those who view it as a constant and pervasive feature of all Islamic faith, an aspect of its common piety. For the purposes of discussion, I will presume the latter view. I do so because this makes the strongest case that Islam in its own way encompasses the dimensions of relation with God we have discussed. From this perspective Islam has an "exoteric" side which defines relation with God in terms of "external" personal practices and an "esoteric" side (notably Sufism) which seeks personal unity with God. Sufism itself has various streams, some of which strongly emphasize personal intimacy with God and some of which move toward a more "impersonal" mysticism of absorption into the divine life, where the distinct human self seems somewhat impermanent.

This reflects the way in which the Islamic tradition takes account of these dimensions of the triune life. The key point is how these are related. The Muslim integration would seem to divide these dimensions between an outer and an inner realization of right relation to God. An external relation of obedience (through the five pillars and *shariah*) is coordinated with an internal relation of loving devotion (and/or perhaps of dissipation of the self in union with God). In its collective life, it is clear that Islam has subordinated two dimensions (the "impersonal" and communion dimensions) to a third, the iconic.[23] Mystical devotion is acceptable as a supplement to the obedience, not a source that might supplant or redefine it. Even apart from that tension, internal spiritual devotion is simply the accompaniment on the human side of the proper obedience to God. From the Muslim view, to posit a similar interiority in God, as the ground of human communion with God, is to transgress on the divine mystery.

It is simplistic to portray Islam as a religion concerned merely with ex-

---

23. However, it is significant to note the depth of "iconic" power that is granted to Muhammad in living Muslim tradition. Though in principle quite distinct from the true icon of the Qur'an, Muhammad's role in Muslim piety does introduce a strongly personal dimension to the Word of God.

ternal duty, making relation with God purely a legal one. The religious end as Islam realizes it involves an intensely personal encounter with God. Humans are made in the image of God, and their goal is to fulfill this image by manifesting certain of its powers. Humans have been gifted with the capacity for speech, for free will, for moral responsibility — capacities that echo divine qualities. The true human destiny is to use these capacities with full recognition of their giver. In a very real but reverent way humans are to imitate God. The religious end involves a loving gratitude toward God, expressed in acts similar to those of God. Some (certainly not all) of the external acts of God are the model for the image of God in humanity. Human speaking, willing, and acting are to conform as far as possible to the model of the divine speaking, willing, and acting. The status of humans as servants of God also imparts a nobility and sovereignty to humans as regents over some of God's creation. Acting as God wills us to act also involves acting in ways analogous to God's own acts. And it involves an intensely interpersonal relation with God, the human standing before God and taking responsibility and accountability before God. This is the focus of Islam's understanding of human closeness to God, as it relates to the religious end.

Salvation (the Christian religious end) involves an internal regeneration of the human person and participation of the human person in the internal divine life (communion) of God, as well as an inner communion with other persons. The image of God in humans is preeminently the communion-nature, the being-as-communion, which makes such an end possible. This is the focus of closeness with God as it relates to the Christian religious end, and the characteristic source of its divergence from the Muslim end.

It is instructive that Christianity and Islam each regard the other as "dualistic" in a negative sense. And, we might add, the consistency of these mutual criticisms, arising as readily from ordinary believers as from scholars, is striking confirmation of a divergence in religious ends in the two traditions. Islam sees in Christianity (particularly modern Christianity) an unfortunate dualism between the spiritual and the worldly. This is evident for instance in the existence of a monastic ideal in Christian tradition and in the comparative reluctance or inability in Christianity to thoroughly prescribe rules for the political and social spheres of human life through religious statutes. From a Muslim view, Christianity relegates religion to a "higher" spiritual sphere, where it may foster noble values but fails to deliver practical obedience to God in the real world. As Seyyed Hossein Nasr says, "Christianity is seen by Muslims as a religion devoid of an exoterism which then substitutes a message of an essentially esoteric nature as the exoteric, thereby creating disequilibrium in human society."[24] By contrast, Islam is a seamless unity, a complete, all-encompassing blueprint that provides a balanced and divinely sanctioned order for all aspects of real life.

Christianity sees in Islam a different kind of dualism between the esoteric and the exoteric, with the former isolated in a private sphere, and so denied transforming or prophetic relevance for the real world. This is evident in the ideal in Islam of a single, unchanging, concrete law, as well as the ideal of a single Muslim cultural core, defined by the Arabic of the Qur'an. In Islam religion is to be more jealously protected than in Christianity from the effects of cultural transformation. Christianity sees itself as a seamless unity as well, but one whose concrete forms are more susceptible to change, the unity resting in the generative dynamic of the living Christ in relation to the canon of Scripture and the organic communion of believers with God through Christ in the church.

These differences regarding the religious end have real effects on the understanding of life here and now, as adherents of both traditions attempt to realize those ends in some measure. This shows up, for instance, in the observation by many Muslim writers that humanity is neither subject to such integral corruption as Christianity presumes, nor fit for the grandiose divinization Christianity seeks. To a Muslim the ultimate Christian religious end appears presumptuous and unnecessary. The life that leads to it looks rather thin and ill-defined, insufficiently extensive in its blueprint for righteousness here and now. To a Christian, the Muslim religious end seems to skirt the internal heart of the divine-human estrangement, the need for reconciliation and regeneration, as well as to limit the scope of God's extraordinary openness to communion with creatures.

The many similarities between Christianity and Islam, particularly in light of Sufism, do not compromise the distinctness of Muslim and Christian religious ends. Both constitute a personal relation with God. As we have seen, the Muslim end plainly excludes a dimension that Christians seek. For this reason, the dimensions of deep relation with God that the two share are integrated differently. As a Christian, I honor the reality of the Muslim religious end, the realization of a profound personal relation with God. Precisely as personal, this relation in some measure also recognizes impersonal dimensions of the divine. On this score, there is a very close affinity between salvation and the Muslim religious end.

Both Christianity and Buddhism seek a religious fulfillment that involves connection with an impersonal face of transcendent reality. In that limited sense, they might be said to seek the same religious end. But of course

24. (Nasr, 1986, p. 5).

this overlap of an element "involved" in dramatically different ways in the two religious aims does not in fact translate to an identical religious end. The same principle operates with the Muslim religious end, though the affinity is much more substantial. A personal relation with a personal God is affirmed by both. The *kind* of personal relation in view is different, sometimes subtly and sometimes dramatically. One can regard the distinction as trivial only if one views distinctions among various kinds of genuine human relations as trivial also. I could be parent to a child, someone's business client, a blood plasma donor, my wife's husband, a governor, a doctor's patient, the executor of someone's will, a teacher's disciple, the judge in a defendant's trial, a trusted friend, a nephew, a child to my parents, a colleague's collaborator. These are all human relations and, in principle, positive ones. But they are distinct; the benefits of one are not identical with those from another. People may choose some relations over others. In addition to preferences, they may reasonably have convictions about the types of relation that are feasible, or objectively engage the fullest depth of human possibility. This situation obtains in our relation with God as well.

The degree of common ground in the Muslim end and the Christian one offers fertile ground for inclusivists in both traditions. They see how relatively easy it might be to use Christian sources to move on toward the Muslim end or, conversely, how Muslim tradition might equip one to pursue the Christian religious aim. There is no doubt that within Islam, particularly within strands of Islam influenced by Sufi and Shi'a elements, one might "anonymously" move toward the pursuit of the Christian end. And there is no doubt that within Christianity, particularly where a comprehensive and concrete biblical mandate for all of human life is sought, one might "anonymously" move toward pursuit of the Muslim end. Such pursuits need not stay anonymous, and they can reach the ends they seek. But this does not mean that Islam and Christianity do not present real alternatives. Instead, it bears out the common conviction of believers that there is often significant importance to "internal" religious differences as well as to "external" ones. It is not necessary to wait for explicit encounter with another tradition in order to face a spiritual crossroad.

The connections between the Muslim religious end and salvation are plain, whether we speak historically or analytically. For this reason, when the two traditions have each considered the other's positive substance (as opposed to the other's errors), they have often had difficulty in discerning anything unique or distinctive. One readily dismissed the other precisely because the other's only legitimate end was thought to be nothing but the same end already contained (with greater clarity) in the "home" tradition of the viewer. The conclusion that a different religion is "another way to the same end" is no necessary recipe for amity. It can sometimes heighten conflict, for it is just as easy to quarrel over which is the better way as over which is the better end.

The Christian end is not already included in the Muslim one, any more than the Muslim end can in its actual uniqueness be subsumed in the Christian one. There is a specific quality to the Muslim religious fulfillment, and Muslim faith and practice provide a far better path to that fulfillment than Christianity does. It seems to me that such recognition is necessary for fruitful understanding. Otherwise, Christian categories allow that Islam may be at most an approximation of something already present in Christianity. As we have described it, the dimensions involved in the Muslim end may be present in Christian faith, but the realization of these dimensions is quite different in the two cases.

It is yet a separate question as to what larger context frames this difference. In many ways this takes us back to our discussion of Dante's imagined cosmology. Are his intermediate destinies part of the geography of heaven or of hell? We could narrow the question further with respect to the Muslim and Christian ends and ask whether the different kinds of personal relations with God sought here amount to the broad difference between an external human relation and an intimate one, or whether they are more of the nature of the varied relations of two beloved, but quite different, siblings to a parent. This is not an issue we need to resolve for our present purposes. On either account, the recognition of distinct religious ends serves us well.

IV

Recognition of the integrity of other religious ends requires us to face, and hopefully to benefit from, the criticisms of Christianity rooted in them. As we have seen, Islam can criticize Christianity as lacking in rigor and practicality in its response to the call for obedience in the dimension of divine-human encounter. Advaita Vedanta criticizes Christianity for lacking clarity and philosophical sophistication, particularly for lacking insight into the pure nature of reality, the impersonal dimensions of divine emptiness and immanence that are everywhere and always the case in the world just as it is. With regard to the actual dimensions of God that these traditions distinctively grasp, their criticisms are correct. Christians can learn from the critique, but cannot expect to extinguish it, for it is rooted in a realized relation with God.

On trinitarian grounds, Christians must acknowledge the dimensions of God in which these criticisms are rooted. These dimensions are real, and we cannot deny them or replace them completely with something else. Christianity's distinction lies in the faith that there is another dimension of the divine life (the communion of the persons) which allows for the relation of communion with God (in Christ). This dimension and the relations it makes possible provide the basis for the co-equality or coinherence of the first two. If Christianity is in error, that error could still leave these other traditions standing. If true, Christianity *requires* the constituent truths they profess. To adopt this view involves a shift away from the common assumption that the realization of a religious end other than the Christian one (if this end has any positive qualities whatsoever) would count as a *disconfirmation* of Christian faith. I am suggesting that it is appropriate to affirm the reality of distinctive religious ends, to interpret them within a Christian context, and to see them as consistent with, even supportive of, Christian faith itself.

Part Four

Eschatology and Plenitude

Chapter Seven

The Glory of the Fullness:
Religious Ends and Plenitude

One final challenge remains in our discussion of religious ends. Even a reader who agrees that various religious ends could be grounded in God's triune nature can raise another objection. If communion with God is the truly ultimate goal offered to all human beings, how can God permit any to miss that communion? Doesn't a variety of final destinies compromise the very unity of humanity itself, making us different kinds of beings? If humans share the same nature, then there must logically be only two options: the true fulfillment of that nature and the lack of such fulfillment. If there is one end God desires for us to share, surely God's providence must refuse to support any others. Therefore the only positive value of religions would be their role in fostering that single human goal (whether it is Christian salvation or some other particular end, including the supposedly neutral one variously proposed in pluralistic philosophies). Otherwise, God is guilty of discrimination. A final eschatological scenario in which religious ends other than salvation were allowed would not be consistent with Christian revelation. God would have failed, leading creation to a defective consummation. For these reasons, this objection concludes, the theory of diverse religious ends is "deceptive and unconvincing."[1]

This is an important objection. Response to it provides a fitting capstone

---

1. This is the conclusion of Jacques Dupuis S.J., who raises this objection strongly in his excellent recent book (Dupuis S.J., 1997, pp. 309-13).

for our study. I will first outline the theological principles that frame my approach, particularly the most distinctive of these principles, theological plenitude. Then in the balance of the chapter I will try to show that an eschatological pluralism is consistent with the guiding theological principles I outlined.

Before proceeding, let me give a brief preliminary response to the two key elements in the objection we have just noted. The first element appeals to God's universal will that all should be saved. Anything other than salvation for all would defeat this divine intention, and so must be ruled out. This is not an argument specifically directed at diverse religious ends. It is a perennial argument for universalism, ruling out *any* ultimate end whatsoever except salvation. Obviously, those who reject the existence of any other end, including any biblical notion of hell or annihilation or eschatological loss, will reject out of hand any diversity among the ends they regard as nonexistent. But universalism has never been a settled doctrine of the church. Among Christian churches it has rarely been excluded as a hope but almost never required as a dogma.[2] In an absolute form, universalism would rule out not just my theological hypothesis but the relevant teaching of virtually all classical Christian theologians and major Christian confessional bodies. In short, this objection carries little weight unless it claims to foreclose the long-running controversy over universalism itself. Since that question plainly remains open, my proposal remains a live option.

This also bears on the question of a common human nature. If the possibility of eternal loss exists, then that loss must constitute a distortion and constraint of the potential in created human nature, or the complete annihilation of that nature. This does not deny human solidarity, for without a common nature there would be no measure to allow talk of "loss" or "fulfillment" at all. To entertain a hypothesis that adds variety to this binary saved/not saved picture raises no new question in principle about our shared humanity. People who reach an ideal fulfillment of their humanity do not thereby become identical. And persons who do not realize the fullest potential of their created nature do not live less than human lives. Belief in our common humanity does not require the belief that there is no human variety within salvation, the belief that there is no final option for humans except salvation, or the belief that there can be only one, entirely negative alternative to salvation.

The second strand of the objection applies the same "all or nothing" rule not to ends but to means. It assumes that anything that is effective or true in any religious tradition has no possible positive use for adherents except to

---

2. The Universalist denomination in the U.S. is a historical example of a group that treated universalism as a constitutive creed.

bring about salvation. Even if there were other religious ends, there would be no means to get to them, because any valid religious practice or belief would always at each instant of adherence move one toward salvation and (at the same time) away from any other possibility. This form of the objection is separable from the first because it can at least contemplate one alternative religious end: damnation. It maintains that the failure to respond positively at all to any religion (or natural law) might lead one to outer darkness, but positive steps could go only in one unequivocal direction. From this perspective, salvation is the sole possible result of any positive spiritual effort. Eternal damnation may be possible, but anything better than eternal fire and less than salvation is anathema.

I reject this objection for two reasons. First, I cannot accept the total annexation of all religions, holding they have no positive purpose whatsoever except the Christian one. Second, the objection ignores the "double effect" that we observe to be real in all human spheres including the religious. That is, it may well be true that every positive human spiritual movement away from sin, evil, and despair is a move closer to salvation than to its polar opposite. It does not follow that such acts might not at the same time lead toward a good that is not identical with salvation. For instance, an individual's realization of greater moral integrity or of artistic creativity or deeper intellectual understanding or clearer meditative consciousness may all be moves "in the right direction" in the Christian geography of salvation. They can at the same time be intentional and effective moves toward "natural" ends or religious ends quite apart from salvation. To put it another way, salvation may presuppose these changes in some measure: these changes do not necessitate salvation. God has not tailored every human artifact and capacity so that it has only two possible uses: a destructive one and a positive one that can serve only for the attainment of salvation but will not contribute to any other good. It is quite right that all truth and beauty and goodness come from God. It is not right that someone who recognizes any portion at all of truth or beauty or goodness then has no choice but to be saved.

In short, I find these objections unpersuasive. But this case can be made more fully below.

I

There are a few basic theological principles that shape my approach to the topics of eschatology we consider in this chapter. Summarizing them briefly will provide a framework for the rest of our discussion.

The first principle is God's universal saving will (the principle that is also the departure point for the objection already noted). God wishes all to be saved, and offers every creature the fullest range of communion with the triune life proportionate to the creature's nature. God seeks the good of all creation. The comprehensive good of all creation is so vast a conception that its dimensions run beyond our capacity for understanding. But God's aim and offer of salvation for every person is one dimension that we have ample scriptural and traditional ground to affirm.

The second principle is the decisive and constitutive place of Jesus Christ as savior. All who are saved are saved in communion with Christ. As we saw in Chapter Two, salvation *means* participation in a web of relationships with God and others that the incarnation makes possible and in which relationship with Christ is a necessary constituent part.[3]

The third principle is the universal accessibility of salvation. If God's will to save is universal, and the decisive saving *act* in Christ is particular, then the theological conclusion follows that there must be means by which these two are connected. The particularity of Christ does not impede the universal aim, nor does a "wider hope" cancel the decisiveness of the incarnation. It is this principle that fuels the varied reflections in theological tradition over the means by which the benefits of this particular event might be made available to all, despite the fact that people stand at radically varying "distances" from it.

The objection that it is unfair for God to allow circumstances of birth or culture to prejudice the possibility of religious fulfillment is well taken. It is interesting to note that this objection has weight only if the religious ultimate is believed to be personal. There is no logical or practical reason that some impersonal, transcendent structure should not be "unfair" in this way, and there would be little meaning to any protest if it were. By a natural, impersonal, and objective process an immunity to some deadly disease might appear in one small human subgroup, unavailable to all others. Those others would stand in a terrible and perhaps irremediable disadvantage. This fact itself would raise no moral claim against the order of things. It would not do so unless the "order of things" was thought to be able to take some intentional care for such matters. Only where agency and will exist could the responsibility to provide equal opportunity exist.

In fact, broad ranges of religious wisdom in Hinduism and Buddhism affirm precisely such "discrimination" in human location. Some human locations are much better suited than others to draw persons to religious fulfill-

---

3. For a fuller discussion of these first two principles, see (Sanders, 1992, pp. 25-30).

ment (though extraordinary progress from unlikely locations may not be ruled out). The conviction is that the impersonal process that allocates persons to these unequal starting points — the karmic process — operates only by reaction to people's own acts in earlier lives. One could hardly complain if this impersonal process were not fair. But it is so, if we look beyond the data of any particular human life, where one person may well be given decisively less opportunity than another to attain the highest religious end. In the longer term, through reincarnation, those disadvantaged now can occupy the more favorable positions. Since as a Christian I affirm that God is personal, I believe that God offers all persons, in their actual individual lives, the same opportunity for salvation. This does not mean that the paths by which people can attain that end must be identical in all or most particulars, only that the way to salvation is open to all with the same chances of final realization.

A fourth principle is the freedom of the creature. God is the source of all good. Christians believe that the triune God is the partner in every transforming human fulfillment. But this does not mean that God is the source and partner in the same manner in all cases. Creation is both a setting forth of the world and a distancing of the world from God, a "letting be" which is essential for creation's freedom. The limitation of creatures is at the same time their glory. Humans are made neither as divine alter egos, already immersed in the inner trinitarian life, nor as impersonal entities, capable only of extrinsic and functional interactions with others or God. We are created in the image of God, that is, as intrinsically constituted by relation. Since our encounter with God is a personal relation, the "rules" of personal relation hold. The nature of the relation is always in some measure shaped by the manner of the creature's participation in it. The construal, perceptions, and intentions a person brings to the encounter will set terms for the relation. In every case, the relation will be what it is in part because of the human contribution to it.

This power given to the human contribution stems from the "withdrawal" we have spoken of as part of God's creative act. It is not a temporary expedience, but an aspect of the being God has granted to creatures. Having created individuals as part of the glory of creation, God honors that reality eschatologically as well. Salvation cancels nothing of this donation of freedom given in creation. The existence of other religious ends upholds that freedom also, even if some ends may confirm a creature's wish to relinquish some of the personal qualities given in that gift.

A fifth principle, or perhaps a corollary of the fourth, is the possibility of loss. On scriptural grounds and consistent with the freedom of the creature, this cannot be ruled out. Salvation is objectively offered to all and all have the same opportunity to attain it, but none are compelled to give up

247

ends they prefer to it. As the universal saving will of God and the particularity of Christ pose a question about the accessibility of salvation, so the universal saving will and the freedom of the creature pose a question about the extreme case of conflict between the two. Here Christians have resisted definitive decision as to whether (or to what extent) the freedom of the creature could thwart the fulfillment of the divine desire in anything or whether God necessarily bends the creature's freedom in every case to perfect subjugation to the divine plan.

Finally, at the intersection of several of these prior principles, I affirm a sixth, a theological principle of plenitude. In brief, "plenitude" means that both salvation and the consummation of creation (to the extent they are different from each other) indelibly bear the marks of difference given in God's creative act and, in a subsidiary way, produced as the product of human freedom. The perfection that God seeks fulfills but does not erase both types of variety. It is neither a uniform condition nor a homogenous being. God aims at the multiplication of kinds of good. Creation is collectively a staggering example of this aim. And consummation mirrors creation in this respect, maintaining the same delight in variety. In affirming that creatures in their particular identities endure in continuing relation with God, Christianity maintains that God chooses a good that consists of God and creatures, over the good which is God alone or the good of God and one sort of creature. This expansive "overflow" can be seen in terms of the intrinsic love and creativity within the divine nature itself, a trinitarian communion of exchange that is already full and yet shares its fullness with no diminishment. From that perspective, it leads us into the trinitarian life we have already discussed in Chapter Four. The plenitude of the divine life is reflected in creation. The communion-in-difference of the triune life is reflected in a unity of diverse goods in creation itself as it comes from God and as it attains to the fullness of God's purpose. Plenitude is both an intrinsic and an economic quality of God as Trinity.

I am aware that the word "plenitude" has some distinct connotations in philosophical discussion. The intellectual history of the idea carries a good deal of baggage. But the word is too apt for our discussion to abandon it. I use "plenitude" in a particular theological sense, which needs to be distinguished from a strictly philosophical meaning.

Arthur Lovejoy's famous and much-debated work, *The Great Chain of Being*, claimed to trace a "principle of plenitude" through Western thought, from Plato to Leibnitz.[4] Lovejoy linked three elements, and claimed that only

---

4. (Lovejoy, 1965).

when they were all present could one talk of plenitude in the strict or fullest sense. The first element was the assertion that in our universe the full range of conceivable *kinds* of being (particularly living being) is actually exemplified. No genuine possibility of being is left unrealized. The second element was the contention that the intellectual world is deficient without the sensible. A realm of essence without embodiment is less perfect or "good" than one with it. A pure idea and its material actualization are superior to the idea alone. The third element is the conclusion that creation is not free or arbitrary but necessary. A good and powerful being, by the definition of "good" used here, must of necessity engender finite beings, and the widest range of them logically possible.

The combination of these ideas into one unified whole is the ideal type of Lovejoy's principle of plenitude. He devotes most of his survey to persons and views that exemplify aspects of this theme but rarely the complete set. Neoplatonism at the beginning and Leibnitz at the end set the standard by which Lovejoy tells his story all along the way. The mindset which reasoned confidently to the principle of plenitude as a kind of logical necessity may seem very foreign to us. But the notion itself encompasses many perennial concrete issues as well as some striking analogies to contemporary discussions, whether those contemporary discussions have to do with "multiple universes" in physics, evolutionary theory in biology, or biodiversity in ecology.

As Lovejoy implies, "good" can have several rather distinct meanings. It can refer to a moral standard. It can refer to the effective relation of form and function (a "good" hammer is one suited well for pounding). It can refer to something that surpasses strict justice, such as mercy or love. But Lovejoy's principle of plenitude assumes the specific meaning of "good" is fecundity, inexhaustible productive energy, the explosive creativity that drives being into all possible niches. In this sense, the good of the whole consists chiefly in the variety of its parts.

In Neoplatonism an original and ultimate divinity "overflowed" necessarily and perhaps unconsciously. In a great chain, it emanated all the possible levels of lesser being, as water might flow downhill from the top of a stepped fountain. In its early struggle with gnosticism, Christianity faced a powerfully mythical version of such a picture. But gnosticism reversed the value judgment on this plenitude, seeing this diffusion of true being into more concrete and material levels as an unfortunate, repellent corruption. With some struggle, Christianity rejected gnosticism's judgments, but aspects of Neoplatonism were undeniably assimilated into Christian theology. The line between Neoplatonism and gnosticism remains a tension point in Christian thought, because the two cosmologies are formally so similar. The positive use of Neoplatonism and the struggle against gnosticism reflected the church's instinct in favor of plenitude.

The generative and creative character of God was a fundamental biblical conviction, and in this sense Christian theologians welcomed plenitude as a divine designation. But they were hesitant about a principle that seemed in fact higher than God, that seemed to decree what God *must* do and to make creation a logical rather than a personal act. Neoplatonic divinity emanates other being impersonally, but remains aloof on its own supreme level. The biblical God creates freely and seeks communion with the creatures. Pseudo-Dionysius, an author certainly far toward the Neoplatonic end of the Christian spectrum, is an interesting case in point. He gives special priority to the love of God not as a compassion or emotion directed at individuals but as the generative generosity that is directed at "levels of being." The first sign of God's love is the desire that there should be others, and not just a few others or just those on the closest possible level to God, but an unimaginable richness of kinds of others. From this perspective, the story in Genesis resounds with the refrain "it was good" not as a judgment on the initial individuals of every kind (it was a good fish, a good bird) but with delight at the filling out of varied niches in creation. It was good that there were fish as a kind (and kinds of fish), birds as a kind (and kinds of birds), and "everything that creeps on the earth."

I make a sharp distinction between the logical necessity implied in a philosophical principle of plenitude, with its "all or nothing" emphasis, and a theological principle of plenitude that does not assume that necessity. Lovejoy is well aware of this difference, though he views it as a distinction between the principle of plenitude and many theologians' inconsistent unwillingness to follow it out to its inevitable conclusion. If, as Aquinas suggests, an angel and a stone are better than two angels, Lovejoy maintains that it follows that God *must* create every possible kind of being, or come up short in goodness or power.[5] Theologians who won't draw this conclusion are simply muddled.

Lovejoy recognizes limitations on the principle. It does not imply that every possible individual being must be created, for instance: only that all possible kinds of being be represented. One person or mosquito more or less doesn't matter, but one species more or less does. And there is another even broader limitation. In any actual universe the realization of some possibilities may logically rule out others as mutually incompatible. The physical atmosphere that makes flying birds possible may make some other theoretical creatures impossible. Plenitude requires the full set of all possible beings that

5. (Lovejoy, 1965, pp. 76-79).

can realistically co-exist in one given world. While divinity is obliged to follow the rule of plenitude, it would be possible to choose among various
worlds that conform to that rule.

Even with these qualifications, Christian theologians generally have rejected a logical principle of plenitude that constrains God in this way. I cannot affirm a principle of plenitude that dictates what God must do and how
God must create. The "necessity" of plenitude in creation is not an abstract
requirement but a personal one. Since creation is the expression of the divine
character, it necessarily reflects the quality of that character. The plenitude of
the divine nature is the communion-in-difference of the three persons. This
fullness encompasses difference and relation in a communion where a single
relation is always overflowing into others. The relation of Father and Son always overflows into the further relations each has with the Spirit. And the
same can be said of each of those relations. There is a circle of communion in
which relation gives rise to further relation. This plenitude does not require
an infinity of persons in God. It only requires true relation in difference and
true communion. Such trinitarian life is then intrinsically open to the further
multiplication of such communion, though it is not necessitated. This is the
Christian belief about creation. The act expresses and reflects the divine nature, but these are free acts and reflections. They are not impelled by logical
necessity but by a qualitatively consistent choice by God to be toward creatures what God is "internally."

There is a dimension of plenitude yet undreamed of in Lovejoy's principle. A universe in which every possible kind of being is also actual is a "full"
or perfect universe, in Lovejoy's terms. But from another perspective it is crucially impoverished: it lacks contingency and space. The best possible painting is not a painting that includes every possible type of brush stroke, or every
possible subject. The choice of what is left out, the space, is also part of the
creative process. There is no necessity for God to fill every niche of possible
being to vindicate God's goodness, as if any possible creation left unmade is a
flaw.[6]

---

6. This whole discussion obviously points us toward the question of theodicy, where
the idea of plenitude has played a major role. The necessity for God to actualize all possible
kinds of being is an excuse of sorts for various evils that may flow from the existence of
less-than-perfect beings. The philosophical principle of plenitude has then been offered as
a solution to the theodicy dilemma. This is the case in claims that this universe is the "best
of all possible worlds." The claim can be made with a straight face on the assumption that
the universe contains the absolute minimum amount of evil required while also realizing
the logically necessary and supreme good of including all possible kinds of beings (igno-
rant and sin-prone ones among them). For the reasons I note above, Christian theology

If it is necessary to have every kind of being, then what of the category of non-necessary being? Must it be included for the fullness to be complete or would its presence destroy the plenitude? If to be possible is to be necessary, there can be no gratuitous kind of being, nothing made that did not have to be made, unless it is the needless duplication of "extra" individuals of the same kind. Christianity may seem deficient in terms of Lovejoy's principle, since it does not accept the realization of all possible kinds as necessary and ideal. On the other hand, it is profligate in its enthusiasm for distinctive individuals within kinds. In contrast with a worldview based on reincarnation, for instance, which efficiently recycles a given number of entities, Christianity sees constant creation of new individuals to multiply the density of relationship.

The Christian notion of creation implies the realization of unnecessary possibilities.[7] All possible being need not be real, and unrealized possibilities are not a metaphysical imperfection. Created being has the quality of gift. God chose creation as a partner for relation out of personal plenitude, the desire for others in their own right with whom to share communion, not from a logical obligation to fill up types of existence. Theology flatly rejects the premise behind philosophical plenitude that insists a longer roster of beings must be a greater good than a shorter one. A hundred kinds of being, in isolation, are by no means as good as fewer kinds in communion. And even isolated relations, actualized from among other unfulfilled options, are better than the same ones made real in a rote acting out of every possibility. Plenitude has to do with God's desire to share the communion-in-relation that characterizes the divine life. And this of necessity requires difference, to multiply relation and communion. But it is not a mathematical equation (or if it is, it is one in which quality of communion and free, contingent relation outweigh mere density of being). The plenitude that Christian faith has in view is one constituted both by variety of kinds of being, variety among individuals, and variety (and depth) of communion among beings across all divisions.

has not generally embraced a "necessity" defense of this sort, though sometimes God's choice in creation is defended with arguments (the best combination of competing goods) somewhat reminiscent of philosophical plenitude. Christian thought holds to the gratuity of creation, even though this might seem to exacerbate the theodicy question. These issues take us too far afield from our current topic to pursue further here.

7. The ontological argument tries to prove that God exists necessarily by virtue of the very idea of God. God is a possibility that must be actual . . . a kind of self-actualizing plenitude. To conceive of God as possible is to know that God must exist. It is interesting that Christian theology views creation (in opposition to philosophical plenitude) through a "non-ontological" argument. We cannot truly understand creation without knowing it did not have to exist. To know the true actuality of creation is to know that it is contingent. Its existence was not required by necessity.

I would formulate a theological principle of plenitude as follows. First, plenitude is a qualitative description of the divine life as triune. It is rooted in the revelation through which we know the Trinity. The unity and character of God are better expressed as a personal communion-in-difference than by reference to a pure divine essence or substance. Plenitude points to this dynamic exchange in communion as the very nature or "fullness" of God. Our discussion of Trinity in chapters four and five tried to provide a basis for understanding this sense of plenitude.

Second, this divine fullness is expressed economically in all that God has made. God has chosen a creation with real freedom. In their freedom for relation and communion with each other, creatures reflect the image of their maker. In addition, the relations between God and creation reflect yet another dimension of plenitude, a communion of the divine and the contingent, the maker and the creatures. The diversity and communion of the triune life have given rise to the plenitude of relations *among* creatures and to the plenitude of relations between creatures and the creator.

Third, salvation itself bears this same characteristic watermark. The saved are an extraordinarily various host of persons in communion with God and each other through Christ, sharing in a network of relations with an unlimited number of individual "flavors" and nuances. Consistent with the quality of plenitude in our first two points, God offers this religious end as the most intimate relation between creature and creator. God chooses to call persons into salvation as this intimate communion-in-diversity, rather than to seek any single kind of perfect relation to God endlessly repeated by every creature. The joy and fulfillment of salvation could not be greater or deeper for any who participate in it. And yet it will be precisely alike for none. Participation in the triune life bears this dramatic mark of commonality with the life of the triune persons: as the persons of the Trinity each are unique and each relation between them in the shared communion is also unique, so will it be in the communion of the blessed with God and with each other.

What we have just said deals entirely with salvation, the Christian religious end. But the fourth element of the theological principle of plenitude extends finally one step further to other religious ends. In harmony with the expansiveness of God's creation in its diversity, God's purpose for creation allows that variety to work itself out in different ways. The variation in creation, including that of each individual, finds its place in consummation. Salvation as Christians hope for it is communion of relation-in-difference with God and with others. So plenitude would be a cardinal feature of religious fulfillment if it were the case that all were saved. Such universal salvation would encompass a rich variety in what precisely being "saved" means for

253

each one. One person's relations with God and with others would retain their unique qualities. But the plenitude that exists within salvation exists in another way outside it. What of the freedom of creatures to either resist relation with God or to limit that relation and frame it in their own terms? This is also a part of God's act of withdrawal and letting be in creation. Nor do we need to assume that God set a limit to this freedom by fiat and an exercise of power. Humans can choose to realize something other than the communion of relation in the divine life that constitutes salvation. Each instance of salvation is concretely different from every other instance. The same principles that lead to that conclusion suggest that instances of "non-salvation" are not all the same.

As I have suggested in reviewing the dimensions of relation to God's triune life, humans can choose religious ends distinct from salvation that are genuine relations with God. Such a choice intensifies a particular dimension of relation and at the same time restricts other possible avenues of communion with God and others. In, with, and under the conditions of creation, God is available for relation with humans in a number of dimensions. Salvation is not simply the presence of *some* relation, over against the absence of any. Short of annihilation, creation can never be out of relation with God. Salvation is shared participation in the range of dimensions of relation with God that constitute the fullest communion open to humanity. The existence of other religious ends alongside this communion is a different but very real plenitude in its own right.[8]

We are now drawing together several points that we have developed in earlier chapters. The universal saving will of God extends to all creatures, consistent with their freedom and variety. There are not two wills in God, for God's judgment of and opposition to evil is directed precisely at whatever stands in opposition to the redemption of creation. God's saving will does not reach a limit or a point at which it changes to condemnation. God's relation to each person is one that seeks endlessly to attain good as fully as possible for the creature, within the terms set by the person's freedom.

God has chosen the plenitude represented by creation itself and wishes to maintain it through the multifarious communion with God in Christ that is salvation. Integral to that same choice, God values the very different kind of plenitude that results when creation's freedom is worked out in the realiza-

---

8. This highlights an interesting question in interreligious discussion. Do traditions understand their own religious end to be one that encompasses significant diversity or not? To what extent is it identical for all who achieve it, and to what extent does it envision distinctions?

tion of a variety of religious ends. The possibility that persons will realize their freedom in something other than salvation is real and accepted by God as a dimension of creation. The actual religious ends distinct from salvation are the concrete face of this possibility. As we have seen in our discussion of the Trinity and of the various ways that we can relate to the triune life of God, the validity and truth of religious ends derive from their actual and particular relation to some aspect of the triune life. Their distinct and unique characters derive from the exclusion of other aspects integral to salvation.

Theologically, plenitude itself has dimensions. It refers to the communion-in-difference of the triune life itself, to the varied dimensions of relation possible between creatures and God made possible by the triune nature, to the diversity of relations possible among creatures and persons, by virtue of their different kinds and individuals. Salvation is the mutual indwelling of these plenitudes, where our varied relations with each other are the vehicles for participation in the varied dimensions of relation with God, which are the means for our fullest sharing in the inner divine life. But even apart from salvation, an exponential fulfillment of this recursive pattern of communion-in-difference, the pattern of plenitude still holds.

The alternatives to salvation are in fact constituents of salvation, standing alongside each other. These ends are not evil or empty. They could not be real unless they were relations to God. They are marked by their *positive* commitment to relation with a particular dimension of God, and a corresponding approach to the other dimensions within the terms of that relation. In salvation, these dimensions are knit together in a web of interpersonal participation, a plenitude of communion. In the variety of religious ends alongside salvation these dimensions are manifest in a spectrum of parallel perfections, a plenitude of differing ultimacies.

These two kinds of plenitude together represent the richest harmonization of the theological principles we have outlined: God's universal saving will, the constitutive place of Christ as savior, the universal accessibility of salvation, the freedom of the creature, and the possibility of loss. All genuine religion, since it grasps some constituent element of saving relation with God, testifies to God's saving will and to the universal accessibility of salvation, and provides avenues by which one may move toward Christ. At the same time, religious diversity honors the freedom of persons to relate to God as they choose, to value the dimensions of divinity on their own terms, and to select the human end they wish. Such alternatives include the loss of dimensions of relation that are declined. A plenitude of religious ends is a reflection of the goodness and the saving will of God, applied in relation to free persons who seek something other than communion with the triune

God. Every relation with God that is sought is fulfilled. Everything is offered. Nothing is denied.

II

We have presented a vision in which there is a plenitude of communion within salvation, but also a plenitude of religious ends alongside it. Is that vision an acceptable picture of the consummation of creation Christians expect? So far we have considered salvation and religious ends primarily as distinct cases. Many readers may have been eager to object that some temporary divergence in such ends may be plausible (in the life to come, as well as in this life), but that such diversity cannot be part of a final eschatological scenario.

In one sense this is a reprise of a very old argument in theology. Some maintain that if in the end every creature is not brought to salvation then God's character and power are somehow diminished, the justice of creation itself violated. Others have argued the necessity for some to be damned, on exactly the same grounds: otherwise God's character and the justice of creation would be compromised.[9] These two sides, the case for universalism and the case for eternal division, each have biblical warrant, though eternal division may have the more extensive support.[10] The theological argument for universalism stresses God's goodness and power; the argument for division stresses human freedom and God's justice. Universalists maintain that their view can retain some meaningful place for justice and judgment. Those who defend division maintain that it can meaningfully be seen as itself an act of goodness and love.

We can illustrate this dialogue with an example. A criticism often advanced against those who defend division goes as follows. The division model supposes that creatures finally do what God wants them to do or they don't. And they are then either rewarded or punished. It is right for God to "im-

---

9. Can a result not in conformity with God's will be a good result? Here again our discussion overlaps with much traditional treatment of theodicy. There are two ways of looking at this. The first is to say it *is* God's will that some be lost and therefore the end is good. The second is to say the good of a free creation, of God granting real independent life to creation, is a great good, but one that intrinsically includes the results of choices against God's wishes. Those results are not substantively good or directly wished by God, but they are good as subsidiary parts of a good that God wills.

10. For a summary of the biblical evidence that gives emphasis to the universalist elements (though without endorsing that conclusion) see (Pinnock, 1992). For a summary that gives the emphasis to division, see (Erickson, 1996).

pose" God's values in this way because what God wants people to do is in fact what is best for them to do. But the criticism says that such imperial dominance, even in a good cause, is procedurally wrong. God owes a certain respect to the creature's own choice. Those who defend eternal division will often agree, and say that hell represents just such respect, allowing persons the integrity of their own choices and the consequences that follow. Universalists will then further object that many who seek something other than communion with God sincerely pursue (and actually achieve) real, if lesser, goods. Since their motives are in some measure good, they hardly seem to deserve an eternal evil, and therefore they ought instead to be promoted to the ranks of the saved.[11] Non-universalists respond that salvation is not primarily a matter of moral attainment but of relation with God. And so the dialogue continues.

The idea of plenitude, the availability of religious ends other than salvation, falls directly into the middle of this argument. This is reflected in the two kinds of criticism it encounters. Some object that it amounts to a quasi-universalism — casting a positive evaluation over non-Christian religious aims and accepting them as in some sense continuous with salvation, as at worst "lesser salvations." It is division and judgment that have been compromised. Others object that the idea is only a somewhat novel version of the standard judgment-and-division model, reserving salvation to Christians and casting aspersions on all other religious fulfillments. It is universalism that has been slighted.

Can humans use their freedom to shape relation with God to the point of permanently frustrating God's intentions? At one extreme, this "shaping" can be a resistance to relation with God so thorough as to approach a denial of the relation itself. Since relation with God is what grounds the creature's very existence, this points toward a negation of being itself. Perhaps this is the only possible negation of God's intention, a self-extinction in which there is finally no "there" left from which to resist God's love, and likewise no longer any actual defiance. Others insist that such a reverse fiat against creation is beyond the creature's power, akin to trying to become invisible by closing your eyes. On this view, all must eventually be drawn into an *apokatastasis* or restoration of all things. Some would further argue that this restoration cannot stop short of universal salvation, with all eschatological loss temporary in character.

---

11. As we saw in Chapter Three, purgatory developed as a key link at this point. It maintained the geography of division, but allowed the population of the saved to be augmented without introducing an indifferentism toward the gaps between those who realized the Christian life much more and those who realized it much less.

In fact, salvation and annihilation represent the true poles of this spectrum. The church has broadly refused to teach that salvation is the destiny of all or that annihilation is the destiny of any. It has accepted the reality of heaven (where salvation is realized) and hell (where communion with God is refused). Hell is in this sense a "middle" option between salvation and annihilation, and its reality must subsist in the realization of some good of creation, however residual. A hell of total negation would be annihilation.

I agree with that part of Christian tradition that views eschatological loss as essentially privative and not punitive in character. Such loss can relate to *delay* in the realization of communion with God (a "purgatorial" possibility) or to an enduring distance from communion with God (alternative ends) or even to the loss of means for communion with God (annihilation). I believe that the nature of the freedom granted by God in creation and the scriptural evidence point toward all three types of loss as real possibilities.

One quite unremarkable conclusion follows from this discussion: my rather atypical thesis about multiple religious ends does not necessarily change these long-running theological arguments about universalism or division or annihilationism one bit. All parties could assimilate the thesis in some form and go on merrily with the same quarrels. For instance, one might view various religious ends as being real but transient. Rather than being actual final destinies, they would eventually sift out into either a simpler two-fold division or to a uniform, universal redemption. The ends might be viewed as having a "purgatorial" nature perhaps. Taken in this way, the hypothesis would introduce a wrinkle that leaves the final issue essentially the same: one end or two.

Even if the religious ends are recognized as permanent destinies, they may still fit into the frame of this debate. Just as the variations within heaven and hell (and the idea of purgatory) which developed in Christian thought were clearly articulated within an overarching "dual option" paradigm, the diversity of religious ends might be understood in a similar way. Where salvation and damnation are the options at issue, questioning the pure homogeneity of each need not disturb the contestants. There is a certain stereoscopic quality to the perspective I offer. From one eye it is an elaboration of what Christians mean by damnation, the absence of salvation. In this vein it can be seen as only a novel wrinkle in the most traditional Christian view of final division, characterizing diverse religious ends as circles in a more complex hell. The thesis could thus be adopted by those who oppose universalism. From the other eye, it can be seen as an unrestrained expansion of the idea of "religious fulfillment" which puts the reality of the specific and distinct religious ends of other religions somewhere on a continuum with Christian salvation as manifestations of God's goodness in relation to creation. This could be seen as a refinement in the description of heaven, and the thesis could then be adopted by universalists. The best picture we can gain on this subject comes precisely through the intersection of these two views. The resulting three-dimensional image is just right, in my view, because of its tension with current theories whose visions of human possibility are too "flat" and because of its consonance with the varied scriptural notes that must have a legitimate place in our theology.

The fundamental question at issue in these debates remains whether the eternal realization of lesser goods than salvation (and greater goods than complete negation) is conceivable in Christian faith. My proposal does not resolve that debate, though it does seek to give it a more concrete context and relevance. I do maintain that in historical-cultural terms and in earthly human experience there are distinct religious ends. I further maintain that distinct religious ends exist also in transhistorical reality (i.e., for persons after death). I would not insist that any or all such varied religious ends *must* in fact be eternal destinies, any more than the church generally has ruled out universal salvation. But I do not think we should rule out the possibility of such pluralism either, as the rest of this chapter makes clear. It is not that it must be so. But in Christian terms it could be so.

The hypothesis of multiple religious ends does not resolve the debate over universalism and division. But I believe it does move us somewhat beyond a traditional impasse. It would enhance theological reflection were the two sides simply to incorporate it within the terms of their ongoing debate, as just outlined. However, I want to consider multiple religious ends in principle as part of a final eschatological scheme. This would set the hypothesis clearly within the division model rather than the model of universalism. This is the option I would like to consider at greater length.

For the purposes of illustration, I would like to take a rather traditional description of eschatological division and show how it would be changed and strengthened through consideration of multiple religious ends. Reformed theologians have in general energetically defended the division option. One wrote, "God decreed of the fallen already involved in their destruction to select some in Christ, in time to call, justify and glorify them with the glory of His gracious mercy; others to abandon to their sins and to damn eternally to the praise of His righteousness."[12] Similar views can be found in nearly all Christian confessional traditions. Reformed thinkers emphasized God's sovereignty and exhorted their hearers to transcend a

---

12. Johannes Henricus Heideggerus, quoted in (Heppe, 1978, p. 146).

merely anthropocentric perspective on eschatological questions.[13] They argued there was justice, fitness, and even beauty in the fact that while God saved sinners who were otherwise bound for hell, yet there were some (or many) who deserved that end and still received it. In the theater of redemption and judgment, God's justice and love were displayed in fuller measure by administering both destinies for humanity than would have been the case in administering only one.

The strength of this approach lies in the seriousness it grants human freedom and in the conviction that God's sovereign power could be vindicated without a uniform result. Like Augustine, classical Reformed thought did not deny the reality of human freedom but maintained that the results of human freedom could not deform God's good plan for creation. Theologians like the one just quoted believed that in the playing out of that human freedom (which calls upon God to be both judge and redeemer) God realized a more majestic and marvelous end than would be the case with less diversity. A traditional way of putting this was to say that the damnation of the ungodly glorifies God as does the unmerited mercy to sinners. To paraphrase Calvin, God chose to be victorious in two ways in creation rather than only one: to show forth his majesty both through just condemnation and through free mercy. In this way, God not only turned human evil into an occasion for good, but in fact made it an occasion for two goods. Here is yet another variant on the idea of plenitude. Calvinists intuitively viewed a God who fulfilled both love and justice, who manifested the divine glory in more than one way, as greater than a God who coped with creation on only one level.

Reformed theologians, jealous for God's sovereignty, were careful to avoid several possible conclusions. One was that God was under an obligation to save any creature. God's mercy is truly a free grace, and not compelled even by a need for God to "live up" to God's purpose in creation. Therefore, damnation must equally be something God is under no obligation to prevent for

13. A certain type of modern secularism celebrates a universe with the marvelous — some would even say "sacred" — natural processes that give rise to life and history. There is no meaning or purpose to this universe, other than what can be projected upon it in our ephemeral existence. Those who want to cling to hope for survival of death, to the continuation of the human species, or to some personal deity only evade the hard but noble truth. Such secularists will say that the universe is glorious nonetheless and one can exalt in the wonder and the oneness of the whole, knowing and accepting that we and our kind will die and be nothing but humus for the next round of cosmic process, as will all the great, the good, the evil, the suffering, and the oppressed of history. There is, or can be in such an attitude a good deal of similarity with a classic Calvinist's focus on the glory of God and God's creation, eschewing any petty concern for human prerogatives or the eternal destiny of one person or another, including one's self.

those who merit it. Another conclusion to be avoided was that the creature, through the free choice to opt for condemnation or salvation, might thereby hold the key to the success or failure of God's purposes. In such a case, God would be entirely at the mercy of the creature for any good to be achieved in creation.[14] For these reasons, such theologians developed an argument as to how the judgment of the wicked redounded to God's glory no less than the redemption of sinners. Judgment and redemption *both* were under God's providential sway and both testified to the goodness of God's creation. Those who were judged had no complaint, for they were treated with profound justice. Those who were saved despite their sin could only wonder at the free grace by which God delivered them. Human freedom is operative in effecting either end. With complete freedom to do what they want, humans still do not have the freedom to do what will not honor God. They do not have the power to diminish God's glory, since both outcomes testify to that glory. In other words, it is a win/win scenario for God's purposes, if not for creatures. Or perhaps it might better be called a no loss/no loss scenario, since in neither case do persons receive less than their due.

This "diversity" has but faint appeal among most today, even those who otherwise insist that God must transcend our conditioned perspectives and who condemn any kind of anthropocentrism. Reformed theologians in the past sometimes drew the case in such abstract terms that it sounded as if our primary concern should be to give God the highest marks for undertaking a feat with the maximum degree of technical difficulty and performing it flawlessly. And it is important to note that the *objection* to this scenario — to exalting the just punishment of sinners — arises naturally from within Christian theology, from the fundamental nature of salvation as relation. The concern of some for the fate of others is an integral feature of salvation itself, communion with God and other creatures.

The objection against the argument for division (and not only the Reformed version of it) appealed to this fundamental feature of salvation and also to the character of God. There are two particularly sharp criticisms on this score. The first is related to the punitive character of the division. Division seems to presuppose that God must will pain and suffering for those who are condemned. God intends and metes out evil to the evil. The justice of God implies the wrath of God. Though the reprobate may well deserve such

14. In contrast with most of those Reformed theologians, I would hold it to be true that God has put the divine purpose "at the mercy" of creatures through the act of incarnation. But by this I mean that God risked the fulfillment of salvation by depending on the free response of Jesus and of believers, not that God depended on particular human responses to vindicate the good of creation *per se.*

retribution, the criticism is that the active administration of punishment is not truly an activity consistent with God's nature. If human sin can coerce God into this posture, against God's ideal will, then God's power is severely compromised. It seems God is compelled to act in a way that is otherwise not a feature of God's true nature. This is the reason that advocates of division argued so strongly for judgment as an intrinsic revelation of God's glory, not as a secondary necessity for a God cornered by human disobedience. The liability of such an argument is that, if successful, it tends to establish wrath as a constitutive aspect of God's nature: not only wrath against sin but wrath against sinners.

The second criticism has to do with the condition of those who are condemned. Damnation means that there are persons who are part of God's creation who are left in an eternal state of active evil, who are barred even from the achievement of goods they did recognize and seek. This is a substantive failing in the fabric of the world. The total sum of the creation's good is actively diminished when the admittedly lesser goods achieved by the reprobate are subtracted from them in punishment for failing to achieve greater goods. As such it seems finally to reflect a defect in God's purposes or in the ability to carry them out, an eschatological defeat. In other words, such a final state cannot be the redemptive or worthy consummation of creation Christians say is promised and realized by God.

How does this perspective change if we bring into it our understanding of varied religious ends? First, the punitive/retributive element is removed. This is something that many Reformed theologians have sought to do in any event, by arguing that the qualities of loss in damnation are intrinsic effects of separation from God, not active divine condemnation.[15] This is true, and provides an adequate account of the extreme possibility of annihilation, at least. But our exploration of alternative ends makes it clear that these are not extrinsic punishments thrust upon persons for some judged failure in belief or act. They reflect God's "letting be" of what we become by our own choice, the realization of the self-determination of the creature. Second, we have introduced the concrete role of religions into the picture, and thereby heightened the sense of God's providential relations with humanity. God always

---

15. And many reject the idea of a punitive hell, in favor of one of affinity. That is, those who are separated from God suffer only the intrinsic consequences of their own choices, and are bound only by their own constant reappropriation of those choices and results. But the most thoroughgoing and profound reconsideration of the whole question is found in Karl Barth's exposition of the doctrine of election, which steadfastly focuses on God's single, positive election of humanity in Christ. See chapter seven, "The Election of God," in *Church Dogmatics* II, 2.

makes a full response to whatever dimension of relation has been accepted by the creature. In this, the tradition's talk of a "merciful judgment" or a "loving judgment" becomes much more clear and concrete. We saw above how Reformed theologians maintained that the pluralism constituted by salvation and damnation ought to broaden rather than narrow our sense of God's majesty. We could say instead that the prospect of persons realizing religious ends alternative to salvation should enhance our sense of God's majesty and love all the more. God's willingness to honor and incorporate this kind of freedom within creation's consummation redounds greatly to God's glory. God is glorified in opening up to creatures participation in the triune life of communion, but also in honoring the free alternative choices of creatures, meeting them not with punishment but with the best possible gifts their choices will allow. Therefore the judgment that God delivers is entirely in keeping with the nature of creation and with the dimensions of plenitude we have discussed above. This plenitude is based on the constant loving will of God, which responds with the greatest possible goodness to every genuine relation to God persons enter.

It seems a sound theological principle that creation would suffer no defect if all were to be saved. However, the Reformed theologians were right that this need not be a simple argument for universalism. Nothing would be lacking to creation were all to be saved. Would creation have failed if not all were saved? Not if all of creation is fulfilled in a manner consistent with the freedom that is part of God's primary act in creation. One may well argue that creation would have failed if God were reduced to coercive punishment of creatures or if creation as a whole spun out to a conclusion that was neither acceptable to God nor consonant with God's character. In fact it reflects greater divine sovereignty for a variety of actual final configurations of creation to be consistent with God's desire for communion, freedom, and a plenitude of good. Is there but one final outcome for the universe, down to the slightest detail, consistent with God's purpose? Or is there a wider range, consistent with creation's capacity to participate in its own future? I suggest that it is actually a greater expression of God's power and nature that creation retains freedom at this level within certain parameters. God assures not an exact result, but the fulfillment of possibilities that are all consistent with God's purposes.

God allows each of us to become what we wish to become. Or, more exactly, God allows each of us to freely form our most profound desires, and then to fulfill them. Short of the total resistance to God that leads to annihilation, each person's aim for fulfillment includes relation with God in some dimension. God's saving will offers all the opportunity for communion in the triune life through Christ. But that same saving will also brings to perfection each true relation with God that a person may freely choose as a final end. And beyond this, God brings the ensemble of such ends and choices to its own pluralistic perfection, integrating the chosen relations and goods so as to create the richest satisfaction of each and all under the terms of their desired fulfillments.

This is the situation that the realization of various religious ends foresees. The plenitude that exists within salvation, the variation in the concrete texture of full communion with God from one unique creature to another, would be augmented with a variation of realized relations with God other than that of salvation. Since such a situation would represent the fulfillment of the highest desires and aim of free creatures, and since it would represent the fulfillment of God's fundamental creative act of granting the creature this self-determination, and since all the relations realized with God are goods in themselves, this represents a true and worthy consummation of creation. There is loss or deficiency in this picture only when some ends are compared with salvation. However objective that discrepancy, persons have full liberty to choose. If salvation is declined in favor of another religious end, this must rest finally on preference for another good. The discrepancy is recognized, but it can be interpreted in favor of the alternative end. There is no evil in such plenitude. The experience of punitive loss could be enforced only if God wished to crush the creature's choice of goods with God's own. And that God does not choose to do.

If God had so made the world as to offer, say, the Buddhist religious fulfillment as the sole and fullest aim open to creatures, creation would be neither unjust nor defective. The diversity of religious ends provides an extraordinary picture of the mercy and providential richness of God. Jesus asks his hearers who among them would give a child who asks for bread a stone in return. And he continues by saying that God, more than any parent, knows how to give good gifts.[16] A Christian theology of religious ends can affirm that no real relation to God goes without its good gift, that God's relation to us is marked by overflowing bounty. Any relation to the triune life receives its own fulfillment.

If the plenitude of religious ends is a good thing, is it necessary for the good of creation, for eschatological consummation, that this plenitude be realized? Is it not only consistent with God's goodness that some not be saved, but is it *necessary* that people not be saved, in order that there be some to fill out the distinct goods of all conceivable other religious ends? Here we touch

16. See Luke 11:9-13 and Matthew 7:7-11.

on a very important point. Theological plenitude in the created realm is not about necessity. There is no requirement that all alternative religious ends be eternally "filled," any more than that every abstractly conceivable individual be created. That these various ends are truly open for persons is a facet of God's creating and redeeming activity. But there is no compulsion on God, from God or for individuals, that predestines the character of this plenitude in all its details.

Here we return to the difference between a philosophical principle of plenitude and the theological one. The philosophical principle of plenitude dictates that whatever is possible must become real. But our theological principle, in which freedom is a feature of plenitude, requires possibilities that are not actualized. Otherwise creation would not have the freedom to take on a determinate character in relation with God, and it is just such freedom that God intends for it. Multiple or "branching" universes have become a staple of speculative physics and science fiction. On some versions of such theories, universes branch at every binary decision point: in one the South won the Civil War while in another the North did. In one, I studied and passed my geometry exam and in another I did not. Here is an infinite plenitude, where literally everything that can happen does happen, in some universe. Even apart from the appalling moral equivalence of this vision, where every conceivable evil inevitably takes place alongside its opposite and no good moral decision or act definitively replaces the corresponding malevolence, this picture is incompatible with a Christian sense of plenitude.

The outcome God has ordained has boundaries, but within them creation traces a path that is unique. It leaves some paths untaken. There is room for surprise, for realities God knows by observation, not by predetermination. God chose this particular creation, to become what unique pattern of goods it chose. The omnipotence and providence of God are manifest in the fact that creation cannot actualize itself in terms inconsistent with the divine plenitude. This means that some ends, such as the creation ending up with none saved, or with no religious fulfillments realized, are precluded. This is a different kind of win/win scenario. Either through the free will of all creatures they are saved (universalism) or through the free will of creatures some are saved and some achieve other religious ends or even negate their relation with God altogether (division). In either case, humans get what they truly desire. And in either case God achieves God's comprehensive aim for creation in its diversity, the aim that every creature attain the highest possible level of good consistent with its freedom and that the consummation of the world reflect in its entirety the good of plenitude that is part of the character given to it by God in creation.

It is not that God micro-manages the operation of each act of free will. It is rather, as theologians like Calvin glimpsed, that God finds free will the uniquely apt instrument of God's own will to realize the good of plenitude. Pure necessity would make creation a mere machine. Granting creation pure randomness could well produce a result entirely out of keeping with the divine nature. But instilling the freedom God does in a creation already marked by God's image leads to a consummation which is a free plenitude of human response to the divine goodness.

We may clarify this in terms that connect with our earlier discussion of plenitude. In the middle ages, theologians sometimes speculated about what God *could* have done, consistent with God's transcendent freedom and power. Could God have chosen a different means for salvation? Could one of the triune persons other than the Son have been incarnate? Those who argued in favor of such counterfactual possibilities defended an absolute divine freedom.[17] That is, they maintained that the addition or existence of *unrealized* possibilities enriches creation more than if every aspect of it were dictated by a logical necessity. From this perspective, a creation that could have been otherwise is greater than one that could not have been otherwise.[18] Even beyond that, a creation which — once made — still carries within itself real alternative possibilities is greater than one that does not.

If we could transpose those medieval questions for our subject, we might ask whether God could have made the world so as to offer human beings only one of the distinct religious ends we have been considering: the Buddhist religious end, for instance. We ask not only whether this would be possible, but whether it would be "good." Or we could ask whether it would likewise have been possible and right for God to have chosen to be known by humans only "economically," that is to say, in various manifestations of transcendent power, of order, of inner light, each remaining self-sufficient and separate for those who were touched by it. I incline to think that God could have done so — both in the sense of having the ability and in the sense that

---

17. See (Heim, 1979), reprinted in (Gamble, 1992).

18. This is just the opposite of the classic argument Lovejoy draws from Leibnitz and others, which implies that the world can be called "good" in some ultimate sense only if in all respects it could not be other than exactly as it is. The perennial theological argument against the iron necessity of the "best of all possible worlds" has maintained that a fuller understanding of "good" — one marked by truer plenitude — requires a world which itself allows for and encompasses various real possibilities and then works these out in a harmony. Again, the common ground on which these questions have been explored is theodicy: How can a world with frail and sinful creatures and the resultant evil be a good world?

such a creation would be good. God could have done these things; no rule obliged God to do otherwise. In referring to a theological principle of plenitude I am only saying that God, unconstrained by some logical requirement, made the free choice to express in creation the plenitude that characterizes the divine life itself. This is an act of consistency with the divine nature, not of obligation to an abstract rule.

Creation is shot through with freedom, including freedom "from" God by virtue of God's withdrawal to give it space for self-determination. Yet creation is also a stacked deck of sorts. It is not predetermined as to every event, but it is organized in such a way that God's plan for creation is realized through and with the freedom it is given. This is only possible because God's purpose in creation is the kind of plenitude we have been discussing. In such a plan, success is consistent with alternative results at a number of points. God's purpose is realized either way.

The deck is stacked in the following ways. First, it is stacked in favor of the realization of *our* desires. There is nothing ultimately extrinsic about the destiny of human beings. The end is thoroughly of a piece with our participation in it. This is the one thing we might say is most absolutely predetermined. We have the freedom to shape our own desires. And having done so, we have no choice but to get what we want. Once we have considered the religions themselves as various ways of relating to dimensions of the triune life, we can see that the deck is stacked in a second respect. It is stacked toward the realization of a religious end that fulfills a true relation with God. To put it another way, no matter what the manner or measure in which we respond to the gifts of the divine life, God has elected to meet our desires with the most complete fulfillment they allow. And finally we can say the deck is also stacked in favor of salvation. That is, from every location and religious perspective the way is open to the fuller communion with the triune God and other creatures through Christ. The good of each religious end's relation with God fits into that wider communion and can be received there. No starting point prevents it. Indeed, all are seeded with the possibility.

At none of these three levels except the first (where we are "condemned to be free") is there any necessity. In the exercise of our freedom we inevitably fulfill God's intent that creation should have its own life. And only with great difficulty may we carry out that freedom without realizing some aspect of the good that God has made available to us. God is, as C. S. Lewis said, very unscrupulous. This stacking of the deck is what advocates of natural theology perceive and emphasize. We are made in the image of God. Every good we perceive and seek is rooted in God and can ultimately lead us to some relation with God. God fulfills every authentic desire to know God. All this is true. But natural theology is in error if it supposes that our desires inevitably attach to nothing but communion with God and can lead us to nothing else. Those who advocate revealed theology are right that because of the freedom God gave creation and because of sin, communion with the triune God requires conversion and grace. True but lesser goods can be chosen in preference to God. Every actual contact or relation with God is not a saving relation. But revealed theology is wrong if it insists that apart from salvation God will do nothing to fulfill human good.

We can now see that the religions are an integral part of God's providential purpose, a reflection of God's universal love. They demonstrate that every movement of human response to God's "Yes" to creation is met by God's further "Yes" as well. We see the particular way in which this is true. Religions represent real relations to aspects of the triune life and aspects of God's economic activity. In this sense they are part of the network by which all can be drawn into closer communion with God and to salvation. But they also represent the fact that God always will relate with creation under the terms of freedom granted it. God will in crucial measure conform God's relation with the person to the person's choice of terms on which to relate to God. In honoring alternative religious ends, God is consistent with the desire for a creation in which plenitude may be realized in diverse ways.

Are religions providential only as avenues that lead to salvation and finally give way to it, or are they providential in offering an eternal pluralism of religious ends? They are providential in both. They are certainly providential as penultimate paths toward salvation and as *possible* eternal alternatives. The realization of salvation for all is in no wise ruled out: we have discussed how diversity and plenitude would be expressed no less within that communion. I have not sought to settle the question between universalism and division, but to set it in different terms, terms that bring the religions directly into play.

As I suggested in Chapter Five, each religion's end involves relation to a particular aspect of the triune divine life. People whose home religious tradition is not Christianity naturally are nurtured in such a way as to focus on the distinctive aspect their faith emphasizes (as Christianity emphasizes communion). This is the place at which relation to the triune God begins within that context, though it need not (and from a Christian view ought not) be the place where such relation also ends. Since each dimension of relation with God is rooted in the trinitarian nature, any particular connection with the triune life can flow increasingly and ultimately into that communion with all the dimensions of the triune God which constitute salvation. This is the way in which salvation is open equally to all, whatever the religious starting point. These dimensions of relation are united in the divine life. The fact that this unity has been manifested to us in Christ, who draws them together in one person, means that Christians look for such convergence. But this in no way requires it.

The religious milieu in which people find themselves is the starting point for the attainment of a religious end, whether that end is salvation or not. Religions have their own integrity, their own orientation toward a particular religious end. They reliably lead adherents toward that goal, with its intensification and fulfillment of relation through a specific dimension of trinitarian life. From a Christian point of view, it is not just that other religions contain "bits and pieces" that can be used against the natural grain of the tradition to lead people toward God in Christ (as also people within the Christian tradition may use some of its elements against the grain toward the attainment of another end than salvation). The internal logic of authentic religious traditions leads them toward profound dimensions of relation with God. It is the *success* of religions in these terms that leads Christians to have confidence in their capacity to serve as a step toward salvation. It is the religious end itself that Christians believe can only with difficulty remain isolated from the entire triune life of which it is one dimension. This fuels the Christian's hope for universal salvation. But "anonymous Christianity" cannot be the accurate global description of another religion. Its ordinary function is to attain its own religious end, not the Christian one.

The options are to receive the communion in the triune God offered to us, or to have what we prefer instead, including another kind of relation with God. Either result, though of inestimable import to the person, fully honors the diversity and freedom that God granted to creation, and therefore glorifies and fulfills God's purpose. We had occasion earlier to note C. S. Lewis's observation that the crucial division among humans is among those who finally say to God "Thy will be done" and those to whom God says "Thy will be done." What we have tried to describe is the fact that variety results in either case. For humans to desire to see God's will done is necessarily to desire that complex communion of unique wills *distinct* from God's, in which each remains entirely itself and yet participates with others. For God to uphold human choices that differ from God's fulfills God's overarching aim to vindicate freedom for the creature. It carries out God's will to make possible what God does not will. And (as our discussion of religious ends has tried to make clear) these choices themselves may contain within them true elements of God's intent, including profound relations with God. When humans choose less than all God offers, it does not mean they choose nothing that God desires. This is the extraordinary mystery and wonder of the divine providence.

Chapter Eight

A Theology of Religious Ends

George Lindbeck offers a thoughtful comment on the outlook of early Christians: "Christians in the first centuries appear to have had an extraordinary combination of relaxation and urgency in their attitude toward those outside the church."[1] He notes that on the one hand Christians did not evidence anxiety over the ultimate fate of believers in other faiths all around them. On the other hand, their missionary witness was urgent and faith clearly a matter of life and death to them. So striking is this combination that Lindbeck speculates early Christians must have shared some unrecorded convictions — perhaps regarding Christ preaching to souls after death — that were never at issue and so remained unarticulated. Those Christians, living as a minority in an intensely pluralistic religious world, invited all to accept the gospel of Christ as the way of salvation. Yet they also had abiding confidence that whatever the outward effects of their evangelism, God would "do right" by all people, would not leave any without a fair opportunity for salvation and would meet humanity at every turn with grace beyond deserving. This confidence in no way hindered the passion to share the gospel message with others.

Lindbeck's point is intriguing, though we can hardly know what the unarticulated convictions of early Christians might have been. The attitudes he notes are real enough. We could go a good way toward supporting a similar disposition in Christians today if we were to develop a theological understanding that genuinely sees other religions as testimony to God's providen-

1. (Lindbeck, 1984, p. 58).

271

tial activity in the world, and sees in their religious fulfillments a tempered hope. The religions offer evidence for God's sovereignty, for the trustworthiness of God's presence and action in the world, a demonstration that in all quarters God cooperates to draw people away from evil. God offers salvation to all through Christ's life, death, and resurrection. And even where that offer is declined or deferred, God draws any positive response, however limited, toward the fullest providential good.

I

I am suggesting that there are four broad types of human destiny. There is salvation, that communion through Christ with God and with others that unites an unlimited diversity of persons and opens each to wider participation in the triune life. Second, we have alternative religious ends, the distinctive human fulfillments of the various religious traditions. Each of these grasps some dimension of the triune life and its economic manifestation, and makes it the ground for a definitive human end. As such, each is an instance of God's gracious, providential support for creatures.

Third, there are human destinies that are not religious ends at all. These are instances of humans clinging definitively to created reality in place of or over against God. Such "hells of idolatry" can exist only by virtue of the created goods themselves (from physical pleasure to individual autonomy to free choice). They take the form of captivity to some aspect of creation completely isolated from God. That captivity sadly shrinks the horizon of possibility given in the created self. Human insistence on using those goods as a shield against any true relation with the God who is their source (or true relation with others) turns them into sparse and barren absolutes. Such destinies are the full satisfaction of human aspiration, when that aspiration has voluntarily and drastically withered. It is an impoverished dream come true.

Since no created good is good as an absolute, the result is distortion. One who wants pleasure entirely "by itself," for instance, wants something that is not actually real, since all created pleasures are by nature linked with God and others. The inhabitants of hell are not denied any of the created good (of sense, for instance) that makes up the pleasure they desire. No matter how many times the same meal is served, the tastes and textures will be reliably the same. But insistently isolated from everything else that makes for a "delicious meal" (from friends to share it, from well-earned hunger to anticipate it, from thanksgiving to God for it), it becomes a rather terrible delight.

Even in realizing such desires, humans uphold at least the relation with God and God's good creation necessary for the existence of their narrow aim.

The fourth destiny does not idolize some created good, but negates creation itself. The only point at which this can conceivably be done is where relation constitutes us as a creature, a being — the point of our relation with God. The possibility at least exists for a settled rejection of the relation that gives us being, a refusal to participate in what makes us possible. That end would be annihilation.[2] The four types of end are thus the negation of the created self, fixation on a created good, a relation with God defined through one of the non-communion dimensions of the triune life, and salvation, the relation with God that is the communion of these dimensions. The first two might be called "godless" ends; the second two realize different kinds of relation with God.

We can clarify this outlook by comparing it with the discussion of a supernatural end (salvation) and a natural end in the theology of Thomas Aquinas. Aquinas is clear that humanity was created for the supernatural end of salvation, the beatific vision, an end that exceeds all human capacity apart from grace. Humans are made for this end, but they have no intrinsic power to achieve it. Humans are made for something that exceeds their independent nature, but is thoroughly possible for them through communion offered by God. In speaking of a natural end for humanity, Aquinas did not mean to compromise salvation as the true goal. Since the supernatural end offered to humanity in salvation exceeds humans' own capacities, the question arises "what *is* possible through those capacities alone?" In one sense this is a thoroughly abstract question, and "pure nature" is an imaginary idea. Humans are never left entirely to their own devices. They are always the objects of grace. In this respect, the natural end is a secondary and theoretical notion.

But the concept is still a meaningful one, in two senses. First (and of great importance in Aquinas's context), it bears on what one can expect from philosophy, the practice of reason on its own. Second, since humans have fallen into sin and are estranged from the way to communion with God, the

---

2. It is important to note that this is not the same thing as a religious end (*nirvana* for instance) that realizes a "return" to humanity's ground in the divine emptiness, in the dimension of kenotic exchange in the triune life. Such an end implicitly *affirms* a relation with God, however partial it is from the perspective of communion. The Buddhist has a unitive intention with regard to emptiness as a transcendent condition. That is different from the nihilism of annihilation as I describe it here. *Nirvana* is a gift of participation in emptiness; annihilation is a rejection of being. The Buddhist lack of recognition of a created self (an error in Christian terms) precludes the active sin of *rejection* of created existence. Its focus is on positive identification with the divine kenotic process.

prospect of a natural end becomes real. By the rejection of grace, humans contrive to make the abstract possibility (a natural end as the ultimate end) actual.

Aquinas's discussion of the natural end aims to make one other crucial point. Though the supernatural end is what God intends and offers to humanity, God's goodness is manifest in the fact that even if we turn to the creature's "own" nature apart from communion with God, and consider an end intrinsic to it, what we encounter is still a good. The imperfect felicity of the natural end is imperfect only in light of what is known by revelation. Frederick Copleston summarizes it this way: "The concrete human being was created by God for a supernatural end, for perfect happiness, which is attainable only in the next life through the vision of God and which is, moreover, unattainable by man by his own unaided natural power; but man can attain an imperfect happiness in this life by the exercise of his natural powers, through coming to a philosophic knowledge of God through creatures and through the attainment and exercise of the natural virtues."[3] The natural end can be entirely subsumed in the supernatural one — there is no reason that all of its imperfect happiness cannot be caught up along the way to eternal happiness. But the point is that left to its own devices, humanity is still a good creation and the end commensurate with it is still a good end. There is no suggestion in Aquinas that humans ought to content themselves with a natural end, but every reminder of God's unstinting goodness.

Aquinas's notion of a natural end marks a kind of border between the first two and the last two of the destinies we outlined above. The natural end is the fulfillment of a relation with God, as that relation can be understood and realized under the conditions set by natural reason. As a destiny centered on relation with God, it falls on the side of religious ends and salvation; as a destiny entirely contained within the terms of created good, it falls on the side of loss and negation. It is a kind of imaginary dotted line, corresponding to no actual human condition.[4] Since a "god" defined solely in natural terms is not the living or revealed God, purely natural religion turns into a kind of idolatry. But it is virtually impossible for any person to practice "natural religion" without contamination from revealed elements (whether borrowed from traditions of revealed religions or received by direct illumination), and

3. (Copleston, 1962, pp. 34-35).
4. By saying it corresponds to no actual human condition I do not mean that I rule out a natural end like the one Dante attributes to Virgil. I simply maintain that the achievement of such an end would never actually take place apart from grace, through pure, autonomous human power.

so such natural religion can often attach itself functionally to one of the religious ends.

I distinguish salvation, communion with the triune God in Christ, from other religious ends, as well as from any natural end. But I distinguish religious ends from the so-called natural end also. These religious fulfillments are beyond attainment by purely natural human capacities. Alternative religious ends define God essentially in terms of one dimension (other than communion) of the triune life. That is, they are rooted in authentic revelation *of* the triune God, but not revelation of God *as* triune. The first distinguishes them from idolatry or a natural end. The second distinguishes them from salvation. They depend on revelation and grace, in two senses. First of all, as human relations with dimensions of the triune life, they depend on God's free self-revelation. This includes but is not limited to general revelation. For instance, even if the dimension of trinitarian "emptiness" is given as a general revelation under the character of all created things, the discernment of that dimension as ultimate, holy, and transcendent (rather than as plain negation) is no simple, natural conclusion. It requires special grace and illumination. Second, this act of revelation and connection, in which God illuminates sinners to recognize an authentic dimension of the divine life, expresses the same divine initiative toward reconciliation and communion that is manifest in Christ.

The triune God is party to the realization of alternate religious ends. They are not simply the actualization of innate human capacities; they are distinct relations with aspects of the triune life. A particular grace of God is operative in them. Second, this divine aid works in some measure to overcome the dynamic of human sin. It is fruitless to speculate whether, apart from sin, human beings could have realized these religious ends "on their own." In fact, sin has touched all dimensions of human life. Therefore attainment of a religious end requires a struggle with disordered human dispositions at every turn, and does not succeed without grace. Third, and perhaps most important for our discussion here, the relation between salvation and other religious ends is more complex than the relation Aquinas presumed between the supernatural and natural ends. For Aquinas the natural end and the supernatural end followed an identical path until a point at which the natural way ended completely and one could go further only by the supernatural way. One could pursue the natural end all the better for doing so as a Christian, subsuming all of its goods readily within the broader supernatural goal.

Virgil, the *Comedy*'s exemplar of the natural end, guides Dante on the single path that leads from lower hell to the very peak of the mountain of purgatory. At the top of Dante's Mt. Purgatory stands the earthly paradise. It is a purely transitional place, a transitory stage before salvation. Souls bound for paradise all pass through, but none stay. Its close twin is the Elysian fields section of limbo, which remains a permanent destination. This is Virgil's abode. He stops at this milestone of natural perfection. The earthly paradise and the Elysian fields together articulate Dante's view of the natural end: one similar reality that is either threshold to salvation or its own final good.

Of course, as Dante and Aquinas were aware, philosophy and the natural end could turn the tables, and propose to subsume revelation and the supernatural end. Reason may recognize no value in the supernatural end that is not already contained and surpassed in the natural end. Then it is religious believers who are viewed as stopped at an earlier milestone, blocked from progress to the natural end by their irrational expectations and flawed understanding.

When other religious traditions are given a status and respect similar to what Aquinas was willing to grant philosophy, the result is a somewhat more complicated picture. We no longer have one unequivocal path, and two ends that represent different stages on it. Instead, we have a variety of religious ends, each of which can serve as a final end or a threshold point toward salvation. The transitional face of these religious goals can be described as follows:

> . . . a particular religious community may foster dispositions that advance its members partly along the way to fellowship with the Triune God. Aims can occur in ordered sequences, and priorities assigned to "higher" aims do not negate or exclude subordinate aims. . . . a person could develop dispositions with a view to a certain aim without the awareness that the attainment of this aim afforded access to another. It might turn out that religious aims pursued as ultimate were themselves encompassed by an end more ultimate yet. Thus, Muslims or Buddhists could be said to develop dispositions conducive to the enjoyment of the true aim of life — fellowship with the Blessed Trinity — even though they do so in the light of conceptions that rule out personal relations either within God or in the ultimate state of enlightenment. The upshot would be that such persons could reach the threshold of the enjoyment of the true aim of life not only despite but also because of dispositions fostered in their communities, even though some of their doctrines are regarded as mistaken or incomplete from the Christian point of view.[5]

But the same religious fulfillment can in fact constitute the final end its tradition seeks. Dispositions conducive to salvation can be developed as sub-

---

5. (DiNoia, 1992, p. 103).

ordinate priorities in service of another religion's higher end. And they can remain subordinate, in the realization of that end. The same "transitional" links we have just described are recognized and valued from the other side, as it were. They are avenues that can lead people over the threshold from what are viewed as lesser religious aims (such as the Christian one) toward the true ultimate offered in *this* religious end.

II

On this basis, we can imagine a new version of the *Divine Comedy*, one that addresses the religions with the care and courtesy Dante showed to human reason. A developed theology of religious ends might now provide the prose skeleton that Thomistic theology provided for the *Comedy*. Dante's afterworld was organized with several principles in mind. The most important one was that the *Comedy* was to be read as a multi-layered work, as Scripture itself was. Like Scripture, Dante believed the *Comedy* should work on four levels. It has a literal meaning as a story. It has a political or "doctrinal" meaning. It has a moral meaning. And it has a mystical meaning. Its genius is the extent to which it does work on various levels, while still remaining one narrative whole, with its own power and unity.

To take one example, virtually all Christian literature prior to Dante did not clearly distinguish hell and purgatory from each other. Dante made them two quite distinct realms. This had to do in part with Dante's acceptance of the contemporary arguments in favor of such a "third place." Dante believed literally in the spiritual realities of heaven and hell and purgation, though he did not believe literally in his physical representations of them (that purgatory is a mountain on an island in the southern hemisphere opposite Jerusalem, for instance). His descriptions of hell, purgatory, and paradise "worked" on both the doctrinal level and on the literal level of his story. But there was yet more. In traveling with his readers through the two distinct places, hell and purgatory, Dante was able to illustrate concretely what distinguishes a purgatorial and hopeful entanglement with sin from a final captivity to it. That is, he was able to communicate on both the moral and mystical levels as well.

We need to be mindful of a similar set of concerns in theology. Although our discussion of religious ends tends to be set most easily as an eschatological story, this is largely a convenience: our imagination moves quickly to the temporal end just as that of Dante's reader moves readily to temporal and geographical ends. But a theology of religious ends bears on several levels at once also. The *Comedy* is literally about the next world; most of its allegorical meanings are about this one. If I use language analogous to Dante's about "place" I do not intend any greater literalness than he does. Dante displayed his images of the afterlife to express eschatological *and* temporal truths. From good theology and good art about the life to come, one could expect to derive insight for practice here and now, ethically and spiritually. The pattern of human destinies I have suggested should also be viewed in this light. It expresses what I take to be sound eschatological speculation, and at the same time it provides a fruitful perspective for understanding interreligious realities in our ordinary lives. We will return to this dimension of the question at the end of this chapter.

So if we were to reorder the *Comedy,* how would we do it? For framework, Dante has his three realms (heaven, purgatory, and hell), with the decisive line dividing the first two from the third. We would keep heaven, the realm of salvation. Then would come a realm encompassing both purgatory and alternative religious ends (about which more in a moment). Then would come a hell, divided somewhat as Dante's was in practice between an upper hell of isolated attachment to created goods and a lower hell of raw negation.

The most dramatic change has to do with the middle kingdom of this imaginative vision. Dante's middle realm, purgatory, was a single mountain with hierarchical order. Heavier sins were purged on its lower circles, and lesser deficiencies near its summit. This reflects the unity that comes from the fact that Dante, like Aquinas, had one natural end (defined by philosophy) in view as the only alternative or modest hope. Our middle realm must be a good deal more pluralistic, with several mountains rather than one. It will be a challenge for our poet to impart to it an elegance and clarity comparable to Dante's mountain. The difference in geography is telling. "Many roads up the same mountain" is a common image. It is used by individual traditions to show that all other paths must ultimately reduce to their own. And it is used with equal enthusiasm by pluralists to show that no path can claim a different end than another. We can also say that for an inclusivist like Dante with his mountain of purgatory and for pluralists with their metaphorical mountain, crisscrossed with the various religious paths leading to the same vague religious end at the top, the one mountain stands for a single truth. There is a single objective character to the world, and religious "preferences" must all work themselves out within that one common reality. This is an important truth. But one world can have more than one mountain.

In our middle realm there are several peaks, for the obvious reason that diverse religious fulfillments stand at their own summits, set so within the texture of their own religious traditions and practices. Each of these peaks represents two options: it can be a penultimate stage in relation to salvation or a final end in its own right.[6] These mountains may be *either* purgatorial or final for those that inhabit them. Therefore, as Dante separated the earthly paradise and the Elysian fields (limbo), our poet will have to find an analogous distinction. In fact, even this purgatorial quality may have two sides. Many religious traditions may expect that after death some interval for purification or development is necessary prior to realization of the true end. The slopes of the individual mountains stand for this process.[7] At the peak, one can pass irrevocably into the specific religious fulfillment, beyond return. As final ends, these fulfillments stand at the top of their own mountains. Each is a separate summit, marking a height of intensification of one type of relation with the divine. This intensification isolates itself from other relations with the divine that have a similar exclusivity.

Below each summit lies a spur or ridge from which those who taste this fulfillment may yet pursue another connection. All the summits are linked by such ridges to the Christian mountain. The Christian mountain is one among others, though we might picture it as lower and broader than the others. Its summit claims finality and particularity, as the others do. The only way toward this higher end is from "lower down" in relation to the other religious ends. Personal communion is the distinctive quality here, and the one that determines the orientation toward the other ends. From the standpoint of those final ends themselves, this is the distinctive quality that makes the Christian mountain a lower or penultimate destination.

It is often argued that religions are most different at their lower elevations, and most alike, even identical, when they reach their highest aims. Others counter that it is just the opposite: two traditions are the same only at their lowest points, down in the valley where you can stand on the junction of two mountains at once. It is at the heights that each becomes most distinct, most absolute in its own particularity. My picture fits with neither of these

6. From any of these non-Christian summits, the other mountains (including the Christian) are likewise viewed as sub-purgatories or as lesser final destinies.

7. These conceptions are particular to individual traditions and take many forms, from the "Pure Land" of Pure Land Buddhism — a penultimate environment in which the attainment of enlightenment is preternaturally easy — to the process of reincarnation itself in Hinduism, and to Christian notions of purgation. It is interesting that John Hick's theology of religion offers its own schema. In Hick's view, after death people experience whatever their religious formation has prepared them to experience. From this point, everyone evolves through further spiritual development toward a hazy horizon in which these remnants of religious particularity fall away and all converge to an identical and ultimate but virtually unspecified religious end. See (Hick, 1976, pp. 415-16) but also see (Hick, 1989) and (Hick, 1990, p. 191).

options. It is true that all who approach alternative religious ends come closer to realizing a concrete relation with God, but it is not the same relation with God in each case. It is true that each peak attains its own distinct and separate perfection, which cannot be combined with another while it remains isolated in its unique purity. But integration or passage between these relations is more possible at higher elevations than at the lowest ground level.

This corresponds to the insight advanced in most religious traditions that on the way to the final end there are higher temptations as well as crude obstacles. Buddhist teaching, for instance, is quite clear about the dangers posed by spiritual attainment. Meditative practice can give individuals supernatural powers and lead to transcendent states of bliss. These reflect progress on the path to enlightenment. Yet if they are taken as ends in themselves — and they have the positive good to exercise that attraction strongly — they divert one from the true end. This is the same insight that John Bunyan's Pilgrim notes at the end of his dream journey: "Then I saw that there was a way to Hell, even from the Gates of Heaven, as well as from the City of Destruction."[8] So, Christian mystics, for instance, though further along the spiritual path in one respect, may be more prone than others to the temptation to isolate their experience of God into the pure absolutism of apophatic emptiness or unitive identity and to turn to another religious end.

From the Christian point of view, the "unification of religions" has two real but different meanings. The various religious aims can be unified in salvation, in the sense that the unique quality of each is included in salvation, so long as it does not take the exclusive form that repels other dimensions of relation with the Trinity. On the other hand, the attainment of the separated and absolute religious ends represents a very different kind of unification, which we discussed in the last chapter. Since each of the creatures has realized a relation with God, they all form part of a diverse whole, centered on the one God and held together by God, though they do not individually participate in a communion of diverse dimensions of relation.

From the Christian summit paradise opens, as a communion in which the relations isolated and intensified at the other peaks are united in one. Where the ridge from another religious mountain connects the two, the ecology on the Christian mountain is very similar to that at the other end of the ridge.[9] But the paths in each case go on to wind completely around the Christian mountain and to pass through the climates of all the other entering

---

8. (Bunyan, 1965, p. 205).

9. And, as we have noted before, this smoothes a way *out* or toward the other religious end for those within Christianity who wish to move in that direction.

ridges. Each *enters* into this communion through the dimension of relation with the Trinity most characteristic of his or her religious experience so far and *rises* only by extending participation in other dimensions, and not just by deepening the most congenial relation. Moral purgation is a part of this process, as Dante illustrates. But our special focus is on a different kind of preparation, developing relation with the full dimensions of the triune life through communion with those who plumb regions we have not or cannot. Though all these dimensions are involved in salvation, salvation cannot be identified with any single one alone.

From the summit of this mountain, like that of Dante's Mt. Purgatory, Christians enter paradise. They are prepared not only by moral purgation but most especially by the tuning of their "ears" to the ranges of communion with the divine life to which they may have been least open before. As we have pointed out at some length in this book, this does not mean that everyone develops the same individual capacities for such communion. Instead, we develop love and mutual participation with those different from us, so that openness to God is multiplied by unity with other creatures. Not even the greatest saint tastes the fullness of God directly in every possible human dimension. The fullness of communion, the approximation to the richness of the triune life itself, is possible only because an individual's capacities can be multiplied in communion with others. One can share in an aspect of God's life that one has little personal aptitude to accommodate, by virtue of communion with another creature who does participate in it. Communion is both salvation and the avenue to salvation. This is the key element in Dante's representation in the *Comedy* of the very distinct "levels" of heavenly bliss on the one hand and the full joy of their communion in unity. This paradigm is exemplified for each of the saved by virtue of their relation with Christ and therefore their derived participation in Christ's relation with God. This is the universal, concrete case and therefore the ground of the communion itself. But it is replicated endlessly, as each person shares communion with specific others without whom some avenue of participation in the divine life would be closed for them.

Paradise will need little updating from Dante's vision, for his ascending spheres and, even better, the celestial rose stress precisely the crucial point. Each person retains a unique profile of relation with God and relation with others. This means that the imprint of various religious traditions, the characteristic penchant for relation with particular dimensions of the triune life, can remain within the personal communion that links all together. Indeed, this variety is an occasion for continual delight.

It is popular in some circles to envision a kind of parliament of world religions in the afterlife — where Jesus and Buddha and Shankara and Mohammad and Confucius and Mahavira and Moses, along with shamans, bodhisattvas, goddesses, Marxists, and spirit guides of all descriptions converse, chant, meditate, and commune together. They share appreciation for one awesome divine reality, each seeing and celebrating the value of the other's truth. Such a vision is religiously biased, heavily skewed by a distinctly Christian flavor. This may sound strange, since many Christians understandably recoil from blending Jesus into a general crowd. What I mean is that this is precisely a picture of personal and interpersonal relation, of participation in difference. As such it is an outright rejection or contradiction of many religious traditions' ultimate aims. By virtue of its very categories, the picture seems flatly inconceivable as a religious end for Buddha or Shankara or a Marxist. In fact for most religious traditions, this scenario could be at most a kind of kindergarten metaphor, a preliminary and quite unsatisfactory state. Of course it is not an adequate description of salvation in Christian terms either, but it encompasses many of salvation's categorical essentials: relation, the integrity of personal selves, communion-in-difference, even a personal relation with Jesus for everyone.

Those who take their way through Buddhist or Hindu or Muslim tradition to the final and distinctive religious ends of those faiths will see their whole journey, rightly, as directed at the goal achieved. For those who follow their way through a Buddhist or Hindu or Muslim tradition and finally follow the ridge that leads them into communion through Christ, their entire journey will seem a providentially ordered way to conversion. Knowledge of God through this religious tradition served as the basis for accepting the fulfillment the gospel offers. Relation with God through the single dimension of divine emptiness or divine immanence, divine purpose or divine agency, drew the adherent toward the personal communion of all these dimensions. The sources in the two itineraries were obviously much the same. The ways in which they were spiritually appropriated were different. To the question as to whether Christians are the only ones who can "put it all together" this way, the answer is definitely not. People in other religious traditions can do so, with God's help. But people who "put it all together" in that manner are in fact becoming Christians, for the vision and realization of communion as the integral end finds Christ as integral with that end. This, it seems to me, is the conclusion suggested by those Sufis or those so-called "hidden Christians" among Hindus for whom Jesus has become not an emblematic but a constitutive part of their religious aim. Sometimes it is relation with Christ that has slowly altered the nature of the aim. Sometimes a changing sense of the religious aim has slowly brought Christ to the center.

Our image of multiple summits reinforces graphically what we have said discursively: those who attain various religious ends have and attain something Christians do not. These individual mountains may well stand higher than the Christian one. From their summits all others surely appear lower. There is a purity, an intensity to these ends that truly is distinctive. The communion that is salvation does not simply subsume everything that those ends achieve in their isolated and absolute identity. That is impossible. For there are benefits, characteristics that spring directly from the intensity and limitation of the particular dimension of relation with the divine life. In the comprehensiveness of communion, none of these dimensions is left aside and each exists in its own unique reality. But none can be said to be the same as when they stand entirely alone.

Alternative religious ends are "higher up and further in" in specific ways that no Christian is likely to approximate. This is why there is no contradiction and should be no hesitancy in Christians taking those of other faiths as leaders, guides, and mentors, let alone neighbors. Dante's two primary guides in the *Comedy* are Virgil and Beatrice, one who has attained a non-Christian religious end and one who participates in salvation. The *Comedy* is clear that Beatrice stands in a position of more comprehensive wisdom, love, and power than Virgil. But there are certain tasks, certain teachings, for which Virgil seems the more apt master. Between Beatrice and Virgil there is only the sweetest courtesy and respect. There is no incident or word of conflict or competition. Both stand in positions of authority toward Dante until, as a temporary visitor, he actually stands in paradise itself. And there the question is moot. Virgil does not enter, for his desire does not draw him there. And Beatrice is eager to show the virtues of others, not to claim her own.

One may well suspect this picture is so harmonious because Dante's Virgil knows his place and is not allowed to question the Christian cosmology in which he is lodged. This leads us to an interesting point. We noted earlier a Muslim author's argument that those in the lower ranks of heaven ought to be unaware that any higher ones existed, lest their joy be tinged with envy or regret. Dante explains at great length how in paradise just the reverse is true. Knowledge of others' joy deepens the delight of all. In our middle realm with its mountains and religious ends at their own summits there is room for a more assertive Virgil. From the perspective of the finality of any one of these religious ends, the alternatives (including salvation) are viewed as secondary. It is not that the reality of salvation and its communion is hidden. The principle of the universal accessibility of salvation assumes that it has been open as a live possibility to those who choose another end. No one fails to know the nature of salvation, the relation God has taken the greatest pains to open to humans. No one is compelled to know that relation *as* the highest end. They may desire and attain something else as their most profound fulfillment, a more discrete relation with the divine life.

This personal evaluative commitment, even if it involves a reordering of divine priorities, is allowed to stand. It is not just the end state that is allowed to stand, but also the conviction of the person who participates in it that it is supreme. The differences that constitute other ends, including salvation, are perceived as deficiency. The inner assurance that I have attained the supreme state and lack nothing obtained by others might characterize some of these religious ends. It is incompatible with salvation. In heaven, people perceive that there are others in some respects better than they, who have better knowledge of some (or all) aspects of God. They can see this also in those attaining other religious ends. Within the communion of salvation, they rejoice in these differences and are nourished by them. The deficiency they perceive in other religious ends is precisely the fact that they are isolated from that communion.

The symmetry of the situation is that the notion of the "best" religious end goes hand in hand with the understanding of the nature of God or the ultimate reality. One will not view salvation as the true religious end unless one believes in the triune God and desires communion with that God. Therefore, with a different view of the ultimate or from the standpoint of a specific alternative religious realization, salvation does not appear a more inclusive or higher end at all. Other religious traditions, if they regard the Christian heaven as real, see it as a transitory and penultimate (purgatorial) good at best, a delusional snare as a final end at worst.

As we noted in an earlier chapter, in some traditional Christian scenarios of the afterlife, the blessed look upon the torments of the damned with satisfaction and the lost look up to the missed delights of heaven with bitter regret. Dante, we saw, already presented a dramatically different picture. If in some metaphorical sense those within various religious ends could see each other, there would be a certain reciprocity in outlook: I rejoice that I am not as these others are. In our middle realm, those who attain other final religious ends are or have been aware of salvation, but they don't perceive their distance from it as a loss. So long as they view that distance as possible loss, salvation would still be open to them. It is the certainty that salvation (along with the other unchosen ends) is a diminished hope, secondary and imperfect alongside this goal, that ratifies a distinct religious end. It becomes final when valued *because* of its difference from salvation.

So does every religious end represent "heaven" for the person who attains it? If by heaven we mean their true desire, the highest good they aspire to, the answer is yes. If we mean the concrete salvation of communion with the triune God, the answer is no. The point is made concretely if we ask whether the Buddha attained salvation, whether he went to heaven. And it is also made if we ask whether Christ eventually transcended attachment to God and humans, the very conditions of relation, and entered true enlightenment. A Christian seeking to express respect for the Buddha might say yes to the first question and a Buddhist expressing respect for Jesus might say yes to the second. With every intention to attribute supreme religious fulfillment to the other, we naturally attribute what we understand (and hope) such fulfillment to be. But people are free to realize their own hopes, not only ours.

It is common to assume that the afterlife thrusts persons into a situation that compels them to accept a cosmic and universal view, an enforced change in outlook. This general assumption is shared by exclusivists and pluralists, who both expect to see their truth unveiled irresistibly to all and adopted by all. Clearly that is not what happens in this life. Nor is it clear why it would happen definitively in the next. It seems equally plausible that our religious formation in this life largely determines the range of what we can assimilate, and the means by which we could do so. This is true even if there is extensive further "purgation" or development that takes place in a future life. Our free formation in this life may prefigure the path to be taken there, or simply shape the window of possibilities open there, leaving some final decisions still open. In either case, the urgency of our religious decision and practice here and now is plain. One may say, "It will all get sorted out later." The catch is that it is the person that I become in the meantime that will be the subject in such sorting, the one whose aims are fulfilled.

Flannery O'Connor has a well-known story titled "All That Rises Must Converge."[10] In one way this phrase describes the picture we have just drawn. All humans who rise above negation or the "hells of idolatry" do converge, in the sense that they all move toward realization of some relation with the divine nature. The Psalmist's cry, "Deliver me from the pit," expresses a hope in negative terms: let me not fall to these depths of negation or idolatry. A number of different "non-pit" possibilities could constitute deliverance in that generic sense, a state of being saved *from* some evil but not *to* communion with the triune God. But all that rises can diverge, as well. All relations with the triune life are not the same. The positive hope of communion with the triune God and God's creatures is *not* necessarily realized by all who avoid idolatry and pure negation. And the religious ends that their traditions regard as ultimate perfection must still carry for Christians a dual aspect, both providential goods and losses by limitation.

10. See (O'Connor and Fitzgerald, 1988).

It may be objected that the vision I propose, with its possibilities for realizing various goods and various dimensions of relation with God, has a fatal flaw: it slights the reality of sin and the wretchedness of the human condition apart from grace. I do not think this is so, on several counts. First, we have recognized annihilation and hell as true options. The condition of fallen humanity, so long as it remains entirely shut in upon its own resources, leads us to long only for the idolatry of created goods or for negation, desires whose very fulfillment deforms or cancels our natures. To the extent we awaken to this reality we despair, unless we have a divine hope.

Does recognition of various religious ends minimize the impact of sin, suggesting that it can be overcome to a significant extent apart from Christ? To begin with, in common spheres of life we already recognize that sin can be vanquished in discrete cases apart from salvation or commitment to Christ. Sin takes many concrete forms, including addiction, dishonesty, malice, and envy. Some people from all religions and no religion prove able to avoid or escape particular sins. Such people may be beneficiaries of unacknowledged grace, but these sinful conditions are overcome without participation in communion with Christ.

But don't religious ends represent a more definitive overcoming of sin? They embody some realized, even perfected, relation with God, and sin is precisely the disruption or loss of such relation. Are not people here being "reconciled with God" without dependence on or life in Christ? Both halves of that question have to be examined. People who achieve other religious ends are not "reconciled with God" in the manner that constitutes salvation. And the relations with God realized in those ends *do* depend on Christ. People can attain these fulfillments without faith in Christ. But sin stands between humans and these ends, as it does between humans and salvation. The work of Christ plays its role in clearing the path to these ends as well as to salvation. Some Christian inclusivists hold that Christ's redemptive work "energized" the religions as avenues to salvation. In this view, Christ has appropriated the religions as ways to draw people anonymously to the Christian end; they can serve no other purpose, despite their apparently different goals. I would make a more restricted claim. The work of Christ is always involved in the overcoming of sin necessary for the achievement of any of the discrete religious ends. The work of Christ is necessary for such ends, but explicit relation with Christ is not constitutive of them.

To understand this we need to refer to the common Christian conviction that only in Jesus Christ do we know either the depth of our corruption or the extent of our redemption. We cannot actually independently know the full scope of our estrangement except as we know the depth of its deliverance.[11] To know our own state in a coldly objective way would be to despair of our good created nature and even of the love God offers. To believe in our destiny of participation in the divine life without recognizing its cost is to lose all humility and mutual compassion. This is expressed in Pascal's dictum that "it is equally dangerous for man to know God without knowing his own wretchedness as to know his own wretchedness without knowing the Redeemer who can cure him."[12] The fullness of salvation corresponds to a thorough inventory of our sin and limitations.

From a Christian view, the very heart of our wretchedness is our personal estrangement from God, our voluntary rupture of that deepest communion with the divine life. The Christian view of other religious ends then is that the achievement of their goods depends upon God's free reconciliation with us in Christ, manifest in the refusal to hold our sins against us. God's readiness to accept sinners into any dimension of positive relation at all, despite our defiance, guilt, or self-destructiveness, is rooted in this definitive act of communion. Some implicit recognition of God's mercy is required for those who attain these ends. That is, recognition of sin at some level is required, as is recognition that divine power or grace makes it possible to overcome that sin and restore relation.

Sin affects us in two ways. It distorts our vision of the end we aim for or desire. It corrupts our ability to maintain our part of any positive relation with God (and others) that we do have the light to seek. Sin skews our vision of the goals we seek, and blocks our attainment even of the real goods we seek. Both aspects of sin must be overcome to some degree in order for any religious end to be realized. From a Christian view sin also remains operative in religious fulfillments other than salvation, particularly on the first count, the nature of the aim itself. The unique core of a religious tradition has constitutive power. Whether it is Buddhist *dharma* or Qur'anic revelation, these sources offer a privileged representation of divine or ultimate reality by constituting a whole network of other symbols and practices.[13] Those symbols represent the ultimate by pointing to the constituting source as authoritative.

11. For a striking contemporary exposition of this theme, see (Alison, 1997).

12. (Pascal, 1988, p. 68). A similar idea is expressed elsewhere this way: "If there were no obscurity man would not feel his corruption: if there were no light man would not hope for a cure. Thus it is not only right but useful for us that God should be partly concealed and partly revealed, since it is equally dangerous for man to know God without knowing his own wretchedness as to know his wretchedness without knowing God" (Pascal, 1988, p. 167).

13. I am here returning to categories taken from Schubert Ogden and discussed in Chapter Two. See (Ogden, 1992, p. 98).

The distinctive sources of religious traditions decisively represent particular dimensions of the life of the triune God. They constitute representations and practices that focus relation through that dimension or ordered pattern of dimensions. These unique sources are also constitutive of the separate and final religious end that a particular religion realizes. Participation in that special fulfillment necessarily involves the "equipment" provided by the distinctive sources of the tradition.

The influence of Christ's work plays an integral role in the process by which any religious believer forms the desire to seek relation with God through a true dimension of the triune life and then carries out the practices that lead to the fulfillment of that relation. Christ may constitute some of the *means* by which people are able to progress on these paths. But Christ is not constitutive of these other religious ends themselves. This is because as separate and distinct final states they exclude each other. The one end that Christ does constitute is the communion of salvation. Christ cannot constitute these religious ends *as* separate and final, since that would be the antithesis of that communion. Because the dimension of relation with God that is affirmed in an alternative religious end is also present in salvation, through communion, Christ can serve in one sense to represent that end, though not to constitute it. This is the reason that those in other religions can so readily appropriate Christ in this limited way, as an adjunct part of the network of symbols centered on their unique religious sources.

The limitation and loss of other religious ends arise because dimensions of sin that are unacknowledged cannot be redeemed, and thus prevent the realization of relation with God through those same dimensions which fill up the integral pattern of salvation. For each of these ends, some dimension or dimensions of God remain hidden. In those aspects, relation with God remains broken and sin thus remains determinative. It is an axiom of Christology that "what is not assumed is not redeemed," meaning that any aspect of human nature subject to sin that was not part of the incarnation could not be healed through it. This was and is an argument for the full humanity of Christ. I am suggesting that there is an interesting reciprocal form of this axiom: those aspects of our own created nature and relation with God whose reality and captivity to sin we do not appropriate as truly ours cannot participate in the redemption Christ offers.

For instance, a Buddhist or a Vedantan classically recognizes neither the dimension of personal communion with the divine nor the dimension of the encounter and accountability of divine and human selves as real or ultimate on the same level as pure emptiness or immanence. It might seem that by this move they neatly avoid any effect of "sin" that might be thought to operate in

288

these (in their view) nonexistent or transitory dimensions. And this conclusion may even be true in the specific sense that sin in these dimensions does not definitively block the achievement of the distinct religious fulfillments of these traditions. A Christian would say that the human refusal to assume these aspects of our nature does not mean that their sinful estrangement is unreal, but only that it will not be changed. That estrangement effectively blocks relation with God in these dimensions. The final loss caused by such sin would be permanent separation from God by non-relationship in those dimensions. There is nothing light about this view of sin, for sin continues to block persons from salvation. Nor is there anything punitive about it. The eternal punishment for sin is nothing but the experience of the condition the sin constitutes and the person desires.

Those in certain other religious traditions sometimes observe that they are not burdened with any concept of "sin" like that in Christianity, or even the categories that frame that notion. From their perspective, Christians suffer delusions of loss of a communion-participation in the divine life or of moral guilt in accountability before God, when in fact there is no such communion or self-to-self encounter. This reinforces the point we are making. Sin and redemption are known together. Where one sees no possibility of estrangement or corruption, there can be no reconciled and restored relation.

At every turn in the world we encounter some aspect of the divine life in its relation to us. But God never crushes our cognitive or spiritual capacities in a self-manifestation that leaves us no freedom to construe that relation in our own terms. The presence of the triune God in creation in such varied dimensions has the perplexing effect of allowing persons to form various and even contradictory visions of God. These can then become molds within which to construe the entire human relation with God. These form the basis for a variety of religious ends, marked by an intensification of a particular kind of relation with an aspect of the divine life. Such intensification is a good thing, except insofar as its realization excludes participation in other equally real dimensions of the divine life. If the intensity is solitary in this way, it diminishes the prospect for communion and participation and therefore prevents salvation. God is not wrathful or punitive toward those who limit their relation with God in these diverse ways. Nor is such a relation bad in itself. We can see then why Christians will tend to see these ends as positive insofar as they are penultimate and transitional phases, but to see them as loss if settled and final. Salvation is distinguished not by being the only actual religious end, but by encompassing in the most inclusive and simultaneously rich ways the variety of the divine life itself.

This is perhaps at least part of what Pascal had in mind in the following:

If there were only one religion, God would be clearly manifest. If there were no martyrs except in one religion, likewise.

God being thus hidden, any religion that does not say God is hidden is not true, and any religion which does not explain why does not instruct. Ours does all this.[14]

III

Earlier in this chapter we noted the multiple levels on which Dante intended his *Divine Comedy* to be understood. Description of the world to come was only one of these levels. In reimagining Dante's vision we are not thinking only of the eschatological future, any more than he was. We are also seeking light on the concrete theological and spiritual questions of religious diversity here and now.

I believe that the strength of a theology of religious ends such as I have sketched is precisely the fit that it reflects between a fruitful theological understanding of religious diversity now and of eschatological destiny then. God's saving will for creation shows up in its proper constancy. God always manifests a loving and merciful purpose that seeks to bring creation into participation in the divine life. God seeks *communion* and never fails to fulfill *relation* to the greatest capacity possible, in harmony with the freedom of the creature. Every response to the divine initiative has its reward. When creatures seek and value even the most limited dimension of relation with God, God both fulfills that aim to the greatest extent its terms allow and offers to expand it through communion in other dimensions. At the same time that this constancy in God's purpose is emphasized, the importance of the particularity of religious traditions, of religious witness, and of spiritual decision and conversion is highlighted as well. Religious differences have decisive value.

I suggested at the beginning of this book that both exclusivist and pluralist theologies of religions lack a fit in connecting views of this world and the next. In the case of strongly exclusivistic views the problem is commending love and respect toward adherents of other faiths and recognizing the virtues and truths richly displayed in their traditions, while simultaneously expecting that the same people will realize only punishment or pain in the next life. The goodness recognized here has no relevance to the fate there. On the other side, pluralists unequivocally affirm the validity of all religions because

14. (Pascal, 1988, p. 103).

they lead to an identical eschatological fulfillment, while at the same time denying any ultimate significance to the specific forms of life and aims that are definitive for each actual faith. It is hard to see how this accords with serious respect for the distinctive features of any tradition on its own terms. The ultimate eschatological good posited in the future has no relevance to the unique qualities of the religions here and now.

By contrast, a theology of religious ends meets the deficiency on each side. First of all, it provides a clear place on the Christian theological map for other religions in their own integrity. The distinctive testimony and practices of various religions must be taken on their own terms. Those traditions need not evaporate either into anonymous Christianity or into shapeless cosmic convergence. Focus falls on their *positive* self-descriptions. They can be taken with full seriousness as alternatives, both here and now and eschatologically. One of the things this means is that these traditions retain sufficient integrity within our theological consideration for us to register the way in which they can judge Christianity as penultimate or distorted, the way in which their religious end stands on its own. It is true that a Christian theology of religious ends cannot go to the extent of endorsing each religion's claim to be the fullest and unsurpassable truth. But it honors those claims and recognizes their roots more concretely than either exclusivism or pluralism. In other words, a theology of religious ends proves more successful than other options in preserving the distinctive qualities of religions, *both* in the manner it treats them when it incorporates them into Christian interpretation and in the manner it recognizes their capacity to stand outside such interpretation and to absorb Christianity into their terms. We are able to register not only the other religion's role as a threshold to Christianity, but its self-understanding as a rival or surpassing alternative to Christianity.

Second, this perspective shows us plainly why the study of other religions belongs in the *theological* curriculum. We have seen the way in which the religions illuminate the Christian trinitarian understanding of God. If we are serious about deepening our own spiritual life, if the church is to grow more deeply into the mystery of the Trinity, the testimony of the religions is essential for internal Christian life. We have also seen plainly why this study must address the traditions on their own terms, through thick description and careful attention to their distinctive qualities. A tradition's witness to its own uniqueness is precisely what our theological study needs to value with special care.

Third, a theology of religious ends goes a considerable way in specifying the meaning of a general affirmation that the religious traditions are part of God's providential purpose. Ordinarily this somewhat bland phrase cashes out to mean basically that other religions serve to prepare people for Christian faith and to nourish generic human virtues of morality and spiritual self-examination. But in our discussion we have viewed the religions as much more integral to providence. We can see how even apart from sin, for instance, something akin to the various religious traditions would have a place in God's purpose for creation, provided always that the true communion of their ends in the life of the triune God were manifest. The religions appear in fact as part of a complex acrostic, in which God has reached out to humanity across all the dimensions of the trinitarian life. The different ways that humans "fill in the blanks" of this puzzle through their varied responses to these dimensions are all woven together in a plenitude, whose glory is compatible with the contingency of many of its specific elements. God's providence uses the religions both for the attainment of salvation and for the attainment of their own ends, each serving God's graciousness.

Fourth, a theology of religious ends provides a sound footing for practical interreligious relations. It gives us no less reason than more wholesale theologies of religious unity to advocate mutual respect, dialogue, peace, and common cause across religions. In fact, though such wholesale theologies frequently exhort us to recognize the "truth of other religions," a theology of religious ends insists on finding much more concrete truth in the religions than those theologies allow: unique, religiously determinative, final truths of the sort that the religions themselves claim and the blanket affirmations of wholesale theologies exclude. This widens dialogue by allowing that it may reveal not only variations on one theme and one result but sharper challenges and crucial options.

For this reason, a theology of religious ends encourages religions to mutually respect something wholesale theologies generally condemn: i.e., each tradition's commendation of the unique fulfillment it offers in contrast to others. A theology of religious ends indicates *why* we should attend to the special witness of specific other religions and offer our own. Such missionary confession is not only valid but necessary in a pluralistic environment. It is necessary both for the depth of learning about the dimensions of the triune life, and for the benefit of those who must in fact choose between real alternatives. We mentioned above the way in which a religious tradition can commend its end as surpassing salvation and can offer an "inclusive" interpretation of Christianity entirely within its own categories. It is appropriate for each tradition to recognize that all others legitimately have such perspectives, while still affirming the substantive truth of its own.

Fifth, a theology of religious ends offers a basis for a renewed theology of Christian mission and evangelism that may prove more adequate for actual engagement with mature religious traditions and also more fruitful in healing some of the internal Christian divisions over these questions. One benefit of this approach is that it encourages greater clarity among Christians about the distinctive nature of salvation. This will benefit Christian spirituality as well as Christian mission, by focusing witness on the positive features of salvation. The good news of the gospel is not saving or dramatic only by contrast with utter loss and torment. Its distinctive character endures in contrast with ends that have their own authentic good. The Christian claim for the uniqueness of salvation through Christ, the vocation to invite others to receive it, the hope that it may be attained "inclusively" by those living within other religious traditions: all these remain integral parts of Christian witness, set on firmer ground.

I think the theology of religious ends corresponds quite closely with the breadth of actual missionary experience. By this I mean that there are many times when Christian faith and salvation are rightly presented to persons as deliverance from a demonic condition, from a present and future of raw negation of God's goodness. But it is also true that Christian witness to the same salvation and its same surpassing glory can take a different flavor in relation to people of religious devotion. In the first case it can rightly evoke the relief of a Gadarene demoniac who comes out from his chained prison among the tombs. Left behind is only loss and evil. In the second case, it may elicit something more like the leaping hearts of those who responded to Jesus' words in the Sermon on the Mount, "Do not think that I have come to abolish the law or the prophets; I have not come to abolish but to fulfill."[15] The example of Jesus in the New Testament shows Christians something of importance not only for mission, but for our own lives of faith. Jesus can say of some people that they are "not far from the kingdom of heaven."[16] And yet, as the instance of the rich young ruler shows, it can be as hard to cross a short distance as a great one.[17] Some who come very close by this reckoning may never come further; some who are far distant will always be restless until their communion is complete.

Clearly there is a difference in relating with people who have no intentional adherence to any religious end, with those who have only a nominal and not a living adherence, or with those who have concretely begun to realize the fulfillment of their particular religious end in their lives. Christian evangelism (like the witness of other religions) typically meets its most obvi-

15. Matthew 5:17.
16. Mark 12:34.
17. Mark 10:17-22.

ous success with people in the first two situations and historically has focused its efforts accordingly. This is understandable. The free conversion of devout religious believers (as in the conversion of a devout Christian to Islam or a devout Hindu to Christianity) is by no means illegitimate, though it is less common. And it usually has a distinctly different quality.

Few religious traditions contend that their religious ends are fully, finally, and comprehensively realized by persons at some point in the course of their lifetimes, in such a way that nothing remains to be deepened or completed. But all believe in and expect at least a provisional participation in the end for devotees. In mature and faithful adherents of other faiths, Christians encounter persons who show this anticipatory participation in the religious ends they seek. We hope that as Christians we too might manifest our anticipatory participation in salvation, the eternal life of communion through Christ with God and others.

In dialogue with such people, the nature of Christian witness is likely to be somewhat different. If, as I have maintained, valid religious ends in fact embody a relation with God in some dimension of the divine life, then Christian witness as flat contradiction of the other's faith is not only likely to be ineffective but is wrong. Though Christians can witness to distinctive features of their faith and of salvation, they will also have to witness in some way through affirmation of the other tradition. And the same assumption requires Christians to acknowledge that they have things to learn, in two primary respects. The first is that there are things to be learned about God and God's relation with us, by virtue of the other religious tradition's highly concentrated wisdom, things that expand and even transform one's Christian faith. The second is that there is a real, distinct, and alternative religious end offered in the other tradition's life, one that can stand over against Christian hope and interpret it as penultimate or inferior.

This is a substantive description of dialogue. Some Christians endorse dialogue with followers of other faiths only insofar as it can be seen as "evangelism by other means." Other Christians would exclude evangelism entirely, except insofar as it might be understood as a subordinate sub-element of dialogue in which one is invited to speak freely about one's private convictions. As I have outlined a theology of religious ends, it should be clear that dialogue necessarily spans both these concerns. It is, and need not be ashamed to be, "witness by other means," inviting testimony to communion with God in Christ. It must also be submission to the witness of the other, in the mode of a learner before superior wisdom. This wisdom extends not only to historical knowledge of the other religious tradition and its practices, but to aspects of the divine life, to truths hidden or never expressed in Christianity. In such dialogue, Christians must be willing to accept their partners as guides with the eagerness that Dante accepted Virgil, as elders and authorities. In return we can offer no power of our own to direct others' path: we can only witness to Christ and the relation with Christ by which we find our way, the way that aims for communion in the life of the triune God.

IV

At its heart, this book is a meditation on the Trinity. From one perspective it asks how the Trinity helps us understand the relation between salvation and the religions. From another perspective, it asks how our study of salvation and the religions leads us to a more profound approach to the Trinity. We can think, or argue, or pray in either direction. The result is always a new depth of riches. The religions teach us about the breadth of the trinitarian life encompassed in the communion of salvation, the end Christians seek but whose extent we can barely grasp. The Trinity teaches us about the integrity of the religions, about the truths at their roots. Together, Trinity, the religions, and salvation teach us about the plenitude of the divine nature and purpose. This plenitude is manifest in the historical drama of religious pluralism and in the marvelous facets of freedom God has patterned for the consummation of creation.

Every human response to the manifestation and revelation of God meets affirmation from God: the "yes" of grace, of humanity's election in Christ for relation with God. Every response to the divine initiative has its reward. Every quest for relation with God that proceeds on the basis of some dimension of God's self-giving to us meets the fulfillment for which it aims and hopes, even if it cannot be persuaded to hope further. Insofar as realization of relation with God in one of the trinitarian dimensions we have discussed resists or refuses communion with God through another dimension, it leads to its own distinctive end. And of course, so long as Christians insist on clinging to distinct identities, to personal relations, to communion and participation in the triune life, they are barred from realizing the distinctive religious ends of other traditions.

Christians can hope for all to be saved. But if in their freedom and their choice of gifts, all are not saved, the consummation of creation will still be a wonder that testifies to the glory of God. Loss and judgment are very real. Looking toward communion in Christ, Christians can rightly "count all else loss" in comparison with what is offered there. But they cannot rightly count all else as nothing or as evil. Loss flows only from the limits that humans impose on God's goodness. Religious ends bear indelible marks of grace and truth. If God had offered creation only one, or only all of these other religious ends, God would have done well. And, to sound Pauline, we would have nothing to complain of. Which of the supreme ends that the great religions of the world seek would we reproach God for allowing? The Christian gospel is not about a God who stints on goodness. It is like that first of Jesus' miracles, when the wedding guests look up in surprise: "you have kept good wine till last."

Works Cited

Alighieri, D. (1950). *The Comedy of Dante Alighieri: Hell*. Aylesbury: Penguin.

Alighieri, D. (1955). *The Comedy of Dante Alighieri: Purgatory*. Baltimore: Penguin.

Alighieri, D. (1962). *The Comedy of Dante Alighieri: Paradise*. Baltimore: Penguin.

Alison, J. (1997). *The Joy of Being Wrong: Original Sin Through Easter Eyes*. New York: Crossroad.

Alston, W. P. (1988). "The Indwelling of the Holy Spirit." *Philosophy and the Christian Faith*. Edited by T. V. Morris. Notre Dame: University of Notre Dame Press, pp. 121-50.

Ariarajah, S. W. (1989). *The Bible and People of Other Faiths*. Maryknoll, N.Y.: Orbis Books.

Augustine, S., and W. J. Oates (1980). *Basic Writings of Saint Augustine*. Grand Rapids: Baker.

Barnes, M. R. (1995). "Augustine in Contemporary Trinitarian Theology." *Theological Studies* 56: 237-50.

Barnes, M. R. (1995). "De Regnon Reconsidered." *Augustinian Studies* 26: 51-79.

Boff, L. (1988). *Trinity and Society*. Maryknoll, N.Y: Orbis Books.

Brown, D. (1989). "Trinitarian Personhood and Individuality." *Trinity, Incarnation and Atonement*. Edited by R. Feenstra and C. Plantinga, Jr. Notre Dame: Notre Dame University Press, pp. 48-78.

Buckley, M. J. (1987). *At the Origins of Modern Atheism*. New Haven: Yale University Press.

Bunyan, J. (1965). *The Pilgrim's Progress*. Baltimore: Penguin.

Burch, G. B. (1972). *Alternative Goals in Religion: Love, Freedom, Truth*. Montreal: McGill-Queen's University Press.

Butterfield, H. S. (1965). *The Origins of Modern Science, 1300-1800*. New York: Free Press.

Capra, F. (1991). *The Tao of Physics: An Exploration of the Parallels Between Modern Physics and Eastern Mysticism.* Boston: Shambhala.

Carman, J. B. (1974). *The Theology of Ramanuja: An Essay in Interreligious Understanding.* New Haven: Yale University Press.

Carman, J. B. (1994). *Majesty and Meekness: A Comparative Study of Contrast and Harmony in the Concept of God.* Grand Rapids: Eerdmans.

Charry, E. T. (1997). *By the Renewing of Your Minds: The Pastoral Function of Christian Doctrine.* New York: Oxford University Press.

Clooney S.J., F. X. (1990). *Thinking Ritually: Rediscovering the Purva Mimamsa of Jaimini.* Vienna: Sammlung De Nobili Institut für Indologie der Universität Wien.

Clooney S.J., F. X. (1993). *Theology After Vedanta: An Experiment in Comparative Theology.* Albany: State University of New York Press.

Clooney S.J., F. X. (1995). "Comparative Theology: A Review of Recent Books (1989-1995)." *Theological Studies* 56: 521-50.

Clooney S.J., F. X. (1996). *Seeing Through Texts: Doing Theology among the Srivaisnavas of South India.* Albany: State University of New York Press.

Clooney S.J., F. X. (1999). *Hindu God, Christian God: Faith, Reason, and Argument in a World of Many Religions.* New York: Oxford University Press.

Cobb, J. (1990). "Beyond 'Pluralism.'" *Christian Uniqueness Reconsidered.* Edited by G. D'Costa. Maryknoll, N.Y.: Orbis Books, pp. 81-95.

Cohen, I. B., K. E. Duffin, et al. (1990). *Puritanism and the Rise of Modern Science: The Merton Thesis.* New Brunswick, N.J.: Rutgers University Press.

Copleston, F. (1962). *A History of Philosophy: Medieval Philosophy from Albert the Great to Duns Scotus.* Garden City, N.J: Image Books.

Corless, R., and P. F. Knitter (1990). *Buddhist Emptiness and Christian Trinity: Essays and Explorations.* New York: Paulist Press.

Cracknell, K. (1986). *Towards a New Relationship: Christians and People of Other Faiths.* London: Epworth.

Cragg, K. (1977). *The Christian and Other Religions: The Measure of Christ.* London: Mowbrays.

Cragg, K. (1980). "God and Salvation (An Islamic Study)." *Salvation in Christianity and Other Religions.* Rome: Gregorian University Press, pp. 155-66.

Cragg, K. (1984). *Muhammad and the Christian: A Question of Response.* London: Darton.

Cragg, K. (1985). *Jesus and the Muslim: An Exploration.* London and Boston: G. Allen & Unwin.

Cragg, K. (1986). *The Call of the Minaret.* London: Collins.

Cragg, K. (1986). *The Christ and the Faiths: Theology in Cross-Reference.* London: Spck.

Cragg, K. (1992). *Troubled by Truth: Life Studies in Inter-Faith Concern.* Edinburgh: Pentland Press.

Cunningham, D. S. (1998). *These Three Are One: The Practice of Trinitarian Theology.* Malden, Mass.: Blackwell.

Davis, C. F. (1989). *The Evidential Force of Religious Experience.* Oxford: Clarendon Press; New York: Oxford University Press.

D'Costa, G. (1990). "Christ, the Trinity and Religious Plurality." *Christian Uniqueness Reconsidered: The Myth of a Pluralistic Theology of Religions.* Edited by G. D'Costa. Maryknoll, N.Y.: Orbis Books.

D'Costa, G., ed. (1990). *Christian Uniqueness Reconsidered: The Myth of a Pluralistic Theology of Religions.* Maryknoll, N.Y.: Orbis Books.

D'Costa, G. (1995). "Christ, the Trinity and Religious Plurality." *Christian Uniqueness Reconsidered: The Myth of a Pluralistic Theology of Religions.* G. D'Costa. Maryknoll, N.Y.: Orbis Books.

D'Costa, G. (2000). *The Meeting of Religions and the Trinity.* Maryknoll, N.Y.: Orbis Books.

DiNoia, J. A. (1989). "Varieties of Religious Aims: Beyond Exclusivism, Inclusivism and Pluralism." *Theology and Dialogue.* Edited by B. Marshall. Notre Dame: University of Notre Dame Press, pp. 249-74.

DiNoia, J. A. (1992). *The Diversity of Religions: A Christian Perspective.* Washington, D.C.: Catholic University of America Press.

Dupuis S.J., J. (1997). *Toward a Christian Theology of Religious Pluralism.* Maryknoll, N.Y.: Orbis Books.

Erickson, M. J. (1996). *How Shall They Be Saved? The Destiny of Those Who Do Not Hear of Jesus.* Grand Rapids: Baker.

Fackre, G. (1978). *The Christian Story: A Narrative Interpretation of Basic Christian Doctrine.* Grand Rapids: Eerdmans.

Gamble, R. C., ed. (1992). *Influences Upon Calvin and Discussion of the 1559 Institutes: Articles on Calvin and Calvinism.* New York and London: Garland Publishing.

Gandhi, M. (1939). *Hind Swaraj, or, Indian Home Rule.* Ahmedabad: Navajwan Publishing House; Weare, N.H.: Greenleaf Books.

Gardiner, E., ed. (1989). *Visions of Heaven and Hell Before Dante.* New York: Italica Press.

Geach, P. (1977). *The Virtues.* Cambridge: Cambridge University Press.

Gellman, J. I. (1997). *Experience of God and the Rationality of Theistic Belief.* Ithaca, N.Y.: Cornell University Press.

Griffiths, P. J. (1990). *Christianity Through Non-Christian Eyes.* Maryknoll, N.Y.: Orbis Books.

Griffiths, P. J. (1991). *An Apology for Apologetics: A Study in the Logic of Interreligious Dialogue.* Maryknoll, N.Y.: Orbis Books.

Griffiths, P. J. (1991). *On Being Mindless: Buddhist Meditation and the Mind-Body Problem.* La Salle, Ill.: Open Court.

Griffiths, P. J. (1994). *On Being Buddha: The Classical Doctrine of Buddhahood.* Albany: State University of New York Press.

Griffiths, P. J. (2000). "Nirvana as the Last Thing? The Iconic End of the Narrative Imagination." *Modern Theology* 16: 17-36.

Gunton, C. E. (1993). *The One, the Three, and the Many: God, Creation, and the Culture of Modernity.* Cambridge and New York: Cambridge University Press.

Harris, H. A. (1998). "Should We Say That Personhood Is Relational?" *Scottish Journal of Theology* 51: 214-35.

Heim, S. M. (1979). "The Powers of God: Calvin and Late Medieval Thought." *Andover Newton Quarterly* 19, no. 3: 156-66.

Heim, S. M. (1985). *Is Christ the Only Way? Christian Faith in a Pluralistic World.* Valley Forge, Pa.: Judson Press.

Heim, S. M. (1987). "The Nature of Doctrine and the Development of Asian Theology." *Bangalore Theological Forum* 19, no. 1: 14-31.

Heim, S. M. (1992). "The Pluralistic Hypothesis, Realism and Post-Eschatology." *Religious Studies* 28: 207-19.

Heim, S. M. (1994). "Salvations: A More Pluralistic Hypothesis." *Modern Theology* 10, no. 4: 341-60.

Heim, S. M. (1995). *Salvations: Truth and Difference in Religion.* Maryknoll, N.Y.: Orbis Books.

Heim, S. M. (1996). "Orientational Pluralism in Religion." *Faith and Philosophy* 13, no. 2: 201-15.

Heim, S. M., ed. (1998). *Grounds for Understanding: Ecumenical Resources for Responses to Religious Pluralism.* Grand Rapids: Eerdmans.

Heim, S. M., National Council of the Churches of Christ in the United States of America. Commission on Faith and Order, et al., eds. (1991). *Faith to Creed: Ecumenical Perspectives on the Affirmation of the Apostolic Faith in the Fourth Century: Papers of the Faith to Creed Consultation, Commission on Faith and Order, NCCCUSA, October 25-27, 1989 — Waltham, Massachusetts.* Faith and Order Series. Grand Rapids: Eerdmans.

Hennecke, E., W. Schneemelcher, et al. (1963). *New Testament Apocrypha.* Philadelphia: Westminster Press.

Heppe, H. (1978). *Reformed Dogmatics: Set Out and Illustrated from the Sources.* Grand Rapids: Baker.

Hick, J. (1976). *Death and Eternal Life.* New York: Harper & Row.

Hick, J. (1989). *An Interpretation of Religion: Human Responses to the Transcendent.* Basingstoke, U.K.: Macmillan.

Hick, J. (1990). "Straightening the Record: Some Response to Critics." *Modern Theology* 6, no. 2.

Hick, J. (2000). "Ineffability." *Religious Studies* 36, no. 1.

Hill, W. J. (1982). *The Three-Personed God: The Trinity as a Mystery of Salvation.* Washington, D.C.: Catholic University of America Press.

Hunsberger, G. R. (1998). *Bearing the Witness of the Spirit: Lesslie Newbigin's Theology of Cultural Plurality.* Grand Rapids: Eerdmans.

Jaki, S. L. (1978). *The Road of Science and the Ways to God.* Edinburgh: Scottish Academic Press.

Jaki, S. L. (1988). *The Savior of Science.* Washington, D.C. and New York: Regnery Gateway.

Jantzen, G. M. (1984). "Human Diversity and Salvation in Christ." *Religious Studies* 20.

Jenson, R. W. (1982). *The Triune Identity: God According to the Gospel.* Philadelphia: Fortress Press.

Jungel, E. (1976). *The Doctrine of the Trinity: God's Being Is in Becoming.* Grand Rapids: Eerdmans.

Kaiser, C. B. (1991). *Creation and the History of Science.* London: Marshall Pickering; Grand Rapids: Eerdmans.

Kasper, W. (1984). *The God of Jesus Christ.* New York: Crossroad.

Keenan, J. P. (1989). *The Meaning of Christ: A Mahayana Theology.* Maryknoll, N.Y.: Orbis Books.

Keenan, J. P. (1995). *The Gospel of Mark: A Mahayana Reading.* Maryknoll, N.Y.: Orbis Books.

Klaaren, E. M. (1984). *Religious Origins of Modern Science: Belief in Creation in Seventeenth-Century Thought.* Grand Rapids: Eerdmans.

Knitter, P. F., and J. Hick (1987). *The Myth of Christian Uniqueness: Toward a Pluralistic Theology of Religions.* Maryknoll, N.Y.: Orbis Books.

Koyama, K. (1971). *Waterbuffalo Theology: A Thailand Theological Notebook.*

LaCugna, C. M. (1991). *God For Us: The Trinity and Christian Life.* San Francisco: HarperSanFrancisco.

Lai, Pan-Chiu (1994). *Towards a Trinitarian Theology of Religions: A Study of Paul Tillich's Thought.* Kampen: Kok Pharos Publishing House.

Lama, D. (1990). "The Bodhgaya Interviews." *Christianity Through Non-Christian Eyes.* Edited by P. Griffiths. Maryknoll, N.Y.: Orbis Books, pp. 166-70.

Lash, N. (1992). *Believing Three Ways in One God: A Reading of the Apostles' Creed.* London: SCM Press.

Le Goff, J. (1984). *The Birth of Purgatory.* London: Scholar Press.

Lewis, C. S. (1946). *The Great Divorce.* New York: Macmillan.

Lindbeck, G. (1984). *The Nature of Doctrine: Religion and Theology in a Postliberal Age.* Philadelphia: Westminster Press.

Link, H.-G., E. Castro, et al. (1985). *Confessing Our Faith Around the World. IV, South America.* Geneva: World Council of Churches.

Link, H.-G., A. W. J. Houtepen, et al. (1983). *Confessing Our Faith Around the World, II.* Geneva: World Council of Churches.

Link, H.-G., E. Tamez, et al. (1984). *Confessing Our Faith Around the World. III, the Caribbean and Central America.* Geneva: World Council of Churches.

Link, H.-G., World Council of Churches. Commission on Faith and Order, et al. (1988). *One God, One Lord, One Spirit: On the Explication of the Apostolic Faith Today.* Geneva: World Council of Churches.

Lovejoy, A. O. (1965). *The Great Chain of Being: A Study of the History of an Idea.* Cambridge, Mass.: Harvard University Press.

Meyendorff, J. (1974). *Byzantine Theology: Historical Trends and Doctrinal Themes.* New York: Fordham University Press.

Milbank, J. (1993). *Theology and Social Theory: Beyond Secular Reason.* Oxford, U.K. and Cambridge, Mass.: Blackwell.

Moltmann, J. (1981). *The Trinity and the Kingdom: The Doctrine of God.* New York: Harper & Row.

Moltmann, J. (1991). *History and the Triune God: Contributions to Trinitarian Theology*. London: SCM Press.

Morgan, A. (1990). *Dante and the Medieval Other World*. Cambridge and New York: Cambridge University Press.

Nasr, S. H. (1986). "The Islamic View of Christianity." *Christianity Among World Religions*. Edited by H. Küng and J. Moltmann. Edinburgh: T. & T. Clark, pp. 3-12.

Newbigin, L. (1954). *The Household of God*. New York: Friendship Press.

Newbigin, L. (1958). *A Faith for This One World*. London: SCM Press.

Novak, D. (1983). *The Image of the Non-Jew in Judaism: An Historical and Constructive Study of the Noahide Laws*. New York: E. Mellen Press.

Novak, D. (1989). *Jewish-Christian Dialogue: A Jewish Justification*. New York: Oxford University Press.

O'Connor, F., and S. Fitzgerald (1988). *Collected Works*. New York: Library of America.

Ogden, S. M. (1992). *Is There Only One True Religion or Are There Many?* Dallas: Southern Methodist University Press.

Otto, R., and F. H. Foster (1930). *India's Religion of Grace and Christianity Compared and Contrasted*. London: Student Christian Movement Press.

Panikkar, R. (1973). *The Trinity and the Religious Experience of Man: Icon-Person-Mystery*. Maryknoll, N.Y.: Orbis Books.

Panikkar, R. (1981). *The Unknown Christ of Hinduism: Towards an Ecumenical Christophany*. London: Darton.

Panikkar, R. (1987). "The Jordan, the Tiber and the Ganges: Three Kairological Moments of Christic Self-consciousness." *The Myth of Christian Uniqueness: Toward a Pluralistic Theology of Religions*. Edited by J. Hick and P. F. Knitter. Maryknoll, N.Y.: Orbis Books.

Panikkar, R., and S. Eastham (1993). *The Cosmotheandric Experience: Emerging Religious Consciousness*. Maryknoll, N.Y.: Orbis Books.

Pascal, B. (1988). *Pensées*. New York: Penguin.

Peters, T. (1993). *God as Trinity: Relationality and Temporality in the Divine Life*. Louisville: Westminster/John Knox Press.

Pinnock, C. H. (1992). *A Wideness in God's Mercy: The Finality of Jesus Christ in a World of Religions*. Grand Rapids: Zondervan.

Race, A. (1993). *Christians and Religious Pluralism: Patterns in the Christian Theology of Religions*. London: SCM Press.

Rambachan, A. (1999). "My God, Your God, Our God, No God?" *Current Dialogue* 33 (July): 38-40.

Rowe, W. (1991). "Paradox and Promise: Hick's Solution to the Problem of Evil." *Problems in the Philosophy of Religion: Critical Studies of the Work of John Hick*. Edited by H. Hewitt, Jr. New York: St. Martin's Press, pp. 11-124.

Russell, J. B. (1981). *Satan: The Early Christian Tradition*. Ithaca, N.Y.: Cornell University Press.

Russell, J. B. (1984). *Lucifer: The Devil in the Middle Ages*. Ithaca, N.Y.: Cornell University Press.

Russell, J. B. (1986). *Mephistopheles: The Devil in the Modern World.* Ithaca, N.Y.: Cornell University Press.

Russell, J. B. (1987). *The Devil: Perceptions of Evil from Antiquity to Primitive Christianity.* Ithaca, N.Y.: Cornell University Press.

Russell, J. B. (1988). *The Prince of Darkness: Radical Evil and the Power of Good in History.* Ithaca, N.Y.: Cornell University Press.

Samartha, S. J. (1991). *One Christ, Many Religions: Toward a Revised Christology.* Maryknoll, N.Y.: Orbis Books.

Sanders, J. (1992). *No Other Name: An Investigation into the Destiny of the Unevangelized.* Grand Rapids: Eerdmans.

Sanneh, L. O. (1989). *Translating the Message: The Missionary Impact on Culture.* Maryknoll, N.Y.: Orbis Books.

Sayers, D. (1955). "Introduction." *The Divine Comedy: Purgatory.* Baltimore: Penguin.

Sayers, D. (1969). "The Meaning of Heaven and Hell." *Introductory Papers on Dante.* New York: Barnes & Noble, pp. 44-72.

Sayers, D. L. (1969). *Introductory Papers on Dante.* New York: Barnes & Noble.

Sayers, D. L. (1969). "The Meaning of Purgatory." *Introductory Papers on Dante.* New York: Barnes & Noble.

Schwobel, C., and King's College. Research Institute in Systematic Theology (1995). *Trinitarian Theology Today: Essays on Divine Being and Act.* Edinburgh: T. & T. Clark.

Smart, N., and S. Konstantine (1991). *Christian Systematic Theology in a World Context.* Minneapolis: Fortress Press.

Song, C.-S., World Council of Churches. Commission on Faith and Order, et al. (1980). *Confessing Our Faith Around the World.* Geneva: World Council of Churches.

Sullivan, F. A. (1992). *Salvation Outside the Church? Tracing the History of the Catholic Response.* New York: Paulist Press.

Thangaraj, M. T. (1983). *Toward a Tamil Christology: The Concept of Guru in Saiva Siddhanta as a Christological Model.* Nashville: Abingdon Press.

Thangaraj, M. T., and G. D. Kaufman (1994). *The Crucified Guru: An Experiment in Cross-Cultural Christology.* Nashville: Abingdon Press.

Thomas, M. M. (1970). *The Acknowledged Christ of the Indian Renaissance.* Madras: C.L.S. for the Christian Institute for the Study of Religion and Society.

Thomas, M. M. (1987). *Risking Christ for Christ's Sake: Towards an Ecumenical Theology of Pluralism.* Geneva: World Council of Churches.

Torrance, A. J. (1996). *Persons in Communion: An Essay on Trinitarian Description and Human Participation.* Edinburgh: T. & T. Clark.

Torrance, T. F. (1985). *Theological Dialogue Between Orthodox and Reformed Churches.* Edinburgh: Scottish Academic Press.

Vanhoozer, K. J. (1997). "Does the Trinity Belong in a Theology of Religions? On Angling in the Rubicon and the 'Identity' of God." *The Trinity in a Pluralistic Age: Theological Essays on Culture and Religion.* Edited by K. J. Vanhoozer. Grand Rapids: Eerdmans, pp. 41-71.

WORKS CITED

Volf, M. (1998). *After Our Likeness: The Church as the Image of the Trinity.* Grand Rapids: Eerdmans.

von Bruck, M. (1991). *The Unity of Reality: God, God-Experience and Meditation in the Hindu-Christian Dialogue.* New York: Paulist Press.

Walls, A. F. (1996). *The Missionary Movement in Christian History: Studies in Transmission of Faith.* Maryknoll, N.Y.: Orbis Books.

Walls, J. L. (1998). "Must the Truth Offend? An Exchange." *First Things* 84: 34-37.

Ward, K. (1990). "Truth and the Diversity of Religions." *Religious Studies* 26: 1-18.

Williams, R. (1990). "Trinity and Pluralism." *Christian Uniqueness Reconsidered: The Myth of a Pluralistic Theology of Religions.* Edited by G. D'Costa. Maryknoll, N.Y.: Orbis Books.

Williams, S. (1997). "The Trinity and 'Other Religions.'" *The Trinity in a Pluralistic Age: Theological Essays on Culture and Religion.* Edited by K. J. Vanhoozer. Grand Rapids: Eerdmans, pp. 26-40.

World Council of Churches (1991). *Confessing the One Faith: An Ecumenical Explication of the Apostolic Faith as It Is Confessed in the Nicene-Constantinopolitan Creed.* Geneva: World Council of Churches, p. 381.

World Council of Churches. Commission on Faith and Order (1987). *Confessing One Faith: Towards an Ecumenical Explication of the Apostolic Faith as Expressed in the Nicene-Constantinopolitan Creed.* Geneva: World Council of Churches, p. 381.

Yagi, S. (1987). "'I' in the Words of Jesus." *The Myth of Christian Uniqueness: Toward a Pluralistic Theology of Religions.* Edited by J. Hick and P. F. Knitter. Maryknoll, N.Y.: Orbis Books, pp. 117-36.

Zizioulas, J. (1985). *Being as Communion: Studies in Personhood and the Church.* Crestwood, N.Y.: St. Vladimir's Seminary Press.

Zukav, G. (1980). *The Dancing Wu Li Masters: An Overview of the New Physics.* New York: Bantam Books.

Index

INDEX

unity, principle of, 160
universal God-human connection, 83-84
universalism, 7, 118, 131, 165, 244, 256-58, 263, 265
Upanishads, 223, 226

Vedantic Hinduism, 54
Virgil, 99, 100, 207, 275-76, 283, 295
virtues, 28
virtuous pagans, 84, 100, 105-6
Vishnu, 160
vision literature, 96-97
Volf, Miroslav, 58, 62n.8, 174n.20
von Bruck, Michael, 188n.31

Walls, Andrew, 139-40

Western theology, 68-70, 138, 168, 172, 173, 192, 228
will, corruption of, 70-71
Williams, Rowan, 150
Williams, Stephen, 35n.40, 179n.23
witness, 293-94
Word of God, implicit presence, 135-36
world, mission to church, 147
world religions, 89, 165
worldview, 24
worship, 200, 231

Zen Buddhism, 158
Zion, 97
Zizioulas, John, 62n.8, 168-74

312